The
Black
Consumer

CONSULTING EDITOR:
Norton Marks,
Notre Dame University

The Black Consumer

DIMENSIONS OF BEHAVIOR AND STRATEGY

edited by

George Joyce

The University of Texas at El Paso

and

Norman A. P. Govoni

Babson College

 Random House · New York

Library of Congress Catalog Card Number: 70–131950

ISBN: 0–394–31130–2

Manufactured in the United States of America. Composed by
Cherry Hill Composition, Pennsauken, New Jersey. Printed &
bound by Halliday Lithograph Corp., West Hanover, Mass.

First Edition

9 8 7 6 5 4 3 2 1

To Wanda, Terry, and our children

Preface

By organizing into a unified whole the available literature that
represents the best thinking on the black-consumer market, this book
serves a two-fold purpose: it identifies those areas that are critical to
successful stimulation of positive buying action in the black-consumer
market, and it contributes to the marketing-planning effort by providing
a framework within which subculture marketing might be better
understood and evaluated by the marketing decision maker.

The Black Consumer is divided into four major parts. The articles in
Part 1 establish the importance of the specific market by examining its
nature and scope and include background information which is essential
to an analysis of special marketing relationships.

The focal point of Part 2 is the social and cultural environments
that characterize this ethnic population segment. Emphasis is centered on
social class structure and psychological influences that account for
specific modes of behavior.

The articles in Part 3 critically analyze consumption patterns,
buying behavior, and motivations, including the similarities and differences
between the black-consumer market segment and other market segments.

The variables that affect the development of marketing strategy for
the black-consumer market are identified in Part 4. These variables
will provide guidelines for successful cultivation of this important market
segment.

An evaluation of the changes and trends that have occurred among
consumers and the implications for future marketing efforts directed
at the black-consumer market are discussed in the Epilogue.

We believe that this book's organizational framework with associated informational content will be especially helpful in bridging the gap between marketing and the black-consumer market.

We wish to thank the authors and publishers for granting us permission to include their selections in the book. In addition, we thank Mr. Christopher Benz of Random House and Dr. Norton Marks of the University of Notre Dame for their expert guidance from the very beginning. Special appreciation goes to Miss Pat Huth for her invaluable assistance in the preparation of the manuscript for publication. We, of course, assume complete responsibility for the organizational framework of the book.

G. J.
N. G.
Summer 1970

Contents

Contents

The
Black
Consumer

Introduction

A basic characteristic of American business is its continual process of dynamic change. And no part of a business organization feels the impact of change more than the marketing function. Recognition that business goals can be achieved only through consumer satisfaction has resulted in an increasing number of firms adopting the marketing concept, which places primary emphasis upon the consumer. Consumer behavior is significantly influenced by environmental conditions that frequently change. Therefore, adjustments are commonplace for businesses to meet the market demands.

A single marketing strategy is not sufficiently adaptable to the variety of environments it wishes to serve or to capitalize on the multitude of opportunities that exist. The black-consumer market segment is an opportunity which marketing would be well advised to examine more diligently; this previously neglected market segment has evolved into one of significant proportion. With proper planning, implementation, and control, marketing can achieve a successful position among these consumers. But a prerequisite for this success is a better understanding of the behavioral characteristics of the black-consumer market.

The United States is a composite of complex, heterogeneous cultures, within which is found a number of subcultures. The largest and most familiar subculture is that of the black population: the more than 23 million blacks in the United States represent a spending potential exceeding $30 billion. As consumers, they account for a considerable share of money spent for consumer goods and services.

Like many other market segments, this consumer market is growing rapidly and is changing constantly. Indeed, its size and continuing growth is a significant force in the American economy. However, evidence suggests that until very recently the black-consumer market has largely been ignored by most marketers. Moreover, purchasing habits of this group are so grossly misunderstood that very few companies have reached anything close to their potential in this market. Traditional assumptions and stereotyped approaches toward winning this ethnic group are no longer applicable. It is apparent that although some marketers have been reaching the black consumer, they are not influencing his purchasing behavior as much as might be expected. Some marketing specialists believe that this market can be reached and influenced through traditional, motivation-oriented mass marketing techniques. However, informed sources suggest that winning black-consumer loyalty requires extra effort.

Belief and conviction must be achieved by marketing practitioners to stimulate blacks to a positive buying action. Every member of the marketing team should be briefed on minority marketing. The key activity for successful marketing to this specific segment is accumulating information on the black consumer that distinguishes and identifies this population group as a market. Recognizing and using detailed information is a vital necessity for sound marketing judgments about black consumers.

PART
1

Nature
and Scope
of the Market

A basic frame of reference for the black-consumer market and an essential perspective for the study and understanding of this particular consumer group are presented in Part 1. The importance of the black-consumer market is suggested and supported by demographic and income data. Once the importance of the market has been established, later articles list social and economic characteristics of the market. These data provide an excellent base for strategy implementation.

An overall view of the black-consumer market is presented in articles by Senator Walter F. Mondale, "The Challenge of the Ghetto to Marketing," and by Eli Ginzberg, "What We Don't Know About the Ghetto." Both of these articles shed considerable light on the characteristics of this market as well as on the methods by which ghetto conditions could be improved. A challenge is issued to marketers to become involved by using their expertise in changing problems into opportunities for the betterment of all concerned. Such an approach requires perceptive, innovative decision making. Although new knowledge will not come easily, attempts must be made to gain knowledge that will permit constructive action on matters affecting the ghetto.

Kelvin Wall, in his article entitled "Marketing to Low Income Neighborhoods: A Systems Approach," points out that the low-income neighborhood is a unique marketing environment, primarily because of such factors as income and life style. In addition to requiring a different marketing mix, marketing to low-income neighborhoods must be based upon a systems approach.

The existence of the black-consumer market is discussed from varying viewpoints by two leading authorities, W. Leonard Evans, Jr., and H. Naylor Fitzhugh, in "The Negro Market: Two Viewpoints." Significant insights can be gleaned from these analyses. The areas of agreement and disagreement between the two authors are summarized for further study and verification.

In an article entitled "Why There Is a Negro Market," by D. Parke Gibson, it is suggested that a separate, distinct black-consumer market exists because of the forced identification of its members, the distinct buying behavior of its members, its size, and its location. In addition, Gibson recommends several ways in which this market segment can be developed more effectively.

The black-consumer market is a reality and should be recognized. When efforts are made to provide this segment with the goods and services it desires, businessmen will find that "Negro Consumers Are Waiting." This article from *Grocery Mfr.* provides interesting empirical evidence regarding the loyalty of black consumers as it is reflected in a study of brand preferences.

The concluding article is a current and comprehensive statistical picture of the population segment referred to as the Negro- or black-consumer market. *The Social and Economic Status of Negroes in the United States, 1969,* is a joint publication of the U. S. Department of Commerce and the U. S. Department of Labor. It presents informative data on the major aspects of black life, including population distribution, income, employment, education, and the family. The statistics provide background data and reveal the changes that have taken place in the social and economic conditions of the black population.

Walter F. Mondale

The Challenge of the Ghetto to Marketing

INTRODUCTION

IN the years since Michael Harrington's "Other America" opened the eyes of a nation, the recognition of domestic poverty has slowly begun to sink into our social awareness.

We know something about poverty now. We know it is

- *Lack of income:* 34 million Americans officially defined as living on "poverty level" incomes;
- *Lack of jobs:* unemployment rates *in* some central city ghettos of 25–35%;
- *Lack of decent housing:* More than 8 million substandard housing units befouling our urban and rural slums;
- *Lack of education:* up to a quarter or more of those who enter 9th grade failing to graduate.

In short, we know poverty has many dimensions, and that its costs can be counted many ways—

- In the individual frustration and fear that lead to riots;
- In the social separation that is making of unity *two* nations, one black, one white;
- In the economic loss of undeveloped human capital, and undeveloped buying power.

Reprinted by permission of the American Marketing Association from *A New Measure of Responsibility for Marketing, Proceedings of the American Marketing Association National Conference,* published by the American Marketing Association, Keith Cox and Ben M. Enis, eds., June 1968, pp. 14–17.

We know the causes of poverty are numerous, interrelated, and difficult to change. We know they are

- *Historical*—the Poor Law tradition that punished people for their poverty and led to a welfare system that now keeps them there;
- *Individual*—the apathy, arrogance, and indifference of those who could have prevented poverty years ago;
- *Institutional*—the vast array of public and private sector organizations which either keep poor people out, or work to keep them poor.

All must share in the collective guilt for this state of affairs both in public and private sectors.

It makes no difference now that most of the decisions creating the situation were unconscious. Poverty is more the result of social "drift" than of individual malevolence.

The fact is that the problem exists, and that it must be attacked now, at every level, and in every sector of our society—individual, organizational, and institutional.

Ladies and gentlemen, I would submit that marketing is part of the ghetto's problem, and must be part of the solution.

MARKETING AND THE GHETTO:
THE NATURE OF THE CHALLENGE

The ghetto is one place Adam Smith's "invisible hand" hasn't reached. The laissez faire system never guaranteed distributive justice. And no ones knows that better than the poor.

Ghettos are like inland lakes, cut off from the marketing mainstream. Walk around a ghetto. What do you see?

- Inefficient stores;
- Low-quality goods;
- Marginal merchants.

Talk to these merchants. What do you hear?

- Poor people mean poor profits;
- High crime rates boost operating costs;
- Riots destroy us for we can't get insurance.

Listen to the poor. What do you learn?

- We are paying more;
- We need jobs and income *in* the ghetto;
- We want to own businesses ourselves.

All of these statements are true. Collectively, they sketch the ghetto market situation.

THE POOR ARE EXPLOITED

As Paul Rand Dixon and others have pointed out, the fact that "the poor pay more is not a slogan, it is a fact."[1]

What the FTC and others have found in Washington, and across the country is this:

- Price markups for durable goods in the ghetto two to three times those in the general market;
- "Easy" credit in the ghetto costing 10–15% more than credit in the general market;
- High pressure techniques and shady practices in the ghetto not tolerated in the general market;
- Punishment by court-ordered garnishments and repossessions in the ghetto at a rate many times that in the general market;
- The poorest of the poor—those with half the "moderate" income getting "taken."

POVERTY FOSTERS EXPLOITATIONS

As the Riot Commission Report points out, exploitation of the poor is a "complex situation":[2]

- Lacking cash, poor people have to rely on credit;
- Lacking steady jobs, the poor are refused general market credit, and must turn elsewhere;
- Lacking cars, poor people can't get to low-cost discount stores in suburbs;
- Lacking consumer education, the poor don't know how to get help from financial institutions, the law, or sources of consumer advice.

GHETTOS DRAG BACK OUR ECONOMY, AND WITH IT, OUR SOCIETY

The ghettos are the undeveloped areas of our nation. Land is expensive. Labor is unskilled. Capital is non-existent. No wonder the ghetto is left with marginal businesses or no business at all.

The cost of the ghettos is enormous. It is the cost of riots; the cost of increased police protection; the costs of lost purchasing power, lost profits, lost income and revenue. The fact is that the ghettos are a lost market, millions of people deep, and billions of dollars wide, and growing every day.

The ghettos cry out for help.

The need is now.

The question is not *whether* we shall move but *when*. The question is not *who* is to blame, but *how* society shall act.

MARKETING AND THE GHETTO:
RESPONSE TO THE CHALLENGE

The ghettos need market development—

- Business and industry located in the ghetto, creating an economic base, and giving residents jobs;
- Capital investment by outside industries in ghetto-owned business, industry, and training ventures;
- Training programs for workers, managers, and entrepreneurs;
- New marketing mechanisms to get goods and services to the ghetto;
- Advertising and merchandising techniques geared to ghetto residents.

Clearly, government can be of some assistance. Many public programs are already aimed at making life in the ghetto more bearable, and, more important, at *eliminating* the ghetto. Programs by the Department of Commerce, the Office of Economic Opportunity, and others stand ready and willing to work with communities, and the business community in addressing the overall problem.[3]

The courts can help create a safer environment in which to work. Strict endorsement of laws curbing unfair and deceptive practices, and truth-in-lending certainly can help.

But the private sector must be in the forefront. As Dr. Kenneth B. Clark, New York University psychologist and educator has pointed out, many ghetto residents have given up on government, the legal system, even the schools and churches. "Business and industry are our last hope," he says.[4]

Ladies and gentlemen, as I read the list of your Association's Committees, I realized what an important part the American Marketing Association could play as part of the private sector effort.

For among the many kinds of needs are needs for skills and talents you Association members have—skills in market research; market education; consumer and industrial marketing; and for professional ethics and standards your Association stands for.

Let me raise some questions:

- How do poor consumers differ from others in their consumption attitudes and habits? Do they do comparison shopping?
- What brands do they buy and why? Market research could help us find out.
- How can the poor best be taught what they need to know to make informed consumer choices? What do minority group suppliers need to know to enter "mainstream" stores? Market educators can help answer this question.
- How can price competition be encouraged and unethical practices curbed? How can we get low-cost credit to the poor? Those who study standards and ethics can help us respond.

- How can service and industry be attracted to the ghetto? How can minority group entrepreneurs "make it" in the mainstream? Consumer and industrial marketing experts are needed as a resource group.

These questions are but the beginning of a list the American Marketing Association can help us develop, and help guide us in answering.

The encouraging thing is that so many of you are already involved. Universities are beginning to act. Business is beginning to move. Both are starting to work with government; and more important yet, to join the community.

Experimental models are many. To name a few:

- In market research, use of ghetto-based research firms, training of Negro employees as researchers. (Eastman Kodak)[5]
- In Market education, use of mobile consumer education vans (Better Business Bureau);[6] technical advice on marketing techniques to food store suppliers (Jewell Tea Company);[7] sophisticated training and counseling the poor for jobs (MIND) (Methods of Intellectual Development);[8]
- In consumer and industrial marketing: building buying power by hiring and training the poor for better jobs (National Alliance of Businessmen under the Chairmanship of Henry Ford II; Minnesota Mining and Manufacturing; Control Data, Minneapolis);[9] building the economy of the ghetto by establishing franchised businesses (Chicken Delight);[10] launching independent businesses (Aero-Jet General sponsoring a tent-making factory);[11] sending mobile retail units into the ghetto; establishing co-operatives in food and other goods.[12]

We are beginning to learn some significant things, though there still is much more to know.

We know working in the ghetto represents a new conception of business' role in society. To put it in the words of William S. Vaughn, Board Chairman of Eastman-Kodak, involvement in the ghetto represents doing "what we should do—keeping in mind our concurrent responsibilities to Kodak men and women, to our share owners, and to our customers— for the benefit of the people involved, and for the betterment of the community of which we are a part."[13]

We know it is different from the dole: To put it in the words of H. D. (Chad) McClellan of the Los Angeles-based Management Council for Merit Employment, it was either "go on paying $400 million a year in Los Angeles Welfare costs . . . or go down and take a realistic look at the potential workers in the slums."[14]

We know it can be profitable: Jewell Tea Company stores were almost untouched in the riots;[15] the Watts (Calif.) Manufacturing Company sponsored by Aero-Jet General is soon expected to make a profit.[16]

We know it takes training everyone—executives, personnel officers, line supervisors, and employees. The Super Market Institute has developed a course 250 top food industry executives and training personnel have taken.[17]

We know it takes communication with the community. Kodak's Business Development Corporation is one way. But every company should have a Community Relations Department, and an Advisory Committee made up of neighborhood residents.

We know it takes involvement with other groups and individuals working to fight poverty. Model Cities and Community Act Programs need your advice. The Urban Coalition needs your support. Legislators— Federal, State, and local can use your help. Legislation is now pending directly related to marketing and the ghetto. The Omnibus Housing bill has in it a riot insurance provision. My own "Domestic Food Assistance Act of 1968" calls for a coalition of public and private sectors to procure and distribute food in new ways. Support is needed for this and other anti-hunger measures. Finally, self-help organizations, like N.E.G.R.O., need your encouragement.[18]

In closing, I wish to draw an analogy. At one time the social problem of auto safety had business lined up on one side, government (both executive and legislative branches) on the other. I was part of that battle, and I know the vehemence with which industry said "it couldn't be done." Safety was simply too expensive, they said.

Social problems are as they are perceived. A recent article in the newspapers shows how the genius of the marketplace finally produced an insight. Auto manufacturers seemingly see something else in the auto safety issue today. Auto safety could be a new form of product differentiation, and a new kind of competition. Thus, in the coming year, American consumers will be offered cars safer to drive. The problem has not changed, but industry's perception has.

I would like to suggest that the same kind of idea can be applied to the relationship between marketing and the ghetto. The problem should not be viewed as a tug of war between government and industry. Rather, it must be viewed as a mutual challenge, one in which business and industry can and must take the lead, just as they have done in auto safety.

What is needed today in the urban ghettos is differentiation of methods, and some competition. The goal of the competition: domestic development, the development of the human and economic potential of the central city core. The methods to achieve this goal: No "one best way," but many, aimed at achieving the social and economic goal. Dozens of different combinations are possible—jobs, business formation, technical assistance alone, or together, residents, private sector, governmental programs alone or in combination.

You of the Marketing Association can no longer ignore the ghetto. You must become involved. The challenge is to change perceptions, to create, to innovate, to transform. The challenge is to change problems into opportunities.

I know you will join with those of us in government, and in the courts, as leaders of the response.

[Notes]

1. "Consumer Credit and the Poor," Hearing before the Subcommittee on Financial Institutions of the Senate Committee on Banking and Currency, April 19, 1968, p. 2.
2. *Report of the National Advisory Commission on Civil Disorders,* 1968, pp. 274–5.
3. See *Riot Insurance,* Hearings before the Senate Commerce Committee, Aug. 29, 1967, pp. 90–116 for descriptions of numerous models of government-business cooperation in meeting these needs.
4. "What Business Can Do for the Negro," *Nation's Business* (October 1967), p. 67.
5. Conversation with Company Regional Representative in New York, May 1968.
6. *Report,* Denver, Colorado Better Business Bureau, 1968.
7. Conversation with Company Executive, May, 1968.
8. *Fortune* (January 1968), p. 159.
9. Conversations with Department of Commerce and Executives, May, 1968.
10. Conversation with Department of Commerce official, June, 1968.
11. *Fortune* (January 1968), pp. 159–160.
12. Office of Economic Opportunity, Community Action Program Consumer Action Program booklets, Washington, D.C.
13. "Kodak Faces the Urban Crisis," pamphlet, unpaged and undated.
14. *Business and the Urban Crisis,* A Special Report by McGraw-Hill, 1968, p. C5.
15. Conversation with Jewell Tea Company executive, May, 1968.
16. *Fortune* (January 1968), p. 159.
17. *Report,* Super Market Institute, Inc., 200 E. Ontario St., Chicago, Ill. 60611.
18. See Peter Bailey, "N.E.G.R.O. Charts New Paths to Freedom," *Ebony* (April 1968).

2

Eli Ginzberg

What We Don't Know About the Ghetto

IT is not surprising that much more heat than light has characterized scholarly as well as popular discussions of the problems of the ghetto. After all the term "ghetto" has been applied to the black community only during the last decade. If we reflect on the reasons that we know so little about the ghetto, the answers are quickly evident.

Since study and research carry a cost, we concentrate on some subjects to the neglect of others. Until recently, the problems of the Negro minority were of little interest and concern to most Americans. Moreover, many ghettos especially in the North and West were absorbing large numbers of in-migrants and a highly mobile population is always difficult to study. In addition, in the United States we have concentrated for all too long on improving the collection and evaluation of aggregate statistics without appreciating that for certain subjects it is the disaggregated figures that count. What is the significance of a single percentage figure of unemployment when the variability by location may be 400 percent and the variability by race as high.

A further explanation is the exacerbation of relations between the races which has made it next to impossible for white investigators to go into the ghetto to collect information. To this difficulty must be added the shortage of trained Negro investigators. And beyond this, we must take special note of the resistance of those in the ghetto to give information. People who have been persecuted by those in authority learn to

Reprinted by permission of the author and the National Association of Business Economists from *Business Economics*, Vol. 4, No. 3, May 1969, pp. 18–20.

keep their mouths shut. If a census investigator knocks on the door of a Harlem apartment and asks how many adults live there, he is likely to receive misinformation if only because the landlady who answers the door believes it desirable to cover up for one or another of her boarders who may be in trouble with a probation official, a collection agency, or his former employer. It is not surprising that we know little about the ghetto and that new knowledge will not come easily.

SOME CONCEPTUAL DIFFICULTIES

It is difficult to define the boundaries of a ghetto. Where does it begin and end? Is the critical element the race of those who live within the area or their income status the criterion? If the answer is—as it probably must be—in terms of density of the racial population, then we will find that many ghetto families are members of the middle and even upper middle income class. Many of the overtones of the true ghetto that bespeak poverty are irrelevant for these families.

There are further difficulties in sorting out the important sub-groups who live in the ghetto. We know little about the ways in which a ghetto is divided among long-term inhabitants of the neighborhood, long-term inhabitants of the city who have recently relocated in the neighborhood, and in-migrants. Without such critical information, it is often difficult to sort out to what extent the problems of the ghetto relate to race and poverty specifically and to what extent they reflect primarily the problems of migrants.

Another question of importance about which relevant information is lacking is how many of those above the poverty line live in the ghetto out of choice and how many would prefer to move out if they could without encountering discrimination in housing in other parts of the city and in the suburbs. While some statistical studies suggest that if income alone were the determinant of location, a large number of ghetto dwellers would relocate, many Negroes prefer to live as members of black communities.

Another facet of ghetto life which we do not understand are the socio-economic relations among the different groups. It has been stated that no Negroes are in the upper echelons of those who control crime in the ghetto, that the effective leadership remains with the white members of the various syndicates. Similarly, there are few hard facts about Negro-Jewish relations in ownership of slum housing, retail stores, and loan and credit operations. Also obscure are the changing relations between the ghetto inhabitants and the politicians at City Hall. Even more obscure are the changing relations among various Negro groups

competing for the allegiance of the ghetto inhabitants. In short, we need
to know much more about the basic power structure of the ghetto and
the transformations that are under way.

SOME ECONOMIC ASSUMPTIONS

No matter how inadequate the data, it needs no more than untrained eyes
and sturdy legs to see that many who live in the ghetto have very little
income, much less than is required to live at a minimum level of decency.
Having acknowledged this overwhelmingly important fact, we can still
profit from looking at certain other dimensions of the income problem.

In the first place, low earnings by individuals are less likely to reflect
low family or household earnings, since the number of employed and
quasi-employed persons are likely to be greater in a ghetto household
than outside the ghetto. The critic might ask about the large number of
female family heads who must bring up their children alone. Even here
we must take account of the following patterns. Frequently the woman's
husband has moved out so that she can become eligible for relief. He
lives nearby and continues his interest in his wife and children to whose
support he contributes. His moving out may have raised the total
"resources" of the family from $3,700 to $7,000 annually. Other women
have "boyfriends" who live with them regularly or intermittently and who
usually make some financial contribution to the family.

LITTLE CASH

Young people, especially young males, can exist with relatively little cash
by having their meals with their mothers or girl friends. If they do not
want to work and if they are not fancy dressers and big spenders, they
can get along with very little cash. And that little cash which they need
or want is not difficult to come by if they are willing to run around the
law. And most of them see no reason not to. They can earn quick dollars
in the numbers racket. If they are willing to take a bigger risk they can
earn more in the narcotics trade. They can work at a legitimate job now
and again for a few days. They insist on getting paid in cash; this means
that no deductions are made from their wages for income tax purposes.

If he does not have a wife and children to support, a Negro youth
with modest consumption demands is likely to work only intermittently.
Why should he submit to the regular discipline of a job which pays little
and offers no prospect of advancement? After he has made the few dollars
he needs, he can leave secure in the knowledge that he can always get
the same kind of poor job if and when he needs cash again.

Too little attention has been paid to the amount of money funneled into the ghetto through various training and community programs. While the total is still far below what would be required to raise all ghetto families above the poverty level, the amounts involved have been substantial. Many young Negroes are able to live on their $25 to $40 weekly training allowances. Others have had an opportunity to obtain one of the new jobs especially created to employ indigenous workers; these youngsters may earn $80 or even more per week. Of course the poor in the ghetto would like to see a vast expansion in such income generating opportunities.

BETTER LABOR MARKETS

One of the major disabilities which hamper people in the ghetto is the poor labor market information to which they have access. They are the last to hear of job openings. And many new jobs located on the city's perimeters never come to their attention. There is a new position in the ghetto occupied by the "job man"—an indigenous worker who tries by word of mouth to inform the people in his immediate area of opportunities about which he has learned from various sources, official and unofficial.

The excessively high rates of unemployment among young Negro girls has not been studied. It may be that the girls balk at private household employment, but they are unable to compete for the white collar positions which abound in the city because of their poor education or other handicaps. By staying at home and running the household and keeping an eye on younger children, they may enable their mothers, aunts, and even grandmothers to be employed. And they too may prefer the odd dollars that they can pick up from periodic work, legal or illegal, to working for a white woman in her home. Here is one more facet of ghetto employment and living that should be studied.

Bad as the ghetto is, miserable as are the lives of many who inhabit it, we must not lose sight of the fact that today approximately 40 percent of all Negro families outside of the South are at the median family income for the total country of $8,000 or above. Admittedly that leaves 60 percent below this level and many at the poverty level or one step above. But the most important fact may well be that within the brief period since World War II, a substantial minority of Negroes has moved into a middle income range.

A critical challenge is to remove the barriers facing many who are in the ghetto not from choice or economic necessity but because of the pervasive discrimination that continues to prevail in the housing market. It is intolerable that Negroes alone should be prevented from spending their money in accordance with their tastes and preferences. The housing market must be opened up. Recent data suggest that it is, though slowly. The density of ghetto areas is being reduced.

It does not follow, of course, that if it is, all Negroes with income sufficient to live elsewhere will seek new homes. Many will stay in the ghetto out of desire to participate actively in the black revolution that is only now gaining momentum. Others will remain because they have an interest in competing for political power and they can best advance their efforts by remaining a part of the community. And some will prefer to remain because they like the neighborhood and the city and have no desire to move.

IMPROVE GHETTO SERVICES

Irrespective of whether more or fewer decide to relocate as the housing bars are lowered, there is no justification for tolerating the characteristically low level of public services in the ghetto. As the black masses organize themselves politically and develop competent and honest leadership, City Hall will have to respond. But much more can and should be done to collect the garbage, police the streets and, above all, improve the schools. It is fatuous to say, as some do, that the ghettos must be destroyed and, therefore, it is not necessary to improve them. The only sound policy is to permit blacks like whites to live where they desire and to provide a decent level of public services for those who remain in the ghetto. Cleaner streets, less crime, and effective schools do not represent gilding the ghetto!

Another doctrine, equally fallacious, is to assume that through government and private help the ghettos can be economically vitalized to a point where they will be able to transform the lives of the people who live there. It may be possible with cheap government loans and large tax concessions to attract a few plants into the ghetto to provide employment opportunities for those who live nearby. And it is surely possible through the combined efforts of the public and private sectors to help some Negroes acquire franchises to start their own businesses or to expand them. And there is no reason that Negro contractors should not have the opportunity to paint the public buildings in the ghetto. There is more than can be done to give ghetto residents the "piece of the action" for which they are now clamoring so loudly. But it is the height of irresponsibility for people who know better to permit the doctrine of the extreme black leaders who proclaim that such development holds the key to the economic future of the black masses to go unchallenged. The future well-being of the Negro masses depends on how successful they are in participating fully in the American economy—that is, in getting jobs, good jobs, and having the opportunity to move up the ladder.

BLACK CAPITALISM

The strength of the black power activists is probably sufficient to .assure that most, if not all, business activity in the ghetto will sooner or later be in Negro hands. At a minimum, Negroes will play a more prominent role in most ghetto enterprises. The steady withdrawal of the Jewish shop-keeper is only an early indication of what is an inevitable trend. That some Negroes will be better off as a result of these transfers goes without saying. What remains moot are the consequences to those without power. Their pride may be enhanced by the black men who will acquire wealth. But it is to be hoped that the new black men of wealth will not charge more or exact higher profits than the white men whom they succeed.

MORE KNOWLEDGE NEEDED

There is no escaping the fact that both white and black America needs more knowledge if it is to act wisely and constructively on matters affect-ing the ghetto. More knowledge is needed on several fronts: on the chang-ing socio-economic conditions in the ghetto, attitudinal changes toward both black leadership and the white community, and with respect to ideology and politics. Despite the current apparent trend toward black nationalism and its many variants, it is likely that the vast majority of Negroes will soon learn that self-imposed segregation has little more to offer than segregation inflicted by a white community. Freedom and oppor-tunity lie in participation, not withdrawal. And most Negroes are likely soon again to press hard to gain the full freedom that is theirs under the law and which is the best guarantee of access to the opportunities that alone will assure them the good things that America has for so long prom-ised and delivered to so large a proportion of its white citizens.

3

Kelvin A. Wall

Marketing to Low-Income Neighborhoods: A Systems Approach

BECAUSE it is generally agreed that marketing in the low-income segment needs improving, we should first review current levels of performance and isolate these by functions. This process provides a clearer picture of the interrelationships of marketing functions as they affect low-income consumers.

Any analysis of this marketing problem is complicated by the fact that low-income family buying patterns tend, in general, to be determined by neighborhoods. These neighborhoods are composed of a "sizeable complement of individuals who differ in one way or another from the neighborhood norm. Nonetheless, even these people tend to conform to their own group behavior pattern."[1] Marketers should, however, carefully appraise their tendency to draw conclusions from the characterictics of a single segment or neighborhood.

Before presenting reasons for developing a systems approach, let's first define the low-income market. My definition of low-income segment, purely on a dollar basis, has to be arbitrary, because of the differences in spending power at different cost of living levels in various parts of the country. Also, both the aspiration level and the life cycle are variables difficult to pinpoint.

Reprinted by permission of the American Marketing Association from *Marketing in a Changing World, Proceedings of the American Marketing Association National Conference,* a publication of the American Marketing Association, Bernard A. Morin, ed., June 1969, pp. 24–27.

LOW INCOME DEFINITIONS TODAY AND TOMORROW

For purposes of this study, we shall consider families earning $5,000 or less annually as components of the low-income segment. By this standard, over nineteen million families were low-income in 1960. This represented close to 41 percent of the total U.S. population at the time.[2] It is estimated that, by 1970, approximately seven million white families and two million black families will still be below the $5,000 income mark. This represents a substantial decrease from the nineteen million families in 1960. The median income by 1970 will be $9,600; however, the U.S. Bureau of Labor Statistics estimates a comfortable living cost of $9,200 for urban dwellers. A little less than half the population will fall below this mark, with 11.6 million white and 3.9 million Negro families below $7,000.

Marketing to low-income neighborhoods demands a consideration of center city populations statistics. By 1970, it is estimated that whites will show a decrease of two million, and the Negro, an increase of 3.3 million in these vital centers. Close to 58.9 million people will live in these areas, with the Negro representing 20 percent of the total.[3]

Much emphasis has been placed on the non-white urban poor in this country; yet, in 1960, 10.7 million white families in urban areas were in this category as compared with 5.5 million blacks.[4]

Of all white families earning over $5,000, the percentage of two wage earners per family ranged from a low of 44.3 percent for the $5,000–$7,000 group to a high of 75 percent for the $12,000–$25,000 group. Most of the ten million-plus white families earning under $5,000 have only one wage earner in their households. Even in the center city of these metro-markets, poor whites outnumber blacks by 1.2 million people.[5]

INFLUENCE OF LIFE STYLES ON MARKETING

When considering the low-income segment, there are a number of socio-economic characteristics and life style factors which encourage a systems approach to marketing. Some of these are:

1. Increased center city low-income population.
2. Low-income groups have experienced a greater increase in income than their cost of living.
3. Their neighborhoods primarily consist of small outlets. Consumers purchase frequently and in smaller units.
4. Community organization exerts pressure for faster economic and social changes.
5. Life style of consumers is need-oriented, peer directed, income-limited, mobility-inhibited, and isolated from the rest of the city.

6. Low-income families are heavily concentrated by region and within the city.
7. Unique communications network exists within the community or neighborhood.

Now let's investigate some of the life style patterns of low-income consumers that are unique in either degree or kind. These patterns, when interrelated with consumer behavior, can be linked to a number of critical marketing functions, such as: distribution, merchandising activities, product mix, packaging mix, advertising programs, sales policies, and dealer relations activities. These various marketing functions tend to interrelate in response to the unique environment of the low-income neighborhood.

"The low-income consumer is a block dweller, who sees himself as part of his immediate environment and neighborhood, rather than a part of the city in general. His peer relationships are close in this limited environment, and as a consumer, he is strongly motivated to shop within these confines."[6] "The poor consumer is less psychologically mobile, less active, and more inhibited in his behavior than well-to-do customers. The stores he considers for possible purchases are always small. The poor people more often buy at the same store."[7] "A comparison of shopping habits of middle class and working class women shows . . . fewer lower class regularly shop in the central business district. The low-income white housewife shops in 'local' stores. The working man's wife or the low-income white wife most frequently prefers to shop in a local and known in store."[8] Because of this narrow territorial view, product availability is an important factor in the marketer's distribution system in low-income areas. Add to this the fact that low-income consumers make frequent shopping trips for smaller package sizes, and you can see the importance of delivery frequency or frequency of sales calls and other sales management policies. Along with product availability, the type of outlet that dominates low-income neighborhoods should also be considered.

REACTION TO COMPANY POSTURE

Community relations has only a minor influence on immediate sales in market segments other than low-incomes. However, such secondary issues as employment policies toward minority groups are particularly important to low-income Negroes, and consequently influence their purchasing behavior.

"A company which advertises in Negro media, contributes to the United Negro College Fund, and employs Negroes is perceived as being concerned with the welfare of Negroes, and therefore is entitled to special concern and patronage." Edward Wallerstein, of The Center for Research and Marketing, went on to state that "Negroes tend to believe that a company which advertises in Negro media will be fairer in terms of its employment practices than most companies . . . further, our respondents said that they would tend to switch to the products of the company which advertised in Negro media."[9] Because Negroes look more favorably on companies which advertise in Negro media and employ Negroes, the marketing man is operating in a climate of increasing intensity. As Thomas F. Pettigrew predicted in 1964, "Negro protests will continue to grow both in intensity and depth." It "will increasingly attract larger proportions of low-income Negroes and shift from status to economic goals." He further stated, "a more intensive use of local and national boycotts of consumer products will be made."[10] His statements clearly indicate the interrelationship between sound community relations efforts and employment practices and sound marketing programs as they effect low-income blacks.

Recent organized boycotts have intensified these attitudes. The physical isolation caused by segregation in housing, either by income or race, has compounded marketers' problems. Another factor is the low-income consumer's "lack of mobility, both physical and psychological."[11] Car ownership is low, and parking space is scarce. This means that besides the general tendency of low-income people to stay within their neighborhoods, there are fewer opportunities for them to travel outside this environment. Therefore, marketing performance in low-income areas must be measured by the success—or lack of it—of retailers in these neighborhoods.

MEETING THE ADVERTISING CHALLENGE

The problem of communicating to residents of these neighborhoods offers a challenge to a variety of marketing and marketing-related functions. Advertising strategy, both from a copy platform and media planning standpoint, is as affected as sales promotion and point-of-sale activities. One reason why this variety of selling activities needs to be tailored to low-income consumers is because of the uniqueness of their life style patterns, including their language and communications patterns and attitudes toward advertising.

The language of this group is *concrete*. They are "less verbally oriented than better educated groups, and their interpersonal exchanges involve smaller amounts of symbolic linguistic behavior."[12] Their day-to-day conversations are less abstract and have less conceptualization. They deal primarily with concrete objects and situations. The fact that they generalize less and are less reliant on the intellectual process, than on observations, often renders some sophisticated advertising and sales promotion efforts of major marketers ineffective.

To fully appreciate the burden that advertising communications must carry into low-income neighborhoods, one should remember that advertising must function as a persuasive vehicle that stimulates the desire to consume, as well as increasing their ability to consume. The educational function that advertising performs in this regard is important. Many low-income housewives, both white and black, look to advertising to fulfill an educational role. Nearly twelve million U.S. adults have less than a sixth grade education, with 2.7 million never having attended school at all. More than 23 million never completed grade school.[13]

Low-income consumers' preference for certain types of models also affects commercial communications. In the case of white blue-collar wives, "advertising which is people oriented is much more meaningful than . . . advertising that communicates a highly technical, impersonal or objective atmosphere."[14] A study conducted by Social Research asserts that "the safest route to high rewards from the Negro audience is to be found in advertisements which feature Negroes exclusively."[15] Naturally this preference should be considered when planning media, advertising, and sales promotions programs.

BRIDGING CULTURAL AND CREDIBILITY GAPS

Understanding the behavior patterns of residents of low-income neighborhoods requires a clear understanding of their attitudes toward the world outside their environment. They often consider it hostile, and think in terms of "we" and "them." "The lack of effective participation and integration of the poor in the major institutions of the large society is one of the critical characteristics of the culture of poverty."[16]

Although it is difficult, a marketer in a low-income area must translate his image from "them" to "we." "Supermarkets operating in disadvantaged areas do not enjoy the confidence of their customers . . . Negroes believe that they are treated as undesirables or untouchables . . . there is a definite credibility gap between what the food chain says they are doing for Ghetto residents and what these people think is being done." Both white and black Ghetto residents have more complaints about their local food stores—"prices are high, service is bad and unfriendly, stores are dirty, and lighting is inadequate."[17]

Both marketers and retailers are faced with a number of problems. In the case of the marketer, has he made certain that the items that appeal most to low-income consumers—the items that fit best into their life style—are available in the right package size? And is the product continuously available for a consumer who has a more frequent shopping pattern than the average?

The pre-conditioning done by the marketer effects the retailer and the consumer. The retailer who has the right variety of merchandise, meaning the merchandise most appropriate to the needs of the low-income community and most readily accepted by that market, will greatly improve his image. Since the food chain store has a poor image among this group, the responsibility of the marketer is more critical. Consequently, such functions as merchandising policies, distribution and sales activities, as well as community relations and public relations functions, are key factors.

BETTER RESEARCH IS SORELY NEEDED

The marketing executive who relies on information derived from his own life experiences is handicapped when faced with the problems of marketing to low-income groups, because their life style is quite different from his middle class one. Nor can he rely on usual sources to help him narrow his informational gap. It is "acknowledged that most market research is now focused on middle and upper income people, but there is increasing awareness of the need to focus more marketing attention on those in low-income groups."[18] This executive discovers that A. C. Nielsen and other store audit services usually do not have a large enough sample in this segment to produce reliable data.

These combined factors clearly indicate the need for a systems approach to dealing with the low-income segment. For example, the system of small outlets, that is, outlets that have a physical space limitation, is interlocked with the fact that merchants usually running them have limited financial resources and management skills. Both their physical and financial limitations usually only allow these retailers to purchase limited quantities at a given time. If the manufacturer's delivery frequency cannot fit these limitations that the retailers operate under, product availability and dealer goodwill become critical problems accentuated by the low-income consumer's propensity to buy often and in smaller units. To attack the problem of product availability, it will be necessary to deal with several marketing functions, such as frequency of delivery, credit policies, and merchandising and display facilities. Changing a single marketing function probably would not be effective.

SUMMARY

A list of factors which influenced our conclusion that there is a need for a systems approach to improve the effectiveness of marketing programs

TABLE 1 *A Systems View of Marketing in Low-Income Neighborhoods*

Sociological-Economic Characteristics	Marketing Implication	Marketing Function or Function Affecting Marketing
Increase Center City Low-Income Population as Middle-Class Out-Migration Continues	Low income segment more important to most major consumer goods marketers and in city retailers.	Distribution/Physical Sales Coverage Advertising Coverage Product & Package Mix Package Size Mix Wholesaler/Jobbers
Greater Increase in Income of Low-Income Group than Cost of Living	This part of the total market will exercise more influence because of increased income and rapid population growth. Competition for their dollars will intensify.	New Products New Outlets Sales Coverage Distribution/Physical Product, Package, Package Size Mix Advertising Coverage
Neighborhoods Have Small Outlets Consumers Purchase Smaller Units	Maximizing sales or profits requires different marketing and sales strategy because of different outlet mix and purchasing patterns.	Distribution/Physical Sales Coverage Dealer Promotions Product, Package, Package Size Mix Sales Promotion Retail Store Audits
Community Organization Pressure for Social and Faster Economic Changes	Mass urban marketers, both retailers and manufacturers, will either respond to these pressures voluntarily or be forced to respond through direct economic action against them.	Product or Service Quality Existing Outlets New Outlets Employment Practices Personnel Training Advertising Content

TABLE 1—Continued

		Advertising Media
		Public Relations
		Sales Promotion
		Joint Ventures
		New Distributors
Life Style	Both retailers and other marketers faced with wider differences in consumer motivations and behavioral patterns between low-income consumers than with any other combination of income groups.	New Products
Need-Orientated		Merchandising Policies
Peer-Orientated		Outlets—Old and New
Mobile-Inhibited		Copy Platforms
Income-Limited		Sales Promotion
Isolated from Rest of City		Fashion/Styling/Colors
		Music
		Advertising Media
		Retail Store Audit
		Market Research
		Public Relations
		Distribution
Low-Income Families Heavily Concentrated by Region and Within Cities	The problems and the needs of low-income people are more similar than unique or distinct among sub groups. The amount of money they have to spend and their relationship with the total community are, in general, their two most important problems.	Sales Promotion
• density increase with low-income		Point-of-Sales
• low-income whites		Advertising Media
• low-income Negroes		Copy Platform
(Both important factors)		Music
		Package Size
		Product Mix
Communications	Conventional media can and do bring messages into the low-income areas. But, these are considered messages from the "outside" and the impact is questionable since their form and language is not their own.	New Media
• neighborhood outlet—part of communications network		New Copy
• conversation topics limited		Sales Promotion
• how as important as what is said		Point-of-Sales
• metaphoric and anecdotical		Music
• peer group network		Public Relations
		Outlets

27

directed at low-income neighborhoods would consist of the following:

1. Marketing administrators responsible for share of market in the major urban centers have to look at how their total system is working in this part of their sales environment.
2. While consumers in low-income neighborhoods are increasing their income more rapidly than their cost of living, there is still a lag in education and income. These two factors will influence a number of marketing functions differently than for other income groups.
3. Life style differences will tend to prevail and marketers will be forced to respond with a different marketing mix. Factors such as varying product or packaging mix policies will be required.
4. Finally, the concentration of low-income families in certain regions of the United States and within certain parts of the city will continue. Communications problems to this group, because of educational differences, will continue to be a challenge for progressive marketers.

Low income neighborhoods will continue to be a problem to marketers who have not adjusted their total system to this segment's needs.

Table 1 provides a summary of the systems view of marketing in low income neighborhoods.

[Notes]

1. Alvin Schwartz, "Study Reveals 'Neighborhood' Influence on Consumer Buying Habits," *Progressive Grocer,* April 1966, pp. 269–272, at p. 269.
2. *United States Census,* 1960.
3. "Changing American," *U. S. News and World Report,* June 2, 1969, p. 69.
4. "Forgotten Men: The Poor Whites," *U. S. News and World Report,* November 27, 1967, p. 76.
5. "Most U. S. Income Found Inadequate," *The New York Times,* November 18, 1968, p. 38.
6. (Unpublished Report), "The Low Income Study," 1969.
7. David Caplovitz, *The Poor Pay More,* New York, The Free Press, 1963. p. 49.
8. Lee Rainwater, Richard P. Coleman, Gerald Handel, *Workingman's Wife,* New York, Oceana Publishers, 1959, pp. 163, 164.
9. "Negro Boycott Could Have Serious Lasting Effect on Sales, Study Shows," *Advertising Age,* September 30, 1963, p. 38.
10. Thomas F. Pettigrew, *A Profile of the Negro American,* Princeton, D. Van Nostrand Co., 1964, pp. 197–199.
11. David Caplovitz, *The Poor Pay More,* New York, The Free Press, 1963, p. 49.
12. Lola M. Irelan, ed., *Low Income Life Style,* Washington, D.C., Health, Education and Welfare, August 1967, p. 72.
13. "The New Market," *Harvard Business Review,* May–June, 1969, p. 61.

14. Lee Rainwater, Richard P. Coleman, Gerald Handel, *Workingman's Wife,* New York, Oceana Publishers, 1959, p. 153.
15. *Negro Media Usage and Response to Advertising,* Social Research, Inc., April 1969, Study No. 362/1, p. 4.
16. Oscar Lewis, "The Culture of Poverty," *Man Against Poverty: World War III,* Bernstein, Woock, ed., New York, Random House, 1968, p. 264.
17. "Poor Still Don't Trust Chains," *Chain Store Age,* February 1969, p. 63.
18. "Lavidge Says Market Researchers Must Focus on Minorities," *Advertising Age,* May 26, 1969, p. 45.

4

Media/Scope

The Negro Market:
Two Viewpoints

LEONARD EVANS has called the "Negro market" a misnomer. He says, "it does not mean a market for Negroes, but rather it is an abnormal consumption in definable geographic areas of national brands at all economic and educational levels." By this definition he sees the market more in economic terms, less in racial or sociological patterns.

Expanding on his Negro market definition, Evans points out that "all markets are geographic," with Negroes, for the most part, living in "geographic densities, cities within cities." If the Negro population was dispersed throughout the 50 states on an equal basis, says Evans, "the resulting scatter would eliminate the market." The publisher and editor of *Tuesday* holds that in marketing terms the Negro is not so much identifiable "by his color" as he is "by his pattern of consumption."

"The Negro buys within and outside the ghetto," says Evans. "If the Negro conformed to the marketing norm, he'd be just another consumer. But he doesn't conform to the norm. He has an abnormal consumption." As an example of this, Evans notes that while the Negro sector of the population is about 11 per cent, "it accounts for 28 per cent of national soft drink volume." And there are many other areas of consumption where Negroes ride decidedly over or under the norm.

The basic reason for "abnormal consumption" in the Negro market vs. the general market is seen by Evans as the result of the Negro's "narrower spectrum of choice." The Negro has "less selectivity in the

Reprinted by permission from *Media/Scope*, Vol. 11, No. 11, November 1967, pp. 70–72ff.

purchase of a home, of a vacation, of travel, dining, entertainment," etc. This results, says Evans, "in a greater expenditure per unit in the things that are available to him." Whites have "more places to put their discretionary income," while Negroes, even in the same income levels as whites, "use their dollars differently because of their narrower selectivity."

Evans, contrary to Naylor Fitzhugh's belief that business is a social institution and marketing to the Negro heightens the sociological phenomenon, does not believe that the social approach fits into the Negro marketing formula. "The Negro," says Evans, *still has to buy a product* despite civil rights and all the attending social problems." Even if the social problems were eliminated, Evans believes that "the Negro will still have the same consumption pattern." The disproportionate consumption of soft drinks by Negroes, for instance, "will not vanish because of integration" just as "my own musical tastes will not change if I moved to the suburbs. I wouldn't feel called on to play Beethoven sonatas on the hi-fi. I'd still want to listen to Duke Ellington and Ray Charles."

Negro and white consumers have different motivations, in Evans' opinion. He reasons that the two races have "completely opposite economic histories," says "you have to remember where each race started from." White civilization developed from the market place, says Evans; Negro civilization from isolated, independent villages. "European society was built around trade, barter and exchange. African society was communal, self-reliant. Today we have these two peoples with their divergent backgrounds set down in a capitalistic society. Of course it's created differences in motivation—and in consumption. And it' hasn't a damn thing to do with civil rights."

With this viewpoint, Evans concludes that the militant turn in the civil rights movement itself does not really alter existing Negro-directed marketing approaches. "Marketing men," says Evans, "should look at this in terms of economics, not in terms of revolution." He sees Negro rioting as "basically economic" and "symbolic of market demand," with the Negro continually seeing the "luxuries of life" advertised but unable to break out of his economic strait jacket to get them. The rioting and looting is a protest and a way to an end. Evans further notes that the rioting is rarely racial. "The clashes have been primarily between the Negro and the law [that stands in his way] and not between Negro and white."

The Negro community, as Evans sees it, is "outside the normal, white-oriented marketing cycle," and this is at the heart of the Negro problem. "The ghetto is non-productive," says Evans. "The Negro is not a producer in the U.S. mainstream. And the profits of a non-productive society flow out. There is presently no way, outside of wages, to get dollars flowing back into the Negro community."

Expanding on this, Evans notes that today "Negroes represent a spending power of $32 billion, yet they own less than 1 per cent of American business." This means that the Negro consumer dollar flows into the general marketing stream, not back into Negro business. "A white newspaper's ad dollars, for instance, invested by advertisers to generate sales among white *and* black consumers, are re-invested by the paper in the white community," according to Evans, and he concludes that "looking at the Negro market on a sociological level isn't going to solve this."

If civil rights tension is not disrupting consumption patterns of Negroes today—and Evans says it isn't—he is not sure what effect current attitudes will have on the future. "We just don't know if the Negro adolescent group of the 1960s will follow the same consumption patterns in the 1970s that their parents follow today. In light of this, of course, it's the job of marketers to evaluate more specifically their Negro customers and how to reach them."

On Negro boycott movements, Evans feels that although a lot of people call for them, "they are ineffective because they are almost impossible to implement on a national level . . . work only in localized instances." But Evans believes that boycott is not the answer to Negro grievances generally. Instead of an auto boycott, as advocated against General Motors recently, Evans thinks Negro goals would be better served "by drives for more Negro dealerships in the cities."

Evans believes that Negro media do have empathy with Negro audiences, but he does not discount the penetration and impact of general media on the same audiences. "It's true," says Evans, "that white newspapers give little exposure to the positive side of Negro life. You generally don't find Negroes featured on the society, financial or real estate pages. Exposure is given to the negative side of the news. Yet if the Negro rejected this [editorial treatment] totally, Negro newspapers would have much greater circulation than they do. As it is, Negro papers account for only a small percentage of the readership in Negro communities."

The majority of the Negro community reads white newspapers, according to Evans. "Actually," he says, "it reads parts of the newspapers, Negro and general, for many different things. In the general press the Negro *wants* to find out the negatives . . . what people say about him. He is two people—an American citizen and a Negro American citizen— and whether he has ethnic identification or citizen identification depends on where he is at given times in given circumstances."

The first "blunder" of advertising and marketing people in assessing the Negro market, Evans feels, "is assuming that the Negro wants to be white. He doesn't want to be white or act white. If anything, he is getting more nationalistic and prouder of his color all the time." Coming back to his original point on white media vs. Negro media, Evans says he observes "a growing segmentation in the Negro market and a growing sophistication. And it takes many media, racially oriented and general, to penetrate the market."

Even if the Negro market is segmenting, largely because of the rise of a Negro middle class, Evans has no doubts about it staying intact as a market. He does not see the Negro community or Negro media disappearing, absorbed into the American mainstream. "You're talking about 23 million people," he says, "30 million in another 10 years. That's too many people with a common culture to be assimilated out of existence. To say the Negro market will disappear in time is to advocate the destruction of Negro culture." Chunks of that culture, Evans points out, notably music and dance, are being absorbed by the white community, preserving its place in the general society. "Co-existence is the order of the day," says Evans.

Evans further believes that more Negro media will come into existence. He notes that out of today's top 100 consumer magazines, only one Negro publication, *Ebony,* has a circulation of over one million. "You can't serve 23 million people with one, million-circulation magazine," says Evans. "The Negro market could absorb two or three additional one- to two-million circulation publications. The Negro media field is underdeveloped and the Negro consumer should have a choice in his media."

Evans himself runs the largest Negro-circulation publication in the U.S., although more exactly the readership—and the approach—is interracial. *Tuesday* is a two-year-old Sunday supplement distributed in 10 major metropolitan newspapers, has a circulation of 1,365,000.

Tuesday's editor and publisher says his publication "interprets Negroes to Negroes, as well as to whites . . . carries a positive message." He notes that while the supplement is directed primarily into Negro neighborhoods, the intent is not segregated circulation. *"Tuesday,"* says Evans, "goes both into the ghetto and out of it," whereas most Negro publications "only go into the ghetto. We're reversing the communication process."

Unlike most Negro publications, where advertising takes on a specific Negro sell using Negro models and tailored copy, Evans says *Tuesday* "provides the editorial climate to receive ads either way," general audience or Negro reader "depending on the advertiser and the campaign objective." But Evans says he's noted "a new era of creativity" coming into Negro market advertising. "There's a trend away from straight use of Negro models," he says. "Some advertisers are finding inventive ways to suggest the Negro milieu and idiom. They're making symbolism—in dress, surroundings, the still life of an ad—perform the ethnic identification job. The Negro audience, like the white audience, wants innovation. Thus the spectrum of appeal is increasing."

Evans welcomes the appearance of Negro models and talent in general advertising, where the inclusion is logical, but he maintains that "there is no evidence of Negroes in general ads increasing sales in the Negro community." He feels that the primary benefit is in "the education of the white reader and viewer, not in the stimulation of Negro sales."

The Negro market can, according to Evans, be analyzed on a white–non-white basis "for comparative purposes," just as you'd have to compare physical markets, New York against Philadelphia, Chicago against Detroit. But Evans feels that most researchers are not sophisticated enough in their Negro market knowledge to analyze the market properly. "Right from the start of an analysis," says Evans, "error can creep in, notably through giving Negroes the same questionnaire used for the white sample." The Negro and the white may be similarly motivated on a question "but the Negro may answer differently purely out of circumstance, his narrower spectrum of choice." Evans maintains that researchers have to be more specific in questioning Negroes.

Evans does not put much faith in public relations as a tool for reaching and working with the Negro market. And here he diverges from the thinking of Pepsi-Cola's Fitzhugh, and the National Assn. of Market Developers, whose current platform deals heavily with the public relations aspects of Negro-market programing. NAMD formerly omitted or sketchily covered public relations in statement papers on the Negro market, but it now accords the subject even greater emphasis than marketing as a dimension of the Negro market.

Says Evans, "NAMD has deemphasized marketing technique and overemphasized public relations. I don't agree with that. I believe that American industry is looking for guidelines and techniques for marketing in this area, and not for long-range, image-building programs."

Naylor Fitzhugh sees the Negro market in terms of consumers and companies, a "communications phenomenon." It involves "two-way communication, consumer to company, company to consumer, with both needing to understand the other." The Negro, says Fitzhugh, is both a consumer and a Negro, "and I'm not sure the two can be separated. The Negro has to be addressed at both levels, with both roles in mind."

Pepsi-Cola's special markets specialist feels that the Negro market has not changed essentially in the turmoil of today's more militant civil rights struggle. "The feelings and yearnings of the Negro are much the same as they always were," says Fitzhugh. "But where the messages coming from the Negro community once ran into barriers, they are now getting through." If there is any change, Fitzhugh contends it's that the "messages" themselves are much more articulate, more dramatic, more powerful. "They demand attention now," says Fitzhugh, "but they're the same messages."

Fitzhugh feels strongly that the real key to a better Negro living standard is through business. "We are a vocal people now," he says.

"But we have to get smart and find out how business works instead of flailing out at the country in general. We must hit on a specific address to business."

Business itself has started making specific addresses to Negroes. Fitzhugh cites the Advertising Council's "Things Are Changing" program as recent progress—a drive enlisting companies in a program to convince minority-group youths that they should prepare themselves more adequately for expanding job opportunities. The program also seeks to convince more companies of the all-round benefits of merit hiring. Fitzhugh is encouraged by the fact that more and more major companies are instituting special programs giving Negroes "a chance to break through the barrier to higher-wage occupations."

Pepsi-Cola, for one, in employment policy, and with a special markets program going into its 20th year, has been among those in the forefront of communicating with the Negro community. Head communicator Fitzhugh, directing a department of 10 people that serves 20 others in the field, says his function is "seeing that Pepsi, through fair, intelligent efforts, gets its full share of soft drink market opportunities represented by the major Negro and Spanish population concentrations."

In looking at the Negro market, Fitzhugh says marketers should realize that most if not all of the so-called racial behavior of Negroes involves their reactions to the inter-racial situation, rather than their spontaneous actions. He further notes that "Negroes are becoming more conscious of the effectiveness of their power as citizens—and as consumers—to achieve ends which they seek as Americans."

The Negro consumer, Fitzhugh feels, will listen to things like company and product boycott appeals voiced by some Negro spokesmen. "But it is hard to say if the Negro will act on the appeal." Fitzhugh says, "Negroes may not like a certain aspect of a company's policy, but they may like some of the company's products. It's highly personal as to which wins over the other." But, he adds, "as people's feelings about interracial issues become intensified, their concern about company policies can be expected to exert stronger influences over their behavior in the market place."

By way of example Fitzhugh recalls that when he was married in Washington, D.C., one major department store in the city held to segregated rest rooms. The Negro community had made known its displeasure but was not demanding anything like a boycott. "Still," he notes, "out of some 180 wedding presents we received, not one was purchased at that store."

Companies offending the Negro do run the risk of lost business, be it a local department store or a national manufacturer. "It has to affect a company's sales effectiveness," says Fitzhugh. "The auto industry, for one, is a highly competitive business. And when a showroom salesman with a criticized company has to face a Negro customer, his job of selling is not going to be as effective as it would be normally. You could say that my job, like the job of Negro marketing specialists with a range of companies, is to keep our organizations from getting into such a negative position."

The fact that a particular phenomenon can have racial overtones—negative or positive—means that it can have an effect on Negro attitudes toward products and companies, according to the Pepsi marketing specialist. And it can also have an effect on Negro attitudes toward media.

Pepsi and Pepsi bottlers use specialized media whenever possible to reach Negro consumers. They regularly use Negro radio, weekly newspapers, magazines and special point-of-purchase material. By using Negro media, Fitzhugh feels that Pepsi is "establishing a line of in-depth communication between the company and the Negro community." He adds that "Negro media know how to get things done in the community they serve . . . and when an advertiser develops good relations with these media, they can help him because they are an integral part of the community." Their merchandising services, sales tips, etc., can be invaluable.

Fitzhugh notes that general or white-owned media do not get the same empathy in the Negro community that Negro-owned media enjoy. "Yet," he says, "it is still true that white-owned, Negro-appeal radio stations today are the *only* mass media which reach Negroes in large parts of the country."

The question sometimes asked, "Will there be a place for Negro-oriented media in a fully integrated American society?" cannot be answered by Negroes alone, according to Fitzhugh. "Will the Negro market disappear someday? The attitudes and actions of white Americans—as well as Negroes—will have a lot of bearing on this question," says Fitzhugh. He points out that "the nation is now in a period of flux making it hard to tell what is progress and what isn't."

It seems to Fitzhugh, however, that Negro media are strengthening and stand to multiply as long as inequality exists. But even with equality, it seems hard to imagine Negro publications, Negro insurance companies and other Negro-owned businesses, wanting to put themselves out of business. Fitzhugh seems to feel that Negro business, for Negroes, will remain in any future social pattern.

The dimensions of the Negro market—what it is, why it is—are often seen differently among Negro market specialists themselves. Some Negro marketing and advertising executives (like W. Leonard Evans, publisher of *Tuesday*) see the Negro market less in racial terms (a Negro as a consumer), more in terms of consumption patterns ("abnormal consumption in definable geographic areas . . . ," as Evans puts it). Fitzhugh disagrees with this approach.

"I see it as partly that, but with many more sociological connotations. Business itself is a social institution and marketing to the Negro heightens the sociological phenomenon because of the role Negroes have in the society."

Fitzhugh calls the Negro market itself a "communications phenomenon," rather than simply a group of identifiable consumers and says "marketers must talk to Negro consumers in the places that count and in the ways that count. Moreover, to say there is *No* Negro market because Negroes buy the same products as whites is also a totally false idea. You must have the right hypothesis about that before you even attempt to analyze this marketing challenge."

"Negroes," says Fitzhugh, "are not a monolithic group of people. But they do have one common characteristic: they do tend to be extremely race conscious and are becoming more so all the time." The Pepsi marketing specialist believes, however, that if the racial factor could be canceled out "you'd probably find that of 100 Negroes and 100 whites in the same consumption bracket buying a new car, for example, all would be buying that car for essentially the same reasons. Add racial overtone," Fitzhugh continues, "such as the auto maker's policy affecting Negroes, and the story would change. The wants are the same but buying motivations can be different."

One of the things that has made a great deal of sense in general marketing in recent years, in Fitzhugh's opinion, is the gradual inclusion of more Negroes in advertising illustration. To be effective, however, Fitzhugh says that integrated ad scenes "must be realistic . . . not contrived or over-drawn . . . a picture Negroes will react to, not resent." A Negro on water skis with a sunny Florida background, for instance, isn't realistic. In Negro-directed ad copy, Fitzhugh points out, beware of preaching. "There are many subtleties to observe or to stay away from."

The best way to handle Negro market communications, according to Fitzhugh, "is with recognition and sincerity." Actions speak louder than words, he notes, "and marketers are only going to be effective in the Negro market if they treat the Negro customers and prospects with dignity."

Apparent Disagreement

- *Market definition:* Evans sees the Negro market more in economic terms—abnormal consumption patterns—less in racial terms, i.e., a Negro as a consumer. Fitzhugh sees the

Apparent Agreement

- *Militant civil rights movement:* Makes no essential change in the Negro community as market for products; no great disruption to current marketing and media approaches.

market in socio-economic terms
and business itself as a social
institution, thus marketing to
the Negro heightening the sociological phenomenon because
of the Negro's role in society.

- *The Negro depicted in general
  advertising:* Fitzhugh feels this
  is realistic and right. Evans
  does also, but says it has no
  evident effect on increased Negro sales, feels it is more for
  "the education" of white audiences.
- *Public relations:* Downgraded as
  a major factor in courting the
  Negro market by Evans; emphasized as one-two punch
  with marketing by Fitzhugh.

- *Boycott pleas:* Unworkable nationally, possible at local level.
- *Negro media:* Strengthening, stand
  to multiply, will not disappear
  in time because Negro market
  will not disappear.
- *General media:* Stress the negatives, seldom report positive
  aspects of Negro life. Negroes
  thus have more empathy with
  Negro media (but do not necessarily reject general media).
- *The Negro himself:* Extremely
  race conscious, increasingly
  proud of his color and heritage.

5

D. Parke Gibson

Why There Is
a Negro Market

IMAGINE a country with a per-capita income slightly more than
the per-capita income of western Europe as a whole and considerably
higher than the per-capita income of Asia, Africa, and Latin America
combined.

Further, imagine this country with six million families or households,
of which more than half own automobiles, which is thirty times more
passenger cars than there are in the Soviet Union and more than in all of
Asia, Africa, and Latin America. One of these families out of every
sixteen has two automobiles, and one out of every one hundred has
three or more autos.

In this country 40 percent of all families own homes and 75 percent
of the homes have television, which is twice as many television sets as
in all of France or Italy and four times as many as in East Germany or
Sweden. Half of these households have automatic clothes washers,
8 percent have food freezers, and 4 percent of the dwellings of these
families are air-conditioned.

These families have more of their members studying in colleges than
the total enrollment in Britain or Italy and slightly less than in West
Germany or France.

This "country" does exist—it is the Negro market in the United
States. From the standpoint of selling goods and services, the countries
abroad and their peoples are often better understood by American busi-

Reprinted by permission of The Macmillan Company from D. Parke Gibson, *The $30
Billion Negro.* Copyright © 1969 by D. Parke Gibson.

ness than is the Negro consumer in America. However, with the understanding of the Negro as a consumer, business can prosper.

People, being the dynamic, complex creatures that they are, are motivated in large measures by emotion, habit, and prejudice from which are derived their ideals and behavior. In the case of the Negro, his highly visible and different outward appearance identifies him as a member of a minority group having an imposed subordinate status in American society. His deepest interests, therefore, center around day-to-day situations concerned with improving his status.

There is nothing hypothetical about this condition or about the Negro's reaction to it. The motivations thus born are vastly different from those formed by the majority population whose experiences were obtained under dissimilar social conditions. Motivations are thus the framework upon which the Negro consumer market is constructed. In this respect the market is a real, impulsive, and often lively one.

The American society today is divided into two basic groups, the white and nonwhite populations, and as a result the two groups, for the most part, operate separately in the patterns of human activity in the basic areas of economics, housing, and social activity.

There is little likelihood that in the near future the Negro community in the United States will be absorbed into the white community, as the white cultural subdivisions in America have been, and this is the basis upon which business and industrial management will have to operate in the sale of goods and services to this expanding market segment.

The fact that Negroes have billions of dollars to spend and that they can be influenced to buy a wide range of products and services through positive programs that recognize them as consumers, identify with them to buy, is a fact that is gaining increased interest and action from American businessmen. Yet there still exists a lack of information and understanding of this market.

Samuel Johnson said, "A nation's ideals are judged by its advertising." The void of Negro orientation in the majority of the nation's advertising itself indicates a lack of marketing know-how or understanding by American business and reflects not only on the ideals of the nation, but those responsible for creating this advertising.

It will be some time before there is any full "integration of advertising," yet there are a group of consumers whose recognition as consumers is needed—the Negro market.

There are four reasons why the Negro market exists: (1) forced identification of the people comprising this market, (2) definable purchase patterns by this group of consumers, (3) the size of this market, and (4) the location of this market within the United States.

American Negroes constitute over 92 percent of the nonwhite population in the United States and 11 percent of the total population. The term nonwhite, therefore, is often used interchangeably with the term Negro.

Eleven percent of the nation's population spread out on an even basis throughout the fifty states would, of course, not constitute a factor. Yet, when one considers that the nation's twenty-two million Negroes are concentrated in seventy-eight cities and that in these markets they become 25 percent of the population, the percentage factor takes on prime importance, since this means that *one person in four is a Negro.*

In speeches throughout the United States, I have pointed out to businessmen some of the purchase patterns of the Negro consumer. Perhaps no other single factor has prompted as much interest in the Negro as a consumer as what he is buying with his money.

Among other statistics, when I have related them, I have said that research indicates that Negroes, as 11 percent of the total population in the United States, consume over 50 percent of the Scotch whisky imported into the nation, consume more than 70 percent of the entire output of the Maine sardine industry, consume more than 49 percent of all the grape soda produced in America, spend 23 percent more for shoes than does the majority white population, and spend up to 12 percent more for food sold in supermarkets to be consumed at home.

Often this dissemination of information has immediately started a machinery of the mind that has resulted in a growing awareness of, interest in, and development of the Negro market.

To sell to the Negro market effectively, the market must be understood—as it has been shaped historically and as it is today—and unfortunately too few companies have either understood or tried correctly to develop the Negro market.

One of the problems that has existed in the needed understanding is what I choose to call "tunnel vision." "Tunnel vision" among market executives, in regard to their thinking toward the Negro, has caused many companies to lose what could have been added sales volume and profit. It has kept many marketing executives operating within a limited scope of activity that can prove even costlier in the future.

What is "tunnel vision"? It is the failure to see the possibilities that lie beyond the narrow scope of old and familiar endeavors. The "tunnel-visioned" executive's outlook is not limited to the Negro market, however.

Marion Harper, former board chairman of Interpublic, once said, "The successor to Willy Loman of *Death of a Salesman* is the man who takes a parochial view of advertising, marketing, and promotion; fails to relate himself to his company's overall marketing mission and relies more on his personal experiences and prejudices than the findings of new marketing techniques."

"Tunnel vision," which proceeds along the narrow-gauge track that excludes the Negro market, can cost both increased profit and goodwill. It could also mean the difference between profit and loss in some product lines.

"Tunnel vision" has limited businessmen to the dim, subterranean thinking that has prevented additional growth and success in what is known as the Negro market. Marketing executives need to leave the tunnel and come out into the wider vistas of what can become additional volume and profit through *effective* marketing to Negro consumers. Increased earnings and profits from the Negro market can come only with a greater understanding, a more realistic attitude, and an honest effort in this direction.

What can business management expect when it comes out of the "tunnel"? One thing is certain—I do not believe advertising as an industry can solve social problems. It is not in that kind of business. Management must be aware of the Negro's thrust in social and racial areas, but it should not try to equate these with the current need to sell more goods and services. Should management do so, it is entering upon an area that could prove dangerous, without proper guidance and the understanding of all the factors that relate solely to marketing.

Coming out of the "tunnel," businessmen will find a group of people, with billions to spend, who are responsive to programs keyed to their interests and who, despite problems, are highly optimistic about the future and what it means to them.

It is important for those who are now selling products, services, and ideas to the Negro market, and for those who would do so in the future, that the basic fact of customer-oriented programming be applied.

There are still many expressions of belief existing in business and industry that segmented marketing—customer-oriented programming directed to the Negro community—is segregation in reverse. *Customer-oriented programs aimed at Negro consumers are not segregation in reverse but simply provide the Negro with what he wants—recognition.*

A myth that has been disspelled somewhat is that companies exercising customer-oriented programs to Negroes bring discredit upon themselves. No company has ever been boycotted for orienting marketing programs to Negro customers. With the widely acknowledged concept that advertising and other means of communication, in order to achieve maximum identification, should be oriented as closely as possible to the interests of the consumer, it is surprising that some executives in business and industry still need to be made aware that this same concept applies in the Negro market.

The Negro wants this concept applied to him, and perhaps the sooner we show respect for people as they are, the faster we will assist the progression toward an "open" or unsegregated society in which business can become more prosperous. Every day we see the evidence of Negro groups intensifying their efforts, through intermittent boycotts of consumer goods, and, in addition, government pressure is being placed on business and industry to change their practices toward Negro Americans.

Negro Americans at this point—and the government as well—seem to recognize that somewhere along the line, the commitment of America to be "American to all" has not been achieved. From our very beginning, proclamations that America was already "American" have always been seen in "general" mass media. It should be clear, therefore, that these mass-oriented communications media, which incorrectly maintain that Negroes and other nonwhites have been accorded these goals and standards which media idealize as typically American, are not able now effectively to reach the minds and articulate the aspirations of twenty-two million Negro Americans now engaged in a determined drive for a basic change in their status.

It becomes important, therefore, that the theory of Negro-oriented communication being segregation in reverse be explored. Understanding of why there is a Negro community is the first step in American business and industry's successful development of the Negro market. What should be understood as well is the "role" of Negro Americans in relation to business and industry and also the assessment of the value of customer-oriented programming by business and industry to this group.

The Negro community exists in America largely because of economics—the business and industry in America of the seventeenth and eighteenth centuries.

Slavery had existed in all parts of the world and was, at that time, as prevalent in South America as it was in the United States. However, compared with slavery that existed in South America, the scars upon the Negro in North America were unusually deep because the United States did not recognize slaves as human beings. Black slaves were treated as property, the same as an animal or other chattel.

South American slavery recognized every human being to have a soul and some freedom. This freedom involved the right to own and inherit property. Thus any slave could work his way to complete freedom and also could inherit property from his legal forebears.

In North America, however, to protect the economic interests of the slaveholder, many artificial means were employed to maintain the economic institution of slavery. Slavemasters had many children, but the American social definition of a Negro, which encompassed "anyone with Negro ancestry," had to be instituted for survival of the American economic system. Thus, everyone of the progeny from interracial contacts was automatically classified as Negro and could not inherit property. Further, and more important, this has made it virtually impossible for Negro Americans even today to become integrated, by the historical means of amalgamation, into the social "mainstream of American life."

The role of the American church to exclude the Negro American was born of the need to consider the slave without a soul. If he were not human, the logic went, why should he need the church? This widely held view, at that time, even affected many churches in the North—and one of our major institutions for social ideals and goals became part of the system that condemned Negro Americans to "exclusion from the mainstream." The artificiality of this total situation has thus affected two of our basic institutions. It also suggests that "artificial" or special means might need to be employed to overcome the widespread vestiges of the North American system of slavery.

American business and industry of the twentieth century did not create a segregated America. The enlightened management of business and industry of today knows that it is always more profitable to employ the most efficient means to do the job, whether it be human talent or the substitution of one machine for another.

Many companies have been forced to reduce efficiency and profits because qualified Negroes could not be employed due to traditional practices of segregation and discrimination. Indeed, the system of separateness has so firmly permeated all of our institutions that many realize, were it not for the changing climate resulting from protests by Negro Americans and the ensuing government pressure to alter the system, business and industry even now could not easily alter many of the outmoded practices of a segregated America.

Race is not an easy subject for many people to discuss. However, if we are to move away from the vast economic and social costs of a now segregated system, we must *recognize* that these conditions do exist, and we must discuss them openly.

The "role" of Negro Americans, as a largely deprived group, has always been a costly item to American business and industry. Business and industry today need trained and skilled people more than ever before, for they are the consumers who will purchase a wide range of products and use services.

Education for every citizen must be stressed more and more. Yet, as Dr. Thomas F. Pettigrew points out in his *Profile of the Negro American* (D. Van Nostrand, 1964),

> . . . slavery in all its forms sharply lowered the need for achievement in slaves. Negroes in bondage, stripped completely of their African heritage, were placed in a completely dependent role. All of their rewards came, not

from individual initiative and enterprise, but from absolute obedience—a situation that severely depresses the need for achievement among all people.

Harvard University social psychologist Pettigrew goes on to say that "strong traces of these effects of slavery, augmented by racial discrimination, have persisted since Emancipation," and he shows how the self-image or esteem of the Negro (which is needed to compete in business and industry) is still depressed via the picture of himself that he gathers from media oriented primarily to white Americans:

> We learn who we are, what we are like, largely by carefully observing how other people react to us. But this process is highly structured for the Negro by the role he is expected to play. When he attempts to gain an image of himself on the basis of his typical contacts with white America, and the general culture, he often receives a rude jolt. While he is totally American in every conceivable meaning of the term, he finds that most Americans are white and that somehow the mere color of his skin puts him into a unique and socially-defined inferior category. And, when the Negro looks around him—except in the spheres of athletics and entertainment—he discovers very few Americans with important positions in his society.
>
> Save for mass media expressly tailored for Negro audiences, he sees only white models in advertisements and only whites as heroes of stories. When he does see Negroes in other mass media, they are likely to be in low-status roles. Little wonder, then, that the question, who am I?, raises special difficulties for him.

Business and industry can only achieve a large measure of profits and success when all people are fully able to produce and to prepare themselves better to purchase the goods and services offered. Every human being born to this earth is going to consume, and unless business and industry, along with all other American people, help all Americans acquire the incentive to achieve the skills to produce and the opportunity to compete equal to their needs, we will have to subsidize these people through relief rolls, aid to dependent children, and many other services that add to our total tax burden—thus reducing profits.

The whole world is rapidly changing in relation to attitudes toward interdependence, and quickness of communication heightens the need for better understanding. Many dark-skinned nations have emerged. Maturity of the colored peoples throughout the world—and their predominance, with over 75 percent of the world's population—should make business and industry in America far more concerned with their relationship with the darker-skinned people here. The tide of events both at home and abroad makes it extremely expensive in this age of automation, increased technology, and rising new political power centers for discrimination to continue.

Negro Americans must change in their attitudes toward themselves and change in their attitudes toward business and industry before we can ever expect movement toward the American ideal. Business and industry, along with other Americans, also must change in their attitudes toward Negro Americans. Problems in communication do exist because of the long-standing, two-sided nature of our society. White Americans must look at the solution to this problem through changes in their attitudes, which can best be done through media oriented to them. It may well be that the best approach for American business and industry to Negro America is through customer-oriented programming.

To assess more adequately the value of customer-oriented programming to Negro Americans, it might be well to look at the backdrop against which Negroes are becoming important consumers despite the conditions. In fifty or more cities more than half of all rental units are substandard; only 70 percent of Negro homes are now rated by the government as "sound"; unemployment runs higher among Negroes than among whites; between 50 and 84 percent of Negro workers are employed performing the hardest, dirtiest, least desirable work, as laborers, operatives, household and service workers; generally, the Negro is still "outside."

The topics of Negro organizations in conventions, in churches, in civic and social organization, and at almost every gathering in the Negro community are geared to "how do we get out of this closed society into an open one?"

Importantly, and this is often overlooked, not only does the public opinion emanating from these groups become important to business and industry, but also the opinion of those who form "the concerned white community" in America, who have also decided it is time for a change and for all to receive equal opportunity.

Some companies have been plagued with unfavorable public opinion in the Negro community and in the "concerned white community," and this has proved disruptive to normal business operations. It could happen to others at any time. The need for establishing communication bridges now is more important than it has been at any time in the past. Too few companies are communicating with the Negro market—which does influence purchasing patterns—or are not doing as much as they could to change their image in this community from which most protests are flowing in this "social revolution."

For business executives simply to say "we do not discriminate; our advertising is geared for everyone; everyone reads daily newspapers [white oriented]; we reach television viewers; we do not want to segregate anyone" is not realistic and does not reflect a true grasp of the situation in light of the changes that are taking place and the practices that continue to be highly evident. While it might have been possile at one time, business and industry can no longer lead Negro thinking through white-oriented media. Negroes continue to experience the futility of this situation.

Guidance is needed to construct programs to the Negro national community properly. Some companies have decided it makes good business sense and have, therefore, taken steps to improve their communications with the Negro market. Admittedly it is not easy to move from a position of never having had communication, correctly practiced, with the Negro community to a full communication that avoids patronization and other sensitivities. If properly handled, it can be done.

Some companies are enjoying excellent relations with the Negro market and others are reaping excellent profits but many companies are continuing to ignore it.

The market will require some self-examination by executives in the years ahead. The companies that have built sales successes through historical accident of distribution and word-of-mouth support will have to ask themselves whether they are going to protect their market share through customer-oriented programming to Negro consumers. Those companies seeking a better profit margin will have to ask themselves if they intend to achieve it through customer-oriented programming in this market.

There is little likelihood that either market franchises can be protected or margin of profits increased if the Negro consumer, primarily an urban consumer whose income is on the rise, is ignored or "segregated" by continuing to be left out of mass advertising.

As consultants to a wide range of companies, advertising agencies, and public-relations firms, as well as nonprofit organizations, we have used several formulas that we believe can help any company to develop the Negro market more effectively.

One of these formulas is: *recognition, identification,* and *invitation.*

The Negro market must be recognized—objectively appraised without reliance on personal experiences and prejudices. The market wants someone to say, "I care about your business."

Harvard Business School's Raymond A. Bauer says, "The distinctive nature of the Negro revolution is that it is not a revolution to overthrow the established order so much as a revolution to achieve membership in that order. Because material goods have such an important symbolic role in our society, it should therefore be no surprise that the acquisition of material goods should in itself be symbolic to the Negro of achievement of full status" (paper, American Psychological Association, 1964).

The company that recognizes this fact and seriously begins to consider the Negro as a consumer is a third of the way to successful development.

The second stage is to regard the Negro consumer in terms of his image of himself, that is, to initiate efforts to give identity to the Negro consumer, as a consumer. The Negro consumer can identify with those programs in surroundings with which he is most familiar.

The third stage is to solicit his business—by invitation—in media and under circumstances with which he is familiar. The invitation, as will be explained in later chapters, can take many forms, but to the Negro it must be a clearcut invitation that takes the "maybe" out of whether it means him or not.

Another formula that we have used successfully in our work for major companies is $\dfrac{PR}{A\&S} + RR = PS$. This is public relations supported by advertising and selling, plus programming to produce a favorable "racial reaction," equals plus sales.

Most Negroes in deciding to make a purchase are influenced either consciously or unconsciously to some degree by their reactions as Negroes. Thus, if a company recognizes the market, creates a favorable climate for itself, and through programming produces a favorable "racial reaction," then this company should have success far beyond any normal pattern.

Case histories that appear in this book [*The $30 Billion Negro*] will show how a number of our clients and other firms and organizations have successfully used these formulas and as a result enjoy success in the Negro market.

6

Grocery Mfr.

Negro Consumers Are Waiting

ALBERT W. JOHNSON, 46, once a St. Louis hospital administrator, acquired an Oldsmobile dealership on Chicago's South Side this summer. Only three other Negroes in the U.S. are new-car dealers.

This illustrates, perhaps as well as anything, the economic situation of Negro Americans today. A few are taking giant steps as new opportunities open, but for the majority the Negro world is a world apart, often barely on the fringe of American life.

Nearly 45% of U.S. nonwhite families have an annual income below $3,000. Only about 7% earn more than $10,000. In 1965, the median family income for nonwhites was $3,396; for whites it was $6,299. But Negro breadwinners have nearly doubled their average weekly incomes since 1950, while whites have had only a 60% rise.

Yet the Negro market is changing. It is a community much more stable than the hot summer scenes of cities in their moments of anguish and chaos. Negroes and whites do not confront each other daily with pounding hearts and grievances.

YOUTH MOVEMENT

And the Negro market is growing rapidly. From 1960 to 1966, its population climbed 14.2%, compared with 8.6% for whites; in the same period, the number of Negro youths aged 14 to 17 increased by 40% compared with 26% for whites.

Reprinted by permission from *Grocery Mfr.*, Vol. 1, No. 10, November 1967, pp. 4–8.

Migration from the South to Northern urban centers is not likely to abate for a few more years. Yet this concentration, which has accelerated since the end of World War II, has placed more than 70% of the Negro population within the nation's major marketing areas, and where super market density is greatest.

However, until the last two decades, the Negro market as a market segment has been virtually ignored except for a handful of companies. Most mass-market oriented companies assumed that their message reached the Negro through television. The weight of evidence now indicates that the companies have been reaching the Negro but not influencing him nearly as much as expected.

NEW ITEM RESPONSE

A good yardstick is how Negroes have responded to new items offered in grocery stores. The Consumer Dynamics Study conducted by Progressive Grocer, Grocery Mfr.'s sister-publication, asked a cross-section of consumers if they purchased any items for the first time during their shopping trip. Over one-third of the customers said yes, but Negroes, at 19.2%, ranked lowest, compared to 25% for industrial workers and a high of 43.8% for young marrieds.

Negro purchasing habits are sorely misunderstood. Traditional assumptions and stereotyped approaches must be discarded in favor of a sounder approach based on market research. Few companies have reached their attainable potential in this market. Many opportunities have been overlooked.

For most national companies, the Negro market has been disguised as part of the mass market. True, it is part of the mass market, everyone is—but the Negro is not everyone, says marketing consultant D. Parke Gibson pointedly.

SECOND EFFORT

Though some marketing specialists cling to the notion that the Negro can be reached through traditional, motivation-oriented mass marketing techniques, the weight of opinion today is that winning Negro consumer loyalty takes extra effort. This change in thinking has already been reflected by several grocery manufacturers; a few have been making efforts in this area for years.

The soft drink companies have been pioneers and they have competed hard for a larger share of the Negro market. They employ every marketing tool—advertising, merchandising, public relations, community work and employment. In addition, PepsiCo, Coca-Cola and Royal Crown all have top-level Negro marketing experts.

Brewers have also put extra tools to work in order to reach this market. Procter & Gamble has recently stepped up its efforts. So have Colgate-Palmolive, Campbell Soup, Sealtest, Nabisco and Pillsbury, among others.

When a grocery manufacturer is dealing with the details of merchandising to Negro Americans, he cannot apply identical practices to all consumers but must learn to recognize motivations that characterize the distinctly different groups that are emerging.

EMPHASIS SHIFT

Among specialists in ethnic marketing, there are differences in emphasis.

Negro marketing consultants feel strongly that very direct efforts must be made. The company's total posture should reflect interest in winning consumers in this market. This means Negro employes, advertising in Negro media, and public relations work within the community.

Kelvin Wall, market development manager for Coca-Cola, reports the old intuitive approach to reaching this market is dead. He and other young Negro marketing specialists rely on thorough market research and develop coherent plans, just as one would do for any other consumer segment.

A good starting point for evaluating the company's position in this market, Wall says, is to ask: How has our latest marketing plan applied to Negroes? This then raises another problem: Is share of market performance as good with Negroes as it is with whites?

"If the answer is yes," says Wall, "then you had better take pains to make sure it stays that way because the competition is getting tougher. If the answer is no, then find out why and get a program into action."

SPECIALIST ROLE

Clarence Holt went to work for BBDO advertising agency 15 years ago as a specialist in ethnic marketing, where he consults on media planning and other programs for reaching special markets. Murray Hillman, vice president, ethnic markets at McCann-Erickson, and his assistant, Tom Sims, are involved daily in advising clients and analyzing ethnic market research data.

There is a Negro market, says Hillman; it is a segment within the mass market. Asked what he would tell a client to do to sell a specific product effectively in this area, Hillman advises:

First, do a complete motivational study, just as you would for any product. Define product benefits, personal reactions and social reactions— find which emphasis is most important for which market. In effect, "bring their needs to the ad."

"A special appeal is not usually necessary. The most important consideration is to find out why they buy. It generally is not fruitful to aim at the Negro as a Negro but at his motivation," Hillman says.

WHAT IS DECISIVE?

Hillman cited a regional beer study among white, Negro and Puerto Rican consumers. Reactions to product benefits were about equal—lightness, body, color, etc. But differences emerged when personal versus social motivations were considered. For example, Puerto Ricans seemed to place little emphasis on the personal satisfaction of drinking beer, but Negroes did; on the other hand, Puerto Ricans placed greater emphasis on the social interaction associated with drinking beer, and Negroes did not.

The lesson to be learned from this, says Hillman, is that it is important to cover as many points as possible and, for the special market, hit the most important one for that area hardest.

Summing up, Hillman suggests that the most important consideration is to determine the decisive versus the nondecisive way to segment the total market. To slice into Negro and white portions may not be decisive —regional, income, age or other factors may be better guidelines.

E. J. Humphries, director of field market operations for the Royal Crown account for D'Arcy advertising, warns that "many professional marketing men tend to overemphasize the differences between Negro and white markets."

TOTAL RECALL

But, he told RC bottlers, Negro media can be an effective way to bolster sales; for the bottlers, radio is especially effective and flexible.

The average Negro listens to radio more than whites and 60% to 70% are regulars. Humphries cited a recent commercial recall study showing that Negroes often had almost total recall of brands mentioned on radio commercials.

When using Negro media, D. Parke Gibson suggests keeping these factors in mind:

- Schedule a discussion, if not a presentation, on the Negro market at annual sales meetings, with prepared material for follow-up use in major markets or sales regions.
- Include Negro-oriented advertising materials along with basic campaigns to be used in the white market.
- Determine problems, as indicated by sales reports, and watch for trends.
- Advise retailers and distributors of company's efforts. Outline the changing picture, and why it is to their advantage to encourage Negro consumers.

Use of a Negro celebrity is another way companies can mount effective programs in this market. Several grocery manufacturers have already done this. Bob Hayes, Dallas Cowboys' football star, appears in Royal Crown POP material, and in the off-season travels across the country doing public relations work.

BABY SAYERS

Althea Gibson was a community relations representative for Ward Baking. Carnation uses Maury Wills and Gayle Sayers, baseball and football stars, in advertisements: "Gayle Sayers was a Carnation Baby, and baby, look at him now!"

Willie Mays has been used by Gillette Safety Razor and Frank Tea and Spice, Elston Howard for Gulden's Mustard. PepsiCo and Coca-Cola have used Negro personalities and singers for some time.

PUBLIC RELATIONS POTENT

Negro marketing consultants say Negro-interest meetings such as this are an ideal time for companies to gain valuable good will.

At last year's midwinter workshop of the National Newspaper Publishers Association, a Negro press group, here is what several grocery manufacturers did:

Seven-Up was host at a dinner, Coca-Cola at a luncheon. Pillsbury sponsored a fashion show and breakfast for the wives of the publishers, who were also guests at a bridge party with Lever Bros. providing gifts.

Schmidt's beer of Philadelphia, Pennsylvania's largest brewer, sponsored the annual National Urban League Guild ball in New York last winter, which was attended by 3,000.

JACKIE ROBINSON

PepsiCo sponsored the "1967 Pepsi-Cola International Golf Tour," with Jackie Robinson as honorary chairman.

Royal Crown hosts dinners for several Negro professional organizations, gives watches to the Negro All-American football team, and helps sponsor local activities, such as high school athlete-of-the-week awards in several cities.

"The posture we maintain with this market segment is extremely important," William M. Kinnaird, director of staff sales for Royal Crown Cola, told the RC bottlers' meeting.

"Today," says Kinnaird, "a company must demonstrate that it wants the Negro's business and is willing to make efforts to gain it and hold it.

"Royal Crown's program is sliced into four essential parts: employment, public relations, sales promotion and media advertising."

Much of the program's energy comes from C. J. (Chuck) Smith, RC director of special markets. ("Negro market promotions are an integral part of the total company marketing strategy," Smith reports.

SEGREGATION A FACT

He believes that residential segregation will continue in its present form without much significant change: "It's a fact of life, at least for the next decade." This is why a company ultimately must use Negro-oriented POP material and media, and become known as a positive factor in the community.

("You simply can't disassociate the social and marketing fabric in the Negro community today. At the very time that the Negro is fighting hardest to win equality, his community and social consciousness are becoming highly developed," according to Smith. "Yet at the same time, Negroes will reflect a company's efforts to promote positive recognition.")

Smith makes two points on why sales programs have failed to reach Negroes:

- Absence of competent internal or external Negro marketing counseling.
- Failure to recognize the Negro market as an exercise in the principles of segmented marketing.

Here is what several other grocery manufacturers have done:

Continental Baking stepped up campaigns this year for Wonder Bread products in New York, Chicago, Boston, Memphis, Los Angeles and St. Louis, scheduling space in Negro newspapers, in Ebony and on Negro-appeal radio.

GOLD MEDAL DEMO

Representatives of Ebony magazine and General Mills put over a plan in Chicago to boost sales for Gold Medal flour. The program consisted of getting major chains and large super markets in Chicago to have in-store demonstrations in predominantly Negro neighborhoods. Although counter to policy, A&P also cooperated in the program, which included Kroger, Jewel Tea and others. In all, 60 stores participated.

Negro food demonstrators distributed free cookies and Betty Crocker's Pie Parade Cookbook. A coupon worth 15¢ toward the purchase of Gold Medal flour was inserted in copies of Ebony distributed in Chicago.

During the month-long campaign, 36,000 Negro families participated in one form or another, and an estimated 15,000 families purchased Gold Medal flour.

Sealtest's use of customer-oriented material has won a substantially improved sales position in the Negro market. Milk and ice cream are supported by Negro-oriented advertising POP material and augmented by merchandising services.

Genesee, a regional brewer, through Wm. Esty advertising, makes use of Negro-oriented newspapers in the Northeast a part of its overall advertising plan. It employs the same ads that it uses in general-appeal media.

SCANTY INFORMATION

One of the difficulties in judging the Negro market is a shortage of meaningful market research. Individual companies, especially soft drink companies, have done exhaustive studies; several media studies are excellent.

Negro-appeal radio station representatives Dore & Allen have developed Negro Consumer Profiles for 300 product categories.

Other good studies on the Negro market include a Negro consumer report on buying habits in five major Negro markets by the research department of Continental Broadcasting. It contains 134 consumer categories, listing 4,009 brands, mostly food products. Another work, conducted by the Service Division of American Research Assocs., shows brand preference and use data for many food products in 10 major Negro markets.

A major section of Progressive Grocer's Consumer Dynamics study focused on The Negro Customer in Cleveland and showed how Negro store sales compare to average sales in 330 product groups. [See Table 1.]

One of the most detailed surveys done so far is the Survey of Brand Preferences Among Chicago Negro Families, published by two professors from the University of Illinois at Chicago Circle. A yet-unpublished survey compared Negro and white buying habits; portions of this have been released to Grocery Mfr.

LOYALTY IS HIGH

The widely discussed loyalty of Negroes to national brands is much in evidence. "In many cases," says Carl Larson, co-author of the study, "Negroes are still skeptical of private label, and when they support a national brand it will likely take something important to make them switch."

For example, measured by pantry inventory, 91% of Chicago Negro families had Quaker hot cereal on hand and only 2% had Cream of Wheat, compared with 75% of white households that had Quaker on hand and 14% Cream of Wheat.

Pillsbury flour was found in 69% of Negro households, but in only 33% of white homes, while General Mills' Gold Medal was in 21% of Negro homes and 34% of white families.

TABLE 1 *How Negro Store Sales Compare to Average Sales in Selected Product Groups*

Product Group	Composite Super Market % to total $ sales	Negro Neighborhood Super Market % to total $ sales	Product Group	Composite Super Market % to total $ sales	Negro Neighborhood Super Market % to total $ sales
Meat	23.67%	28.30%	Fruits, canned	1.33	1.24
Produce	8.90	6.81	Household supplies	2.25	1.68
Fruits	3.78	3.02	Jams, jellies, spreads	0.98	1.02
Lawn and garden	0.08	0.02	Juices, canned	0.93	1.25
Vegetables	5.04	3.77	Macaroni products, dry	0.57	0.46
Dairy	9.68	10.00	Meat, prepared food, canned	1.54	1.54
Frozen foods	3.95	3.10	Milk, canned & dry	0.55	1.04
Grocery	47.20	45.77	Paper products	2.07	1.94
Baby foods	0.76	0.58	Pet foods	1.12	0.94
Baking mixes	1.38	1.50	Salad dressings	0.61	0.56
Baking needs	0.38	0.29	Shortening and oils	0.67	0.97
Beer, wine, mixes, etc.	0.88	1.23	Snacks, desserts	1.89	1.08
Bread and rolls	3.13	3.51	Soaps and detergents	2.93	2.98
Cakes	1.44	1.17	Soft drinks	2.15	2.08
Candy, chewing gum	1.04	1.07	Soup, canned and dry	0.91	0.50
Cereals (cold)	1.48	1.05	Sugar	1.25	1.68
Cereals (hot)	0.11	0.22	Vegetables, canned	1.71	1.83
Cigarettes, cigars	5.38	5.13	Vegetables, dried	0.42	0.55
Condiments, pickles, etc.	1.59	1.73	Non-foods	6.60	6.02
Crackers, toasted products	0.55	0.51	HaBA	2.24	2.49
Cookies	1.12	0.88	Housewares	1.45	1.40
Fish, canned	0.64	0.73	Promotional merchandise	1.37	1.98

Source: Progressive Grocer, Consumer Dynamics Study of Kroger stores in Cleveland.

(Negro Americans generally express greater national brand loyalty than whites. Moreover, loyalty associated with quality or brand image is stronger than loyalty associated with low prices or bargains. Negroes tend to stick with their brand, but forsake price loyalty quickly when economic factors turn upward. Blue collar white consumers tend to be more conservative and slower about making this switch. /

STICK WITH YOU

Ebony magazine, whose market research team has studied Negro consumers in depth, says this about brand loyalty among Negroes:

"We have studies which show that Negroes consistently will buy the brands that are nationally advertised, the ones that have the prestige connotation and the brands about which they can feel pretty sure."

This is because "Negroes have deep psychological needs," says Ebony publisher John H. Johnson, "and ofen feel left out or forced outside" as expressed by today's social revolts. "Often the association of a name product with himself provides a lift."

In addition, brand loyalty and quality consciousness are closely tied, Johnson says. "Nationally advertised brands are generally associated with quality, and you will find that many Negroes are sensitive to quality and select the brands they can trust.

"You will also find Negroes to be more health-conscious than many other consumers. The relation of quality foods to their own health is almost inseparable."

Time and again it has been pointed out that television is popular with Negroes but commercials have failed to influence them as much as the white audience. D. Parke Gibson and other Negro marketing consultants are quick to point out what is missing: identification.

"THAT'S NOT US"

To remedy this, several national advertisers have begun using integrated spots in the big urban markets. However, there are doubts whether this is really a decisive factor unless the scene is realistic. Too often the reaction among Negroes is "that's not us."

Some companies still worry that integrated commercials can do their image more harm than good. Negroes, they say, are accustomed to watching generally white or product focus commercials. These companies believe that it is more fruitful to reach the Negro through his own media. The soft drink companies have been very successful using this combination. Procter & Gamble recently went this route, using Negro magazines and radio for Tide.

This approach parallels what Negro media men for years have insisted is the best method.

"We feel," says the manager of a New York City Negro-appeal radio station, "that if you're serving the Negro market, you want a Negro speaking to a Negro."

MERCHANDISING MEDIA

In a study of Negro-appeal radio in New York, the manager of WLIB told this story about Arnold Bakers' move:

"A few years ago Arnold never bothered with the Negro market because they assumed that their products were too high-priced for the Negro consumer. We persuaded them to initiate a trial campaign on the station for one year. The results were so spectacular that Arnold now runs advertising schedules on all three New York Negro-appeal stations."

Most Negro-oriented radio stations offer shelf talkers for local super markets that tie in the station call-letters with a sponsor. WWRL talkers have included Campbell Soup, Ken-L-Ration, Aunt Jemima flour, Muellers spaghetti, Libby's corned beef hash, peas and fruit cocktail, Quaker grits, and Carolina rice.

According to the Journalism Department of Lincoln University, Jefferson City, Mo., there are now 172 Negro newspapers published in the U.S. with a combined circulation of nearly two million. They are published in 36 states and the District of Columbia; California leads the list with 17 papers.

Most Negro newspapers are weeklies, though there are dailies in Atlanta and Chicago. The two-year-old Negro newspaper supplement called "Tuesday" is offered as an ethnic medium within the regular Sunday newspaper. It is inserted into 11 metropolitan newspapers, including Chicago, Philadelphia and Milwaukee.

SHOWCASE MEDIUM

In the magazine field, Negro media really means Ebony. It is the Negro market's showcase medium and claims a subscriber median income of $6,648, compared with $3,700 for all Negroes. Ebony has made an extensive effort to win advertisers in the food field, and within the last year has taken great strides in this direction. The magazine also maintains a staff of 10 trained merchandising men who cover 11 major cities, each with large Negro populations. These men act as local marketing experts and cultivate contacts with jobbers, brokers, wholesalers, and chain and independent retailers.

Employment is a subject that usually crops up when a company looks at this market segment. Rev. Martin Luther King's "Operation Breadbasket," in fact, listed three grocery manufacturers as target companies in its drive to boost Negro employment—Del Monte, National Dairy and Kellogg. Product boycotts, however, have not materialized.

Dr. King chose these companies because Negroes are good customers for their products, "not because their records of fair employment are necessarily different from the records of other companies."

This is essentially a carry-over from the days when the young Adam Clayton Powell urged Negroes, "Don't buy where you can't work."

QUICK SETTLEMENTS

When such employment questions arise today, they are usually settled quietly. Civil rights groups have proven sympathetic to the problems confronting grocery manufacturers, and the companies in turn have made sincere efforts to create more and better opportunities for Negroes.

A question mark on the horizon is how successful the Negro-owned Jet Food super market network will be in meeting the needs of poor Negroes in the big cities. There are now 12 markets either on the drawing board or under construction. It is estimated that as many as 20 will be opened in areas with a high concentration of Negroes by the end of 1968. Stores are generally franchised and owned by local Negro businessmen. Jet Food was created in 1966 to bring top-quality food to central-city areas at competitive prices. A secondary aim is to provide more jobs for urban Negroes and offer the chance to participate in store ownership.

7

Bureau of the Census
Bureau of Labor Statistics

The Social and
Economic Status of Negroes
in the United States

INTRODUCTION

THE progress of the Negro toward full social and economic equality with other Americans has been one of the major issues of the 1960's. Impressive progress has been made, but wide discrepancies remain. This report, prepared jointly by the Bureau of the Census and the Bureau of Labor Statistics, is the third in a series of statistical reports about the social and economic condition of the Negro population of the United States. Current data are presented in the following tables showing the changes that have taken place in population distribution, income, employment, education, and the family for the Negro population segment.

The statistics indicate once again that the important gains made by Negroes in earlier years in their level of living have been retained and in most instances have increased. They are more likely to be receiving higher incomes, holding better jobs, living in better housing, and finishing high school and college than they were a decade ago. Negroes continue to move into the higher status jobs as new opportunities are open to them. They are also more likely to be working full time rather than part time.

However, Negroes are still disadvantaged compared with white Americans in terms of educational and occupational attainment. They are

Reprinted by permission from *The Social and Economic Status of Negroes in the United States*, 1969, Series P-23, No. 29, a joint publication of the Bureau of the Census, U. S. Department of Commerce, and the Bureau of Labor Statistics, U.S. Department of Labor.

more likely than whites to be among the poor and the disabled and to live in crowded homes in poverty neighborhoods of large cities.

Some instances of the progress discernible in 1968, and the existing gaps, follow:

INCOME AND POVERTY

In the past 8 years, family incomes have generally risen, with percentage gains somewhat higher for Negro and other races than for whites. About one out of every three families of nonwhite races had an income of $8,000 or more in 1968. Negro family income reached an average (median) of $5,400 in 1968, about double the median at the end of World War II. However, this was only 60 percent of the white family median of $8,900. In the South, where half of the Negro population still lives, the Negro median family income was only about half the white level.

In part, income differences reflect the lower educational achievements of the older generation of Negroes. But even with one or more years of college Negro men 25 to 54 years old have incomes lower than whites. Despite the gains of the past few years, the movement toward income equality is still very slow.

In 1968 there were nearly 25.5 million poor people in the United States, and 3 out of every 10 were of nonwhite races. About 1.5 million poor children of Negro and other nonwhite races are in households where family income is below the poverty level. In many cases, other family members work, in addition to the family head, without lifting the family out of poverty. About one-sixth of all Negro families with two or more earners are poor. About half of the poor of nonwhite races and approximately one-third of the white poor receive public assistance.

Among families with female heads, the incidence of poverty is high —more than half of such families were below the poverty level in 1968. An increasing proportion of families are headed by women, who earn less than men, whether black or white. A Negro woman working all year full time earns only about two-thirds as much as her male counterpart.

EMPLOYMENT AND UNEMPLOYMENT

The rise in employment of Negro and other races has continued into 1969. Employment gains for this group averaged about 200,000 a year in the past few years, with the gains concentrated in the upper half of the occupational pyramid—among white collar (notably clerical), craftsmen, and operative jobs. Many Negroes are in business for themselves, most operating small service-oriented businesses.

The unemployment rate for Negro and other races was lower in 1968 and 1969 than in any other years since the Korean War, and the number of unemployed fell below 600,000 for the first time since 1957. The unemployment rate continues to be about double the rate for whites.

The highest unemployment rates of any group in the labor force are those of teenagers of nonwhite races. To some extent, high teenage unemployment rates reflect that one out of every three of those looking for work is also in school—completing an education rather than replacing it with a permanent occupation. Among heads of households (married men with spouse present), the unemployment rate for nonwhites in 1969 was 2.5 compared with 1.4 percent for whites.

EDUCATION

The increase in school enrollment is especially noticeable among Negroes, particularly the very young and those at the college level. About 20 percent of children three and four years old of Negro and other nonwhite races were enrolled in school in 1968. The emphasis on advanced education is reflected in the fact that about 450,000 Negroes are now in college—two-thirds of them in predominantly white institutions. The percent of Negro men 25 to 34 years old completing four or more years of college has increased markedly since 1960.

In 1969, 60 percent of Negro men 25 to 29 years old had at least finished high school, compared with about 50 percent in 1966.

I. POPULATION

The percent of Negroes in the total population has remained about the same since 1900. [See Table 1.] The percent of Negroes living in the

TABLE 1 *Total and Negro Population,*
1900, 1940, 1950, 1960, and 1966–1969*

	TOTAL	NEGRO	PERCENT NEGRO
1900[1]	76.0	8.8	12
1940[1]	131.7	12.9	10
1950[1]	150.5	15.0	10
1960	178.5	18.8	11
1966	194.1	21.3	11
1967	196.1	21.7	11
1968	198.2	22.0	11
1969[2]	199.8	22.3	11

* In millions.
[1] Data exclude Alaska and Hawaii.
[2] 5-quarter average centered on January 1969.
NOTE.—Data exclude Armed Forces overseas. Data for 1950, 1960, 1966–1969 also exclude Armed Forces in the U.S. living in barracks and similar types of quarters.
Source: U.S. Department of Commerce, Bureau of the Census.

South has continued to decrease slowly; however, 52 percent of all Negroes still live in the South. [See Table 2.]

TABLE 2 *Percent Distribution of the Negro Population, by Region, 1940, 1950, 1960, 1966, and 1969*

	1940[1]	1950[1]	1960	1966	1969
United States	100	100	100	100	100
South	77	68	60	55	52
North	22	28	34	37	41
Northeast	11	13	16	17	19
North Central	11	15	18	20	21
West	1	4	6	8	7

[1] Data exclude Alaska and Hawaii.

[2] NOTE.—Except where noted, when data for regions are shown in this and succeeding tables, the standard Census definition for each region is used. In that definition, the South includes the States of the Old Confederacy as well as Delaware, the District of Columbia, Kentucky, Maryland, Oklahoma, and West Virginia.

In this report, numbers or percentages may not always add to totals, because of rounding.

Source: U.S. Department of Commerce, Bureau of the Census.

While the percent of Negroes has been declining in the South, it has been rising elsewhere. Nevertheless, Negroes are less than 10 percent of the population in the North and West, but almost 20 percent in the South. [See Table 3.]

TABLE 3 *Negroes As a Percent of the Total Population in the United States and Each Region, 1940, 1950, 1960, and 1969*

	1940[1]	1950[1]	1960	1969
United States	10	10	11	11
South	24	22	21	19
North	4	5	7	9
Northeast	4	5	7	9
North Central	4	5	7	8
West	1	3	4	5

[1] Data exclude Alaska and Hawaii.

Source: U.S. Department of Commerce, Bureau of the Census.

Metropolitan areas have grown more rapidly than the rest of the national population, and the increase has been primarily in the suburban areas. The Negro population in central cities has increased by 2.6 million persons since 1960 while the white population in central cities has shown a decline of 2.1 million. [See Table 4.]

TABLE 4 *Population of the United States, by Metropolitan-Nonmetropolitan Residence, 1960, 1964, and 1969**

	1960[1]	1964[2]	1969[3]	PERCENT CHANGE		AVERAGE ANNUAL PERCENT CHANGE	
				1950–60	1960–69	1950–60	1960–69
Negro	18,793	20,514	22,331	25.5	18.8	2.3	2.0
Metropolitan areas[4]	12,168	13,970	15,594	46.2	28.2	3.8	2.8
In central cities	9,687	11,282	12,317	50.4	27.1	4.1	2.7
Outside central cities	2,481	2,688	3,278	31.6	32.1	2.7	3.2
Nonmetropolitan areas	6,625	6,541	6,736	–0.3	1.7	(Z)†	0.2
White	158,051	167,146	175,311	17.6	10.9	1.6	1.2
Metropolitan areas[4]	99,740	106,406	111,736	24.3	12.0	2.2	1.3
In central cities	47,463	47,632	45,348	4.7	–4.5	0.5	–0.5
Outside central cities	52,277	58,774	66,387	49.8	27.0	4.0	2.7
Nonmetropolitan areas	58,311	60,735	63,577	7.6	9.0	0.7	1.0

* Numbers in thousands.
† Z Less than 0.05 percent.
[1] For comparability with data from the Current Population Survey, figures from the 1950 and 1960 censuses have been adjusted to exclude members of the Armed Forces living in barracks and similar types of quarters.
[2] Five-quarter average centered on April 1964.
[3] Five-quarter average centered on January 1969.
[4] Population of the 212 SMSA's as defined in 1960.

Source: U.S. Department of Commerce, Bureau of the Census.

The average annual out-migration from the South of persons of races other than white declined from 146,000 in the fifties to 88,000 in the sixties. [See Table 4.]

TABLE 5 *Negro Population and Estimated Net Out-Migration of Negro and Other Races from the South, 1940–1969**

	1940	1950	1960	1969[1]
Negro population in the South	9,905	10,222	11,312	11,630

	1940–50	1950–60	1960–69
Average annual net out-migration from the South of Negroes and other races	159.7	145.7	88.3

* Numbers in thousands.
[1] Excludes Armed Forces living in barracks and similar types of quarters.

Source: U.S. Department of Commerce, Bureau of the Census.

Negroes in metropolitan areas are concentrated in the central cities where 55 percent of all Negroes now live. Whites live predominantly outside central cities in metropolitan areas. About three-fourths live either in suburbs or small places. [See Table 6.]

TABLE 6 *Percent Distribution of Population by Location, Inside and Outside Metropolitan Areas, 1950, 1960, and 1969*

	NEGRO			WHITE		
	1950	1960	1969[1]	1950	1960	1969[1]
United States	100	100	100	100	100	100
Metropolitan cities	56	65	70	60	63	64
Central cities	43	52	55	34	30	26
Suburbs	13	13	15	26	33	38
Outside metropolitan areas	44	35	30	40	37	36

[1] Based on 5-quarter average centered on January 1969.

Source: U.S. Department of Commerce, Bureau of the Census.

Negroes today are 21 percent of the total population of central cities in metropolitan areas, compared with 12 percent in 1950. The corresponding figures for cities of metropolitan areas of 1,000,000 or more are 26 percent in 1969 and 13 percent in 1950. The proportion of the suburban population that is Negro has remained about the same since 1950. [See Table 7.]

TABLE 7 *Negroes As a Percent of Total Population by Location, Inside and Outside Metropolitan Areas, and by Size of Metropolitan Area, 1950, 1960, and 1969*

	PERCENT NEGRO		
	1950	1960	1969
United States	10	11	11
Metropolitan areas[1]	9	11	12
Central cities	12	17	21
Central cities in metropolitan areas of—			
1,000,000 or more	13	19	26
250,000 to 1,000,000	12	15	18
Under 250,000	12	12	12
Suburbs	5	5	5
Outside metropolitan areas	11	10	9

[1] Population of the 212 SMSA's as defined in 1960.

Source: U.S. Department of Commerce, Bureau of the Census.

The Negro population is considerably younger than the white population; the median age of Negroes is 21 years while that of whites is 29. [See Table 8.]

TABLE 8 *Population by Age and Sex, 1969**

			PERCENT	
	Negro	White	Negro	White
Male				
All ages	10,660	85,189	100	100
Under 14 years	3,987	23,954	37	28
Under 5 years	1,435	7,665	13	9
5 to 13 years	2,552	16,289	24	19
14 to 15 years	510	3,411	5	4
16 to 19 years	869	6,065	8	7
20 to 24 years	766	5,863	7	7
25 to 34 years	1,189	10,393	11	12
35 to 44 years	1,065	10,155	10	12
45 to 64 years	1,658	17,788	16	21
65 years and over	618	7,560	6	9
Median age	19.8	28.2	(X)†	(X)
Female				
All ages	11,671	90,123	100	100
Under 14 years	3,964	22,944	34	25
Under 5 years	1,427	7,342	12	8
5 to 13 years	2,537	15,602	22	17
14 to 15 years	498	3,309	4	4
16 to 19 years	924	6,146	8	7
20 to 24 years	916	6,981	8	8

TABLE 8 (Cont.) *Population by Age and Sex, 1969**

			PERCENT	
	Negro	White	Negro	White
25 to 34 years	1,359	10,717	12	12
35 to 44 years	1,279	10,526	11	12
45 to 64 years	1,936	19,280	17	21
65 years and over	794	10,218	7	11
Median age	22.4	30.3	(X)	(X)

* In thousands. Five-quarter average centered on January 1969.
† X Not applicable.

Source: U.S. Department of Commerce, Bureau of the Census.

II. INCOME

The ratio of family income of Negro and other races to white has risen since 1965. The ratio is still only 60 percent for Negro families alone. [See Table 9.]

TABLE 9 *Median Income of Families of Negro and Other Races As a Percent of White Family Income, 1950–1968**

	NEGRO AND OTHER RACES	NEGRO
1950	54	(NA)†
1951	53	(NA)
1952	57	(NA)
1953	56	(NA)
1954	56	(NA)
1955	55	(NA)
1956	53	(NA)
1957	54	(NA)
1958	51	(NA)
1959	52	(NA)
1960	55	(NA)
1961	53	(NA)
1962	53	(NA)
1963	53	(NA)
1964	56	54
1965	55	54
1966	60	58
1967	62	59
1968	63	60

* Annual figures shown are based on the Current Population Survey.
  † NA Not available. The ratio of Negro to white median family income first became available from this survey in 1964.

Source: U.S. Department of Commerce, Bureau of the Census.

The greatest disparity between Negro and white family income is in the South, where the Negro median family income is only about half that for whites. [See Table 10.]

TABLE 10 *Median Family Income in 1968, and Negro Family Income, 1965– 1968, As a Percent of White, by Region*

	MEDIAN FAMILY INCOME, 1968		NEGRO INCOME AS A PERCENT OF WHITE			
	Negro	White	1965	1966	1967	1968
United States	$5,359	$8,936	54	58	59	60
Northeast	6,460	9,318	64	68	66	69
North Central	6,910	9,259	74	74	78	75
South	4,278	7,963	49	50	54	54
West	7,506	9,462	69	72	74	80

Source: U.S. Department of Commerce, Bureau of the Census.

Although the dollar gap between white median family income and median family income of Negro and other races has increased since 1947, the proportionate increase was greater for Negro and other races. The percent of families of Negro and other races receiving less than $3,000 income is less than one-half the equivalent 1947 figure. [See Table 11.]

TABLE 11 *Distribution of Families by Income in 1947, 1960, and 1968**

	NEGRO AND OTHER RACES			WHITE		
	1947	1960	1968	1947	1960	1968
Number of families (in millions)	3,717	4,333	5,075	34,120	41,123	45,440
Percent	100	100	100	100	100	100
Under $3,000	60	41	23	23	16	9
$3,000 to $4,999	23	23	22	28	16	11
$5,000 to $6,999	9	16	17	23	21	14
$7,000 to $9,999	5	13	18	15	26	24
$10,000 to$14,999	3	6	15	11	17	26
$15,000 and over		2	6		7	16
Median income	$2,514	$3,794	$5,590	$4,916	$6,857	$8,937
Net change, 1947–1968:						
Number	(X)†	(X)	$3,076	(X)	(X)	$4,020
Percent	(X)	(X)	122.4	(X)	(X)	81.8

* In 1968 dollars.
† X Not applicable.

Source: U.S. Department of Commerce, Bureau of the Census.

In 1968 about one-third of all families of Negro and other races had incomes of $8,000 or more, compared with 15 percent in 1960. In the North and West, two-fifths of the families of Negro and other races had incomes of $8,000 or more in 1968. [See Table 12.]

TABLE 12 *Percent of Families with Income of $8,000 or more, 1947–1968**

	NEGRO AND OTHER RACES	WHITE		NEGRO AND OTHER RACES	WHITE
United States:			United States—		
1947	6	20	Continued		
1948	4	18	1964	20	47
1949	4	18	1965	21	50
1950	4	20	1966	25	53
1951	4	21	1967	29	55
1952	5	23	1968	32	58
1953	8	26			
1954	7	26	South:		
1955	8	30	1966	14	44
1956	9	34	1967	17	48
1957	10	32	1968	19	50
1958	10	33			
1959	12	37	North and		
1960	15	39	West:		
1961	15	41	1966	36	56
1962	14	42	1967	40	58
1963	17	45	1968	43	61

* Adjusted for price changes, in 1968 dollars. An $8,000 income in 1968 was equivalent in purchasing power to about $5,100 in 1947.

Source: U.S. Department of Commerce, Bureau of the Census.

The income disparity between Negro and white families tends to become greater for all families and for husband-wife families as the age of the family head increases. [See Table 13.]

TABLE 13 *Median Income of Negro Families As a Percent of White, by Type of Family and Age of Family Head, 1968*

	ALL FAMILIES	HUSBAND-WIFE FAMILIES
All Ages	60	72
14 to 24 years	70	88
25 to 34 years	62	78
35 to 44 years	59	72
45 to 54 years	62	70
55 to 64 years	57	59
65 years and over	65	63

Source: U.S. Department of Commerce, Bureau of the Census.

III. EMPLOYMENT

Employment has increased in the past 9 years, and unemployment has declined for workers of all races. The number of employed persons of Negro and other races rose 1.5 million in the 9-year period—increasing 21 percent compared with 18 percent for whites. [See Table 14.]

TABLE 14 *Number of Employed and Unemployed Persons, 1960–1969**

	EMPLOYED		UNEMPLOYED	
	Negro and Other Races	White	Negro and Other Races	White
1960	6.9	58.9	.8	3.1
1961	6.8	58.9	1.0	3.7
1962	7.0	59.7	.9	3.1
1963	7.1	60.6	.9	3.2
1964	7.4	61.9	.8	3.0
1965	7.6	63.4	.7	2.7
1966	7.9	65.0	.6	2.3
1967	8.0	66.4	.6	2.3
1968	8.2	67.8	.6	2.2
1969	8.4	69.5	.6	2.3
Change 1960–1969:				
Number	+1.5	+10.6	−.2	−.8
Percent	+21	+18	−27	−27

* In millions. Annual averages for 1960 to 1968; January–November averages for 1969.

NOTE.—The information on employment and unemployment is obtained from a monthly sample survey of households. All persons 16 years of age and over are classified as employed, unemployed, or not in the labor force for the calendar week containing the 12th of the month.

The unemployed are persons who did not work or have a job during the survey week, and who had looked for work within the past 4 weeks, and were currently available for work. Also included are those waiting to be called back to a job from which they had been laid off or waiting to report to a new job.

The sum of the employed, excluding military, and the unemployed constitutes the civilian labor force.

Source: U.S. Department of Labor, Bureau of Labor Statistics.

In the period 1960 to 1969, the percent of workers of Negro and other races in the highly skilled, well-paying jobs increased much more sharply than the percent of white workers in these jobs. The percentage decrease in the number of persons employed in laborer and farm occupations was much greater for persons of Negro and other races than for whites. [See Table 15.]

Despite years of occupational upgrading, about two-fifths of the persons of Negro and other races remained in service, laborer, or farm occupations in 1969. This was more than twice the proportion of whites in these occupations. [See Table 16.]

TABLE 15 *Employment by Occupation, 1969, and Net Change, 1960–1969**

| | Employed, 1969 | | CHANGE, 1960 TO 1969 | | | |
| | | | Number | | Percent | |
	Negro and Other Races	*White*	*Negro and Other Races*	*White*	*Negro and Other Races*	*White*
Total	8,369	69,452	1,442	10,602	21	18
Professional and technical	692	10,031	361	2,893	109	41
Managers, officials, and proprietors	254	7,721	76	832	43	12
Clerical	1,078	12,282	575	3,023	114	33
Sales	163	4,488	62	365	61	9
Craftsmen and foremen	704	9,485	289	1,346	70	17
Operatives	1,998	12,379	584	1,843	41	17
Service workers, except private household	1,525	6,371	311	1,535	26	32
Private household workers	712	900	−270	−91	−28	−9
Nonfarm laborers	876	2,809	−75	207	−8	8
Farmers and farm workers	366	2,986	−475	−1,349	−56	−31

* Annual averages for 1960: January–November averages for 1969.

Source: U.S. Department of Labor, Bureau of Labor Statistics.

TABLE 16 *Percent Distribution of Employment by Occupation and Sex, 1969**

| | NEGRO AND OTHER RACES | | WHITE | |
	Male	Female	Male	Female
Total employed (thousands)	4,768	3,601	44,075	25,377
Percent	100	100	100	100
Professional, technical, and managerial	11	12	29	19
Clerical and sales	9	22	13	44
Craftsmen and foremen	14	1	21	1
Operatives	28	18	19	15
Service workers, exc. household	13	25	6	15
Private household workers	—†	20	—	3
Nonfarm laborers	18	1	6	—
Farmers and farm workers	7	2	6	2

* January–November averages.
† Represents zero or rounds to zero.

Source: U.S. Department of Labor, Bureau of Labor Statistics.

The proportion of workers of Negro and other races in each occupation is becoming more like their proportion in the total labor force. By 1969, when 11 percent of the employed were of Negro and other races, 10 percent of the teachers and 7 percent of the craftsmen and foremen were of these races. However, a larger than proportionate share of the lower-paid, less-skilled jobs were still held by Negroes and other races in 1969. [See Table 17.]

TABLE 17 *Negro and Other Races As a Percent of All Workers in Selected Occupations, 1960 and 1969**

	1960	1969
Total, employed	11	11
Professional and technical	4	6
Medical and other health	4	8
Teachers, except college	7	10
Managers, officials, and proprietors	2	3
Clerical	5	8
Sales	3	4
Craftsmen and foremen	5	7
Construction craftsmen	6	8
Machinists, jobsetters, and other metal craftsmen	4	6
Foremen	2	4
Operatives	12	14
Durable goods	10	14
Nondurable goods	9	14
Nonfarm laborers	27	24
Private household workers	46	44
Other service workers	20	19
Protective services	5	8
Waiters, cooks, and bartenders	15	14
Farmers and farm workers	16	11

* Annual averages for 1960 and January–November averages for 1969.

Source: U.S. Department of Labor, Bureau of Labor Statistics.

Nonfarm workers of Negro and other races in business for themselves tend to concentrate in services and in retail and wholesale trade. [See Table 18.]

TABLE 18 *Self-Employment by Industry, 1969*

| | NUMBER (THOUSANDS) | | PERCENT DISTRIBUTION | |
	Negro and Other Races	White	Negro and Other Races	White
Total	387	6,782	100	100
Agriculture	94	1,818	24	27
Mining	—†	15	—	—
Construction	36	653	9	10
Manufacturing	10	256	3	4
Durable goods	9	156	2	2
Nondurable goods	1	100	—	1
Transportation	23	162	6	2
Trade	78	1,575	20	23
Finance, insurance, and real estate	7	254	2	4
Private household	6	23	2	—
Other service	135	2,026	35	30

  * January–November averages.
  † Represents zero or rounds to zero.

Source: U.S. Department of Labor, Bureau of Labor Statistics.

IV EDUCATION

During the 1960's there was a considerable increase in the enrollment of persons above the compulsory attendance age. In 1960, 35 percent of Negro youths 18 and 19 years old were enrolled in school. In 1968, however, this proportion had increased to 45 percent. [See Table 19.]

TABLE 19 *Percent Enrolled in School, by Age, 1960, 1966, and 1968*

| | NEGRO | | | WHITE | | |
	1960[1]	1966	1968	1960	1966	1968
3 and 4 years	—*	[1]14	19	—	12	15
5 years	51	65	69	66	74	78
6 to 15 years	98	99	99	99	99	99
16 and 17 years	77	85	86	83	89	91
18 and 19 years	35	38	45	39	48	51
20 to 24 years	8	8	12	14	21	22

  * Represents zero.
  [1] Negro and other races.

Source: U.S. Department of Commerce, Bureau of the Census.

Among 3- and 4-year olds, the percent enrolled in school is higher for Negroes than for whites. This is due in part to the high enrollment of Negroes in the Head Start Program.

Negro children are more likely to be enrolled in public elementary schools and less likely to be enrolled in parochial and other private elementary schools than whites. In 1968, 97 percent of Negroes in elementary school were in public schools, compared with 86 percent of whites. For both Negroes and whites, enrollment in parochial and other private schools tends to increase as family income increases. [See Table 20.]

TABLE 20 *Percent of Pupils Enrolled in Grades 1 to 8, in Public, Parochial and Other Private Schools, by Family Income, 1968*

	NEGRO		WHITE	
	Public Schools	Parochial and Other Private Schools	Public Schools	Parochial and Other Private Schools
Total (thousands)	4,569	147	24,628	4,053
Total (percent)	97	3	86	14
Under $3,000	100	—†	92	8
$3,000 to $4,999	98	2	92	8
$5,000 to $7,499	96	4	88	12
$7,500 to $9,999	95	5	85	15
$10,000 to $14,999	88	12	83	17
$15,000 and over	86	14	79	21

† Represents zero or rounds to zero.

Source: U.S. Department of Commerce, Bureau of the Census.

The proportion of both whites and Negroes who have completed at least one year of college was greater in 1969 than a generation earlier. In 1969, 21 percent of Negroes 20 and 21 years old had completed at least one year of college. Among those 35 to 44 years old only 11 percent of Negroes had attended college for one year or longer. Despite the improvement in the proportion with some college training, 18 percent of the white and 42 percent of the Negro 20 and 21 year olds had not completed high school. [See Table 21.]

TABLE 21 *Percent Distribution by Years of School Completed for Persons 20 Years Old and Over, by Age, 1969*

	LESS THAN 4 YEARS OF HIGH SCHOOL	HIGH SCHOOL, 4 YEARS	COLLEGE 1 YEAR OR MORE	MEDIAN YEARS OF SCHOOL COMPLETED
NEGRO				
20 and 21 years old	42.1	36.6	21.2	12.2
22 to 24 years old	43.9	37.1	19.1	12.2
25 to 29 years old	44.3	40.1	15.7	12.1
30 to 34 years old	49.8	36.7	13.5	12.0
35 to 44 years old	62.8	26.8	10.5	10.6

TABLE 21 (Cont.) *Percent Distribution by Years of School Completed for Persons 20 Years Old and Over, by Age, 1969*

45 to 54 years old	70.8	18.9	10.3	9.1
55 to 64 years old	85.2	8.7	6.2	7.6
65 to 74 years old	89.7	5.5	4.9	6.1
75 years old and over	92.4	4.1	3.5	5.2
WHITE				
20 and 21 years old	18.1	41.6	40.1	12.8
22 to 24 years old	19.6	44.8	35.7	12.7
25 to 29 years old	23.0	44.8	32.1	12.6
30 to 34 years old	27.3	44.9	27.6	12.5
35 to 44 years old	33.9	41.0	25.1	12.4
45 to 54 years old	40.7	39.3	20.0	12.2
55 to 64 years old	55.2	27.5	17.3	10.9
65 to 74 years old	67.6	18.9	13.4	8.9
75 years old and over	75.1	13.8	11.1	8.5

Source: U.S. Department of Commerce, Bureau of the Census.

V. THE FAMILY

About 70 percent of all families of Negro and other races are headed by a man with a wife present, compared with 90 percent of white families. The proportion of female-headed families of Negro and other races has increased since 1950. [See Table 22.]

TABLE 22 *Composition of Families, 1950, 1955, 1960, and 1966–1969**

	HUSBAND-WIFE		OTHER MALE HEAD		FEMALE HEAD[1]	
	Negro and Other Races	White	Negro and Other Races	White	Negro and Other Races	White
1950	77.7	88.0	4.7	3.5	17.6	8.5
1955	75.3	87.9	4.0	3.0	20.7	9.0
1960	73.6	88.7	4.0	2.6	22.4	8.7
1966	72.7	88.8	3.7	2.3	23.7	8.9
1967	72.6	88.7	3.9	2.1	23.6	9.1
1968	69.1	88.9	4.5	2.2	26.4	8.9
1969	68.7	88.8	3.9	2.3	27.3	8.9

* Percent.

[1] Female heads of families include widowed and single women, women whose husbands are in the armed services or otherwise away from home involuntarily, as well as those separated from their husbands through divorce or marital discord.

Source: U.S. Department of Commerce, Bureau of the Census.

At incomes below $3,000 only half of Negro families are headed by a male as compared with three-fourths of white families. At the higher income levels about nine-tenths of the Negro families are headed by men. [See Table 23.]

TABLE 23 *Families by Sex of Head, by Income Group, 1968*

	NEGRO			WHITE		
	Total	Female	Male	Total	Female	Male
All families	100	29	72	100	9	91
Under $3,000	100	56	44	100	27	73
$3,000 to $4,999	100	36	64	100	17	83
$5,000 to $6,999	100	22	78	100	12	88
$7,000 to $9,999	100	11	89	100	6	94
$10,000 to $14,999	100	9	91	100	4	96
$15,000 and over	100	7	93	100	3	98

* Percent.

Source: U.S. Department of Commerce, Bureau of the Census.

About 70 percent of children of family heads of Negro and other races and 90 percent of children of white family heads live with both parents. [See Table 24.]

TABLE 24 *Percent of Children of Family Heads Living with Both Parents, 1960–1969*

	NEGRO AND OTHER RACES	WHITE
1960	75	92
1961	76	92
1962	73	92
1963	70	92
1964	71	92
1965	71	91
1966	71	91
1967	73	92
1968	69	92
1969	69	92

NOTE.—Unmarried children under 18 years old living in families.

Source: U.S. Department of Commerce, Bureau of the Census.

Selected References

American Negro Reference Guide (Mimeograph), Vol. 1, Nos. 7, 8, 9, New York: World Mutual Exchange (March, April, May 1961).

Badger, S. "Negro Market: Fifteen Billion Dollar Market," *Negro Historical Bulletin,* 18 (October 1954), 12.

Barnes, Nicholas L. *Some Potentialities and Limitations of the Negro Market in Chicago.* Chicago: T and T, 1953.

Becker, Garry S. *The Economics of Discrimination.* Chicago, University of Chicago Press, 1957.

"Blacks in America," *Social Science Quarterly,* Vol. 49 (December 1968).

Business and Defense Services Administration, *A Guide to Negro Marketing Information.* Washington, D.C.: U.S. Department of Commerce (September 1966).

Business and Defense Services Administration, *Bibliography on Marketing to Low-Income Consumers.* Washington, D.C.: U.S. Department of Commerce (January 1969).

Cervantes, Alfonso J. "To Prevent a Chain of Super-Watts," *Harvard Business Review,* 45 (September–October 1967), 55–65.

"Characteristics of Families Residing in 'Poverty Areas,' March 1966," August 24, 1966 (Series P-23, No. 19), Washington, D.C.: U.S. Department of Commerce, Bureau of the Census.

Cohen, Stanley E. "Business Must Act to Keep Ghetto's Distrust of Crooks from Hurting All," *Advertising Age,* 39, April 15, 1968, 16.

Dallaire, Victor J. "U.S. Negro Market: Growing Targets for Advertisers," *Printer's Ink,* September 15, 1955, 52.

Davis, John P., ed. *The American Negro Reference Book.* Englewood Cliffs, N.J.: Prentice-Hall, Inc., 1966.

"Do Negroes Compose a Separate Market?," *American Druggist,* 158, July 29, 1968, 65.

Gibson, D. P., and associates. *Confidential Report of the Negro Market.* (October 1962).

Gibson, D. P. "The Expanding Negro Market in the West," *Western Advertising,* 82 (June 1964), 19–22.

Grayson, W. P. "Despite Integration Negro Is Separate Market," *Advertising Age,* 34, June 3, 1963, 104.

Hall, Claude H. "Guide to Marketing for 1959: The Negro Market," *Printer's Ink,* 265, October 31, 1958, 137–138.

Holte, C. L. "Negro Market: To Profit from It, Recognize It and Service Its Needs," *Printer's Ink,* 262, April 4, 1958, 29–32.

"Is There a U. S. Negro Market?," *Sponsor,* 18, August 17, 1964, 32–35.

Korenvaes, P. "Negro Market," *Dun's Review and Modern Industry,* 82 (November 1963), 61–62.

"Market Basics," *Sponsor,* 15, October 9, 1961, 16–21.

Negro Buying Power (Mimeo) Report No. L-18, Atlanta, Ga., Southern Regional Council, 1960.

"Negro Gets Toehold in Harlem Retailing," *Ebony,* 21 (March 1966), 149–152.

"Negro Impact on Market," *Broadcasting,* 64, June 17, 1963, 96ff.

"The Negro Market," *Time Magazine,* 79, February 9, 1962.

"Negro Market: Business Counts Its 19 Million Customers," *Newsweek,* 58, July 31, 1961, 67–69.

"Negro Market Data: Still Inadequate, but Starting to Flow," *Sponsor,* 13, September 26, 1959, 12–13.

"Negro Market: Executive Guide to Marketing—1965," *Printer's Ink,* 288, August 28–September 4, 1964, 9.

"Negro Market: Prime Target," *Chemical Week,* 93, September 7, 1963, 77.

"Negro Market Sought Because of Hard Headed Economics: An Interview with J. H. Johnson," *Advertising Age,* 36, November 29, 1965, 3ff.

"Negro Marketing Basics," *Sponsor,* 14, September 26, 1960, 17–28.

"Negro-White Differences in Geographic Mobility, 1964." Washington, D.C.: Area Development Administration, U.S. Department of Commerce.

"$2 Billion Negro Furnishing Market Seen by Ebony," *Advertising Age,* 34, March 25, 1963, 88ff.

Urban Negro Market Potential. New York: Johnson Publishing Co., May 1959.

Social
and Cultural
Aspects

The social and cultural dimensions of any segment of society are significant because they influence behavior. The articles in Part 2 focus on these aspects and examine the social stratification system, attitudes, and aspirations of the black population. Effective communication with black consumers depends upon the ability to recognize and adjust to the social and cultural conditions that characterize black society.

"Low-Income Outlook on Life," by Lola M. Irelan and Arthur Besner, describes the life style of our lower-income population relative to the rest of American society. Inherently poor people are at the bottom of society's economic ladder. Because of associated aspects, their views are significantly different. Their purposes, plans, and objectives influence their behavior and provide a set of recognizable life-style conditions.

The literature on the subject provides considerable evidence of social stratification and its importance to marketing. In "The Black Community: Social Stratification," Alphonso Pinkney compares the social systems of rural and urban blacks as well as those of blacks and whites, and he contrasts characteristics of the lower-, middle-, and upper-class blacks.

The social factors that influence behavior in the marketplace are generally of such significance that businessmen incorporate them in their decisions. Eric Lincoln's article, "The Negro's Middle-Class Dream," compares the aspirations of the black to the white middle class and discusses the values associated with this social stratum.

Norval D. Glenn and Donald L. Noel, in "Negro Prestige Criteria: A Case Study in the Bases of Prestige" and "Group Identification Among Negroes: An Empirical Analysis," respectively, provide empirical bases for the study and understanding of the black-consumer segment. Glenn reveals that the most important prestige criterion among blacks is formal education. As contrasted with the white-consumer segment, this criterion is significant because of the greater variation in the educational achievements of blacks.

The psychological aspects of Glenn's article and Noel's group identification subject area provide some interesting insights. Both contributions are well documented and highly analytical. Background information is empirically tested and bench marks are provided for future study.

The black-population segment has its separate institutions and associations; consequently, it is not unusual to discuss this segment as a subculture in terms of the total American population. The final article in this part, "The Subsociety and the Subculture in America: Negroes," provides a summary of the social and cultural characteristics of the black and analyzes various aspects of numerous studies in the current literature.

8

Lola M. Irelan
Arthur Besner

Low-Income Outlook on Life

CURRENTLY, in our national concern for the alleviation of poverty and economic dependency, the need to know and understand what life looks like from the bottom of society is a crucial one. We can induce meaningful change only if we understand the situation where we intend it to occur. It is unlikely, for example, that we can change or reduce rates of dependency and poverty without knowing what the conditions of dependence and deprivation mean to people caught up in them. Nor can we bring any class of people into a different relationship to society without knowing the quality of the existing situation.

As yet, knowledge of this sort is fugitive and tenuous. Much needed research has yet to be designed. There are gaps and flaws in the exploratory research which has been done. The findings on hand are suggestive rather than definitive. There is enough known, however, to warrant inventory and judicious application. It behooves us to systematize and use such knowledge as we do have. In the long run, such a step will serve to refine and increase it.

This paper summarizes available findings, largely from studies in the United States, bearing on the approach to life of the poor, the people at the bottom of society's economic ladder. It will discuss the connection between the condition of poverty, the views of man and society which arise there, and the apparent effect of those views on the lower class version of American goals and values.

Reprinted by permission from *Low-Income Life Styles,* a publication of the U.S. Department of Health, Education, and Welfare.

LIFE CONDITIONS OF THE POOR

In our society, a continuously low income is directly associated with certain life situations. Poorer, more crowded living quarters, reduced access to education and recreation, occupational restriction to simpler, manual types of work—these and similar characteristics of the very poor are sufficiently obvious to need no underlining. The result of these circumstances is a set of life conditions which is not so obvious. They consist of four general limitations: (1) comparative simplification of the experience world, (2) powerlessness, (3) deprivation, and (4) insecurity. These limitations are, of course, relative. Indeed, they can be discerned only because of the different extent of their existence at the several levels of society.

1. Limited alternatives   The poor, of all the strata in society, have the slightest opportunity to experience varieties of social and cultural settings. Their own setting is one of the least intricacy and flexibility. Throughout life, they experience a very narrow range of situations and demands. Their repertoire of social roles is limited. They seldom participate in any activity which takes them out of the daily routine. They rarely play roles of leadership, or fill any position calling for specialized functioning. On their jobs they confront less complex situations and have fewer, less diverse standards to meet. Socially, they seldom go beyond the borders of kinship and neighborhood groups—people very like themselves.[1]

2. Helplessness   The position of the poor vis-à-vis society and its institutions is one of impotence. They have practically no bargaining power in the working world. Unskilled and uneducated, they are the most easily replaced workers. The skills they do have are minimal, of little importance in productive processes. On the job itself, the very poor man can exercise little autonomy and has small opportunity to influence conditions of work. He is close to helpless even to acquire information and training which would change this situation. He has neither the knowledge nor the means to get it.

3. Deprivation   It is reasonable to suspect that this general condition, almost universally associated with poverty, is felt with particular intensity in American society. Deprivation is, after all, relative. When it is defined as lack of resources relative to felt wants and needs, it is evident that America has one of the greatest gaps between generally accepted goals and the extent to which the lower class can realistically expect to attain them. As a nation, we stress, perhaps inordinately, the value and virtue of high attainment. We expect and applaud efforts at self-improvement and upward social mobility. Commercial advertising attempts to stimulate and increase desire for status achievement. The richness of life in the rest of society is well displayed—on television, in newspapers, on billboards, in store windows, on the very streets themselves. All this, plus awareness that some people have actually succeeded in the strenuous upward move, makes the condition of the unachieving poor one of unremitting deprivation. Their relative deprivation is, perhaps, the condition which more than anything else affects the life-view of the poor. Constant awareness of their own abject status and the "failure" which it rightly or wrongly implies understandably leads to embarrassed withdrawal and isolation.

4. Insecurity People of low income are more at the mercy of life's unpredictability than are the more affluent. Sickness, injury, loss of work, legal problems—a range of hazardous possibilities—may overwhelm anyone. But to the poor man they are especially fearful. His resources are more sparse. His savings, if any, are quickly expended in any sizable emergency. Certain conditions of his life make emergencies more likely. His work skills are more expendable, sometimes more dependent on seasonal demands. He is more likely to lose his job on short notice. An emergency expenditure of funds may mean the postponing of rent payments and the fear of eviction. He is unable to secure for himself and his family the regular, preventive health measures which would fend off medical emergencies. He often finds that he cannot successfully navigate the channels involved in using public sources of emergency help, such as clinics and legal aid agencies.[2]

LOW-INCOME VIEW OF MAN AND SOCIETY

Constant, fruitless struggle with these conditions is likely to produce estrangement—from society, from other individuals, even from oneself. The wholeness of life which most of us experience—the conjunction of values, knowledge, and behavior which gives life unity and meaning—is less often felt by the poor. They see life rather as unpatterned and unpredictable, a congeries of events in which they have no part and over which they have no control.

Conceptualized as "alienation," this view of life is repeatedly found associated with lower social and economic status.[3] It is multifaceted—despair can be generated and felt in many ways. Generally, however, it seems to have four different forms of expression. The alienation of the poor is graphically seen in their feelings of: (1) powerlessness, (2) meaninglessness, (3) anomia, and (4) isolation.

1. Powerlessness   The objective condition of helplessness in relation to the larger social order leads naturally to the conviction that one cannot control it. The poor are widely convinced that individuals cannot influence the workings of society. Furthermore, they doubt the possibility of being able to influence their own lives. Correspondingly, they are likely to voice such pessimistic views as, "A body just can't take nothing for granted; you just have to live from day to day and hope the sun will shine tomorrow."[4]

2. Meaninglessness   Powerlessness, the feeling of being used for purposes not one's own, usually is accompanied by conviction of meaninglessness. The alien conditions in which an individual may be caught up tend to be unintelligible. He does not grasp the structure of the world in which he lives, cannot understand his place in it, and never knows what to expect from it. Oriented, by need, to the present, he is relatively insensitive to sequences in time. He often does not understand the continuity of past experience and current ones. And, not only does the poor man feel unable to control future events, he cannot even predict them.

3. Anomia   The term "anomie" was originally coined to describe situations in which social standards have been broken down, or have no influence upon behavior.[5] It has subsequently been pointed out that this normless condition is a probable result of the failure of prescribed behavior to lead one to expected goals.[6] The life view of individuals caught in such a discrepant situation is likely to be cynical, perhaps fatalistic. For example, the poor man who is taught in many ways that economic success is the most desirable thing in life—and then is barred from legitimate means of achieving it—may come to expect that illegal behavior is necessary to reach approved goals. The situation, moreover, induces people to believe in luck. The poor are in no position to comprehend the whole of society's structure and operation, or to understand its dysfunctions. Since they also have little control over it, its impact on them is frequently fortuitous. Understandably, they are quick to credit their difficulties to fortune and chance.[7]

4. Isolation   More than any other segment of society, the very lowest economic stratum is socially isolated. The poor man not only fails to comprehend society or his community, he is out of touch with it. He reads fewer newspapers, hears fewer news programs, joins fewer organizations, and knows less of the current life of either the community or the larger world than more prosperous, better educated people do. Nor do the poor associate among themselves more than minimally.[8] Experiencing separation from society and each other, it is natural for them to feel alone and detached. And feeling no identity, even with each other, they view the world as indifferent and distant—"No one is going to care much what happens to you when you get right down to it."[9]

GOALS AND VALUES

What are the aims of life in such circumstances? In a situation of relative helplessness, knowing themselves worse off than the rest of society, living on the edge of chronic emergencies, and seeing their own circumstances as formless and unpredictable, how do the poor shape their lives? What values do they hold? What goals do they seek? Essentially, they seek and value the same things as other Americans. Naturally enough, since they are American poor, they absorb characteristic American values and preferences. And, just as naturally, the realities of low economic status are visible in the lower class version of American dreams and designs. The result is a constricted but recognizable variant of society-wide goals and standards.

Increased sophistication of research on lower income and deprived groups is correcting a long-held impression that the poor place no value on occupational and educational achievement. While the poor do have a more modest absolute standard of achievement than do those who are better off, they want relatively more improvement in their condition. They value the same material comforts and luxuries. Psychologically, they seek the securities that appeal to other Americans. They hold, with little qualification, to the same proprieties of social conduct.

Interest in improving one's status, however, seems to have different sources at different social levels. To the middle-class youth, the idea of having a better job than his father is appealing, sometimes absorbing. Such achievement is attractive in itself. A lower-class youngster has more urgent, material reasons for wanting an improved future. His present is painfully unsatisfactory. His urge toward better, stabler occupations is not so much drive for achievement as flight from discomfort and deprivation. It is probably stronger for that difference.[10]

Reality—expenses of education and training, lack of resources—usually keeps less well-off high school students from aspiring to the highest level professions. But, more than their middle-class fellows, lower-class high school students want better jobs than their fathers'. They are more likely to value increased income. In significantly greater numbers, they are unwilling to enter the same occupations as their fathers.[11]

Although they may not expect to achieve it, most low-income people value advanced education. It has been found that up to 65 percent of parents will say they want a college education for their children.[12]

Materially, the lower classes are not satisfied with poor housing or living conditions. High on their list of desirable improvements are better housing and neighborhoods. Inside their homes, they value the same things as the general run of Americans—comfortable and durable furniture, a television set, an array of electrical appliances, and, to give life grace as well as comfort, a few ornaments and art objects. Tastes in style are definitely American—modern furniture, colored telephones, pole lamps, systematic color schemes.[13] It sometimes happens, as in more affluent circumstances, that materialistic values win out over real human needs. Parents stint on children's clothing to save money for a car. Older children are pressed too early into adult responsibilities because both parents are working away from the home.[14] A woman postpones an operation for herself because the family must have a car or a radio.[15]

In common with other Americans, the lower class enjoys excitement and values the opportunity to escape routines and pressures of day-to-day existence. Spectator sports, television, visiting—all are valued leisure-time pursuits.[16]

Probably the most basic value held by the poor is that of security. Even more than "getting ahead," they value "getting by," avoiding the worsening of an already unstable situation.[17] They are unwilling to take risks, and seek security rather than advancement—also a frequent pattern in economically better-off segments of the population.[18]

The moral code of the very lowest class is a moot subject. It has been said that they have an entirely separate set of moral and ethical values. They have also been described as subscribing so fully to the general American code that they are frustrated by it.[19] The most realistic conception seems to be that which credits them with an adapted version of society's rules of behavior. They value stable marriages, perhaps even more highly than do middle-class Americans. They do not, however, reject out of hand other forms of sex partnership. A sliding scale seems to exist, whereon a good common-law marriage is valued less than legal union, but more than a transient arrangement. Illegitimacy is not devalued to the extent that it is elsewhere. Legitimate families are the ideal, but there is also some merit ascribed to the parent who acknowledges and supports children born out of wedlock.[20]

LIFE THEMES

The anomaly of life at the poverty line is evident. When people live in conditions of such obvious helplessness, when they are themselves so aware of their condition as to feel alienated and apart from society, how can they retain, much less implement, the values of that society?

The apparent answer is reinterpretation. Paths to achievement, to security, to any goal—the very quality of the goal itself—are refracted by the lower class view of life. They are interpreted in the light of what the poor man considers to be facts about life. The helplessness which he feels, the insecurity he experiences, the meaninglessness of life—all have their effect upon the way he lives and behaves.

There are four distinctive themes peculiar to lower class behavior, all apparently the result of a deprived, alienated condition: fatalism, orientation to the present, authoritarianism, and concreteness.

The genuine powerlessness experienced by the lower class is the source of persistent fatalistic beliefs. The natural counterpart of feeling helpless is belief in uncontrollable external forces. The attitude is reminiscent of belief in fate. People cannot avoid what is going to happen to them. Resignation is the most realistic approach to life.[21] Even when optimism is expressed, it is likely to be in terms of the working of chance —"A poor person should never give up hope; there's always a chance that a lucky break will put him on top."[22] This attitude acts as a definite brake on occupational and educational aspirations, and retards health care. In various other ways fatalism minimizes efforts to cope with deprivation and its consequences.

Hand in hand with fatalism goes a persistent tendency to think in terms of the present rather than the future. It is, after all, fruitless to pay attention to the distant future or try to plan life when fortune and chance are considered its basic elements. Also, when so much of one's resources must be expended simply to survive the present, little is left over for the future.[23] Results of this ad hoc orientation are pervasive. It handicaps people for the planning required in systematic economic improvement. It works against the frugality and rainy-day planning which could offset economic dependency. In the home, it results in child-training in terms of immediate reward and punishment. Children quickly evince their own present-time thinking. This low concern for future goals has been shown to be related to low academic achievement[24]—and the cycle continues.

The authoritarian theme is a strong underlying factor in interpersonal relationships of the poor. Generally defined, it is the embodiment of belief, more prevalent in the lower classes than elsewhere, in the validity of strength as the source of authority, and in the rightness of existing systems. It seems to arise from simplification of life experiences, in which one learns to prefer simple solutions to problems, and from constant subordination of the poor. Authoritarianism is incarnate in the habit of classifying people as either "weak" or "strong," in belief that deviance or disobedience should be severely punished, and in reliance on authority, rather than reason, as the proper source of decisions. It has traceable effects on family relations, child-rearing patterns, and relation to community institutions—schools, clinics, the police, welfare agencies, even to churches.[25]

Concreteness, stress on material rather than intellectual things, is a believable but little-discussed theme of lower class life. It is natural to people preoccupied by material problems. It shows itself in verbal patterns, in distrust of intellectualism, and in occupational values.

The concrete verbal style of the poor has been well-documented.[26] It is characterized by less abstraction, fewer concepts, more frequent reference to concrete objects and situations, and a less discursive manner. It includes fewer generalizations, relies less on intellectual process than on observation, and is more tied to the world of immediate happenings and sensations.

Consistent with its patterns of speech, the lower class inclines to withhold its admiration from "eggheads," reserving it instead for the practical, down-to-earth man of action. What counts is not abstract, intellectual pursuits, but the hard tangible products of action. Results are important.[27]

This pragmatic orientation has a vital effect upon the occupational values of the lower classes. They have been found, at as early an age as 10 years, to value occupations for more tangible rewards rather than for intellectual or emotional ones. That is, a boy will aspire to a certain profession because of what it offers in terms of money and prestige rather than the nature of the work itself.[28]

SUMMARY AND IMPLICATIONS

Our lower income population is insecure and comparatively powerless in relation to the rest of American society. Realizing their submerged position, they have come to feel apart from society rather than part of it. From their own helplessness, they have generalized to the belief that most of life is uncontrollable. They are convinced of their own impotence so that, while they accept typical American values, they are frequently lethargic in trying to attain them.

It would be incautious, in view of the sparseness of our knowledge, to say just what program implications such knowledge has, or what techniques of improvement are most likely to succeed. But it would be irresponsible to close this discussion without underlining the precautions it suggests:

1. The entire life situation of the poor must be considered if any part of it is to be changed. Their attitudes arise in no vacuum but are logical results of real circumstances.
2. Lower class citizens must be brought off the periphery into the structure of the community. Nothing which the community does for them can be durably effective until they are a functioning part of the community.
3. Energetic patience must prevail. The alienated adult cannot be completely reeducated. His children can be somewhat swayed. But it is with his grandchildren that one can really have hope.

[Notes]

1. Dotson, Floyd. "Patterns of Voluntary Association Among Urban Working Class Families," *American Sociological Review,* vol. 16, October 1951, pp. 687–693.
2. These four conditions of lower class life were pointed out by Albert K. Cohen and Harold M. Hodges, Jr., in "Characteristics of the Lower-Blue-Collar Class," *Social Problems,* vol. 10, no. 4, Spring 1963, pp. 303–334.
3. Bell, Wendell. "Anomie, Social Isolation, and the Class Structure," *Sociometry,* vol. 20, no. 2, June 1957, pp. 105–116. Simpson, Richard L., and Max Miller. "Social Status and Anomia," *Social Problems,* vol. 10, Winter 1963, pp. 256–264. Dean, Dwight G. "Alienation: Its Meaning and Measurement," *American Sociological Review,* vol. 26, no. 5, October 1961, pp. 753–758.
4. Quoted in Cohen and Hodges, *op. cit.,* p. 322.
5. Durkheim, Emile. *Suicide.* Translated by John A. Spaulding and George Simpson. The Free Press, Glencoe, Ill., 1951, p. 253.
6. Merton, Robert K. *Social Theory and Social Structure.* The Free Press, Glencoe, Ill., 1949, p. 128.
7. *Ibid.,* pp. 138, 148–149.
8. Wright, Charles R., and Herbert H. Hyman. "Voluntary Association Memberships of American Adults: Evidence from National Sample Surveys," *American Sociological Review,* vol. 23, June 1958, pp. 284–294. Leighton, Dorothea, *et al. The Character of Danger.* Basic Books, New York, 1963, p. 384. Myers, Jerome, and Bertram Roberts. *Family and Class Dynamics in Mental Illness.* John Wiley, New York, 1959, pp. 178–179.
9. Seeman, Melvin. "On the Meaning of Alienation," *American Sociological Review,* vol. 24, no. 6, December 1959, pp. 783–791. Simpson, Richard L., and Max Miller. "Social Status and Social Alienation," paper read at the meetings of the Southern Sociological Society, Miami Beach, Fla., 1961.
10. Gould, Rosalind. "Some Sociological Determinants of Goal Strivings," *Journal of Social Psychology,* vol. 13, May 1941, pp. 461–473.
11. Empey, LaMar J. "Social Class and Occupational Aspirations: A Comparison of Absolute and Relative Measurement," *American Sociological Review,* vol. 21, December 1956, pp. 703–709.
12. Bell, Robert R. "Lower Class Negro Mothers' Aspirations for Their Children," *Social Forces,* vol. 43, May 1965, pp. 493–500.
13. Lewis, Hylan, "Culture, Class, and the Behavior of Low-Income Families," paper read at the Conference on Lower Class Culture, New York City, 1963, pp. 26, 34.
14. *Ibid.,* p. 37.
15. Koos, Earl Loman. *The Health of Regionville.* Columbia University Press, New York, 1954, p. 35.
16. Riessman, Frank. *The Culturally Deprived Child.* Harper and Row, New York, 1962, p. 28.
17. Kahl, Joseph A. *The American Class Structure.* Rinehart and Company, New York, 1959, pp. 205–210.
18. Centers, Richard. *The Psychology of Social Classes.* Princeton University Press, Princeton, 1949, p. 62.
19. This controversy is summarized in Hyman Rodman, "The Lower-Class Value Stretch," *Social Forces,* vol. 42, no. 2, December 1963, pp. 205–215.
20. Lewis, *op. cit.,* p. 29. The problem of lower-class attitudes toward "deviant" behavior is currently being researched by Dr. Hyman Rodman of The Merrill

Palmer Institute (Cooperative Research Project No. 243, Welfare Administration, U.S. Dept. of Health, Education, and Welfare).

21. Miller, Walter. "Lower Class Culture as a Generating Milieu of Gang Delinquency," *Journal of Social Issues,* vol. 14, no. 3, 1958, p. 11. Rainwater, Lee. *And the Poor Get Children.* Quadrangle Books, Chicago, 1960, p. 52.

22. In research supported by the Welfare Administration (Cooperative Research Project No. 125, Leonard Goodman, principal investigator) it has been found that poor people are more likely, by 13 percent, to express "strong agreement" with this statement. At less than the .05 level of confidence, the difference is statistically significant:

Economic level and degree of agreement with the statement, "A poor person should never give up hope; there's always a chance that a lucky break will put him on top."

Economic level*	Percent indicating—	
	Strong agreement	Little or no agreement
Poor (N = 169)	31	69
Not poor (N = 166)	18	82
Percent difference	13	13

* According to the measure developed by James Morgan *et al.,* in *Income and Welfare in the United States.* McGraw-Hill, New York, 1962, pp. 188–196.

23. LeShan, Lawrence L. "Time Orientation and Social Class," *Journal of Abnormal and Social Psychology,* vol. 47, 1952, pp. 589–592.

An example of this trait is a recent finding by Leonard Goodman (Welfare Administration Cooperative Research Project No. 125): Economic level and agreement with the statement, "Nowadays a person has to live pretty much for today and let tomorrow take care of itself."

Economic level	Percent indicating—	
	Agreement	Disagreement
Poor (N = 169)	48	52
Not poor (N = 166)	34	66
Percent difference*	14	14

* Significant at less than the .05 confidence level.

24. Teahan, John E. "Future Time Perspective, Optimist, and Academic Achieve-

ment," *Journal of Abnormal and Social Psychology,* vol. 57, November 1958, pp. 379–380.

25. Lipset, Seymour M. *Political Man.* Doubleday and Company, Garden City, N.Y., 1960, pp. 97–130.
26. Bernstein, B. "Language and Social Class," *British Journal of Psychology,* vol. 11, September 1960, pp. 271–276.
27. Miller, S. M., and Frank Riessman. "The Working Class Subculture: A New View," *Social Problems,* vol. 9, Summer 1961, pp. 86–97.
28. Galler, Enid H. "Influence of Social Class on Children's Choices of Occupations," *Elementary School Journal,* vol. 51, April 1951, pp. 439–445. Morse, Nancy C., and Robert S. Weiss. "The Function and Meaning of Work and the Job," *American Sociological Review,* vol. 20, April 1955, pp. 191–198.

9

Alphonso Pinkney

The Black Community: Social Stratification

THE black community, like the white community which surrounds it, has always maintained a degree of social stratification. During slavery the primary distinctions among the Negro slaves were based on those who worked as house servants and those forced to work as field hands. The house servants were most often mulattoes who represented a favored class in the eyes of the slaveholders. The field hands were the black illiterates who were considered less than human beings. This distinction between slaves was frequently fostered by slaveholders and served as a divisive force between the slaves.

Among the "free" blacks during slavery, several types of distinctions were discernible. As among the slaves, distinctions were made between mulattoes and blacks, with the former enjoying higher status. There were also distinctions between skilled workers and artisans and domestic workers and unskilled laborers. Finally, many of the free Negroes were direct descendants of wealthy white planters. They frequently maintained extensive property holdings and slaves.[1] Although white ancestry was not enough to confer higher social status among the free Negroes, it was frequently associated with greater education and mechanical skill.

After emancipation, class distinctions among Negroes frequently followed the patterns established during slavery: those based on wealth, occupation, "respectability," and skin color. However, another factor assumed prominence. Negroes who had been free before the Civil War distinguished themselves from those who were freed with the emancipation.[2]

Reprinted by permission of Prentice-Hall, Inc., Englewood Cliffs, N.J., from Alphonso Pinkney, *Black Americans.* © 1969.

The restoration of white supremacy, as well as the migrations of the blacks from rural to urban areas and from South to North, had the effect of minimizing class distinctions among Negroes. Yet the black community, like its white counterpart, has continued, through a variety of criteria, to distinguish among its members.

Several studies have focused attention on status distinctions in the black community.[3] In judging one another, black people use many of the conventional social-class criteria utilized by white Americans, such as income, occupation, education, wealth, family background, style of life, refinement, property ownership, organizational affiliations, respectability, and morality. Some criteria, however, such as white ancestry, skin color, and cultural similarity to whites, are peculiar to the Negro community. In recent years black nationalism has made inroads into the black community, especially in urban areas. This development has led to a deemphasis, if not a cessation, of these characteristics as criteria for status.

THE RURAL BLACKS

Studies of rural black communities reveal the presence of the three social-class levels found in the society at large. In a study of rural Negroes in eight counties in five Southern states, Charles S. Johnson delineated three classes and estimated the percentage of Negroes in each class as follows: upper class, 6 percent; middle class, 12 percent; lower class, 82 percent.[4] The upper-class blacks were those possessing a family social heritage that was known and respected in the community and a high educational and occupational status. These persons were usually medical doctors, school-teachers, and successful landowners. The middle class consisted of propri-etors of small businesses, white-collar workers, schoolteachers, and some skilled artisans. The lower class was composed of unskilled and semiskilled workers and domestic workers. Also within this group were found the sharecroppers and tenant farmers.

Dollard also posited the existence of three social classes among Negroes in the small town which he studied in the 1930's, but he concen-trated on the middle- and lower-class Negroes.[5] In this community the lower-class Negroes were those individuals with the lowest skill levels, forming the "broad base on which society in this area rests." The middle-class people were mainly teachers and ministers, who attempted to isolate themselves from the lower class and what they considered lower-class values.·

Davis, Gardner, and Gardner report that in rural Mississippi social classes were present among Negroes but that the differentiation among classes was slight.[6] In rural Southern communities fewer criteria exist for distinguishing among blacks than are found in urban areas. However, such criteria as education, property ownership, and skin color still constitute a basis for social stratification.

THE URBAN BLACKS

Since the vast majority of black people are urban dwellers, and since the greater complexity of urban life is conducive to greater stratification, it might be expected that somewhat more elaborate stratification may be discerned among blacks in urban areas. Although there are regional differences in stratification among urban Negroes, in general the class distinctions hold in the South and elsewhere. Frazier makes the point that skin color diminishes as a status variable as one progresses from the Deep South to the Border South to the North.[7] In addition, economic opportunities for Negroes have generally been greater in the North than in the South; therefore, greater occupational differentiation has made for some differences in stratification. Finally, compared to the South, the black man in the Northern city is a relative newcomer. Southern Negroes in some ways have a more established system of stratification. It is possible, however, to make some general statements about class distinctions which hold for urban Negroes throughout the United States.

Most of the studies of social stratification among urban Negroes delineate a small upper class, a proportionately small but growing middle class, and a large lower class that encompasses the vast majority of Negroes. The black upper class includes professionals, especially medical doctors, dentists, and lawyers; public administrators; civic leaders; businessmen; educators; and politicians. (These people would be considered middle class in terms of their standing in the general society if race were irrelevant.) In describing the upper class Negroes in Chicago, Drake and Cayton have this to say:

> If one wished to ascertain just what people constitute Bronzeville's upper class, it might seem practicable to group together those persons who have the most money, those with the greatest amount of education, those with the "best" family backgrounds, and those who wield the greatest political power —and attach to this group the label UPPER CLASS.[8]

This group, they write, included some 5,000 people in the 1940's, most of whom were medical doctors, lawyers, newspaper editors, civic leaders, and politicians. Their prestige was based on education, professional status, and style of life, rather than on income, although some of them earned as much as $50,000 yearly.

Frazier describes the black upper class in Washington, D.C., which he feels to be typical of other border cities, as comprised of "a relatively large professional class and a clerical group of the same relative size as Chicago and New York. Consequently, those of upper-class status include almost entirely people of professional status, businessmen, and those in clerical occupations."[9]

Upper-class Negroes tend to associate with other upper-class Negroes. Entertaining is done in the home, except for the public events which they sponsor. They are Protestants, usually Congregationalists, Episcopalians, and Presbyterians. They are active in social clubs, especially fraternities and sororities, and they support civil rights activities through the National Association for the Advancement of Colored People (NAACP) or the Urban League.

Middle-class status among Negroes in Chicago, according to Drake and Cayton, is not necessarily limited to those persons of appropriate income and occupation. "Rather, the middle class is marked off from the lower class by a pattern of behavior expressed in stable family and associational relationships, in great concern with 'front' and 'respectability,' and in a drive for 'getting ahead.' All this finds an objective measure in standard of living—the way people spend their money, and in *public behavior*."[10] The middle class in Chicago consisted of a wide variety of occupational categories, including professionals, independent businessmen, clerical workers, service workers, and laborers. Frazier agrees that style of life is the most crucial element in identifying the Negro middle class. He writes, "Because of their fairly secure and adequate incomes, Negroes of middle-class status are able to maintain what they regard as a desirable mode of life. This desirable mode of living includes . . . certain standards of home and family life."[11]

With increasing urbanization there has emerged a rather well-defined middle class among Negroes. In large cities there is a large group of clerical, skilled, and public service workers, in addition to professional workers in virtually every field. Because these occupations provide adequate incomes and economic security, the black middle class has developed stable family lives. There is among the black middle class an overriding concern with "respectability" and a serious desire that their children receive the educational advantages which they were frequently denied.

Middle-class blacks value home ownership and are concerned about maintaining the proper associational relationships necessary for advancing themselves. They are likely to be members of church congregations, including Congregationalist, Episcopalian, and Presbyterian, but, unlike the upper-class Negroes, most middle-class blacks are Methodists and Baptists. Within these two denominations they frequently attend churches which cater to the middle class. Like the upper-class Negroes, the middle class expend considerable time and energy on social clubs and other social organizations, especially fraternities and sororities.

Because of the precariousness of the status of middle-class blacks, their overriding concern is with maintaining respectability. This concern has frequently led to a self-hate characterized by contempt for lower-class Negroes. One writer takes a rather harsh view of the rising Negro middle class and the fantasy world which, he insists, they share with upper-class Negroes. He writes:

> The emphasis upon "social" life or "society" is one of the main props of the world of make believe into which the black bourgeoisie has sought to escape from its inferiority and frustrations in American society. This world of make believe, to be sure, is a reflection of the values of American society, but it lacks the economic basis that would give it roots in the world of reality. In escaping into a world of make believe, middle-class Negroes have rejected both identification with the Negro and his traditional culture. Through delusions of wealth and power they have sought identification with white America, which continues to reject them. But these delusions leave them frustrated because they are unable to escape from the emptiness and futility of their existence.[12]

The lower-class Negro, comprising at least two-thirds of the urban black population, is at the bottom of the class structure in the black community. It is of the lower-class Negro that so many stereotypes have developed. These are the blacks who are chronically unemployed, who do the back-breaking jobs and are still defined as "lazy"—and who make up a disproportionately high proportion of the welfare rolls in urban areas. The lower-class Negro is most often the recent migrant from the rural South, seeking to improve his status in the city. Among lower-class Negroes disorganized family life is prevalent.[13] It is also to the lower-class blacks that widespread social pathologies are attributed.[14] Finally, it is the lower-class Negro who in many ways is the major target of the War on Poverty. For, historically, these are the individuals who have received fewer social rewards than any other group. They are crowded into the slums of the largest cities and are only noticed when acts of violence (real or imagined) are attributed to them.

Drake and Cayton describe the complexity of the lower class in the black community in Chicago. In addition to those with middle-class aspirations and to the stable "church folk," one finds "the denizens of the underworld—the pimps and prostitutes, the thieves and pickpockets, the dope addicts and the reefer smokers, the professional gamblers, cutthroats, and murderers."[15]

Writing about the residents in America's urban Negro slums, especially New York's Harlem, Kenneth Clark describes the lower class as being "subject peoples, victims of greed, cruelty, insensitivity, guilt, and fear of their masters."[16] Perhaps the most salient characteristics of the lower-class blacks are their powerlessness, hopelessness, and depair. They lack the organization and organizational participation of middle- and upper-class Negroes. Even religious institutions have failed to assist them in coping with their many problems, especially in urban areas. They tend to affiliate themselves with "store-front" Fundamentalist churches which are generally powerless in the larger community. Furthermore, they tend to be rejected by middle- and upper-class Negroes, who feel that identification with the lower class would lower their status.[17]

DIFFERENCES IN SOCIAL STRATIFICATION: BLACKS VS. WHITES

Social stratification in the black community differs in some regards from that found in the white community. Because of the overrepresentation of Negroes in the lower class, stratification tends to be based to a greater degree on behavioral patterns and social factors, rather than on income and occupation, which usually are considered crucial determinants in the white community. Social stratification in the black community is more likely to be determined by style of life and family background. Although a few Negroes who have amassed great wealth or achieved fame in the larger society might be considered upper class by objective standards, most blacks who are considered upper class within their own community would not be so considered if they were white. Schoolteachers are a notable example. Within the black community they are frequently considered to be upper class; white schoolteachers are rarely so considered. Similarly, many individuals working as skilled workers, service workers, and even laborers are considered to be middle class because of their behavior patterns.

However, behavior patterns, while still salient, are losing force. Support for this contention is found in a recent view of published literature dealing with prestige criteria among Negroes. This study reveals that in 16 of the better-known community studies, Negroes traditionally used different criteria for evaluating one another than did whites.[18] However, the trend is clearly toward increasing acceptance of the same three main criteria used in the general community. Thus education is emphasized more frequently than any other status element, followed by occupation and income, respectively. Other criteria reported (in order of importance) are respectability or morality, refinement or "culture," skin color or white ancestry, family background, and property ownership.[19] Among white Americans occupation and income have received importance equal to that of education, and frequently more so.

With increasing urbanization, regional redistribution, educational achievement, and occupational differentiation, there is a trend toward the development of socioeconomic status groupings among urban Negroes that will parallel those among white Americans.

As with American communities in general, the black community varies depending on whether it is in the South or outside that region and on whether it is urban or rural. However, certain recurrent patterns exist in black communities throughout the United States. In a study of the Negro community in 11 cities of varying sizes and different regions, Williams reports clearly discernible patterns appearing in each of them.[20] Several of these characteristics are of relevance to the present chapter [chapter 3 in *Black Americans*]. The black community tends to be socially isolated from the larger community. Separate social institutions have developed among Negroes to meet needs not served by the larger community. The church continues to play a dominant role in the institutional life of the rural black community but a declining role in the urban community. The black community adheres to a system of social stratification not unlike the larger community. Its members distinguish among themselves on the basis of certain achieved and ascribed criteria.

In addition, the black community in America is like a colonial possession in that it tends to be economically and politically dependent upon the larger community. Its residents provide a source of cheap labor, and, depending on the needs of the larger community, unemployment may be widespread. The residents of the black community are crowded into a geographical area distinguishable from the general community by poor housing conditions and the lack of services provided. Education is controlled from the outside, and the police often assume the posture of occupying forces. In short, all important decisions—political, economic, and educational—affecting the black community are made for its residents by white Americans who have become known as the "white power structure." In periods of disorder (usually in summer) specially trained and equipped police and military forces are rushed in to quell the disturbances with armed force, but little thought is given by public officials to the conditions that produce these disorders.

[Notes]

1. E. Franklin Frazier, *The Negro in the United States* (New York: The Macmillan Co., 1957).
2. *Ibid.*, pp. 276–78.
3. See, for example, the following: Allison Davis, Burleigh Gardner, and Mary Gardner, *Deep South* (Chicago: University of Chicago Press, 1941); John Dollard,

Caste and Class in a Southern Town (New Haven, Conn.: Yale University Press, 1937); St. Clair Drake and Horace Cayton, *Black Metropolis* (New York: Harcourt, Brace, 1945); W. E. B. Du Bois, *The Philadelphia Negro* (Philadelphia: University of Pennsylvania Press, 1899); E. Franklin Frazier, *Negro Youth at the Crossways* (Washington, D.C.: American Council on Education, 1940); Hylan Lewis, *Blackways of Kent* (Chapel Hill, N.C.: The University of North Carolina Press, 1955); Hortense Powdermaker, *After Freedom* (New York: Viking, 1939); John Rohrer and Munro S. Edmondson, eds., *The Eighth Generation Grows Up* (New York: Harper, 1960); Robert Warner, *New Haven Negroes* (New Haven, Conn.: Yale, 1940).

4. Charles S. Johnson, *Growing Up in the Black Belt* (Washington, D.C.: American Council on Education, 1941).
5. Dollard, *op. cit.,* p. 83.
6. Davis, Gardner, and Gardner, *op. cit.,* p. 238.
7. Frazier, *The Negro in the United States,* p. 291.
8. Drake and Cayton, *op. cit.,* p. 526.
9. Frazier, *The Negro in the United States,* p. 286.
10. Drake and Cayton, *op. cit.,* pp. 661–62 (italics in the original).
11. Frazier, *The Negro in the United States,* p. 301.
12. E. Franklin Frazier, *Black Bourgeoisie* (Glencoe, Ill.: Free Press, 1957), p. 237.
13. See especially U.S. Department of Labor, Office of Policy Planning and Research, *The Negro Family: The Case for National Action* (Washington, D.C.: Government Printing Office, 1965).
14. Clark, *op. cit.,* Chap. 5; Frazier, *The Negro in the United States,* pp. 286–87; 303–4.
15. Drake and Cayton, *op. cit.,* p. 600.
16. Kenneth B. Clark, *Dark Ghetto* (New York: Harper and Row, 1965).
17. Middle- and upper-class Negroes repeatedly express contempt for lower-class Negroes. Such feelings are frequently expressed in the case histories reported in Abram Kardiner and Lionel Ovesey, *The Mark of Oppression* (New York: World Publishing, 1962), especially Chap. 6; see also Frazier, *Black Bourgeoisie,* pp. 224–29.
18. Norval Glenn, "Negro Prestige Criteria: A Case Study in the Bases of Prestige," *American Journal of Sociology,* Vol. 68 (May 1963), 645–57.
19. *Ibid.,* p. 647.
20. Robin M. Williams, Jr., *Strangers Next Door* (Englewood Cliffs, N.J.: Prentice-Hall, 1964), pp. 252–54.

10

C. Eric Lincoln

The Negro's
Middle-Class Dream

A FAMOUS professor at a large university used to begin one of his lectures in social psychology with a description of the characteristics of a typical American family. After he had described the family's income, address, religion, the kind of car they drove, organizations to which they belonged and the occupation of the father, he would then demand to know what social class the family belonged to. But before the students could answer, the professor would add as an apparent afterthought: "Oh, yes, I forgot to mention that this is a *Negro* family!" Inevitably, the students were stymied. What had begun as a simple problem became insolubly complex by the addition of the word "Negro."

Where do Negroes fit into the prevailing American class structure? Most sociologists say they don't. Negroes have a *parallel* social structure, somewhat—but not entirely—analogous to that of whites. This social parallelism, or two-caste society, is created by the color barrier which, with the rarest exceptions, prevents lateral movement from class to class between Negroes and whites. As a prominent Negro matron said in Detroit, "We Negroes and whites visit each other at times, and frequently we belong to the same civic organizations and attend the same functions, but the lines are there, and no one has to say where they are."

The Negro class structure had its roots in the institution of American slavery, which, in ignoring the African's cultural presumptions, leveled all classes, and force-fused highly disparate individuals and groups into one conglomerate mass—"the Negro slave," or simply, "the Negro," a word which, in America, became synonymous with "slave" or the "descendant of slaves." Prince and servant, Eboe and Mandingo, Moslem and spirit-worshipper were all the same to the slave master, who saw them only as commodities to be bought and sold, or as a labor supply for his vast plantations.

Whatever the basis of past distinctions, the Negro social structure in America had to evolve out of conditions connected with plantation life, and within a context which recognized the absolute superiority of the white slave owner (although not necessarily that of the small, nonslave-holding white farmers, who supplied the "overseer" class, and who were looked upon by house servants and slave owners alike as "poor white trash").

The Negro's "society," then, had four more or less distinct social classes. In ascending order, they were: (1) field hands (who had least contact with the socializing influences of the white environment); (2) mechanics and artisans (bricklayers, carpenters, iron workers, bakers, etc., who were frequently hired by the month or the year to merchants or builders in the cities); (3) valets, butlers, maids, cooks and other house-hold servants (whose frequent personal contact with whites made them the most "acculturated" class); and (4) free Negroes (who had bought their freedom or had become free by manumission—often because of faith-fulness or some heroic exploit).

As slaves, the house-servant class had by far the highest proportion of mulattoes. While this did not by any means exempt them from the normal rigors incident to being slaves, including sale, the light-skinned mistresses of the slave masters were often granted petty privileges and their children were more frequently given their freedom than those of any other class.

At the end of the slave period, the mulattoes sought to establish themselves as a distinct occupational and social class within the Negro subculture. For the most part, they continued as servants and retainers to their erstwhile masters—as dressmakers, barbers, coachmen and the like. For more than a generation they clung tenuously to a certain degree of status derived from catering exclusively to the "quality" folk (as they had done in slavery) under the then current slogan of (serving) "mighty few white folks and no niggers a'tall!"

By the turn of the century, however, as the economy of the South began to revive, the mulatto "retainers" were progressively displaced by European immigrants and poor whites who were suddenly willing to do "Negro work." From that date neither occupation nor color has been a reliable index of social standing among Negroes.

Today, a light skin is not an automatic key to social status. In this day of the Negro's increasing race pride and his subtle impulse to nationalism, a light skin *can* be a handicap, especially if it is associated with "recent" miscegenation. Mass education and the indiscriminate rise to power and money of significant numbers of Negroes irrespective of their grandparents' station in the slave society have all but destroyed the effectiveness of the Negro's private color bar. Leadership in civil rights as well as in the professions has long since passed from the mulatto class. As a matter of fact, the number of mulattoes in the general Negro population seems to be declining steadily, and there is no evidence that legal integration will soon replace clandestine miscegenation in restoring the ratio of light color.

There is no unanimity of opinion as to what proportion of today's Negroes fall into the traditional "lower," "middle" and "upper" classes of the Negro social structure. Prof. Tillman Cothran, head of the graduate department of sociology at Atlanta University, estimates that "not more than 25 per cent of the Negro population can be called middle class by any reasonable standards. And not more than 5 per cent can be called upper class."

Other sociologists have argued that if one applies the full spectrum of criteria by which the white social structure is measured—ranging from income to education, affiliation, residence, etc.—the Negro middle class is reduced to 4 per cent or 5 per cent of the Negro population, and the Negro upper class vanishes altogether.

Such an estimate is, I think, too drastic. If the theory of parallel social structure is valid (and there seems to be no other way to measure "class" in an essentially segregated society), certainly it can be shown that Negroes and whites of similar education and income exhibit many of the same desires, restraints, conformities and general patterns of behavior.

America's self-image is that of an essentially equalitarian society best represented by the middle class. Most Americans concede that there are a few snobs and millionaires at the top, and a few poor people in Appalachia, or somewhere, at the bottom, but America is middle class, and most Americans identify themselves as belonging to the middle class.

Implicit in this identification is a belief in "democracy" and "fair play," and also the expectation of "the good life"—a home, a car, a regular vacation, an education for the children, regular promotions, and maybe even extras like a boat or a summer place. Despite the pessimism of the sociologists, more and more Negroes share this dream, and to an increasing degree they are making it come true for themselves and their children.

The Negro middle class is made up primarily of Negro professionals, with school teachers probably constituting the largest single bloc. Teachers, along with doctors, lawyers, college professors, small businessmen, ministers, and postal workers have traditionally made up the bulk of the Negro middle class.

However, the recent availability of new kinds of jobs not previously held by Negroes has begun to modify the character of this group. Technicians, politicians, clerical and sales personnel, social workers, labor-union officials, minor government bureaucrats, and an increasing managerial class in such agencies as Federal housing and local units of national corporations have helped broaden the occupational range of the Negro middle class.

Under the Kennedy-Johnson Administration a few Negroes have been appointed to the upper echelons of Government officialdom, and within the past two or three years a few Negroes have reached executive status in white corporations. A recent dinner in New York honored seven Negroes who were vice presidents or held managerial positions in major firms. In Washington, Dr. James Nabrit, president of Howard University, and Dr. Frank Jones have been elected to the board of directors of a major bank. And in that city, several Negroes have been elected to the Board of Trade.

It is difficult to set a salary range for a given social class because social status does not depend upon money alone. Some upper-class whites are impoverished, but their families have once held fortunes and they have traditions of culture and attainment. Since the American Negro's family traditions seldom antedate the Civil War, Negro society puts an undue emphasis on money and material acquisitions. It is often said by Negro critics themselves that "anybody with a dollar, no matter where he stole it, can belong to Negro society."

Most Negroes, like most other Americans, earn their living legitimately, of course, but because of job discrimination and lack of skills, the total income of the typical middle-class Negro family will be substantially lower than that of a typical white family of the middle class. An arbitrary figure of $7,500 a year as the average income of a middle-class family would severely limit the number of Negroes who could be called middle-class.

Some Negro families do exceed a $7,500 income, but the vast majority of those who do are families in which both husband and wife work full time. Very frequently among home-buying Negroes, the head of the family works at two jobs, and occasionally at three. Such supplementary work or "moonlighting"—often driving a taxi, waiting on tables, tending bar or bellhopping—is known as "a hustle," a term quite familiar to the Negro middle class.

In many of the large cities of the North such as New York or Boston where undeveloped land is nonexistent, the middle-class Negro, who has the means and the desire to live elsewhere, is locked in the black ghetto. Only with difficulty can he find a house or apartment outside the ghetto in a white community. As a consequence, many Negroes despair of ever leaving the slums, no matter what their education or income.

Money that would normally go for a new house is spent in the hopeless task of refurbishing antiquated apartments, or in conspicuous consumption which somehow helps them to forget the horror of living in the nation's Harlems. (In the South, the housing problem is not nearly so acute. Space for building can be had in most Southern cities, although it is likely to be in a segregated community.)

The style of living of the Negro middle class does not differ radically from that of its white counterpart. Bridge is a favorite pastime among both men and women. Those who have the leisure belong to innumerable social clubs. An increasing number of Negro men play golf and participate in water sports where facilities are available. In the South, fishing and hunting are favorite pastimes, but only if one has the full regalia of dress, and all the latest equipment shown in the sports magazines.

To a far greater degree than whites, Negroes maintain affiliation in the graduate chapters of their college fraternities and sororities, and these organizations are important indexes of social stratification. Women of a given sorority tend to marry men of its fraternal opposite number. Together, the eight major Negro sororities and fraternities constitute the nucleus of any imaginary "blue book" of Negro society.

The children of the Negro middle class are taught to aspire to middle-class standards. They take lessons in piano and creative dancing on Saturday mornings and attend carefully planned parties on Saturday night. A few are sent East to private schools.

Sometimes the interpretation of middle-class values takes an unusual twist. A Negro matron in a Memphis department store, for example, refused to corral her two children who were busily chasing through the store and littering the aisles with merchandise. She explained: "The white kids do it and the salesclerks think it's cute. I don't want my children inhibited by feeling that they can't do anything any other kids can do."

In Washington, among those aspiring to the middle class, or those who are recently "in," status is measured by the quantity and the cost of whisky served one's guests. The most conspicuous feature in such a home will be the bar appointments, and it is considered equally insulting for a guest to refuse a drink as it is for the host to offer his guests "cheap whisky." One Washingtonian gained prominence in his set by consistently being first to serve rare and expensive imports before they were well known in the Negro community. He learned what was "in" by frequenting an exclusive liquor store patronized by high Government officials.

It used to be said that the difference between a Negro making $50 a week and driving a Cadillac and a white man making $100 a week and driving a Chevrolet was that the Negro, having nowhere to live, needed the bigger car to sleep in! On Atlanta's West Side, where the Cadillac (or Lincoln) frequently comes with a split-level ranch house, it is popular to have the main (or "status") car match the house in color and appointments.

A second car for the Negro professional family is not unusual. Unlike most white middle-class families having two cars, the Negro's second car is likely to be as big and expensive as his first. An expensive automobile to drive to work is often as much a matter of personal prestige for the working Negro woman as for her husband. Hence, it is common to see large numbers of Pontiacs, Oldsmobiles and Mercurys parked near the schools where Negro women are employed as teachers.

A cottage at Oak Bluffs, on Martha's Vineyard, or in Maine or Upper Michigan can be claimed by a few. A very small number of Negroes go to Europe and to the Caribbean or Mexico on vacation. A sort of pilgrimage to Africa has high status value for those seeking to "understand their pre-Western heritage."

Some Negroes are in the middle class because there is nowhere else for them to go. These few might be considered "upper class" but there is a certain incongruity in talking about a Negro "upper class" so long as the color barrier operates to bar Negroes who are otherwise qualified from full participation in American social life. "There may not be an upper class," says Clarence Coleman, southeastern director of the National Urban League, "but there is a 'power élite' which abstracts itself from the rank and file of the middle class and participates to an important extent in the decision-making of the white power structure where Negroes are concerned."

Certainly this power élite does exist. But where it was not created by the white establishment, its power derives from white recognition and respect. Militant civil-rights leaders have discovered this again and again when the white establishment has refused to negotiate with the Negro community except through "recognized channels."

The Negro middle class, like any middle class, is preoccupied with making secure its hard-won social position. This is a characteristic of middle-class aspirations.

Because of this preoccupation the Negro middle class has been criticized frequently for not being more deeply and realistically involved in the struggle for civil rights. The criticism is well placed, for given more manpower, more money and more dedication, it is obvious that more walls could be breached. But this is not the whole story, and the lack of total involvement may not be an accurate index of middle-class feelings and intensions.

Much of the criticism has come from within the ranks of the middle class itself. The Urban League's Clarence Coleman sees the middle class as the buffer between the militants, whose aspirations are frequently unrealistic in terms of present possibilities, and the power élite which seems concerned to protect itself and its privileged positions from too rapid social change.

James A. Tillman Jr., executive director of the Greater Minneapolis Fair Housing Program and a frequent writer on problems of social change, describes the Negro middle class as "that class of Negroes who have bought the inane, invalid and self-defeating notion that the black man can be integrated into a hostile white society without conflict."

Tillman denounces the power élite as "the fixers and go-betweens who cover up rather than expose the violent nature of racism." They are, he declares, "the most dangerous clique in America."

Tillman's sentiments are echoed by Cecil Moore, militant civil-rights attorney and head of the Philadelphia N.A.A.C.P. Moore, who himself came from an accomplished West Virginia family, insists that "the Negro middle class, and all those who consider themselves above the middle class, 'subsist on the blood of the brother down under,' the brother they are supposed to be leading. Who do these Negroes think they're kidding?" he asks, and then answers his own question. "They're kidding nobody but the white folks who are willing to pay 'philanthrophy' to keep from having to come to grips with the central problem, which is 'full and complete citizenship for all Americans, *right now!* '"

Despite all such criticism, however, the Negro middle class has borne the brunt of the civil-rights protest. Critics of the so-called "Black Bourgeoise" have not always given them credit for the maturity and social responsibility upon which the Negro's fight for first-class citizenship has finally depended. The civil-rights fight, at least insofar as it visualizes an integrated society, is a middle-class fight. The N.A.A.C.P., CORE, the Urban League and the followers of Dr. Martin Luther King are all middle-class. (Indeed, the lower-class Negro has yet to be stirred by the promise of integration. He is more concerned with such immediate needs as jobs and housing than with abstract values like integration. He looks neither to Martin Luther King nor to Roy Wilkins; in fact, the leader of the black masses has yet to appear.)

In Atlanta and other Southern cities during the massive sit-ins of 1962–63, housewives baked pies, made sandwiches and provided transportation for the students. Negro businessmen donated food, gasoline and other supplies. Then doctors, nurses, professors and businessmen walked the picket lines. Similar middle-class support has assisted the activities of CORE in New York, Cleveland and other cities in the North. Voter registration is essentially a middle-class project.

Middle-class leadership and support of the civil-rights movement has not been without ambivalence. Desegregated schools frequently mean that Negro teachers will lose their jobs. Negro businessmen often lose their most competent clerical help to recently desegregated industries.

Negro restaurants, drug stores, real-estate firms and the like may be adversely affected by desegregation. Some Negro churches have lost members to white churches. In a fully integrated society, the Negro middle class would lose its identity. Indeed, it would cease to exist.

Some Negroes recognize all this, of course, and fight against it. Nor can it be said that the majority of the middle class is active in the rights struggle. What can be said is that the struggle is for the most part led, financed and supported by the Negro middle class and, of course, its white allies.

Certainly, Negro leadership has become a "profession," and in some cases a lucrative one. Yet most Negroes trying to help improve things are in search of neither fame nor fortune and may be themselves disadvantaged by the race issue. A. Maceo Walker and Jesse Turner of Memphis, for example, both executive officers of a sensitive banking business that has important white as well as Negro depositors, comes to mind. These men and others like them have little to gain for themselves personally, yet they have given leadership to the civil-rights movement in their city for years. Other cases could be cited across the country.

In Washington, I talked with the distinguished Negro attorney, Belford Lawson, and his wife, Marjorie McKenzie, who, as associate judge of the Juvenile Court there, is no less distinguished. The Lawsons were undisturbed about the "black backlash" against the Negro middle class, although they felt that the middle class was just beginning to realize its responsibilities to the Negro masses. Nor did they recognize a middle-class backlash against the lower class (which has been roundly criticized by some Negroes for rioting in the streets and undoing the patient and painful accomplishments of middle-class leaders).

"We must press on to the next phase," Lawson said. "And it would be foolish to wait until all of us have reached the place a few of us have reached today. Negroes, like other people, move at different rates of speed. Our circumstances vary. Now we have a handful of civil rights and no money. Our next front is economic. We want to buy stocks in banks and corporations and sit on their boards. Every time a Negro reaches an executive position in a major corporation, he is in a better position to help that Negro in the streets without a job."

Mr. Lawson believes that it is time to stop complaining and to move into the American mainstream. "Breaking into the white man's economy" he believes to be essential to any further progress on the part of Negroes. "In Washington," he says, "where many social and cultural affairs are integrated, many doors would open if the Negro would only push on them."

Negroes are pushing—for status and respectability and economic security. They are less concerned with integration for integration's sake than they are with being comfortable—middle-class—and unhindered in enjoying all that America has to offer. The riots in the city streets are not the work of sinister Communist agents, except where such agents move in to exploit an already festering social situation. Nor are they the work of hopheads and hoodlums bent on the destruction of the fruits of years of patient interracial effort.

They are the social expressions of pent-up anxiety and frustration which derive from the hopelessness of the conditions under which those people live. *They* cannot hope for "the good life." *They* cannot appropriate the "middle-class image," the American norm for democratic living.

I sat recently in a comfortable middle-class home in northwest Washington talking with Jerry Coward and his wife, both school teachers in the District of Columbus school system. "You know, when we moved into this neighborhood five years ago," Jerry said, "the whites all threatened to move out. A few stayed. And since that time, two brand-new white families have moved in, right down the block. Professional people, too. When white people start moving into, instead of away from, a Negro neighborhood, I guess we've got it made."

I guess they have.

11

Norval D. Glenn

Negro Prestige Criteria: A Case Study in the Bases of Prestige

Since the publication in 1941 of the first two Warner community studies,[1] community prestige stratification has occupied a prominent place of interest among American students of social stratification. Despite the conceptual and methodological weaknesses of the Warner studies, and the unwarranted generalizations that Warner and others have drawn from them, they focused attention upon a highly significant social phenomenon. Prestige, the Warner studies showed, can be looked upon as the unifying stratification variable, the variable that makes it meaningful to speak of an integrated community system of stratification rather than of disparate systems for the different stratification variables.

Because of the unifying function and the summary nature of prestige, its relationships to other variables are of major importance in stratification theory. A question of primary theoretical relevance is: What accounts for the relative importance of the variables that are the bases of prestige?

An examination of the prestige criteria used by American Negroes to evaluate one another can throw light upon this question. The relative importance of the variable bases of prestige is or has been considerably different among Negroes than among whites. Accounting for this difference can be of value in accounting for variations in prestige criteria in general.

Reprinted by permission of The University of Chicago Press from *The American Journal of Sociology*, Vol. 68, No. 6, May 1963, pp. 645–657.

THE BASES OF NEGRO PRESTIGE

Although, there is no dearth of Negro prestige-stratification studies, their conceptualization is, without exception, hazy and their methods are, at best, only moderately rigorous. Many of the reports of these studies merely enumerate the characteristics of people at the differnt prestige levels, failing to distinguish between what Powdermaker has called *primary* and *secondary* class characteristics, that is, between the bases of prestige and its correlates and consequences.[2] Such a distinction can be made empirically only with difficulty, but it is of theoretical importance. For instance, if most high-prestige Negroes are found to be light-skinned, it is important to know whether their prestige is based to a large extent upon their skin color or whether it is based largely upon other attributes, which, for historical reasons, mulattoes are more likely to possess than other Negroes. The relationship between prestige and the associated attributes is further complicated by the probable tendency for correlates and consequences of prestige to evolve into prestige criteria. In other words, if all or most high-prestige people exhibit a certain type of behavior, for whatever reason, such behavior may become requisite to, or at least an aid to, the acquisition of high prestige.

Despite the difficulty of distinguishing bases from correlates of prestige, we have been able to find sixteen Negro prestige stratification studies where the researchers clearly believe they have identified the more important bases of prestige. These studies and the major prestige criteria identified by each are given in Table 1. Several well-known Negro stratifi-

TABLE 1 *Major Criteria of Prestige Discovered in Sixteen Empirical Studies*

STUDY AND DATE OF PUBLICATION OR COMPLETION	MAJOR CRITERIA*
DuBois: Negroes in Philadelphia's Seventh Ward, 1899	Respectability, income, occupation, style of life, education, general social efficiency
Daniels: Boston Negroes, 1914	Occupation, wealth, education, refinement
LaGrone: Negroes in Marshall, Texas, 1932	*Education,* cultural similarity to whites (especially with respect to morals)
Burke: Tulsa Negroes, 1936	*Education, wealth,* occupation
Dollard: A small town in the Deep South, 1937	Property ownership, occupation, white ancestry, education, morality
Powdermaker: A small town in the Deep South (same community studied by Dollard), 1939	*Sex morality and stable family life, education,* occupation, forms of religious worship
Frazier: Louisville Negroes, 1940	Wealth, family background, skin color, occupation
Warner: New Haven, Connecticut, Negroes, 1940	Morality, refinement, education, income, occupation

Davis, Gardner, and Gardner: A small town in the Deep South, 1941

Education, occupation, manners and refinement, skin color, morality, status of employer

Johnson: Rural Negroes in eight southern counties, 1941

Family social heritage, education, occupation, income, property ownership, stability of residence, cultural standards

Drake and Cayton: The Chicago Black Belt, 1945

Education, wealth, occupation, standards of behavior, organizational affiliations, skin color

Hill: A small all-Negro community in Oklahoma, 1946

Cultural pattern, wealth, education, family status, leadership

Jones: Negroes in a small Viriginia town, 1946

Education, wealth, occupation, family tradition

King: Negroes in a southern city, 1953

Education, occupation, source of income

Lewis: Negroes in a southern Piedmont community, 1955

Respectability, education, occupation

Rohrer and Edmonson: New Orleans Negroes, 1960

Occupation, education, income

---

* Criteria that are clearly more important than the others are italicized.

Source: Francis D. Burke, "A Survey of the Negro Community of Tulsa, Oklahoma" (unpublished M.S.W. thesis, University of Oklahoma, 1936), pp. 29–30; John Daniels, *In Freedom's Birthplace* (Boston: Houghton Mifflin Co., 1914), pp. 174–83; Allison Davis, Burleigh B. Gardner, and Mary R. Gardner, *Deep South* (Chicago: University of Chicago Press, 1941), p. 246; John Dollard, *Caste and Class in a Southern Town* (3d ed.; Garden City, N.Y.: Doubleday & Co., 1957), pp. 83–87; St. Clair Drake and Horace R. Cayton, *Black Metropolis* (New York: Harcourt, Brace & Co., 1945), pp. 515, 520–26, 543–46, 712; W. E. B. DuBois, *The Philadelphia Negro* (Philadelphia: University of Pennsylvania Press, 1899), pp. 310–15; E. Franklin Frazier, *Negro Youth at the Crossways* (Washington, D.C.: American Council on Education, 1940), pp. 25–28; Mozell C. Hill, "A Comparative Analysis of the All-Negro Society in Oklahoma," *Social Forces,* XXV (October, 1946), 70–77; Charles S. Johnson, *Growing Up in the Black Belt* (Washington, D.C.: American Council on Education, 1941), p. 73; Clifton R. Jones, "Social Stratification in the Negro Population: A Study of Social Classes in South Boston, Virginia," *Journal of Negro Education,* XV (Winter, 1946), 4–12; Charles E. King, "The Process of Social Stratification among an Urban Southern Minority Population," *Social Forces,* XXXI (May, 1953), 1253–63; Cyrus W. LaGrone, "A Sociological Study of the Negro Population of Marshall, Texas" (unpublished Master's thesis, University of Texas, 1932), p. 35; Hylan Lewis, *Blackways of Kent* (Chapel Hill: University of North Carolina Press, 1955), pp. 234–37; Hortense Powdermaker, *After Freedom* (New York: Viking Press, 1939); pp. 62–69; John H. Rohrer and Munro S. Edmundson (eds.), *The Eighth Generation* (New York: Harper & Bros., 1960); pp. 48–61, and Robert A. Warner, *New Haven Negroes* (New Haven, Conn.: Yale University Press, 1940) pp. 184–90.

cation studies, including the study of Chicago Negroes by Warner, Junker, and Adams,[3] are so vague concerning the determinants of prestige that they could not be included.[4]

Those criteria emphasized in more than one study and the number of studies in which each is emphasized are given in Table 2. Education is emphasized most frequently (in all but one of the sixteen studies), and occupation and wealth or income rank second and third. The exact frequencies should not be taken too seriously since the decision as to whether a criterion was or was not emphasized was necessarily made on a subjective basis. However, the ranking of education, occupation, and wealth or income above the other criteria is very likely to reflect the empirical rank order. Also, education very likely does rank first in importance (or has until recently), since the studies most frequently identify it as the Number 1 criterion. For instance, King writes of his study of Negroes in a southern city:

> The informants generally stressed or implied that education is the chief item, followed by occupation and source of income, that makes for social differentiation. The rating of occupations tends to be determined by the amount of education basic to the occupation.[5]

Drake and Cayton point out that in Chicago in the early 1940's a heavier weighting of education than of occupation was a peculiarity of the Negro social-status (prestige) scale. They write:

> Securing an education is the most effective shortcut to the top of the Negro social pyramid. Money and occupation are important, but an educated man without a high-status occupation or a very large income, might be admitted to circles that a wealthy policy king or prize fighter would find it hard to enter.[6]

Those authors who do not list education as the most important criterion generally list it very near the top. For instance, Powdermaker writes that education "is second only to the code of sexual behavior as an index of status, and is the chief means of advancing one's social position."[7] No one places either occupation or income above education in order of importance.

That Negroes value education more than high occupational status tends to be corroborated by a study in which Rosen found that Negro mothers had high educational but low occupational aspirations for their sons relative to the aspirations of mothers in several ethnic groups.[8] Relative aspiration and relative evaluation are not necessarily the same, of course. The Negro mothers may have had higher educational than occupational aspirations for their sons mainly because they perceived greater opportunities for educational attainment.

The prestige criteria found by the different studies listed in Table 1 vary considerably. However, it is difficult to discern whether the variations reflect regional differences, differences among communities of varying sizes, temporal changes, or simply differences in the perceptions of the investigators. That the latter accounts for some of the variations is evidenced by the fact that both Dollard and Powdermaker studied the same community.

The studies show no clear-cut pattern of temporal change in criteria. Education and occupation are emphasized in the two earliest as well as in the several latest studies. The six studies that do not emphasize income or wealth range from one of the earliest (1932) to one of the latest (1955). Respectability or morality is emphasized in the earliest (1899) and in the next to the latest study (1955). On the other hand, "culture" and refinement appear to have declined in importance, being emphasized in only one study after 1941 and in none after 1946. White ancestry and skin color are emphasized neither in the earlier nor in the latest studies. The absence of stress on these attributes in recent studies supports the rather general agreement in the literature that Caucasoid features are declining in importance as Negro prestige criteria.[9]

Not enough very recent studies are included in Table 1 to form a basis for conclusions about current trends in Negro prestige criteria. Nor can much speculation about these trends be found in the recent literature. Frazier claims that income and its concomitant style of life have emerged as the most important Negro prestige criteria, having surpassed education and occupation.[10] This conclusion is impressionistic, however, and may or may not be correct.[11] For a reason that is discussed below, income probably has increased in importance as a Negro prestige criterion, but it may not yet be more important than education and occupation.

When the studies are divided into those of southern, northern, and border communities (see Table 2), some ostensible regional differences

TABLE 2 *Frequency of Emphasis of Negro Prestige Criteria in Sixteen Empirical Studies, by Region**

	NO. OF STUDENTS IN WHICH EMPHASIZED			
CRITERION	Four Northern Studies	Three Border Studies	Nine Southern Studies	Total
Education	4	2	9	15
Occupation	4	2	8	14
Wealth or income	4	3	3	10
Respectability or morality	3		5	8
Refinement or "culture"	2	1	2	5
Skin color or white ancestry	1	1	2	4
Family background		2	2	4
Property ownership			2	2

* Only those criteria emphasized in two or more studies are listed.

appear. Wealth or income is emphasized in all of the studies of northern and border communities but in only three of the nine southern studies. Family background is emphasized only in the border and southern studies.

This may reflect a general North-South difference in the relative degrees of achievement as opposed to ascription of prestige.

Of the prestige criteria listed in Table 2, only one, skin color or white ancestry, is peculiarly Negro. While each of the others is, to some extent, important in white prestige evaluations, their rank order of importance among whites appears to be different. In reports of white prestige-stratification studies, strong emphasis upon education is conspicuously absent. Primary emphasis is placed upon wealth, income, family background, and a variety of other variables that can be subsumed under "style of life." For example, Davis, Gardner, and Gardner point out that among the whites of "Old City" the social strata were delineated primarily by economic variables at the lower and middle levels and by family background at the highest level.[12] Education was of secondary importance and could be used to aid upward mobility only if the person had or could obtain the requisite economic status for the level to which he aspired.[13]

Warner, in his study of prestige stratification in Morris, Illinois, found several variables more highly correlated than education with the Evaluated Participation (E.P.) ratings (which are essentially measures of prestige). The correlation of the E.P. with education was +.78, whereas it was +.91 with occupation, +.85 with source of income, +.85 with house type, and +.82 with dwelling area (each variable having been rated on a seven-point scale).[14] Although correlation must not be equated with causation, it is likely that the variables most highly correlated with the E.P. were the most important bases of prestige.

A means of estimating the relative importance of education and income as prestige criteria that is available for whites is not available for Negroes. The relative importance of these two variables as bases of occupational prestige is probably similar (although not necessarily identical) to their relative importance as bases of personal prestige. In the NORC (North-Hatt) occupational prestige study published in 1947, a number of occupations were rated as to prestige by a national sample.[15] Forty-five of these occupations are comparable or roughly comparable with occupations used in the 1950 Census reports. Among these, the prestige ratings and the median incomes of male experienced workers in 1949 correlate with a value of +.83. The correlation of the prestige scores with the median years of school completed in 1950 is exactly the same—+.83.[16] The identity of the two correlations indicates that income and education were of about equal importance among whites as bases of occupational prestige, and probably also of about equal importance as bases of personal prestige.

It seems, therefore, that education was relatively more important as a basis of prestige in the white population as a whole than in the small communities studied by Warner and by Davis, Gardner, and Gardner. However, education was not markedly more important than income for whites, as it apparently was for Negroes.

POSSIBLE REASONS FOR THE PRE-EMINENCE OF EDUCATION AS A NEGRO PRESTIGE CRITERION

There is little doubt that, up until recently at least, formal education has been more important in Negro than in white prestige considerations. Three possible explanations for this difference come to mind. First, Negroes may value education more than do whites because it is scarcer among Negroes. Second, education may be of greater utility to Negroes in the acquisition of other valued attributes that are bases of prestige (although the reverse is usually assumed to be true). Third, Negroes may be more differentiated than whites in educational attainment, and the importance of a valued attribute as a prestige criterion may depend, to a large extent, upon how unequally it is distributed.

RELATIVE SCARCITY

Greater scarcity cannot in itself account for the great prestige value of education to Negroes. It can explain why a Negro at a given educational level enjoys greater prestige in the Negro community than his white counterpart enjoys in the white community, but it cannot account for education being more important than income in Negro prestige considerations nor for education being a more important Negro than a white prestige criterion. Income is even scarcer than education among Negroes, if the white levels of income and education are used as standards in determining scarcity. In 1950, non-whites had an estimated 7.6 per cent of the total years of school completed by persons twenty-five years old and older, whereas in 1949, non-whites had only about 5.4 per cent of the total personal income.[17] In 1950, the median years of school completed by non-whites twenty-five years old and older was 71 per cent of the white median, whereas in 1949, the median income of non-white families was only 51 per cent of that of white families.[18] If income after taxes rather than total income were considered, the relative scarcity of non-white income would be less. However, one may safely assume that in 1949–50 formal education was at least not much scarcer than disposable income among Negroes.

RELATIVE UTILITY

The question of the relative utility of formal education to Negroes and to whites is somewhat more complicated. The data in Table 3 shows that in 1950, according to our Index of Occupational Status, non-whites between the ages of twenty-four and thirty-five at each educational level had a lower occupational status than whites.[19] This means that young non-white adults were, on the average, getting less reward in occupational status than whites from a given amount of education. However, these data also reveal that, at some levels, an added increment of education was

TABLE 3 *Index of Occupational Status* for Persons 25–34 Years of Age, by Color, Sex, and Educational Level, 1950*

YEARS OF SCHOOL COMPLETED	NON-WHITES			WHITES		
	Index Value	Change from Next Lower Level		Index Value	Change from Next Lower Level	
		Abso- lute	Per Cent		Abso- lute	Per Cent
Males:						
Less than 5	80			88		
5–7	85	5	6.3	92	4	4.5
8	89	4	4.7	94	2	2.2
1–3 years of high school	92	3	3.4	101	7	7.4
4 years of high school	98	6	6.5	108	7	6.9
1–3 years of college	107	9	9.2	121	13	12.0
4 years or more of college	136	29	27.1	141	20	16.6
Females:						
Less than 5	63			87		
5–7	65	2	3.2	84	− 3	− 3.4
8	69	4	6.2	85	1	1.2
1–3 years of high school	72	3	4.3	92	7	8.2
4 years of high school	83	11	15.3	107	15	16.3
1–3 years of college	105	22	26.5	119	12	11.2
4 years or more of college	128	23	18.0	130	11	8.5

* The Index of Occupational Status was derived in the following manner: The occupational status value for a worker = $(a/A + b/B)/2$ when

  a = median income for workers in his occupational group (1949)
  A = median income for all experienced workers
  b = median years of school completed by workers in his occupational group (1950)
  B = median years of school completed by all experienced workers
The Index of Occupational Status = Mean Occupational Status Value for workers at an educational level.
The index values were computed for males using male income and education data and for females using female data.

Source: Computed from data in Donald J. Bogue, *The Population of the United States* (Glencoe, Ill.: Free Press, 1959), pp. 513–14; and United States Department of Commerce, Bureau of the Census, *Census of Population: 1950,* Special Report P-E No. 1B, *Occupational Characteristics,* pp. 107–21, 183–90, 215–22.

likely to bring a greater gain in occupational status to the non-white than to the white person. This can be seen from the absolute and percentage differences between the Index of Occupational Status at each educational level and the index at the next higher level.[20] The differences indicate that going from less than five years of school to five to seven years or from five to seven to eight years of school had on the average more occupational utility to non-whites. Graduation from college, likewise, seems to have brought much greater occupational gain on the average to non-whites than to whites. For males, all other added increments of education had, according to this measure, more utility to whites, whereas for females, going from four years of high school to one to three years of college had more occupational utility to non-whites.

Another measure of occupational differences between adjacent educational levels is given in Table 4. This measure, Duncan's Index of Dis-

TABLE 4 *Index of Dissimilarity* Between Adjacent Educational Levels for Persons 25–34 Years of Age, by Color and Sex, 1950*

Years of School	Males		Females	
Completed	Non-whites	Whites	Non-whites	Whites
Less than 5	15.0	13.8	9.5	18.4
5–7	11.9	5.3	10.5	8.5
8	10.2	15.0	7.0	17.3
1–3 years of high school	15.8	17.7	19.2	37.3
4 years of high school	18.2	28.5	34.5	25.2
1–3 years of college	49.8	39.9	45.3	38.1
4 years or more of college				

* The Index of Dissimilarity is the percentage of workers at one educational level who would have to change occupational groups in order for their distribution to equal that of workers in the other educational level.

Source: Computed from data in Donald J. Bogue, *op. cit.*

similarity, is the percentage of individuals at an educational level who would have to change occupational categories in order for their occupational distribution to equal that at the adjacent level.[21] Weaknesses of this measure are that it takes into account all intercategory differentiation, horizontal as well as vertical, and it does not distinguish between vertical differences of varying magnitudes. Nevertheless, it leads to substantially the same conclusions as those arrived at from the examination of the

Index of Occupational Status: (1) college graduation was more important vocationally to non-whites than to whites; (2) one to three years of
college had more utility to white than to non-white males and more utility
to non-white than to white females; (3) one to three years of high school
or completion of high school had more utility to whites, both male and
female; (4) completion of elementary school had more utility to non-
whites; and (5) going from less than five to five to seven years of school
had more utility to non-white than to white males. The only disagreement
between the two measures is on the relative utility to white and non-white
females of going from less than five to five to seven years of school. The
Index of Dissimilarity indicates that this added increment of education
had more utility to white females, whereas the differences between the
values of the Index of Occupational Status at the two levels indicate
the opposite.

These data make it obvious that the conclusion that formal education has more occupational utility to whites than to Negroes is too sweep-
ing a generalization. Added years of schooling at some levels apparently
are, or have been, more conducive to Negro than to white occupational
advancement (above the occupational status that could have been attained
at the lower educational level). This makes the high Negro evaluation of
education less of an enigma. That a college degree should be more highly
valued by Negroes than by whites is strictly rational, for the degree brings
about, on the average, a greater increment of occupational gain to a
Negro. The fact remains, of course, that, on the average, the Negro college
graduate has a lower occupational status than the white graduate.

At this point, a pertinent question arises: Must the occupational
utility of education be as great to Negroes as to whites in order for education to bring as much occupational prestige to Negroes? The answer
apparently is "No." Since high occupational status is much scarcer among
Negroes, many occupations are likely to have higher prestige value to
Negroes than to whites. The occupations represented in the upper prestige
stratum according to thirteen empirical studies of Negro communities are
given in Table 5. Some of the occupations listed for several of the studies,
both early and recent, would give whites only lower-middle-class status.
Examples are artisans, storekeepers, and people in clerical occupations;
these require less education than most of the occupations that afford
upper-stratum status to whites, thus making education more useful to
Negroes than to whites in the acquisition of occupational prestige.[22]

With income, as with occupational status, the payoff to non-whites
was less than to whites at each educational level.[23] However, unlike occupational status, additional years of schooling in 1949 were consistently
associated with less additional median income for non-whites than for
whites. Anderson has shown that from each educational level to the next

TABLE 5 *Occupational Composition of Upper Negro Prestige Stratum According to Thirteen Empirical Studies*

STUDY AND DATE OF PUBLICATION OR COMPLETION	OCCUPATIONS REPRESENTED IN THE UPPER STRATUM
DuBois: Negroes in Philadelphia's Seventh Ward, 1899	Persons not engaged in menial service
DuBois: Negroes in Athens, Georgia, 1902	Teachers, physicians, barbers, tailors, carpenters, shoemakers, waiters, ministers, blacksmiths, postal employees, *et al.*
Daniels: Boston Negroes, 1914	Lawyers, physicians, salaried employees, business proprietors, literary and musical people
Powdermaker: Negroes in a small town in the Deep South, 1939	Teachers, education officials, doctors, dentists, businessmen
Frazier: Louisville Negroes, 1940	High-school teachers and principals, college faculty, pastors of prominent churches, more successful physicians and dentists, executives of large Negro businesses
Warner: New Haven, Connecticut, Negroes, 1940	Doctors, lawyers, dentists, social workers, teachers, ministers of large, long-established churches, wealthy proprietors and businessmen
Davis, Gardner, and Gardner: A small town in the Deep South, 1941	Professional men, planters, storekeepers, contractors, artisans, and employees of the federal government
Johnson: Rural Negroes in eight South-	Doctors, teachers, and school principals, successful landowners
Drake and Cayton: The Chicago Black Belt, 1945	Doctors, lawyers, school teachers, executives, successful business people
Jones: Negroes in a small Virginia town, 1946	Professionals, businessmen, contractors, school teachers
Frazier: Negroes in Washington, D.C., 1949	Professionals, businessmen, people in clerical occupations
King: Negroes in a southern city, 1953	Physicians, dentists, lawyers, college presidents, college instructors, high-school teachers, insurance executives, professionally trained ministers
Rohrer and Edmonson: New Orleans Negroes, 1960	Professionals, managers, proprietors

Source: Daniels, *op. cit.*, p. 181; Davis, Gardner, and Gardner, *op. cit.*, p. 457; Drake and Cayton, *op. cit.*, p. 522; DuBois, *The Philadelphia Negro*, p. 310, and *The Negro in the Black Belt: Some Social Sketches* (Bulletin of the Department of Labor, No. 22 [Washington, D.C., 1902]); Frazier, *Negro Youth at the Crossways*, p. 23, and *The Negro in the United States*, p. 286; Johnson, *op. cit.*, pp. 73–74; Jones, *op. cit.*, p. 8; King, *op. cit.*, p. 352; Powdermaker, *op. cit.*, p. 65; Rohrer and Edmonson (eds.), *op. cit.*, p. 26; and Robert A. Warner, *op. cit.*, p. 189.

higher one the increment of additional median income generally was more than twice as great with whites as with non-whites.[24] The percentage difference from each level to the next higher one was more similar for whites and non-whites, but in each case the difference for whites was greater.[25] The apparent anomaly of the income increment consistently being greater for whites and the occupational increment at some levels being greater for non-whites can be accounted for by a greater disparity between white and non-white incomes at the higher occupational levels.[26] The greater occupational increment to non-whites at some educational levels remains important in spite of the fact that it was not accompanied by a greater income increment. Occupation can be an important basis of prestige independent of prestige it brings through income.

Furthermore, it does not necessarily follow from the smaller non-white income increment associated with additional years of schooling that the additional education brought less income-based prestige to non-whites. Since income is much scarcer among Negroes, a given amount of income, no doubt, has more prestige value to a Negro than to a white person. Therefore, if additional education was *consistently* associated with additional income (although a lesser amount) among Negroes, income utility could account for as much of the prestige value of education to Negroes as to whites. Since it is not feasible to measure the association of education with income among all adult Negro and all adult white individuals, we have measured the association among broad categories of individuals; namely, the male experienced workers in the eleven "occupational groups" used in the 1950 Census reports. Among these categories of non-whites, median income in 1949 and median years of school completed in 1950 correlated with a value of +.79. Among these categories of all experienced male workers, the correlation was +.83.[27] These correlations suggest that education and income were about equally associated among whites and non-whites. However, since the correlations of group and of individual characteristics may differ considerably, this conclusion cannot be made with certainty.[28]

The above discussion suggests that occupational and income utility may account for about as much or even slightly more of the prestige value of education to Negroes as to whites. However, it seems unlikely that this utility accounts entirely for the apparently much greater importance of education as a basis of Negro than of white prestige. Furthermore, the occupational and income utility of Negro education can hardly account for the ranking of education above both occupation and income as a Negro prestige criterion.

RELATIVE DIFFERENTIATION

It is obvious that a population must be differentiated to a certain minimum extent with respect to an attribute before that attribute can serve as a basis for invidious distinctions. Because Negroes in the American South were fairly homogeneous with regard to income, wealth, occupation, and education until the early decades of this century, the major bases of prestige were, of necessity, other attributes such as skin color, ancestry (free or slave, household or field slave), status of employers, and the like.[29] Income, occupation, and education emerged as the dominant criteria only where and when the Negroes became fairly well differentiated in these attainments. Perhaps, in most places, the educational differentiation proceeded most rapidly.

It is easy to go from the obvious requirement for minimal differentiation to the proposition that the prestige value of an attribute varies directly with the differentiation of the population with respect to the attribute. If this is a correct proposition, earlier and greater differentiation of Negroes in education than in occupation or income could account for the pre-eminence of education as a Negro prestige criterion. However, the proposition is not an obvious truth and should be regarded as only a hypothesis. Furthermore, it is not certain that educational differentiation of Negroes proceeded much more rapidly than occupational and income differentiation.

Since occupation is not a quantitative variable, educational and occupational differentiation cannot be compared precisely. And, unfortunately, data that can be used to estimate the relative degrees of Negro and white educational and income differentiation are not available for years prior to 1949–50. However, the data in Table 6 provide a reasonably

TABLE 6 *Estimated Percentages* of Income and of Formal Education Possessed by the Uppermost Segments of Adult Individuals, Whites and Non-Whites, 1949–50*

	EDUCATION (1950)		INCOME (1949)	
INDIVIDUALS	Entire United States	South	Entire United States	South
Upper 10 per cent:				
Whites	16.8	17.8	30.4	32.8
Non-whites	21.4	23.7	27.9	24.1
Upper 50 per cent:				
Whites	66.8	68.8	80.8	82.7
Non-whites	77.4	76.7	82.2	81.5

* The frequency tables from which the education estimates were made have an open-ended upper interval of 16+ years of school completed. The average value of cases in this interval was estimated as 16. The frequency tables from which the income estimates were made have an open-ended upper interval of $10,000 or more. The average value of cases in this interval was estimated as $14,000 for whites and as $12,000 for non-whites.

Source: Estimated from data in United States Department of Commerce, Bureau of the Census, *Census of Population: 1950,* Vol. II, *Characteristics of the Population,* Part I, *U.S. Summary,* pp. 163, 237, 298, 363.

good estimate of relative degrees of educational and income differentiation of whites and non-whites in 1949–50. The greater the percentage of an attribute that resides with an uppermost segment of a population, the more unequally the attribute is distributed. Therefore, the higher the percentages in Table 6, the greater was the differentiation.

According to the estimated percentages in Table 6, non-whites were more differentiated than whites in education. The difference remains even if whites with 16+ years of school are estimated to have an average of 17 years of school, an estimate undoubtedly too high![30] On the other hand, if our estimates are substantially correct, there was no appreciable difference in the differentiation of whites and non-whites in income. In fact, non-whites were almost certainly more differentiated than whites in *disposable* income, since more of the white income extended into the higher tax brackets. Therefore, if prestige value is a function of differentiation, education should have been a more important prestige criterion to non-whites, and income should have been about equally important to whites and to non-whites, or somewhat more important to non-whites. This may have been the case.

According to our estimates, both whites and non-whites were more differentiated in income than in education, although the difference was greater with whites. This would lead us to expect income to be more important than education as a prestige criterion among both non-whites and whites; in fact, education apparently was more important than income for non-whites (or Negroes) and the two variables were of about equal importance for whites. However, the differentiation of both whites and non-whites in disposable income was less than in total income and disposable income may be more important in prestige considerations. Because of the income taxes that take much or most of added increments of income, and possibly for other reasons, income exhibits what may be called "diminishing marginal prestige value." To illustrate, $5,000 added to a $5,000 income brings much greater increased prestige than $5,000 added to a $50,000 income. Possibly with disposable income also, $5,000 added to $5,000 brings greater increased prestige than $5,000 added to $50,000, but this is less certain. By contrast, education does not exhibit diminishing marginal prestige value. Not all added years of school have the same prestige value, but the prestige value of added years does not decrease uniformly from lower to higher levels. For instance, a year of college added to twelve years of school has more prestige value than a year added to three years of school. Consequently, if income could be stated in units of equal prestige value, and if education could be stated in the same manner, there probably would be considerably greater differentiation of both whites and non-whites in the education-prestige units than in the income-prestige units.

An additional consideration is that the educational differentiation of non-whites may have been greater relative to their income differentiation prior to 1949–50. A comparison of the data given in Table 6 for the South with those given for the entire country suggests that such a change probably occurred. In 1949–50, non-whites were lesss differentiated in income in the South than in the country as a whole, and we know that, with regard to many Negro social and economic characteristics, the trend has been away from the southern and toward the national pattern. A trend toward greater income differentiation could account for income becoming a more important Negro prestige criteria, if, as Frazier claims, income has become a more important criterion.

This treatment of relative differentiation illustrates that attempts to deal empirically with the relative differentiation of two populations with respect to a variable or of one population with respect to two variables are complicated by a number of factors and that the results of such attempts have uncertain meaning. However, the discussion does suggest that greater differentiation of Negroes than of whites in education and greater differentiation of whites than of Negroes in income can account, partially, or wholly, for the one-time differing rank order of importance of the two prestige criteria among Negroes and whites.

SUMMARY AND CONCLUSIONS

Formal education (apparently) has been the most important determinant of Negro prestige, at least until recently, ranking above occupation, income, and all other prestige criteria. Among whites, by contrast, occupation and income have been as important as education, and possibly more so.

These differences in the ranking of Negro and of white prestige criteria could be accounted for solely by variation in the relative differentiation of the different bases of prestige. In fact, the data presented in this article are compatible with the hypothesis that the importance of a variable as a prestige criterion depends upon how unequally the variable is distributed.

However, social phenomena rarely are amenable to simple, one-factor explanations, and there is little reason to believe that variation in the weighting of prestige criteria is an exception. Therefore, a more tenable restatement of the above hypothesis is: *All other pertinent factors remaining constant,* the importance of a variable as a prestige criterion varies directly with how unequally the variable is distributed. Other relevant factors are relative scarcity and relative utility. Additional factors possibly are pertinent.

The data given in this article do not disprove the importance of relative scarcity as a determinant of the weighting of a prestige criterion. Education probably has been more important than income as a basis of Negro prestige *in spite of* income being scarcer. Had other pertinent factors been equal, the scarcer attribute probably would have been the more heavily weighted prestige criterion. However, degrees of differentiation in income and in education were not equal, and, apparently, relative scarcity is less important than relative differentiation as a determinant of the weighting of a prestige criterion.[31]

The role of utility (for the acquisition of other valued attributes) in determining the importance of a prestige criterion is in no way minimized by the data presented here. Added increments of education at several levels have been associated with greater occupational gains to Negroes than to whites, a little known fact that can partially account for education having been a more important prestige criterion among Negroes. Furthermore, because of the greater scarcity of income and high occupational status among Negroes, a given increment in income or in occupational status is likely to bring more added prestige to a Negro than to a white person. Therefore, education may bring greater rewards in occupational and economic prestige to Negroes than to whites.

[Notes]

1. W. Lloyd Warner and Paul S. Lunt, *The Social Life of a Modern Community* (New Haven, Conn.: Yale University Press, 1941); and Allison Davis, Burleigh Gardner, and Mary Gardner, *Deep South* (Chicago: University of Chicago Press, 1941).
2. Hortense Powdermaker, *After Freedom* (New York: Viking Press, 1939), p. 70.
3. W. Lloyd Warner, Buford H. Junker, and Walter A. Adams, *Color and Human Nature* (Washington, D.C.: American Council on Education, 1941).
4. In addition to those criteria listed frequently in Table 1, "style of life" is likely to be a major Negro prestige criterion. Those attributes that constitute style of life are not listed in the table because the authors identify them only as characteristics of prestige strata and not as bases of prestige.
5. Charles E. King, "The Process of Social Stratification among an Urban Minority Population," *Social Forces*, XXXI (May, 1953), 352.
6. St. Clair Drake and Horace R. Cayton, *Black Metropolis* (New York: Harcourt, Brace & Co., 1945), p. 516.
7. *Op. cit.*, p. 65.
8. Bernard C. Rosen, "Race, Ethnicity, and the Achievement Syndrome," *American Sociological Review,* XXVI (February, 1959), 47–60.

9. E.G., see Davis, Gardner, and Gardner, *op. cit.*, p. 246; Drake and Cayton, *op. cit.*, p. 506; Alvin Boskoff, "Negro Class Structure and the Technic-Ways," *Social Forces*, XXIX (December, 1950), 131; E. Franklin Frazier, *The Negro in the United States* (rev. ed.; New York: Macmillan Co., 1957), p. 291; and Maurice R. Davis, *Negroes in American Society* (New York: McGraw-Hill Book Co., 1949), pp. 417–18.

10. E. Franklin Frazier, *Black Bourgeoisie* (Glencoe, Ill.: Free Press, 1947), p. 199.

11. A recent study by Shirley Caldwell of Negro Freshman women at the University of Illinois lends support to Frazier's conclusion. Twenty of thirty-six women interviewed seemed to value a college education mainly as a means to high occupational and economic status rather than as a direct means to higher prestige. Fifteen of the thirty-six said they would drop out of college if they could find a suitable job that did not require a college education ("Why Negro Freshman Women Come to College" [unpublished paper, 1961]). However, the small and non-random sample of this study makes it an inadequate basis for generalization.

12. *Op. cit.*, pp. 70, 75–76.

13. *Ibid.*, p. 187.

14. W. Lloyd Warner, Marchia Meeker, and Kenneth Eells, *Social Class in America* (Gloucester, Mass.: Peter Smith, Publisher, 1957), p. 168.

15. National Opinion Research Center, "Jobs and Occupations: A Popular Evaluation," *Opinion News*, IX (September 1, 1947), 3–13.

16. Income and education data were taken from United States Department of Commerce, Bureau of the Census, *Census of Population: 1950*, Special Report P-E No. 1B, *Occupational Characteristics*, pp. 107–114, 183–190. The median years of school completed are given for some occupations as 16+. In such cases, the actual median was estimated. For instance, the median for physicians and surgeons was estimated as 20 years, for college professors as 18 years, for dentists as 19 years, for public school teachers as 16.5 years, and so on.

17. Estimated from data in United States Department of Commerce, Bureau of the Census, *Census of Population: 1950*, Vol. II, *Characteristics of the Population*, Part I, *U.S. Summary*, pp. 237–414. The frequency table from which the educational estimate was made has an open-ended upper interval of 16+ years of school completed. The average value of cases in this interval was estimated as 16, which is slightly low for both whites and non-whites and somewhat lower for whites than for non-whites. The frequency table from which the income estimate was made has an open-ended upper interval of $10,000 and over. The average value of cases in this interval was estimated as $14,000 for whites and $12,000 for non-whites.

    Several times in this article data for non-whites are used as bases for conclusions about the Negro population. This is justifiable since 95.5 per cent of the non-whites in the United States in 1950 were Negroes (United States Department of Commerce, Bureau of the Census, *Statistical Abstract of the United States: 1960*, p. 28).

18. United States Department of Commerce, Bureau of the Census, *Statistical Abstract of the United States: 1960*, p. 108; and *Current Population Reports, Consumer Income*, Series P-60, No. 35 (January 5, 1961), pp. 6–7.

19. See Table 3, n.*, for the formula for the Index of Occupational Status. Since the index values are derived from the distributions of workers among the eleven "occupational groups" used in the 1950 Census reports, differences between the white and the non-white values do not fully reflect the extent of the differences between the whites and non-white occupational distributions. In some of the

occupation groups, the distributions of whites and non-whites among the detailed occupation groups differed considerably in 1950. However, the differences were less at each educational level than among all workers.

20. Although we make inferences here concerning the occupational utility of education by comparing occupational distributions at different educational levels, the data are not direct evidence of the occupational utility of education. Persons at one educational level may differ in their occupations from those at another level partially because of differences in native intelligence, motivation, and the like. In other words, differences in other attributes may be common causes of some of the differences in educational attainment and in occupational status.

Furthermore, it should be kept in mind that the inferences made here concerning the increases in occupational status that were likely to come from added education apply to one or a small number of individuals rather than to a large number. If enough people were to move up educationally to alter appreciably the educational distribution, the occupational payoff of education at the higher levels no doubt would diminish.

21. This index is defined, among other places, in Otis Dudley Duncan and Beverly Duncan, "Residential Distribution and Occupational Stratification," *American Journal of Sociology,* LX (March, 1955), 494.

22. Morgan C. Brown replicated the NORC occupational prestige study with a sample of Negroes in Columbus, Ohio. He found that the Negro prestige ratings for most occupations did not differ greatly from the NORC ratings and that the Negroes rated more occupations much lower (five points or more) than much higher than the NORC respondents ("The Status of Jobs and Occupations as Evaluated by an Urban Negro Sample," *American Sociological Review,* XX [October, 1955], 564–65). However, the occupations that the Negroes rated much higher are ones in which Negroes are highly or moderately well represented, and therefore they are occupations into which upwardly mobile Negroes are likely to move. By contrast, the occupations that the NORC respondents rated much higher are either agricultural occupations or ones in which Negro representation is very low, and therefore they are occupations into which few Negroes are likely to be upwardly mobile. Consequently, Brown's data do not refute the hypothesis that a given increment of increase in occupational status is likely to bring more added prestige to the Negro than to the white person.

23. For 1949 income data by educational level and color see C. Arnold Anderson, "Regional and Racial Difference in Relations between Income and Education," *School Review,* LXIII (January, 1955), 39. The difference between the white and non-white median incomes was least at the lowest educational level and increased up the scale of education. For instance, in the South the ratio of the non-white to white median income was .822 at the level of one to four years of school but was only .501 with college graduates. In the North and West the corresponding ratios were .854 and .597.

24. *Ibid.* For instance, in the South the difference between the median incomes of white high school and college graduates was $1,929, whereas the non-white difference was only $859. In the North and West the white difference was $1,852 and the non-white difference was only $774.

25. In the South the median income of white college graduates was 55 percent greater than the median income of white high-school graduates, but the non-white percentage was almost as great—46 percent. In the North and West the white and non-white percentages were 50 and 31 percent, respectively. At the other educa-

tional levels, the disparity between the white and non-white percentages ranged from slight to moderate (see *ibid.*, Table 1).

26. For instance, in 1949 the ratio of the median income of employed non-white males who were professional, technical, and kindred workers to the median for all males employed in that category was .575; and for managers, officials, and proprietors the ratio was .500. By contrast, the ratio was .911 for private household workers, .716 for farm laborers, .810 for other laborers, .776 for service workers, and .721 for operatives and kindred workers. The lower relative non-white incomes in the higher occupational groups are partially accounted for by non-whites being concentrated in the lower-paying detailed occupations within the groups. However, there was a great disparity between white and non-white incomes in many of the detailed occupations. For instance, the ratio of the non-white to the total median income (for males) for physicians and surgeons was .589, for clergymen it was .581, for funeral directors and embalmers it was .632, and for teachers it was .717 (source: United States Department of Commerce, Bureau of the Census, *Census of Population: 1950*, Special Report P-E No. 18, *Occupational Characteristics*, Tables 19 and 21).

27. Computed from data in United States Department of Commerce, Bureau of the Census, *Census of Population: 1950*, Special Report P-E No. 1B, *Occupational Characteristics*, pp. 107–21, 183–90, 215–22. The regression of median income on median years of school completed was $158.45 with non-whites and $341.55 with all male workers. This indicates that an increase of one year of schooling was associated with less than half as much increase in income with the non-whites as with all male workers.

28. For a discussion of the sometimes great discrepancy between correlations among categories of individuals and among the individuals in those categories see W. S. Robinson, "Ecological Correlations and the Behavior of Individuals," *American Sociological Review*, XV (June, 1950), 351–57.

29. Johnson, *op. cit.*, p. 257, and Frazier, *op. cit.*, pp. 394–95.

30. According to this estimate, the upper tenth of the whites had 19.5 percent of the total years of school completed by whites, and the upper half had 75 percent.

31. It should be pointed out that scarcity and differentiation are not completely independent dimensions. High differentiation of a population in regard to an attribute necessarily entails relative scarcity among some members of the population. On the other hand, if the standard of abundance is some quantity aside from the central tendency of distribution of the attribute in the population (such as level of need or the central tendency of the distribution of the attribute in another population), low differentiation may occur with either scarcity or abundance.

12

Donald L. Noel

Group Identification Among Negroes: An Empirical Analysis

SOME kind of positive group identification or loyalty is a prerequisite for the stability of any specific group in a multi-group environment. Indeed, "society—social structure of every sort—rests upon loyalties: upon attitudes and actions directed at supporting groups, ideas, and institutions" (11, p. 5). Nevertheless, despite the universality of group loyalty, social scientists who study minority groups have generally stressed negative group identification—variously labeled withdrawal, rejection or self-hatred. Actually a minority group provides its members an abundance of both gratifying and depriving experiences and group identification—positive as well as negative—is a product of these experiences. Minority group members are, then, caught in a conflict which theoretically gives rise to "a typically ambivalent attitude . . . toward their own group" (16, p. 177).

This ambivalence implies that group identification is a multi-dimensional phenomenon which cannot be adequately characterized in terms of a single continuum ranging from group self-hatred to group pride (see also 1, p. 492). Moreover, a survey of the literature reveals discussion of several types of both positive and negative group identification. The various types of pride (ethnocentric, nationalistic, militant and non-defensive) appear to be largely independent but the various types of self-hatred (personal, general, segmental and defensive) appear to be intrinsically related, perhaps scalable. We suggest, then, that group identification and

Reprinted by permission of The Society for the Psychological Study of Social Issues from *The Journal of Social Issues,* Vol. 20, No. 2, April 1964, pp. 71–84. Numbers in parentheses refer to sources listed in the reference notes on pages 140–141.

its positive component are multi-dimensional while group self-hatred may be uni-dimensional. A brief review of the various types of group identification generally supports this contention.

Ethnocentric group pride or chauvinism has been discussed by many writers (e.g., 2, 13 and 18) and may be characterized as the tendency to assert or defend the in-group, right or wrong, and to accept positive stereotypes about the in-group. *Nationalistic* pride is illustrated by Negroes whose race pride is "built on the contemporary achievements of Negroes *in the caste system*" (19, p. 93) and is linked to ethnocentric pride via the Negro who manifests pride in the positive acts (as defined by whites) of any Negro anywhere. Both nationalistic and ethnocentric pride imply a tendency to clutch at any and all straws in an attempt to combat an underlying feeling of inferiority.[1] *Militant* group pride, a type originally suggested by Rose, centers around the expression of identification via concern with protest and is exhibited by participants in the sit-in movement, the NAACP and other minority protest organizations and activities. Finally, *non-defensive* group pride is exhibited by the individual who "shows satisfactions derived from group membership, without claiming race superiority or showing excessive defensiveness" (13, p. 176). Such ideal group loyalty is rare, particularly in minority groups.

Widespread negative identification, on the other hand, is unique to minority groups. Lewin, who introduced the concept of group self-hatred, views antipathy toward one's own group as a resultant of (1) the adoption of majority attitudes and values; and (2) the inability to escape membership in the group even though membership results in severe restrictions on personal opportunity (16, pp. 164, 176–177, 189, and 191–192). Lewin alludes, without elaboration, to the existence of several varieties of self-hatred (16, pp. 186–187) and subsequent writers have systematized this area to some extent. In particular R. B. Johnson's concept of the generalizability of the self-hating sentiment appears to be a useful mode of classification (15, pp. 236–238). Using this concept, which is implicit in Lewin, we can distinguish personal, segmental and general disparagement or self-hatred.[2] *Personal* self-hatred is focused on rejection of one's self and can readily be explained in terms of Meadian social psychology as the incorporation of the negative attitudes and responses directed toward the minority individual by members of the majority group. *Segmental* disparagement involves the rejection of a specific segment of the in-group (e.g., the "lower class") while *general* disparagement involves rejection of the entire in-group with the exception of one's self and perhaps one's intimate in-group associates. Both general and segmental disparagement are explicable in terms of the scapegoating mechanism. Although the majority group may be too powerful to be attacked by a minority individual prevented from attaining personal goals because of his minority status, the in-group provides an alternative outlet for aggression—and group disparagement is one means of expressing this aggression.

A fourth type of negative reaction to group membership, *defensiveness,* is characterized by a tendency to deny any disadvantages in group membership and refusal to perceive any differences between the minority and the majority group (13). This type also manifests some elements of group pride and therefore appears to constitute a mild form of *ambivalence* in contrast to the severe ambivalence of those who manifest both strong group pride and constant group disparagement. A number of writers (e.g., 13, 15 and 18) discuss this response and generally conclude, like Lewin, that ambivalence is commonplace among minority persons.[3]

AN INDEX OF GROUP IDENTIFICATION

The theoretical expectation of widespread ambivalence demands that a thorough empirical analysis of minority group identification utilize independent measures of group pride and disparagement. Accordingly group identification is assessed in the present study via separate three item indices of *militant* group pride and *general* disparagement. Group pride is manifested by a negative response to two or all three of the following items:

1. I don't worry much about the race problem because I know I can't do anything about it.
2. Do you ever get the feeling that it is just not worth fighting for equal treatment for Negroes in this town?
3. Negroes shouldn't go in business establishments where they think they're not wanted.

Group disparagement is manifested by an affirmative response to two or all three of the following items:

1. Negroes blame white people for their position but it's really their own fault.
2. Negroes are always shouting about their rights but have nothing to offer.
3. Generally speaking, Negroes are lazy and ignorant.

The items in each of these sub-sets are significantly related to each other and the two sub-sets are inversely related with a chi square value (46.6) significant beyond the .001 level.[4] This relationship is subject to challenge, however, as an artifact of response set.

Inasmuch as militancy is established solely by negative responses and general disparagement by positive responses, our *Identifiers* (i.e., persons who manifest group pride but not disparagement) conceivably could include a sizeable proportion of "naysayers" and our *Disparagers* (i.e., persons who manifest group disparagement but not pride) a sizeable proportion of "yeasayers" (see 6). If this were true only the *Ambivalents* (i.e., persons who manifest equivalent amounts of pride and of disparagement) would be validly identified by our index. The data indicate, however, that response set is of negligible importance in the present measure of group identification. The responses of Identifiers ($n = 229$) and Disparagers ($n = 106$) to each of nine items requiring a positive or negative response indicate that Disparagers affirmed only two of the items significantly more often than the Identifiers while the reverse, contrary to the response set hypothesis, occurred four times.[5]

The current need in studies of group identification "is to describe and measure the variables—in personality tendencies, in group structures, and in the total situation—that determine the extent of group solidarity and group withdrawal" (23, p. 224). Thus, data collected as part of the Cornell Study of Intergroup Relations from a probability sample of 515 Negroes in Bakersfield, California and Savannah, Georgia have been analyzed to test various hypotheses regarding the relation of group identification to certain aspects of personality structure and the social milieu.

PERSONALITY AND GROUP IDENTIFICATION

Himelhoch has advanced the general hypothesis that among the members of a disprivileged group "the personality needs which foster prejudice toward out-groups also engender prejudice toward the in-group" (14, p. 80). Inasmuch as frustration and authoritarianism have reigned as the major psychological correlates of out-group prejudice for the past twenty-five years, we shall test this hypothesis by examining the relationship of each of these two variables to group identification.

As regards frustration, Lewin maintains that:

> A person for whom the balance [of forces toward and away from group membership] is negative will move as far away from the center of [group] life as the outside majority permits. He will stay on this barrier and be in a constant state of frustration. Actually he will be more frustrated than those members of the minority who keep psychologically well inside the group (16, p. 193).

Although Lewin recognizes that adjustment to the group is conditioned by personality factors, he clearly stresses the causal priority of group identification in its relation to personality. This interpretation has been challenged by subsequent empirical studies and indeed the relationship *per se* has been challenged (22, pp. 304–308). The Cornell data do not allow us to establish causal priority but they clearly support the Lewinian hypothesis as regards the relation of frustration and group identification.

TABLE 1 *Frustration Is Negatively Related to Group Identification*

	FRUSTRATION			
	General[a]		Race-linked[b]	
Group Identification	Yes (216)	No (299)	Yes (298)	No (217)
Identifiers	32%	53%	37%	55%
Ambivalents	37	34	37	32
Disparagers	31	13	27	12
	$\chi^2=32$; $p<.001$		$\chi^2=22.7$; $p<.001$	

[a] Respondent is considered to experience "general" frustration if he *agrees* with the following item: Sometimes I feel so frustrated I just feel like smashing things.

[b] Respondent is considered to experience "race-linked" frustration if he agrees with the following item: When one Negro does something wrong, the whole Negro race suffers for it.

Both parts of Table 1 indicate that the frustrated are more than twice as likely as the non-frustrated to be Disparagers.

The second of the two items indexing frustration is especially interesting in that it approximates a pure measure of the frustration attributable to the fact of racial group membership. Negroes who believe that "the whole race suffers whenever any Negro does something wrong" are much more likely to manifest negative group identification than those who do not share this belief, and it was thought that this might account for a large part of the relationship between general frustration ("smash things") and group disparagement. This was not the case, however, as the "smash things" item significantly differentiates the identification types in both partials of the "race suffer" item.

Previous empirical studies of Jews and Negroes (13, 14 and 18) indicate that authoritarianism is also positively associated with group disparagement and Radke-Yarrow and Lande report a similar association between authoritarianism and ethnocentric group pride. The data presented in Table 2 confirm the positive relation between authoritarianism and disparagement, but the qualitative distinction between militant and ethnocentric group pride is clearly demonstrated by the negative relation between authoritarianism and the present index of pride. Where Radke-Yarrow and Lande observe that "the [ethnocentric] individual who *'thinks'* his group is best also accepts many of the stereotypes directed against it, and 'hates' it, and, on occasion, resists identification with it,"[6] the Cornell data suggest that the individual who expresses a willingness to militantly *act* in behalf of his group is rarely beset by such ambivalence. The relationship between group pride and authoritarianism shown here also implies a relationship between group pride and generalized prejudice significantly different from that generally reported (see 4, pp. 153–154).

TABLE 2 *Authoritarianism Is Negatively Related to Group Identification*

	AUTHORITARIANISM[a]	
Group Identification	High (247)	Low (268)
Identifiers	28%	60%
Ambivalents	40	30
Disparagers	32	10
	$\chi^2 = 66.5$; $p < .001$	

[a] Respondent is rated high in authoritarianism if he gives the indicated response to 2 or all 3 of the following items: (1) children should obey *every* order their parents give *without question* even if they think the parents are wrong (agree); (2) Some say you can't be too careful in your dealings with people while others say that most people can be trusted. From your experience which would you agree with more (can't be too careful); and (3) Prison is too good for sex criminals. They should be publicly whipped or worse (agree). This third item was not asked in Bakersfield so the following item was substituted: When things go wrong for me, I usually find it's my own fault (disagree). This substitution weakens the overall relation with group identification because the substitute item is positively related to self-hatred as well as to militancy.

GENERALIZED PREJUDICE AND GROUP IDENTIFICATION

Studies of the relationship between in-group and out-group attitudes have been confined almost entirely to majority group persons. Moreover, these studies have focussed exclusively on ethnocentrism which posits a positive association between in-group glorification and out-group rejection by definition. Adorno, *et al.,* make this explicit by stating that:

> Ethnocentrism refers to group relations generally; it has to do not only with numerous groups toward which the individual has hostile opinions and attitudes but, equally important, with groups toward which he is positively disposed (2, p. 102).

Several writers have generalized this relationship to the entire genus of group pride. Thus Bierstedt says that "prejudice 'for' entails almost inevitably prejudice 'against' " and that:

> It is unreasonable to ask us both to take pride in our own groups and their accomplishments and at the same time to refrain from considering them superior. It is the superiority in which we take the pride. And if our groups are superior they must be superior to something that is inferior. . . . (3, pp. 473, 469; see also 9 and 20).

However, the inverse relation between in-group and out-group attitudes which is characteristic of ethnocentrism should not be considered inherent in group pride inasmuch as pride is multi-dimensional. Indeed, other writers hypothesize very different relations between in-group and out-group attitudes. Lewin, for example, argues that identification with the in-group is positively associated with friendly relations with out-group members (16, pp. 166–167). Rothman stands between Bierstedt and Lewin with the claim that data collected from some 200 Jewish adolescents clearly support the hypothesis of "no correlation between in-group identification and either out-group attitudes or out-group associations" (22, p. 309, and 21). Rothman cautions that minority group identification is complex and many sided but neither he nor Bierstedt nor Lewin explicitly argue that different types of in-group pride might relate differently to out-group attitudes.

The Cornell data allow us to test these competing hypotheses by relating our measure of group identification to an index of generalized prejudice. The index of generalized prejudice was formed by combining indices of anti-white and anti-minority prejudice. Anti-white prejudice was measured by three social distance items which ask:

Do you think you would ever find it a little distasteful:

1. to eat at the same table with a white person?
2. to dance with a white person?
3. to have a white person marry someone in your family?

Anti-minority prejudice was measured by the following items:

1. This country would be better off if there were not so many foreigners here.
2. Generally speaking, Mexicans are shiftless and dirty.
3. Do you think you would ever find it a little distasteful to go to a party and find that most of the people are Jewish?

Respondents are considered prejudiced on either measure if they give an affirmative answer to two or all three of the items with the single exception that a Bakersfield Negro is considered prejudiced toward whites if he endorses even one of the "distastefuls."

TABLE 3 *Among Negroes Generalized Prejudice Is Negatively Associated with Group Identification*

Generalized Prejudice[a]	GROUP IDENTIFICATION		
	Identifiers (229)	Ambivalents (180)	Disparagers (106)
High	18%	25%	42%
Medium	28	42	32
Low	54	33	26
	$\chi^2 = 39.2, p < .001$		

[a] Respondent is classified high in generalized prejudice if he exhibits both anti-white and anti-minority prejudice, medium if he exhibits anti-white or anti-minority prejudice but not both, and low if he exhibits neither kind of prejudice. The indices of anti-white and anti-minority prejudice are described in the text.

Combining these two indices reveals a positive association ($p < .001$, $C = .31$) between anti-white and anti-minority prejudice and also allows us to isolate three degrees of out-group rejection. When out-group rejection is then related to in-group identification the data, presented in Table 3, manifest the positive relation hypothesized by Lewin. Identifiers are twice as likely as Disparagers to score low on generalized prejudice and only half as likely to score high. The positive relation between group disparagement and out-group rejection is well established (e.g., see 8, 14 and 18), but the relation between out-group rejection and group pride is apparently a function of the type of group pride. Moreover, where Rothman suggests that heightened minority group identification (type unspecified) may deteriorate intergroup relations by promoting separation and social insulation, the present data suggest that a *militant* group pride uncontaminated by group disparagement is functional for the integration of the total society.

SOCIAL STRUCTURE AND GROUP IDENTIFICATION

A basic proposition of sociology in general and reference group theory in particular asserts that the groups we (aspire to) belong to exert a significant influence on our actions and attitudes. This should be no less true of attitudes toward in-groups *per se* than of attitudes toward other objects. Thus it is our purpose in this section to analyze the effect upon group identification of differential location in the social structure is indexed by region, social class, interracial contact and organizational participation.[7]

In light of the regional variations in the pattern of race relations in the United States, it seems reasonable to hypothesize a more negative group identification among Southern Negroes than among those in other sections of the country. This is not substantiated, however, as Bakersfield and Savannah Negroes distributed among the three group identification types in an almost identical manner. Nevertheless, there are distinct but cancelling regional tendencies with respect to the components of group identification. The difference regarding group pride is in the expected direction although not significant ($p < .10$); but, contrary to our hypothesis, the Bakersfield respondents are significantly ($p < .01$) more likely to manifest group disparagement than are the Savannah respondents. This community difference remains unexplained although it might be that the existence of more effective organizations for combatting discrimination in the Southern community may partially account for the reversal of our expectation.[8] This possibility plus the significant relationship between group identification and participation in protest organizations, shown in Table 4, suggests that organizations which successfully combat discrimination may minimize self-hatred in the minority community in general.

TABLE 4 *Membership in the National Association for the Advancement of Colored People Is Positively Associated with Group Identification*

Group Identification	NAACP MEMBER	
	Yes (77)	No (438)
Identifiers	60%	42%
Ambivalents	34	35
Disparagers	6	23
	$\chi^2 = 13.4, p < .001$	

If we make the seemingly reasonable assumption that Negro Americans generally participate in all-Negro organizations, we may hypothesize that membership in organizations in general (i.e., regardless of type) is positively associated with group identification. This is consistent with Grodzin's observation that loyalty to the group is founded upon loyalty to the various constituent sub-groups (11, p. 29). The data support the hypothesis when membership in at least one organization is the only criterion applied. However, when members of the NAACP are deleted from the sample and the data reanalyzed, the relationship is no longer significant although it does approximate significance ($p < .10$).

Social class as an important dimension of social structure has also frequently been posited as a major determinant of group identification. Generally it has been argued that upper-class minority persons are more likely to exhibit group disparagement than are lower-class persons.[9] The rationale for this belief stresses that members of the upper class see lower-class behavior as the cause of prejudice and discrimination and, therefore, they blame the lower class for their own low *intergroup* status. This implies that lower-class persons less often view either their own behavior or that of the upper classes as the cause of prejudice and discrimination and, therefore, they manifest group disparagement less frequently. As Table 5 indicates, the Cornell data do not support this position. When we use education and occupation as separate indices of class status, the data not only indicate that upper-class Negroes are significantly more likely to identify with the in-group (a topic rarely discussed in the literature) but also that they are *less* likely to disparage the in-group than are lower-class Negroes.

Two cautions pertaining to the interpretation of the relationship between class and group disparagement are necessary. First, attitudes toward the in-group—whether minority or majority—may simply reflect interclass hostilities (see 23, p. 219 and 19, p. 91). Thus, since it has been suggested that class distinctions are more important in the Negro than in the white community (7, p. 416), it is conceivable that our index of group disparagement is primarily measuring inter-class hostility. Although we

TABLE 5 *Social Class, As Measured by Education and Occupation, Is Associated Positively with Group Identification*

	Social Class				
	Education[a]		Occupational Status[b]		
Group Identification	High (105)	Low (410)	High (53)	Medium (99)	Low (147)
Identifiers	72%	37%	77%	41%	40%
Ambivalents	24	38	19	43	37
Disparagers	4	25	4	15	23
	$\chi^2 = 45.7$; $p < .001$		$\chi^2 = 27.2$; $p < .001$		

[a] High education category includes high school graduates and those who attend college; all others are classified as low in education.

[b] High occupation category includes professionals and proprietors, and white collar; medium includes skilled and semi-skilled workers; and low occupational status includes laborers and domestics. N is reduced to 299 because not all respondents were employed.

cannot completely partial out the effect of the class factor in the present study, it is clear that in-group disparagement is not entirely attributable to class because a considerable proportion of Negroes endorse statements which relate to (alleged) shortcomings primarily due to their own class. For example, over 20 per cent of the upper status Negroes—who should initiate and lead an action program—agree that "Negroes are always shouting about their rights but have nothing to offer." A second caution regarding the class-disparagement relationship concerns the fact that we are dealing with general self-hatred (i.e., disparagement) and, therefore, cannot confidently draw conclusions about personal self-hatred. It is not usually clear which type of self-hatred is being discussed in the literature, but Frazier indicates the relevance of the distinction in stating that the repression by upper-status Negroes of hostilities felt toward whites results in a self-hatred "which may appear from their behavior to be directed towards the Negro masses but which in reality is directed against themselves" (10, p. 226). This distinction offers a possible but not convincing explanation of the contradiction between our finding and the expectation derived from the literature.

While most minority persons must of necessity maintain certain functional contacts with members of the dominant group, a much smaller proportion experience intimate interpersonal contact across group lines. Reference group theory suggests, however, that these few will be particularly disposed to self-hatred due to the *relative* nature of status and deprivation. That is, Negroes who experience intimate interracial contact will be more aware of their own lack of opportunities and privileges, as compared to their white friends, and, therefore, more likely to express resentment of their status via group disparagement. Table 6 indicates that the available data definitely do not support this theoretical derivation. Indeed, participa-

TABLE 6 *Interracial Social Contact Is Positively Related to Group Identifica-tion, but Friendship Contact Is Not Significantly Related to Group Identification*

	INTERRACIAL CONTACT			
	Social[a]		Friendship[b]	
Group Identification	Yes (77)	No (438)	Yes (236)	No (279)
Identifiers	55%	43%	42%	46%
Ambivalents	38	34	37	33
Disparagers	8	23	20	21
	$\chi^2 = 9.0; p < .02$		$\chi^2 = 0.89; p < .70$	

[a] Respondent is classified as having social contact with whites if he does something of a social nature (e.g., going to a sports event together or visiting in each other's homes) with any of the whites with whom he has contact.

[b] Respondent is classified as having friendship contact with whites if he considers his closest white contact a friend as opposed to being someone he just knows to speak to.

tion in informal social relations with whites proves to be associated posi-tively with group identification. The attribute of having at least one white friend as opposed to none does not manifest this relationship to group identification but neither does it support the derived hypothesis. The "friendship" index is, moreover, a questionable indicator of interpersonal intimacy as it is not related to anti-white prejudice whereas social contact is negatively related ($p < .001$) to prejudice.

SUMMARY AND CONCLUSIONS

Data collected from 515 Negroes in two American communities provide an opportunity to test a number of hypotheses regarding the correlates of minority group identification. A review of the literature suggests that group identification is a multi-dimensional phenomenon and, therefore, our find-ings cannot be generalized beyond the confines of *militant* group pride and *general* disparagement. However, within the limits of this pattern of group identification, the Cornell data justify three major conclusions.

First, the data confirm Himelhoch's hypothesis that among minority persons the personality characteristics associated with rejection of (i.e., prejudice toward) out-groups are also correlates of rejection of the in-group. Both authoritarianism and frustration manifest strong negative re-lations to group identification. Second, this is paralleled by a striking similarity of the social correlates of out-group and in-group attitudes among Negroes. In contradiction of prevalent hypotheses, education, occupation and interracial (social) contact are positively related to group identification and organization membership and age also bear approximately the same relation to group identification as to anti-white and anti-minority prejudice.[10] The similarity of social correlates is less clear-cut with respect to sex, marital status and region. However, the Cornell data indicate that the relation of sex to prejudice is highly variable dependent upon the dimension of prejudice involved and that the marital status and regional correlates of prejudice toward whites do not extend to prejudice toward minority out-groups.

Consistent with the first two conclusions, the third conclusion is that in the population studied attitude toward the in-group is positively related to attitude toward out-groups. This challenges the belief that the rejection of out-groups is an almost inevitable concomitant of in-group pride and suggests that an unequivocally positive group identification can be functional for societal integration. The differences in the findings and inferences of the present study as compared to previous researches underscore the necessity of specifying the type (s) of group identification under consideration. Such specification is pre-requisite to further advances in our understanding of the causes, processes, and consequences of group identification.

[Notes]

1. Thus Rose says that "the blatant, nationalistic claim to the cultural achievements of Negroes with whom there is no cultural contact . . . indicates an unconscious assumption . . . that race is important for achievement . . . and a feeling that they are inferior and must hunt far afield for something to be proud of" (19, p. 92). See also (18, pp. 268–269).

2. Lewin's concept of self-hatred is misleading as a generic label inasmuch as most types of negative identification refer to rejection of the group and not the self *per se*. Thus we prefer group disparagement to group self-hatred as a generic label.

3. Grossack recognizes the existence of an ambivalent type but he argues that both disparagement and ambivalence are less common than they are generally considered to be (12, 13). The opposite of ambivalence, *neutrality* or the absence of both positive and negative group sentiments, is a theoretically possible type of group identification but is probably rarely found among the members of any stable group.

4. The chi square test of significance is used throughout this paper and a relationship is considered significant only if it attains the .05 level of significance as determined by two-tailed analysis.

5. The total of six significant differences greatly exceeds chance expectation but the nine items were *not* chosen to attain significant differences. Rather they were chosen by the criteria of relevance (i.e., requirement of positive or negative response), availability, and the lack of previous use in the data analysis.

6. See 18, p. 268; emphasis added. It seems reasonable to hypothesize that the extent of group disparagement among ethnocentric individuals is a function of the in-group's position in the power structure of the total society. Ethnocentric persons are generally authoritarian and, inasmuch as authoritarians tend to identify with the strong and reject the weak, such persons might logically be expected to reject a weak (minority) in-group as well as weak out-groups. This implies that group disparagement is rare in the majority group and more common among low status minority groups (e.g., Indians and Negroes) than among those of higher status (e.g., Jews and Japanese-Americans).

7. Basic sociological variables as sex, marital status, and age bear no sizeable relation to group identification (with the single exception that even when education is held constant Negroes aged 55 or over are more likely to manifest group disparagement than are younger Negroes).

8. Analysis of field worker's notes indicate that Savannah Negroes are better organized to combat discrimination than Negroes in Bakersfield and this is substantiated by the fact that 95 percent of the Southern but only 58 percent of the Western respondents felt that the local NAACP Chapter was doing at least a "fairly good" job. The figures were 41 and 20 percent respectively for a "very good" job. Consistent with this idea of community variations in organizational effectiveness, previous studies are inconsistent in their findings regarding regional differences in group disparagement among Negroes (see 23, pp. 213–215).

9. See 5, p. 510; 19, pp. 64–66; and 24, p. 314. On the other hand, Grossack (13) diverges from general opinion by hypothesizing that the less privileged strata are most likely to disparage the in-group.

10. The relevant data regarding the social correlates of out-group prejudice among Negroes are presented in chapters III and V in 17.

[References]

1. Adelson, J. "A Study of Minority Group Authoritarianism" in M. Sklare, ed., *The Jews.* Glencoe: The Free Press, 1958, pp. 475–492.

2. Adorno, T. W., Frenkel-Brunswik, E., Levinson, D. J., & Sanford, R. N. *The Authoritarian Personality.* New York: Harper & Brothers, 1950.

3. Bierstedt, R. *The Social Order.* New York: McGraw-Hill, 1963, second ed., pp. 469–474.

4. Christie, R. "Authoritarianism Re-examined" in R. Christie and M. Jahoda, eds., *Studies in the Scope and Method of "The Authoritarian Personality."* Glencoe: The Free Press, 1954, pp. 123–196.

5. Clark, K. B. "Racial Prejudice Among American Minorities." *International Social Science Bulletin,* 1950, 2, pp. 506–513.

6. Couch, A., & Keniston, K. "Yeasayers and Naysayers: Agreeing Response Set As Personality Variable." *Journal of Abnormal and Social Psychology,* 1960, 60, pp. 151–174.

7. Davie, M. R. *Negroes in American Society.* New York: McGraw-Hill, 1949.

8. Ditz, G. "Outgroup and Ingroup Prejudice Among Members of Minority Groups." *Alpha Kappa Deltan,* 1959, 29 (#2), 26–31.

9. Fairchild, H., *Race and Nationality.* New York: Ronald Press, 1947.
10. Frazier, E. F. *Black Bourgeoisie.* Glencoe: The Free Press, 1957.
11. Grodzins, M. *The Loyal and the Disloyal.* Chicago: University of Chicago Press, 1956.
12. Grossack, M. M. "Perceived Negro Group Belongingness and Social Rejection." *Journal of Psychology,* 1954, 38, 127–130.
13. Grossack, M. M. "Group Belongingness Among Negroes." *Journal of Social Psychology,* 1956, 43, 167–180.
14. Himelhoch, J. "Tolerance and Personality Needs: A Study of the Liberalization of Ethnic Attitudes Among Minority Group College Students." *American Sociological Review,* 1950, 15, 79–88.
15. Johnson, R. B. *The Nature of the Minority Community.* Unpublished Ph.D. thesis, Cornell University, 1955.
16. Lewin, K. *Resolving Social Conflicts.* New York: Harper & Brothers, 1948.
17. Noel, D. L. *Correlates of Anti-White Prejudice.* Unpublished Ph.D. thesis, Cornell University, 1961.
18. Radke-Yarrow, M., & Lande, B. "Personality Correlates of Differential Reactions to Minority Group Belonging." *Journal of Social Psychology,* 1953, 38, 253–272.
19. Rose, A. *The Negro's Morale: Group Identification and Protest.* Minneapolis: University of Minnesota Press, 1949.
20. Ross, R., & Van den Haag, E. *The Fabric of Society.* New York: Harcourt, Brace and World, 1957, pp. 64–74.
21. Rothman, J. "In-Group Identification and Out-Group Association: A Theoretical and Experimental Study." *Journal of Jewish Communal Service,* 1960, 37, 81–93.
22. Rothman, J. "Minority Group Status, Mental Health and Intergroup Relations: An Appraisal of Kurt Lewin's Thesis," *Journal of Intergroup Relations.* 1962, 3, 299–310.
23. Simpson, G., & Yinger, J. M. *Racial and Cultural Minorities.* New York: Harper & Brothers, 1958, rev. ed.
24. Walter, P. A. F. *Race and Culture Relations.* New York: McGraw-Hill, 1952.

13

Milton M. Gordon

The Subsociety and the Subculture in America: Negroes

THE separation of America's 20 million Negroes (approximately 11 per cent of the total American population)[1] from the white population in the United States in meaningful primary group contacts and the existence of a separate Negro social world with its own institutions and associations has been attested to in such community studies and over-all surveys as those of Myrdal (a massive compilation based on many separate studies),[2] Drake and Cayton,[3] Frazier,[4] Davis and the Gardners,[5] Dollard,[6] Davie,[7] C. Johnson,[8] and R. Johnson.[9] Served by Negro weekly, semi-weekly, or daily newspapers, the leading ones like the *Pittsburgh Courier,* the Chicago *Defender,* the Baltimore *Afro-American,* and the Norfolk *Journal and Guide* having a national or regional distribution, and by Negro magazines such as *Ebony* (sometimes referred to as the Negro *Life*), *Our World, Jet, Hue,* and *Tan,* this ethnic society resounds with news of "the race" and its doings, frivolous and otherwise, and its progress against the discrimination which emanates from the "other world" which is controlled and populated by whites.

In the South this segregation is stipulated by "Jim Crow" laws, whose legality, until 1954, was unthreatened, and by customs and folkways resting on a base of racial hostility and antipathy on the part of the great majority of white people toward Negroes. Since the early 1950's, court decisions, mass demonstrations, and the impact of the federal government through the operation of military installations, civil rights laws, and executive decisions have begun to have some effect on the enforced separation in secondary group areas of contact: formal attendance at school, riding in public conveyances, using public facilities, etc. There is no evidence, however, that the existence of separate white and Negro social worlds of primary group contacts and communal associations and institutions has been affected in any significant way by these developments.

In the North, the line that divides Negroes from whites has no legal sanction, and in areas of secondary contact varies widely from city to city and even within a given community. Fair employment practices laws have begun to lift the "job ceiling," and Negroes in the large cities are extending the boundaries of their traditionally segregated housing areas and occasionally setting up new pockets of settlement, although few have been able to buy homes in the upper-middle-class sections of suburbs. Public facilities, with the occasional exception of bathing beaches, are generally open to Negroes. But, again, in the private worlds of intimate social contact, non-vocational organization life, and meaningful institutional activity, Negroes and whites generally remain apart. Even in the smaller communities, if there is any significant number of Negro residents, a Negro communal life takes shape. Robert Johnson, in his report of a study of Negro life in a middle-sized upstate New York city declares that "The 'Negro community' is an isolated one. . . . Questionnaire evidence shows not only that contacts with whites are quite limited in quantity and in depth, but also that Negroes viewed many issues more as part of a psychological community of 1200 members than as part of a Hometown community of 60,000."[10] For instance, such statements or phrases by Negro respondents as "It's all over town," "the prettiest girl in town," or "the meanest man in town," had reference not to the entire city but to the Negro community. And, Johnson adds significantly, "The term 'we' usually turned out, under probe, to refer to Hometown Negroes or to Negroes throughout the country, rather than to Hometown in general."[11]

One of the most telling indexes of communal separation is the rate of intermarriage. Marriage between Negroes and whites is still legally prohibited in 22 states of the union, most of them in the South and the West.[12] These laws will probably eventually be declared unconstitutional. However, even where there is no legal ban on such unions, their rate, at present, is very small. While no over-all national rates are available, such studies of Negro-white marriages as have been made in particular communities where their legality is unquestioned indicate that their rates vary from none to, at the most, three or four out of every hundred marriages involving Negroes.[13] The percentage of whites involved in such marriages becomes, of course, insignificant.

The internal differentiation of the Negro group into social classes has been described in community studies such as those of Drake and Cayton in Chicago,[14] Davis and the Gardners,[15] Dollard,[16] and Powdermaker[17] in small communities in the South, and in over-all surveys by Myrdal,[18] Frazier,[19] and Davie.[20] As in the white society, class boundaries are not hard and precise, the various classes "shade into" one another, and substantial mobility takes place from one class to another as the socio-economic condition and occupational and educational attainment of the individual or family shift in the fluid dynamics of American social life. Nevertheless, the broad outlines of the Negro class system are unmistakable. The following brief account leans heavily on the studies mentioned above.

Even before the abolition of slavery, internal differentiation along socio-economic lines had begun to take place among Negroes. The free Negroes of both the North and the South, many of them mulattoes, constituted a group apart and were themselves internally differentiated according to occupation and property ownership. Within the slave group distinctions were recognized which set off from each other the privileged house servants (many of whom could claim partial white ancestry and who were able to observe and imitate the "refined" cultural behavior of their white masters), the skilled artisans, and the lowly field hands. During the years following the Emancipation, the great masses of Negroes were unskilled farm hands, and above this group such criteria as free ancestry, lighter skin color, property ownership, descent from the partially acculturated house servants, and occupational considerations, all constituted the basis for status claims and social separation. Particularly in the larger southern or border cities such as Charleston, New Orleans, Washington, and Atlanta, where a more elaborate stratification system was developed, upper-class Negro society was a "blue-vein" society—that is, it was made up of mulattoes and was highly color-conscious.[21] Occupationally, however, prior to World War I, from the point of view of the white social world, the Negro community contained little differentiation on which to base social divisions. Tailors, barbers, waiters, and undertakers mingled with a few physicians, teachers, and business men in the Negro upper class of the day.

Large-scale Negro migration from the rural South to the cities of both the North and the South which began during World War I in response to the need for additional unskilled labor in the factories and processing plants of the nation created a sizable Negro proletariat which could serve as a base for increasing numbers of Negro professionals such as doctors, lawyers, teachers, ministers, and social workers, and Negro "service" businesses such as undertaking, cosmetics, insurance, banking, and small proprietary establishments. The Negro business class, however, has never been large. The practical necessities and ideological currents of the World War II period and its aftermath, together with the increasing political participation of the northern Negro, produced further gains for Negroes in semi-skilled factory jobs, skilled trades, lower white collar work, sales work, and the professions. The result of these twentieth century trends has been to proceed some distance toward "normalizing" the Negro class structure—that is, to differentiate the group occupationally to a much wider degree than had previously been the case, and to strengthen the power of education and occupation as criteria of social class position and increasingly diminish the role of skin color and considerations of descent. An additional occupation group in the Negro community, because of job discrimination probably proportionately larger than in the white community, consists of the "shadies," those who operate, at various levels of the enterprise, the "numbers," bootlegging, and other illegal or questionable businesses. The result of all these developments is the Negro class system as it exists today. All levels of it, of course, are not found in the smaller communities. The following description is applicable to a large northern metropolis.

The Negro upper class is a relatively small group composed primarily of families whose male heads are engaged in some professional occupation such as medicine, dentistry, law, teaching, social work, publishing, and government service, but also includes successful Negro business men, writers, entertainers of national renown, and, with varying degrees of access to the social life of the rest, the top level of the "shadies." Not infrequently the wives work, also in professional pursuits. This is not a leisure class, nor with some exceptions a wealthy class, and obviously in occupational type (and also, as we shall see, in life style) it is very similar to the upper-middle class of the white social world.

If they have a church affiliation, members of this class tend to belong to Episcopal, Congregational, and Presbyterian congregations which, situated in totally or predominantly Negro neighborhoods, are likely to be totally or predominantly Negro in membership. Services are conducted with the traditional decorum associated with churches of these denominations. The Negro minister in charge will be college and seminary trained. The social life of this class is centered around alumni groups of Negro college fraternities and sororities (the young and even middle-aged members of this class are by now mostly college trained) and an elaborate system of men's clubs, women's clubs, and, in some cases, couples' clubs, together with informal social cliques, all of which tend to be confined in membership to members of their own class. Many of the members of this class are "race men"—that is, they are active as members and leaders in Negro advancement organizations such as the National Association for the Advancement of Colored People and the National Urban League, and, as in white society, social events such as large dances frequently become the occasion for fund-raising drives for these organizations or others of a "protest" or charitable nature serving the Negro community. In recent years, with increasing prosperity, the social events of this class, according to one observer, have become increasingly elaborate,[22] and in the larger cities the Negro upper class, in parallel fashion to the white upper class, have instituted their own Debutante Balls, such as the Philadelphia "Pink Cotillion," in which the daughters of the socially prominent and ambitious are formally "presented" to Negro society.

The dominant emphasis in the Negro middle class is "respectable" public behavior, stable family life, and planning for the future, either of oneself or one's children. Occupationally, it includes a wide range of ways of making a living; there are lower white collar workers, proprietors of small business establishments, skilled and semi-skilled workers, policemen, firemen, watchmen, Pullman porters, and other occupational types. Church-goers among this group are likely to belong to all-Negro Baptist and Methodist churches which frequently are large and may contain lower class members as well. (In such a case, the pastor has a difficult time adjusting the type of service to the conflicting cultural demands of both groups.) The associational life of this class is highly elaborated, and social clubs and fraternal lodges which parallel the fraternal orders of the white lower middle class abound. Some "shadies" hover on the edges of this social world. The middle class is larger than the upper class, and it is safe to assume that it is growing in relative size. However, it is still considerably smaller than the large Negro mass at the bottom of the Negro social structure which still makes up the bulk of the Negro population.

The world of the northern and metropolitan Negro lower class reflects its southern rural background. Its speech is the dialect of the lower class rural South, though its present residence is the northern urban slum. Its family and sexual patterns reflect a way of life in which the male adult frequently wanders in search of work and in which the female domestic is the surer breadwinner. Desertion, divorce, common-law marriage, illegitimacy, and violent domestic strife are routine, and the woman tends to be the dominant and stable element in the family unit. Since she is out of the house a good deal of the time earning the family income, children are frequently unsupervised and delinquency rates are high. The men, when they have work, are employed in various semi-skilled or unskilled manual labor jobs or as porters and janitors. For some, particularly the women, religion serves as an emotional outlet and an anchor of respectability. If they do not belong to one of the Baptist or Methodist churches, they support the numerous small store-front churches of the Holiness or Spiritualist variety, where the theology is Fundamentalist and the preacher, who is likely to have little education himself, knows how to whip up the congregation by means of a rambling disquisition into a "shoutin" mood— a frenzied exhibition which may include vigorous random movements as well as loud and semi-coherent expression of religious fervor. Membership in formal organizations other than the church and, lately, the union, is not characteristic of this class. It should be mentioned that there is a more stable element in this class which is trying to "live decent" or "get ahead" in spite of the handicaps of the physical and social environment. Finally, at the other end of the scale are the lower class "shadies"—the prostitutes, pimps, dope addicts, and criminals whose propinquity must be tolerated in the crowded, powerless world of the racial slum, regardless of how their behavior may be evaluated by the bulk of its beleaguered residents.

It would be too much to claim that the substantial separation of the classes within the Negro group in primary relationships and associational life has been demonstrated in rigorous quantitative fashion by the studies and surveys to which we have had reference. However, with due allowance for the imprecise nature of class boundaries in American life and some overlapping as the result, particularly, of the activities of socially mobile individuals, it may be said that the cumulative testimony of these surveys and fields reports points unmistakably to the existence of such substantial separation from each other of the intimate communal life of the classes we have described.

In evaluating the extent of the acculturation process, it will be recalled that we are using the subculture of the "core society"—middle-class white Protestants—as the touchstone. Subcultural behavior may be examined, we suggest, on three levels: extrinsic traits, or external behavior; intrinsic traits based on value systems related to inner psychological attitudes; and the nature of institutional life within the subsociety. We do not claim that the acculturation process has proceeded so far that all differences in values and norms between the middle classes, for instance, of all minority ethnic groups and the white Protestant middle class have disappeared. For one thing, the psychological and sociological experiences of belonging to a minority group must inevitably affect one's way of looking at the world, even apart from the effect of the specific content of the minority group's cultural heritage. Thus we would expect Negroes and Jews to have more liberal attitudes on civil rights issues involving ethnic segregation than Protestants, regardless of class level. Lenski, in a recent study, has demonstrated, on the basis of research on a representative sample of the population of Detroit, that there are statistically significant differences in attitudes (that is, in percentages of the given group who favor or do not favor a certain course of action) toward a complex of economic, political, familial, and educational issues related to "the Protestant Ethic" and economic advancement under capitalism among white Protestants, white Catholics, Jews, and Negro Protestants.[23] Many of these differences remain when class is "controlled"—that is, when comparisons are made among the four ethnic groups on the same class level. Davis and Havighurst, in an earlier study carried out in Chicago, comparing child-rearing practices among four groups: middle-class whites, middle-class

Negroes, lower-class whites, and lower-class Negroes, found that while all differences between Negroes and whites did not disappear when class was controlled, nevertheless, that "there are considerable social class differences in child-rearing practices, and these differences are greater than the differences between Negros and whites of the same social class."[24] They go on to add that "the striking thing about this study is that Negro and white middle-class families are so much alike, and that white and Negro lower-class families are so much alike."[25]

On the basis of the accumulated evidence, including the descriptions of institutional life in the community studies cited above, we would conclude that the subculture of the Negro upper class has many similarities, particularly in values relating to external behavior and to institutional life, to that of the white Protestant upper-middle class. The subculture of the Negro middle class appears similar in many ways to that of the white Protestant lower-middle class. Some differences in degree in particular value-areas still exist between Negroes and other groups, even at the middle-class level. The subculture of the Negro lower class testifies eloquently to the power of prejudice and discrimination to retard the acculturation process both in external behavior and internal values.

[Notes]

1. Donald J. Brogue, *The Population of the United States,* Glencoe, Ill., Free Press, 1959.
2. Gunnar Myrdal, with the assistance of Richard Sterner and Arnold Rose, *An American Dilemma,* New York, Harper and Brothers, 1944.
3. St. Clair Drake and Horace R. Cayton, *Black Metropolis,* New York, Harcourt Brace, 1945.
4. E. Franklin Frazier, *The Negro in the United States,* New York, The Macmillan Co., 1949; and *Black Bourgeoisie,* Glencoe, Ill.; Free Press, 1957.
5. Allison Davis, Burleigh B. Gardner, and Mary R. Gardner, *Deep South,* Chicago, University of Chicago Press, 1941.
6. John Dollard, *Caste and Class in a Southern Town,* New York, Harper and Brothers, 1937.
7. Maurice R. Davie, *Negroes in American Society,* New York, McGraw-Hill Publishing Co., 1949.
8. Charles S. Johnson, *Patterns of Negro Segregation,* New York, Harper and Brothers, 1943.
9. Robert Johnson, "Negro Reactions to Minority Group Status," in Milton L. Barron (ed.), *American Minorities,* New York, Alfred A. Knopf, 1957, pp. 192–212.
10. Robert Johnson, *op. cit.,* p. 199.

11. *Ibid.*
12. Jack Greenberg, *Race Relations and American Law,* New York, Columbia Universtiy Press, 1959, pp. 344, 397–8.
13. Ruby Jo Reeves Kennedy, "Single or Triple Melting Pot? Intermarriage Trends in New Haven, 1870–1940," *American Journal of Sociology,* Vol. 49, No. 4 January 1944); August B. Hollingshead, "Cultural Factors in the Selection of Marriage Mates," *American Sociological Review,* Vol. 15, No. 5 (October 1950), p. 621; Milton Barron, *People Who Intermarry,* Syracuse, N.Y., Syracuse University Press, 1946; Gunnar Myrdal, *op. cit.,* pp. 606 and 1360–61; Maurice Davie, *Negroes in American Society,* p. 410; Louis Wirth and Herbert Goldhamer, "The Hybrid and the Problem of Miscegenation," in Otto Klineberg (ed.), *Characteristics of the American Negro,* New York, Harper and Brothers, 1944, pp. 276–81; Gerhard Lenski, *The Religious Factor,* New York, Doubleday, 1961, p. 36.
14. Drake and Cayton, *op. cit.,* pp. 495–715.
15. Davis, Gardner, and Gardner, *op. cit.,* pp. 208–51.
16. Dollard, *op. cit., passim.*
17. Hortense Powdermaker, *After Freedom,* New York, Viking Press, 1939, *passim.*
18. Myrdal, *op. cit.,* pp. 689–705.
19. Frazier, *The Negro in the United States,* pp. 273–305; *Black Bourgeoisie, passim.*
20. Davie, *Negroes in American Society,* pp. 415–33.
21. By "color" is meant here not only skin color itself, but the whole complex of Caucasian facial features and hair form.
22. Frazier, *Black Bourgeoisie,* pp. 195–212.
23. Gerhard Lenski, *The Religious Factor,* New York, Doubleday, 1961.
24. Allison Davis and Robert J. Havighurst, "Social Class and Color Differences in Child-Rearing," *American Sociological Review,* Vol. 11, No. 6 (December 1946), p. 707.
25. *Ibid.,* p. 708.

Selected References

Back, Kurt N., and Ida Harper Simpson. "The Dilemma of the Negro Professional," *Journal of Social Issues,* 20 (April 1964), 66–70.

"Black Power in the Market Place," *Sales Management,* 97, September 15, 1966, 36.

Bloom, R. "Race and Social Class as Separate Factors Related to Social Environment," *American Journal of Sociology,* 70 (January 1965), 471–476.

Blue, John J., Jr. "Patterns of Racial Stratification: A Categoric Typology," *Phylon,* 20 (Winter 1959), 364–371.

"Burgeoning Middle Class Boosting Negro Buying Power," *Sales Management,* 93, Part I, November 20, 1964, 77–78.

Clark, Kenneth B. *Dark Ghetto: Dilemma of Social Power.* New York: Harper and Row, Publishers, 1965.

Davidson, William. "Our Negro Aristocracy," *Saturday Evening Post,* 235, January 13, 1962, 9–16.

Dykeman, Wilma, and James Stokely. "New Southerner: The Middle Class Negro," *New York Times Magazine,* August 9, 1959.

Edwards, G. Franklin. "The Changing Status and Self-Image of Negroes in the District of Columbia," *Journal of Intergroup Relations* (Winter 1962–1963).

———. *The Negro Professional Class.* Glencoe, Ill.: Free Press, 1959.

Frazier, E. Franklin. *Black Bourgeoisie.* Glencoe, Ill.: Free Press, 1957; reissued, New York: Collier, 1962.

———. "The Negro Middle Class and Desegregation," *Social Problems,* 4 (April 1957), 291–301.

———. "The Status of the Negro in the American Social Order," *Journal of Negro Education,* 4 (July 1935), 293–307.

Frumpkin, Robert M. "Race, Occupation, and Social Class in New York," *Journal of Negro Education,* 27 (Winter 1958), 62–65.

Glenn, Norval D. "Some Changes in the Relative Status of American Negroes," *Phylon,* 24 (Summer 1963), 109–122.

Hill, M. C., and T. D. Ackiss. "Social Classes: A Frame of Reference for the Study of Negro Society," *Social Forces,* 22 (October 1943), 90–92.

"Integration Issues Haunt Advertisers," *Printer's Ink,* 284, July 19, 1963, 7–8.

"Keeping an Ethnic Market Friendly," *Printer's Ink,* 278, January 19, 1962, 53–54.

King, Charles E. "The Process of Social Stratification Among an Urban Southern Minority Population," *Social Forces,* 31 (May 1953), 352–355.

Kleiner, R. J., and H. Taylor. *Social Status and Aspirations in Philadelphia's Negro Population.* Philadelphia: Commission on Human Relations, 1962.

Lees, Hannah. "The Making of a Negro Middle Class," *Reporter,* 31, October 8, 1964, 41–44.

Meier, August. "Negro Class Structure and Ideology in the Age of Booker T. Washington," *Phylon,* 23 (Fall 1962), 258–266.

Montague, Joel B., and Edgar G. Epps. "Aptitudes Toward Social Mobility as Revealed by Samples of Negro and White Boys," *Pacific Sociological Review* (Fall 1958), pp. 81–84.

"Negro Middle Class Is New Marketing Target: Study by a Leading Station Rep in Negro Appeal Radio (Bernard Howard Co.)," *Sponsor,* 18, November 23, 1964, 22.

"Negro Self Image," *America,* 107, November 10, 1962, 1023.

Parker, Seymour, and Robert J. Kleiner. "Status, Position, Mobility and Ethnic Identification of the Negro," *Journal of Social Issues,* 20 (April 1964) 85–102.

Record, Wilson. "Social Stratification and Intellectual Roles in the Negro Community," *British Journal of Sociology,* 8 (September 1957), 235–255.

Solzbacher, Regina. "Occupational Prestige in a Negro Community," *American Catholic Sociological Review,* 22 (Fall 1961), 250–257.

Warner, W. Lloyd. *American Life: Dream and Reality.* Rev. ed., Chicago: University of Chicago Press, 1962.

———, and Leo Srole. *The Social Systems of American Ethnic Groups.* New Haven: Yale University Press, 1946.

"Why an Ethnic Appeal Is Working," *Printer's Ink,* 279, June 1, 1962, 54–55.

Young, Whitney M., Jr. "The Role of the Middle-Class Negro," *Ebony,* 18, September 1963, 66–71.

Consumption Dynamics

The articles in Part 3 emphasize the consumption dynamics of the black-consumer market. Consumer behavior is a function of many variables, not all of which are readily identifiable. There is a great need for relevant information that documents the motivations, behavior, and purchase patterns of black consumers and compares black and white consumers. The excellent empirical studies in this part provide useful information regarding consumption patterns and practices.

"Consumer Motivations in Black and White—Part 1," by Henry Allen Bullock, is an in-depth investigation of how the cultural system of each race determines the differences in the purchase behavior of blacks and whites. It also reveals that many advertisers have a distorted view of the black as a consumer. Bullock bases his findings on responses of more than 1,600 blacks and whites to various psychological tests and depth interviews.

The second part of Bullock's investigation issues the challenge to businessmen to apply the insights gained from the study of the differences and similarities of black and white motivations. The major conclusion suggests that the creation of an "integrated" marketing program, appealing to both blacks and whites, is the only effective, long-run way of reaching the black consumer. According to Mr. Bullock, the differences in white and black marketing behavior arise from blacks' needs of belongingness and security.

In "Racial Factors in Shopping Behavior" Laurence P. Feldman and Alvin D. Star present empirical evidence that black and white shopping behavior is very similar at upper-income levels. However, the similarity tends to disappear at lower-income levels, suggesting that as blacks better themselves economically the differences in shopping behavior between the two groups become negligible. The study concentrates on the income variable, however, and the author explains why this base of reference may be too narrow.

"Racial Brand Usage and Media Exposure Differentials," by Carl M. Larson, emphasizes the importance of accumulating information about the black consumer, since meaningful marketing decisions cannot be made without adequate knowledge of this consumer group. The article surveys a broad range of products and differences between blacks and whites with respect to their preferences for products and brands and analyzes store preference between the groups.

In "The Marketing Dilemma of Negroes" Raymond A. Bauer and his coauthors, Scott M. Cunningham and Lawrence H. Wortzel, make a strong case that blacks as a group have accepted white middle-class values but are at a disadvantage in attaining them. These writers indicate that the basic dilemma of blacks is whether they should try to attain these values.

"An Examination of Race as a Factor in Negro-White Consumption Patterns," by Broadus E. Sawyer, reveals that factors other than race combine to determine consumption patterns. Although he does not rule out race, uncontrollable factors such as self-evaluation, age, education, occupation, dependents, location, and income expectation are responsible for the differences in consumption patterns of blacks and whites.

Marcus Alexis, in "Some Negro-White Differences in Consumption," gives an excellent analysis based upon many studies by noted authorities in which budget data are summarized in an attempt to determine how black and white consumers allocate their incomes to various budget items, including savings, food, housing, clothing, recreation and leisure, house furnishings and equipment, and transportation. He derives many conclusions and suggests that race is an important consumption variable warranting more attention.

"Some Consumption Pattern Differences Between Urban Whites and Negroes," by James E. Stafford, Keith K. Cox, and James B. Higginbotham, demonstrates that a combination of societal constraints, cultural traditions, and differences in values, preferences, and psychological needs has resulted in substantially different consumption patterns between blacks and whites. The black consumer, when viewed from a businessman's standpoint, is identifiable not so much by color as by pattern of consumption.

The final article suggests an opportunity to market a product to the black consumer that characteristically has not been considered possible in the past. "Negroes and Fashion Interest," by Bernard Portis, attempts to determine whether blacks really represent a desirable, special market for expensive and fashionable goods. He cites some popular beliefs about black purchasers of fashion goods and gives data from a survey of the black fashion market. He concludes that fashion consciousness can best be understood on an individual rather than on a racial basis. The research is well structured, and the subject area is unique because of the implications of marketing products with fashion considerations to population segments that are identified as low income.

14

Henry Allen Bullock

Consumer Motivations in Black and White—Part 1

DURING the past three decades, advertisers have made noticeable attempts to gain favor with that special market offered by America's 17 million Negroes. Some have sought this goal mainly through the Negro press. Others have turned to radio. A few have employed Negro models in their visual copy and, in scattered instances, have ventured so far as to present these models via television advertising. However, they have not felt secure in such ventures. They know that the market is special, but they have been in doubt how special it really is. Even now they do not know whether good strategy calls for renewed emphasis on old techniques or creative dedication to new ones.

Before advertisers can feel secure in the knowledge of how best to reach the Negro market, they must first truly understand the differences and similarities between the motivations of Negroes and whites. They dare not assume that, as consumers, both races behave the same; for, as our studies show, they do not in many instances. But just what are these differences? That is what Part 1 of this article reveals.

Then, in Part 2, businessmen will be challenged to apply these new insights in ways that are socially and economically desirable. Specifically, the creation of an "integrated" marketing program, that appeals equally to blacks and whites, will be advanced as the only effective, long-run method of reaching the Negro consumer. Both parts draw on extensive original research, which will be described in some detail at the appropriate point.

DANGERS OF EXTREMES

Because ad-men have not really understood the motivations of Negroes as consumers, they have tended to vacillate between dangerous extremes. At one end of the policy continuum are those who approach the market by direct appeal, selecting media and copy especially for Negroes. At the other are those who use indirect appeal, beaming to the general market in the faith that Negroes too are thereby reached. Let us consider why, though vast sums are invested to implement each approach, neither has made a significant impact on the mind and behavior of the Negro consumer.

OVERPLAYING THE HAND

Those using direct appeal tend to go too far. They assume the Negro market to be more special than it is, and by this assumption miss the heaviest and most persistent purchasers. Two advertising patterns illustrate this fact:

Inherent in one of these is the apparent belief that most Negroes are highly superstitious—prone to use self-medicaments as cure-alls, patent drugs for building sex potency, and hair oils or face creams to make them look like white people. Examples of these appeals are abundant. In 1959, a nationally circulating Negro weekly carried the following advertisements:

"Lucky Hand Brand Oil—has been used by thousands of satisfied customers."

"Troubled? Love? Money? Problems? I'll help. Solution available if instructions followed."

"Asthma—write for. No Risk, No Cost Trial Offer. No matter if you consider yourself 'hopeless.'"

"Presto Face Cream Bleaches, Beautifies. Makes skin like velvet."[1]

Messages like these tend to fail in the long run because they appeal mainly to an unstable minority who are neither able to buy very much nor inclined to stick with any product very long. On the other hand, they alienate the more stable majority whose ego cannot accept the self-image they impose. Consequently, this pattern has been useful only for those sellers whose ethical values motivate them to seek a quick "killing," and then to withdraw or change the name of their product.

Another pattern using direct appeal operates through a series of radio outlets generally known as "Negro stations," mainly located in such Southern cities as Atlanta, Baton Rouge, Beaumont, Houston, Memphis, Mobile, and New Orleans, but also with some outlets in Northern cities. The basic policy of these stations probably represents the most colorful feature in the history of "Negro advertising." Beamed primarily to Negro audiences, the broadcasters utilize a program pattern consisting principally of gospel music, rock and roll, and gulps of poorly read news.

The shows are conducted by disc jockeys who take personality names that actually are the property of the station. One of the most famous of these personality creations is "Dr. Daddy-O," first presented through the sponsorship of the Jackson Brewing Company of New Orleans. Using a Cab Calloway style, the originator of this character attracted large audiences through his snappy jazz selections, his "hep-cat" lingo, and the novelty of a Negro's being on radio. The personality seeds which he planted at New Orleans were so fertile that a second Dr. Daddy-O sprang up at Houston.

Since that time an entire army of eccentric radio personalities has paraded across the "colored air." Mama Lou, Okey Dokey, and Hot Ziggity sprang up in New Orleans; Cousin Carrie and Rooty Tooty appeared in Baton Rouge; Deacon Sam, Big Daddy Dandy, and Miss Mandy began beeping over Mobile; and Groovey George, Dizzie Lizzie, and Hotsy Totsy went into orbit around Houston.

This is a Mardi Gras technique of advertising. Although those who wear these personality masks come and go, the personalities themselves continue to broadcast, undisturbed by personnel changes. The mask and not the talent makes the character.

Since its appeal is highly specialized, this type of advertising pattern also experiences limited effectiveness. It misses the middle-class Negro altogether. The brands that are usually advertised this way do not suit his social aspirations. Members of the more responsible upper class, along with a goodly portion of those composing the bulging middle class, are actually made hostile toward sponsors who use these disc personalities to push their products. They feel that this method shows disrespect for the Negro community and places an unwholesome stigma on it.

This was brought out very clearly by a group of Negro consumers who discussed the matter in a freewheeling interview session. "I for one," complained a participant, "would like to stand on the housetop and castigate every radio station in Houston that keys its market toward the Negro." Another participant confirmed this, saying: "I'd like to give them a piece of my mind." Showing the force of alienation inherent in this type of radio programing, still another advised: "Do like I do. Don't buy the product."

The general opinion expressed by members of all upper- and middle-class session participants was: "I don't listen to them." Some Negroes have actually joined in organized movements to get these types of programs off the air. Thus, the sphere of influence of such programs is generally confined to lower class consumers and to children. And, although this type of advertising must be successful for particular companies, the customers it attracts are of the "dollar down—dollar per week" variety.

THROWING AWAY THE CARDS

Just as there are advertisers who overplay their hand in quest of Negro patronage, there are also those who throw their cards away. The latter group, using indirect methods, pour their spiels into the general channel of mass communication on the assumption that Negroes as well as whites are being reached and influenced by it. The assumption that they are being reached may be valid; the faith that they are being favorably influenced is misplaced.

So far, copy used this way fails to trigger the motivations of Negroes. It has prevented their identification with the sponsor or his product and has left them either indifferent or in doubt. Here are some examples:

- One Negro woman of a dark complexion expressed this left-out feeling when she responded to a soap advertisement on TV by asking: "Now how can *any* soap make my skin white like that?"
- One group of Negro men assembled in a barber shop also illustrated this left-out feeling. After viewing a television commercial that claimed some type of relief to be just a gulp away, one member of the group queried: "I wonder if they mean us?"

NEW RESEARCH NEED

Reality forces on us an awareness that national advertising has to be very subtle in its appeal to Negro consumers if it is to avoid losing the more lucrative white market. So the big question is: How can advertisers win Negro identification while avoiding white alienation?

We faced this question and gained insights for its answer when we were given a grant by two sellers of advertising space (the OK-Radio Group and the Motion Picture Advertising Service Company) for the purpose of determining whether or not whites and Negroes differ in their consumer motivations, and what types of advertising programs should be beamed to them.

This article is an abbreviated report of our expedition into this little-explored region of consumer behavior. It seeks to bring into focus some of the basic motivations inherent in the collective psychologies of black and white; to show how these motivations express themselves in the consumer orientations and behavior of those composing the two races; and to suggest some advertising policies that may protect sellers against throwing out the baby with the bath water. These objectives, though somewhat academic in nature, placed pressures on us similar to those now experienced by those advertisers whom we have sought to help: we had to drop old methods and pick up new ones.

INADEQUATE BRAND STUDIES

We sought help from existing literature on the Negro market, but found none. Practically all of this literature consists of "nose-counting" surveys that simply supply facts on population, purchasing power, brand

preferences, and, occasionally, accessibility to advertising media. It soon
became quite apparent to us that such facts alone have scant relevance to
motivational problems, since many of them were gathered more to influence advertisers than to inform them. Specifically:

> The first studies of the Negro market were done by the Negro press early in
> the 1930's. Responding to a psychological climate of intense racial pride,
> these efforts made a decided bid for the patronage of advertisers. Pushed
> by two forces—the need to sell advertising space and the Negro's aspiration
> to present himself as a first-class buyer—Negro weeklies launched a pro-
> gram designed to influence advertisers to use these issues as a gateway to
> the Negro consumer. Publishers learned that the Negro market survey was
> their best bait. Therefore, they used this lure to prove that Negroes *are*
> sensitive to advertising just as whites are; that they are *very* brand-conscious;
> and that they *do* buy quality merchandise. Consequently, a tabulation that
> favored Negroes as buyers of name brands was considered a gem in Negro
> market research. It was judged to be far more important than any statement
> that answered the question *"why."*
>
> Leading this movement were surveys of the Interstate United News-
> papers, the Afro-American Company of Baltimore, and the *Pittsburgh
> Courier.*[2] The magazine *Ebony,* coming closer to the "why" than any of the
> rest, broke into the ring of modest sellers of advertising space. Its aggressive
> publisher, John H. Johnson, emerged as an authority on selling to Negroes.
> The *Time* story of the premier of the showing of Johnson's film, "The
> Secret of Selling the Negro Market," gave deserved impetus to this image,
> and his article advising sellers to tailor their sales effort to this special mar-
> ket increased the confidence of advertisers in his leadership.[3]

Although surveys like these identified brands that were momentarily
most popular among Negroes, they still failed to meet the problem of
"why"—to account for this form of intense consumer bias. Thus, while
brand preference studies made advertisers conscious of and somewhat
acquainted with the Negro market, they have not given them an understanding of it. Now that the introductions have been made and advertisers
have come to be on speaking terms with the Negro consumer, all are
experiencing the shocking realization that host and guest do not speak the
same language. Sellers would *like* to tailor their sales efforts to influence
Negro consumers, but they do not know what *kind* of suit to make.

Brand preference statistics do not seem to supply a stable pattern. If
one survey shows a given brand leading in the market one week, next
week's survey may reveal an entirely different brand in command. Furthermore, people like to make good impressions. They often say they use certain brands in order to gain prestige, rather than to be factual. When we
asked consumers to name the radio stations to which they listened most,
almost invariably they listed the largest stations in town. But when asked
to name the program they followed most, the greater proportion of the

"big station" listeners identified small stations that are beamed mainly to lower class audiences.

There are also times when changes occur in the psychological climate of a community, causing corresponding changes in buying patterns and brand selection. We interviewed 1,000 Negro householders of the Houston area and observed that over half of them were using bread produced by a particular bakery.[4] Less than three months later, hardly 3% of these householders were found using this brand. The reason? The bakery had become a victim of some unpleasant rumor concerning racial integration. Serious instability like this in the field of brand preference statistics has kept the programs of many advertisers ineffective, for the same reason that it renders brand surveys *per se* inadequate for making management decisions.

NEW VANTAGE POINTS

Since brand preference statistics have proved inadequate to supply answers to the kind of questions which advertisers now raise, we have found it necessary to erect new vantage points from which to view the Negro market. If advertisers are to secure proper guidance toward winning favor with both Negro and white consumers, those who would seek to help them must conceive of marketing research as an explanation of consumer behavior rather than a count of it.

The consumer must be viewed not as an "economic man" behaving rationally in the market, but as a particular kind of person who buys goods and services according to the needs he has acquired or the attitudes he has shaped under the impact of special kinds of experiences. I am taking the position here that although some of these needs and attitudes vary racially and influence blacks and whites to respond in different ways to advertising media and copy, there are common denominators which, if properly manipulated, will make it possible for sellers to win favor with both groups through a common program.

Evidence that we are on the right track comes from many sources. Psychologists have known for over a quarter of a century that people respond selectively to their external world, that they hear, see, and feel according to how they have been trained. Human perceptions, judgments, and even decisions appear to be conditioned by the way individuals have been brought up and the kinds of persons they have become.[5] Signs are abundant that this principle is operative in consumer behavior. More recent researchers have concluded repeatedly that consumers purchase commodities and patronize establishments according to how they have learned to perceive them. They have shown that a particular product or retail store is actually a different perceptual object to different people.[6]

As we examine data like these, we find great confidence in the thesis that psychological factors such as personal attitudes, aspirations, and anxieties acquired through cultural experiences give shape to consumer behavior. Therefore, we designed our inquiries so as to look more into the minds of people than at their shopping lists. We have given some attention to the differential conditions characterizing black and white community life because these are the breeding grounds of motivational differences. They seem to supply nourishment for what people want to be, what they feel they need, and what they believe will enhance their self-realization. Objective observations have validated these suspicions by bringing into sharp focus the attitudinal differences of the two groups and the common denominators which sellers must manipulate if they are to win one without losing the other.

TWO WORLDS OF COLOR

Consumer motivations come in black and white. Although human needs are basically the same for all people everywhere, these drives tend to become plated with the compulsions, checks, and guidance systems of different cultures. It is this cultural overlay that forms the foundation for all motivational differences between groups. This happens in the case of Negroes and whites because the two races live in worlds that are somewhat culturally separate; needs develop that are, in some instances, peculiar to each race.

I shall discuss (1) the needs of both Negroes and whites to "belong" —albeit in different ways—and how each race trades to "belong"; and (2) how insecurities of both races influence their behavior as consumers, and how in each case the consumer trades money and credit for security.

STUDY DESIGN

As noted earlier, we went out into the field to get the facts we needed.

Although Houston constituted the main research site, data were also drawn from four other Southern cities: Atlanta, Birmingham, Memphis, and New Orleans. There were 1,643 persons who responded to our incomplete sentence blanks—1,106 Negroes and 537 whites. Approximately one half of those composing each racial group were drawn from the various socio-economic classes of Houston, and the remainder were equally distributed over the other cities according to the same pattern of class strata. Depth interviews were held with 300 of these persons—200 Negroes, 100 whites—who were similarly drawn from the above cities. Negro and white members of this latter group were also exposed to the MMPI test, the pictures that constituted the TAT-style test, and our collection of display ads, as described subsequently. Freewheeling sessions were composed of Houston Negroes only.

The conclusions presented in the study are generally applicable to Northern as well as Southern consumers. Separation of the two races in Northern areas is almost equally as pronounced, and the pressures of economy, technology, and social-cultural changes are certainly not confined to the Southern region. It is reasonable to assume that black and white consumers, in both the North and the South, are strongly motivated by the desire to belong and feel secure. Such regional differences as may exist must be matters of degree rather than kind.

NEED TO BELONG

Belongingness, one of the most common motivational forces with which advertisers must deal, hits black and white consumers at different spots but with equal force. Thus:

- Negroes want group identification; whites, feeling that they already have this, want group distinction.
- More specifically, Negroes want to be identified with the general American society and all its peoples, while whites want to remain generally acceptable but particularly exclusive.

Several conditions have functioned to keep alive these respective motivational inclinations and all of them involve the status definition that identifies accepted relations between the two races. The Negro's urge to become an integral part of American life obviously begins with the nation's historic policy of racial separation. Ours, by tradition, has been a nation of many peoples. However, despite all the cosmopolitanism which we have manifested in accepting these peoples as full partners in our democratic enterprise, Negroes have been apart from the general society. They have experienced the least opportunity to become like all Americans. In fact, one distinguished scholar, who was brought here from Sweden to study such matters, concluded that the American policy is to exclude Negroes from assimilation.[7]

Bowing to this involuntary isolation, therefore, Negroes have tended to develop ways of living and attitudes consistent with their own situation. Since they have not been allowed to swim in the main stream, they have been forced to make the eddy waters of American society their own private swimming pool.

Only a skeletal analysis of such living conditions is required to remind us of their tremendous potential effects on the minds of blacks and whites alike. Millions of Negroes have moved from the rural South to the cities of that region, but in doing so have only reinforced the wall of racial separation which tradition has erected across the face of the nation. They have tended to concentrate in fewer though larger places. Almost half the urban Negroes of Louisiana reside in New Orleans. Atlanta, Birmingham, Memphis, and Richmond each holds over one fourth of all urban Negroes in their respective states.[8]

More important is the brutal fact that residential segregation, also involved in the urban shift, causes the formation of a series of colored islands in a great white urban sea. Although these islands are more numerous in the South, one can also find them in other regions. Some of us may be more familiar with New York's Harlem or Chicago's Southside than we are with Houston's Fifth Ward, Atlanta's Auburn Avenue area, or even New Orleans' Rampart District, but conditions are similar. In Houston there are approximately 190,000 Negroes living within the city's corporate limits, but 42% of them are almost equally distributed over two traditional areas located near the central business district.

CONFLICTING SELF-IMAGE

The Negro's need to belong grows directly out of the badge of inferiority which his communal isolation forces on him. *Both* blacks and whites are conscious of this badge, and from this awareness stems a tremendous psychological force. *Both* races feel the pressure to define all things white as "good" and all things black as "bad," and from this contrast conception grows the first significant motivational aspect of racial segregation.

There are developed within the minds of the colored people conflicting self-images. They are forced to hate and love themselves at the same time. Here are a few illustrations of this fact:

Negro children grow up in a constant world of color whose limitations they are trained to dislike. They see color in themselves, and many of them are influenced to give it a negative quality by those who would correct their behavior. "Just like a Negro," they are told when scolded for some misdoing, and they often catch an earful of the epithets frequently used to symbolize their race and its complexion. Although they gain many of these negative images directly from their parents and other Negro adults who dominate their world, these children do a thorough job of teaching themselves—mostly through a pattern of verbal aggression called "the dirty dozens." This is a game in which contestants assault each other with symbols of "black" tied neatly into dramatic phrases of disparagement.

Thus, color consciousness dawns early in the minds of the Negro children and forms a reference scale by which they judge the "nice" and "notnice." Objectively evidencing this is the Doll Test which Kenneth and Mamie Clark conducted in order to observe racial identification as it relates to ego development and self-consciousness in Negro children. By allowing them to select a doll from among four models—each of which was exactly alike, except that two were brown with black hair and two were white with yellow hair—the experimenters were able to identify the children's color values. The results showed a definite tendency for the majority of the children to prefer the white dolls, considering them "most nice," desiring to play with them most, and judging them as not "looking bad."[9]

Lurking in the background, however, is the other half of the Negro's split self-image. It is here that the Negro child learns to reshape this image in tones which he considers more acceptable. Evidence of this reshaping may be seen indirectly when we observe race consciousness in the field of Negro achievement. Even as Negroes reject their color, they find it necessary to protect with equal vigor the dignity of their racial heritage. This appears, as if suddenly, when they are given a chance to evaluate the achievements of their race in comparison with that of others.

This was brought out when a group of 267 Houston Negro junior high school boys were given lists of boxers and baseball players and were asked to rate who was best at each of these sports. The pattern of choice was the same in each instance: Negro athletes were far more highly rated than were whites, although objective judgment based on actual performance would have resulted in a different rank order.

Another study of skin color judgment, this one among Negro students of Fisk University, brings the tendency to reshape self-image even more sharply into focus. Here the findings showed that Negroes tend to judge the complexions of others in terms of their own. Persons lighter than the rater are judged as "light"; those who are darker are judged as "dark." The individual's own color always represents the center point of the reference scale. Nevertheless, ratings of attractiveness are clearly affected by objective skin color. Those whom Negroes judge as attractive are lighter than average but are not at the extremely light end of the color continuum.[10]

Whites contribute to this love-and-hate conflict by the value they place on certain types of Negro achievement. Although they attribute to Negroes a general status of "inferiority," their image of the race is not entirely consistent. In a field of physical prowess such as athletics, or in fields of special talents such as singing, dancing, and other forms of entertainment, they admit Negro "superiority" without apparent fear of shaking their position in the general society. For example:

- When white junior high school principals were asked to comment on the ratings of athletes given by the Negro boys, one summarized the common reply when he said: "I think the boys showed good judgment. I could hardly disagree with them."
- Over three fourths of the white householders who were asked by the interviewers to list the five leading opera singers of the world named Marian Anderson, and two thirds of the whites listed Nat (King) Cole as one of the leading popular singers.

It is significant that one white, defending his choice of a Negro singer, and following the way of many Southern whites, added freely: "Negroes have made more progress since they've been free than any other people in a similar period of time." This probably represents a pep talk which says in effect: "Conditions for the Negro are not so bad after all." This idea, too, has its weight. It creates an imbalance within the Negro mind.

WHITE EXCLUSIVENESS

The black motivation of belongingness has its white counterpart. One specific attitudinal pattern illustrates this well. It is the Southern white consumers' strong and persistent feeling that they belong exclusively to themselves. The sense of superiority which communal apartness fosters seems to make many of them more ethnocentric than Negroes and even less tolerant of people and ideas outside their local orbit. They want to remain to themselves, apart from nonwhite groups.

Their ethnocentrism, however, reaches beyond these boundaries to shape not only their reactions to neighbors at home but also their concepts of foreigners abroad. We observed this in their response to certain items in a test which used the technique of incomplete sentences. For example, when white consumers are asked to complete this sentence, *"If I could change the world, I would . . . ,"* the most representative of their replies to it are as follows:

- "Make it so that people would not park in front of my driveway."
- "Stop the neighbors' children from cutting across my lawn."
- "Eliminate federal control over our lives."
- "Destroy the United Nations."
- "Do away with one worldism."
- "Change the Supreme Court."

On the other hand, the most frequent replies of Negroes to the same sentence ran this way:

- "Make all people the same."
- "Establish brotherhood."
- "Do away with war."
- "Break down segregation."

Here, again, we have evidence that Negroes want to burst the bonds that confine their world. Whites want to keep their own world untarnished by "out-groups."

However, this form of alienation does not seem to satisfy completely the motivation of belongingness which whites possess. Another attitudinal pattern appears to be operating. It is the urge to belong with those at the top of the heap. They seek to identify with the "ideal American family," as one white consumer expressed it, but their definition of "ideal" is based on the status symbols of material achievement. For example:

- One man put it more explicitly: "The poor want to be well-to-do and the well-to-do want to be rich. If you have one automobile in your garage, the object is to get another."
- A white male consumer, showing some strain from climbing the class ladder, stated a compulsiveness of this motivational dimension when he said: "This is a state of affairs in which, whether you want to or not, you run as fast as you can to keep from being run over." Despite the apparent strain, this philosophy emerged as his definition of progress.
- One white housewife, a social leader in Houston's fashionable Memorial area, concurred with this view when she admitted to our interviewer: "My position just will not let me rest. I must always be on the prowl for something new."

In short, different consumers used different words, but the theme of compelling and distinctive belongingness was paramount.

MARKET ORIENTATIONS

The drive to belong gives black and white consumers special kinds of market orientations. One of the most important of those fostered among Negroes is the pronounced inclination to trade across racial-cultural boundaries. They are inclined to cross the boundary line both as to the kinds of goods they buy and as to the places where they buy them. Of course some of this grows directly out of segregation, where rapid population growth places unrelenting, insurmountable pressure on area resources and facilities. Most, however, is attributable to the self-rejection side of the Negro's split self-image.

Because of the combined weight of these two forces, Negroes trade in an atmosphere of scarcity and compulsiveness. One would not overstate the case, for example, if he were to say they have a "real estate mania." New apartments made available to them fill quickly, no matter how high the rent. Houses vacated by whites are readily purchased by them, although the prices, in many cases, would appear to be out of their reach.

Is this simply a response to the housing shortage? To some extent, of course, but what it also signifies is the fact that they think it makes them less like themselves—more like white people and the general community norm.

Furthermore, many upper- and middle-class Negroes have developed "country club ways" without a country club. They like to appear "out of type" before their guests or when visitors come to town. Consequently, they attempt to surround themselves with visible symbols of whiteness.

Those who feel they can afford the luxury try to maintain a country club at home. The playroom has become a fad, and domestic bars for dispensing drinks have achieved the status of standard equipment. Lawns are fenced and hedged to accommodate outdoor snacks and entertainment, and almost every householder of these classes aspires to give his place a festive air. Thousands of Southern urban Negro consumers go into the furniture, appliance, food, and liquor markets in search of products capable of feeding their country club aspirations.

We cannot, in all objectivity, overlook the Negro's firmly established conviction that goods and services offered by white institutions are, on the average, better and more trustworthy than those offered by institutions operating within his own area. Over 96 cents of every dollar that Southern urban Negroes spend, except in cases of racial boycotts, goes to "outland" institutions—all in the search for belongingness. Further, where they find acceptance, they concentrate their patronage, to a greater extent than the white customers of the same stores do.

NEED FOR SECURITY

Another need which we observe to be operative in the consumer behavior of Negroes and whites is that of security. Some degree of insecurity seems to grow directly out of their respective social-cultural settings, and additional anxieties are apparently fostered by the goal blockages which they encounter in their pursuit of belongingness.

The Negro's insecurity begins basically at home. It is planted in his personality structure there, and its effects are spread to encompass a great portion of his life in the larger society. Our findings have led us to believe that this is not the case with whites. Instead, serious forms of anxieties seem to develop somewhat later through the compulsion to push ahead and out of those changes in our national and international life which they define as threats to their status position.

The seed bed of the Negro's fears appears to be the instability inherent in his family life, but the fertile soil in which these fears really grow must be identified as the even greater uncertainty which he experiences later. The normal pattern of father and mother roles is characteristic of the families of both races, but the Negro family deviates more sharply from this norm. Its members are dependent solely on the mother to a greater extent.

The main reason for this is that a larger proportion of Negro families are headed by females. One fourth are so headed as compared with 14% of the whites. (These are averages based on 664,415 white and 237,355 Negro households of five leading Southern cities.[11]) There figures represent a greater tendency toward family dissolution among Negroes. Rates of desertion, divorce, and widowhood are higher among Negro families, and the mother is more likely to be left with children for whom she is the sole source of support. Many of these mothers are very young—some barely out of their adolescence. Over 25% of them are under 25 years of age as compared with 5% of the white mothers who shoulder such a responsibility.

The personality-building power of this domestic pattern rests on its tendency to forge extremely close relationships between mother and child through its impact on child-rearing practices. It is in this way that maternal dependency is taught and the matriarchy arises as the Negro child's greatest source of stability and anchorage. Studies have shown that in matters of infant care, relationships between Negro mothers and their babies are closer and more natural than in the case of white mothers.[12]

Although this matriarchal feature gives Negro children some degree of security during their infancy, it exposes many of them to greater insecurity during their adolescence. They have to go to work at a relatively early age and, even when their mothers remarry, find no additional security. Stepfathers are sometimes reluctant to support stepchildren. The small proportion of Negro elementary school children who enter junior high is an indicator of the eroding effect of employment on children who are only entering the teens.

ROLE CONFUSION

Influenced by such conditions, many of these children enter their adult life with personalities already twisted by the insecurities from which they suffer. The responses of our subjects to the Minnesota Multiphasic Personality Inventory test clearly suggested this.[13] Scores made by Negro males and females showed mutual acceptance of the maternal dependency that has traditionally characterized the family life of most of them. The interest pattern of Negro men appears more feminine, and that of Negro women more masculine, than in the case of whites.

Other responses to this test were even more indicative of the impact of insecurity on the Negro's personality structure. Here Negroes scored higher than did whites in tendencies toward suspiciousness, oversensitivity, and some idea that people are against or, in extreme cases, trying to injure them.

Although our findings are based on relatively small samples, data presented by clinical psychologists tend to give further support to our conclusions concerning the greater degree of maternal dominance among Negroes. In a comparison of the frustration-aggression patterns of larger samples of Negroes and whites, researchers found racial and regional variation among subjects who responded to the Rosenweig Picture-Frustration Study:

> The Negro female, true to her traditional role in the monarchy, once again emerges as the dominant figure of the family—the one who meets frustration head-on. She directs her energy toward the sources of her frustration to a significantly greater degree than her white counterpart who is more inclined to turn her aggression on herself. Northern males, both black and white, join the Negro woman in this personality inclination, but the Southern Negro male is the most passive and self-blaming of them all.[11]

Of course, in contrast to the strong *maternal* role among Negroes, there is a pattern of white paternal dominance. So it may well be that, in the culture which Americans have built in the South, only the Negro woman and the white man are free.

ECONOMIC ANXIETIES

Some degree of insecurity is fed into the experiences of Negroes and whites as a result of the differences in how fully each race shares in the economy. While whites worry about earning enough money to "get ahead," Negroes worry about getting enough money to keep what they have. In building its racial division of labor, the Southern city has developed a neat occupational rank order that reflects a top and bottom pattern so far as Negroes and whites are concerned. In such cities as Atlanta, Birmingham, Houston, Memphis, and New Orleans, about 75% of all white male workers are employed at the level of craftsman or above, but only 20% to 30% of the Negro male workers achieve this status. The addition of female workers to the totals affects the percentages hardly at all.

True, the expanding economies of Southern cities are gradually drawing more Negroes into the upper occupational classes; but since this also happens to white workers, the percentages remain constant. Though the change increases the Negro's income from gross wages, it does not alter his relative social or economic position. Negro workers, therefore, derive their insecurity from this marginal position. They must cross racial boundaries, both spatial and social, in order to make their living. Their employers and supervisors are almost invariably white. Naturally, then, most Negroes define their position as uncertain and expendable.

This insecure view of their economic role persists even when employment policies are standardized. As an example, when Negro union workers were asked what they thought of their employer's new policy of hiring according to performance on a standard test, they generally agreed that it provided a good excuse for holding them back. Some Negro workers are so convinced that there is an immovable economic lid over their heads that they seldom, if ever, apply for jobs at levels higher than those usually filled by Negroes.

There are other worries that result more directly from short rations. Although Negroes have become somewhat adjusted to deprivation, poverty for a goodly portion of them is a constant threat. Obviously, their lower income places tremendous pressure on the family that tries to live according to the current American standard. Temporary unemployment is a serious and ever-present threat. Illness is feared not so much as a harbinger of death as it is a cause of lost paychecks. The financial reserves of most Negroes are so small that unemployment compensation is, as some of them say, "a poor harbor."

Still, Negro families attempt to partake of all the gadgetry that characterizes American living standards. They tend to encumber through credit obligations a large portion of their future earnings. The anxieties that stem from this strain are best illustrated by the middle-class Negro worker who said: "We've bought so much stuff on time that to miss a payday makes us want to change out telephone number." These are not all of the Negro's economic fears, but they are the big ones—anxieties that grow chiefly out of the possibility that what one has will be taken away.

WHITE FEARS

The comparable worries of white consumers are basically characterized by the fear of not keeping up or moving ahead. Contrary to outside appearances, desegregation in real estate inspires fears equal to those inspired by public school affairs. Such changes are putting pressure on white residential sections, causing a noticeable degree of anxiety among those who cannot conveniently find escape from the Negroes who are rapidly becoming their neighbors. These people are not afraid solely of proximity to Negroes, per se, but of falling down the class ladder as a result of living among or near them. Some white homeowners we interviewed offered remarks like these:

- "We stay on edge all the time. You can never tell when somebody will sell to Negroes, and in that case my daughter will suffer embarrassment before her associates."
- "We can't move right now. The other places we have looked at are so high. I don't mind living with colored people, but I'm worried all the time, wondering what my friends will think."
- "We paid more for this house than we should, but there is the advantage of not having to worry about all kinds of people moving in here."

Expressions like these illustrate an important point: they show that the white consumer's path to exclusiveness is not entirely strewn with roses. There are thorns that elicit fear.

We feel safe in the conclusion that the respective cultures of each race have planted fears and, to some degree, have erected defenses against them. The differences are in terms of degree rather than kind, although there are some instances in which the security of one means insecurity for the others.

How, then, does this matter of security show itself in buying habits? When Negroes and whites go into the market place, there are essentially three patterns of insecurity that appear; fear of economic imbalance, uneasiness over store-customer relations, and fright imagery associated with particular kinds of products. These three anxiety patterns, though somewhat different in content, decisively join Negro and white consumers in the retail market. This common quality emerged when, in response to depth interviewing, both Negroes and whites gave extended views about credit buying, department store shopping, customer-salesman relationships, and the use of particular consumer products.

CREDIT BUYING

Negro consumers displayed almost common agreement about the use of credit as a method of bolstering their insecurities. Almost three fourths favored credit buying, but felt obliged to display an elaborate system of rationalization to justify themselves. They generally concurred that credit, if not abused (meaning that the income of the purchaser can stand another weekly or monthly note), is a wonderful means by which poor people can get some of the things they want. Here are some representative comments by Negro housewives:

- "It is not too bad to buy on credit if you budget that credit—if you keep up those notes. The only way a poor person can buy is on credit."
- "I think it is always best to buy by cash, but poor people must buy on credit. It is one of the best ways for us to buy, but we should never go too far in debt where we can't make our payments."
- "Fine thing—good. First of all, I do think it's a good thing to establish a good credit record. You can buy almost anything. Even if you have money, it gives you time to have money and pay your bills. It does give you a secure feeling, and you can get things you want."

Over 70% of white consumers approved of credit buying as readily as did Negroes. However, the rationalizations behind their approval appear designed to protect their egos rather than their economic balance. According to them, buying on credit is all right provided others would only be as intelligent about it as they themselves are. People should watch interest rates carefully and not overburden themselves with payments. This kind of rationalization often shifts to the type of object purchased, implying that size of monetary obligation should govern one's credit buying. One white consumer using this system of reasoning told us: "It's dangerous. Better for people to pay cash unless it's an automobile or something big." Only a few turned economist and justified credit buying on the basis of financial need. One representative of this group said: "I would have to need it." Further inquiry, however, showed "need" to mean "want." This is the factor that makes the transaction a "sharp" one and the purchaser a "discriminating shopper."

DEPARTMENT STORE SHOPPING

Apparently, the human relations atmosphere of the large department store elicits some feeling of insecurity from consumers of both races. It places Negroes on the defensive and makes whites more aggressive.

Negroes carry their feeling of rejection into the trading relationships which they experience across racial-cultural lines. One reason for this is what some call their "high visibility"; that is, in telling us of their reactions to downtown shopping, many Negroes confessed that they felt conspicuous—as if all eyes were on them. Consequently, they experienced a compulsion to be on their "best behavior," or to meet higher standards than the situation ordinarily required. For example, for fear that their children will be accused of stealing, they tell the children not to pick up or handle objects when shopping in a department or variety store.

Most Negroes, however, face downtown shopping with some feeling of security, especially when buying in stores at which they usually trade. In speaking of her "at-homeness" in one of the stores, a Negro woman told us:

"When I first started trading there, I felt kind of strange. The place was so big and everybody seemed so busy, I thought they wouldn't notice me. But after a while I learned to like the place. I know where everything is and everybody seems glad to help me."

Even those who do not feel at home will admit that shopping experience in a store tends to ease tensions. One shopper who typifies this group volunteered this statement:

"When I would go there, I would get mad. I knew, with all the people they had to wait on, they would make the colored folks wait until last. But they didn't do that. Nowadays, they seem to take you as you come."

According to whites, the atmosphere of bigness and formality characterizing most department stores presents no awe which they cannot overcome. But they do have to come to terms with it. Apparently, most of them make the adjustment by retreating behind the greater weight of consumer demand offered by the white race in this country. "I tell myself that the clerks are there to serve me," reported a housewife of the middle-upper class; "if it were not for us they would have no jobs." Another who represented this group observed: "I feel almost as if I own the store when I go in it. I have this account there, my credit is established, and I feel like the store would not exist without me."

There are some consumers, however, whose sense of security comes from the store itself—from the type of confidence which the store inspires. One shopper characterized the feelings of this group when she gave us this account:

> "I went to the book department. No one watches you up there. I have always wondered why people don't cart away books or something because you know they are small and everything. I sort of looked around me a couple of times, and I thought, 'Well these people just trust you,' you know . . . and you can wander all through this pretty book department. . . . But, of course, since I feel that I sort of own the place, my feeling is that I do want to pay for these things because I want this to be a good store so I can come back here. So I just sort of feel this obligation; yet I feel completely at ease when I go in the store."

SALESMEN RELATIONSHIPS

Other defensive tactics were observed when our consumers gave us an account of their feelings about contact with salesmen. We guided each in his narrative by having him suppose that a salesman wanted to sell him some large item costing $200 or more. Each was asked to relate the prior experience essential for his willingness to talk with the salesman about the item; what kind of person the salesman would have to be; how he would have to talk; and what he, the consumer, would expect from the relationship.

Negro and white responses were so similar that only in a few instances could anxiety patterns be identified racially. Both groups agreed that readiness to talk with a salesman would depend on an emerging need. They appear much more amenable to making contact with a sales-man if, before the contact, their old car or refrigerator had given them trouble. "The item would have to be something I really need—for exam-ple, if my refrigerator went bad and it cost too much to fix it," is the way a Negro housewife expressed her emerging need. Saying virtually the same thing, a white housewife made this response: "I would talk with him especially if I had been caught flat with my car broke down and I had to get somewhere in a hurry. You don't forget these things.

You always say I'm going to get rid of this thing the first chance I get."

There were exceptions in both camps, however. A minority of the whites agreed that they would talk with a salesman provided they had already decided they were in the market for the item. A small but proportionally larger group of Negroes based their readiness on the condition of the family budget. "I never carry but one major bill at a time," reported a housewife of this group. "So my first experience would be no major bills on hand. But if a salesman wanted to show me an item, I would listen to his sales talk."

Another set of racially common response patterns involved the kind of person the salesman would have to be in order to win attention. Consumers of both races stressed personality traits—neatness, manners, honesty, and intelligence. Racial differences appeared only with regard to the security needs these traits were to serve. Specifically:

- For Negroes, the needs are confidence and trust. Therefore, they regard the salesman as a counselor whose personality inspires faith in his character or, at least, in his appeal.
- Whites need affability and concession. They want to see the salesman as a person "on their side"—one who knows his product, but uses his knowledge in favor of the potential purchaser rather than the seller. Instead of playing up the product at all points, they want him to play it down at some.

Illustrating these interpretations, one Negro housewife said: "He would have to be honest and neat. I would have to be told everything possible about the product. He would have to convince me." Another said: "He would have to be very nice and a well-talking salesman, very kind, and explain clearly the things about it, like the guarantee, the terms, and how good it was. I prefer a middle-aged rather than a too young man."

The personality phase of a white housewife's narrative went this way: "He would have to be clean, neat, and intelligent. He would have to know the mechanics of the item, be able to explain it. He should use no high-pressure tactics. His view of the product should be as critical as mine. Flaws should be admitted and even pointed out."

It is on the third level of the consumer-salesman relationship that the buyer's security needs manifest themselves most clearly. Those of both races want to feel secure as a result of the transaction. Whites want security in their belief that they themselves made the decision to buy; that they have used good judgment and have driven a hard bargain. "I would expect to have a feeling of satisfaction from the purchase," reported a white male. "I would want to feel that I spent our money well, and that those who trust my judgment think so too." Another told us: "I would expect to get complete satisfaction in service and guarantee—no regrets; no feeling that I have been taken."

Negroes seek their security in the belief that they have not misplaced their confidence, and that the terms are low enough. "I would expect good service," said one. "I would expect the product to stand up, to give long service like the salesman promised, and I would expect the payments to be as agreed on." Also emphasizing personal confidence, another explained: "I would expect the product to be what he said it was, to last like he said, and for the payments to run no longer than he said."

What is most important about these replies is the emphasis which consumers place on the salesman as a person. Only three whites and two Negroes mentioned the company which the hypothetical salesman represented. This suggests that when a salesman makes contact with a prospective buyer, *he* becomes the company. For that moment, at least, the destiny of his company is in his hands. Another important observation is that practically all of the consumers spoke deploringly of high-pressure sales tactics. Yet each one seems to expect the salesman to be a kind of lecturer or counselor. It seems that each buyer wants to have his mind made up for him, but he would like to feel that he did the job himself.

PRODUCT ATTITUDES

Some degree of consumer insecurity is carried into the product area, but with more apparent racial difference. Thus, whenever the theme of health appeared in depth interview responses, it was invariably tied into the consumer's discussion of products. And, since one health anxiety common to both black and white consumers is the fear that if illness or death comes, it will come through the mouth or nose, we took a look at the specific attitudinal patterns related to food, cigarettes, and air conditioners. Is there a real difference between the degree of anxiety which the two races feel in relation to these products? Let us take a look:

Food. Many Negroes tend to view food basically as a means of sustenance, and eating mainly as a way of meeting biological needs. Beyond this point, eating is unnecessary and indulgent.

We asked each Negro consumer: "What do you think of people who eat and drink just to satisfy their appetites?" The answer most common to the Negroes was: "It's a bad habit." Although one third of them (mostly from the upper classes) dismissed the topic by insisting that people should eat when hungry, more of the lower class went far beyond this point. "If he drinks," replied one, "he has a habit of eating as he drinks. Overdrinking leads to overeating; soon you have a glutton on your hands." The majority of these consumers, however, not only interpreted the behavior as overeating, but also warned against the health hazard they believed to be involved. A good example is the Negro man who insisted: "He shouldn't overindulge because in his old age he may come up with a pressure condition." Running through most of these answers was a clear signal that food is for the body rather than for the appetite. It may be that many Negroes see food mostly as a biological necessity because they have not always had enough of it in their lives.

Differing somewhat, a greater proportion of the white consumers conceive of eating as a self-indulgent and pleasurable experience. When the sustenance image does emerge, it is generally applicable to the vitamin and reducing-fad fields. When asked about eating and drinking to satisfy appetites, many whites seemed startled and replied: "What other reason is there for eating and drinking?" Only now and then did we get such responses as "guilty of gluttony," "a sign of neurosis," or some other sign of disapproval. As if suspecting negative intentions behind our question, one white man responded defensively by saying: "This is not necessarily glutty. It could be pleasure." Another became even more defensive, and warned the interviewer: "You're getting personal."

Statements like these suggest an indulgent attitudinal pattern which separates eating from its basic biological function and makes it a special ritual which serves a pleasant end. As more Negroes enter the upper classes, and as the entire population gets a greater share of our economic gains, we believe black and white motivations along these lines will grow more alike.

Smoking. Though they differ in their food concepts, black and white consumers seem to share a common fear about cigarettes and what they term "excessive smoking." Despite the fact that most of them smoke, many define the pack-a-day habit as dangerous. "Too many," complained one Negro man. "My doctor is on me about that now." Another who shared this fear replied: "Too much. It is either a dangerous habit or the individual is too nervous." Several others said: "A little too much," and most of them added that a person smoking at this rate must be emotionally disturbed. In general, Negro consumers pushed the pack-a-day habit into the region of abnormal consumption, but their attitudes were probably not shaped by the lung cancer scare. Less than 10% of them expressed fear of lung cancer. Theirs was not a fear of death but an anxiety about physical or neurological incapacitation.

Where cigarettes are concerned, whites drop their attitude of indulgence and join Negroes in a fraternity of fear about the pack-a-day habit. Even the few who are least concerned call it "foolish." One white man, somewhat more poetic than the others, stated: "These smokers live in a cloud of smoke and die in a pile of ashes." The real objectors (and these are in the majority) base their anxiety on the lung cancer concept. They are the death-watchers. "I think it is a waste of money and dangerous to the health," commented one man after citing the literature that built up his lung cancer scare; "I know a man who has cancer now from smoking too much. I'm expecting him to die any minute." Statements like these reflect the attitudes of many white consumers who, having little apparent fear of illness, stand in awe of a more sudden death—a death by accident or by some act of the technological web in which they feel caught.

Air Conditioning. A greater proportion of Negroes than whites have health anxieties with regard to air conditioners. When asked what they think of people who work or live in rooms ventilated almost entirely by air conditioning, Negroes usually gave negative responses. The continuum of rejection extended from "I don't think much of that" to the idea that use of air conditioning should be tempered by a basic reliance upon "fresh air." Representing the prevailing attitude, however, was the Negro housewife who said: "I don't think that's good. Some types of air conditioners have acid in them." Instead of preaching air temperance on the basis of health, a minority took the Spartan view. They felt that too much reliance on it is overindulgent and bespeaks a lazy person.

Most whites took this self-indulgent view also, but they favored the indulgence. "Lucky dogs" they called people who are "fortunate" enough to enjoy air conditioning regularly. A few of them, however, turned negative and referred to these people as "goldfish." But this reference, too, is made more out of a spirit of envy than an aim to ridicule. "They are spoiled, but I think it's wonderful. I wish I could afford to do it." This was the response of one white housewife whose view was shared my most.

NAME BRANDS

So far as the brand concept is concerned, black and white consumers are not far apart. The pressures of their security needs prevent them from buying prestige entirely at the expense of utility and economy. They revealed this by the way they answered when asked what they thought of the housewife who seldom buys unless the product bears a well-known brand.

Almost 20% of the Negroes belittled the policy as such, tagging such buyers as gullible. As one housewife said: "I think she is naive. If everyone bought as she does, the newer manufacturers wouldn't survive. She is probably following advertisements blindly." Another who put it more directly said: "She buys it because she thinks she is getting the best. I think she is just buying the name." The majority of Negroes subordinated brand buying to the economy of the housekeeping. One housewife said: "It is a good thing as long as it does not disrupt the budget." Another to whom economy was even more important seemed to let price be the sole determinant. "Well, I shop for bargains—not brands," she reported; "if a well-known brand is not on sale and one that is not so well known is on sale, I buy the one that's on sale." Another who associated brand name and high prices told us: "If a person has the money to pay for these high-price brands, I guess she has her reason."

It is important to note that about 35% of the Negroes interpreted brand buying as a status symbol and an expensive undertaking, but at the same time most of them identified brand name with quality. Their major worry seemed to be: "Can I afford to pay for the choice?"

White consumers, on the whole, concurred with Negroes in the view that brand buying has its economic facet. The major difference seems to be a matter of where the defense line is erected. Most whites approved of the practice, and tended to base their acceptance, as in the case of credit buying, on a rationalization that casts them in the role of a discriminating shopper. Over 60% appear to think this way. In commenting on the brand-buying type, a white consumer of this group summarized the position well when she said: "If she has tested varying brands and comes to these choices out of preference, this is good business. If she has not, but has bought out of habit, she is timid and unimaginative." Another, reinforcing this position contended: "If she is buying brands blindly, she is not an experienced shopper. She has too much faith in advertisements."

Most whites, however, emphasized the economy of brand buying, saying that buying this way is the logical thing to do. They called the brand buyer "cautious," "a quality-seeker," or "a penny-wise shopper." They seem to believe that knowing brands is a mark of consumer sophistication, and that shopping by brand is an indication of consumer maturity. Taken as a whole, both Negro and white consumers react to brand buying defensively. The former want to defend their budgets. The latter want to defend their egos.

CONTRASTING IMAGERY

Through their imagery concerning a large-purchase item like automobiles, Negro and white consumers once again showed an economic compulsion to temper their desire for prestige with their need for security. In 1959, they saw certain cars as "luxury liners"—the kind prominent people usually buy; they saw others as "best buys"—the kind that represent the most car for the money. As shown graphically in Exhibit 1 Cadillac, Lincoln, Buick, and Imperial were placed in the former category. Nevertheless, the cars most of them owned were Fords and Chevrolets, and these also ranked highest as best buys. Only in the case of Negro owners of Buicks were prestige and best-buy ratings approximately the same.

We were able to clarify the security motivation better when we had consumers complete the following sentence: *The ——— is the car that ———.* We entered a specific model of car in the first blank, and they entered a characteristic description in the second. The results for three cars of the low-price field are given in Exhibit 2.

Note that for Ford both Negroes and whites give priority to the same qualities, though not with the same strength. (Plymouth and Chevrolet enjoy positions very similar to Ford, but with Negroes according a larger vote than whites to "easy to operate," as well as to "economical to oper-

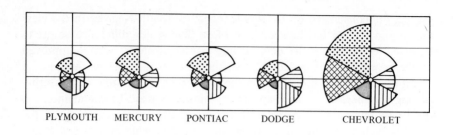

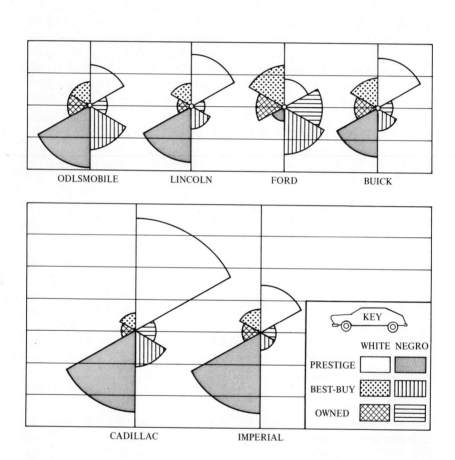

EXHIBIT 1 *Consumer Images As Reflected in the Percent Choosing Certain Automobile Models in Terms of Prestige, Best-Buy, and Ownership*

EXHIBIT 2 *How Negroes and Whites Characterized Certain Makes of Cars in 1959*

CHARACTERISTIC	FORD		MERCURY		DODGE	
	Negro	White	Negro	White	Negro	White
Economical to operate	67%	39%	0%	3%	33%	33%
Uneconomical to operate	0	11	17	15	0	2
Easy to operate	17	33	11	5	20	22
Hard to operate	0	15	5	5	4	5
Attractive in design	5	1	50	11	41	33
Unattractive in design	11	1	17	61	2	5

ate.") Note, however, the really sharply contrasting mental picture for Mercury in the area of design. Negroes labeled the Mercury as "sharp," "sophisticated," and "swinging." Whites negated this judgment by calling the car "horrible," "too bunglesome," "too chromy," or "too showy."

These may be overdramatic comments on the part both of whites and of blacks, elicited by the nature of the research itself. But, by the same token, there is no possible doubt left as to the clear division on *some* products and on *some* market qualities between the two races. This makes it all the more important that marketers should be able to follow an integrated advertising policy and appeal to "consumer motivations in black and white" with a single, economical, effective approach, as I shall try to describe in Part 2.

[Notes]

1. The *Pittsburgh Courier,* September 12, 1959.
2. See *The National Negro Market* (New York, Interstate United Newspapers, Inc.); also *Surveys of Select Cities* by the Afro-American Company, the *Pittsburgh Courier* and *Chicago Defender.*
3. John H. Johnson, "Does Your Sales Force Know How to Sell the Negro Trade? Some Do's and Don'ts," *Advertising Age,* March 17, 1952. (Reprint through courtesy of Johnson Publishing Company, Inc.)
4. See Henry Allen Bullock, *Pathways to the Houston Negro Market* (Ann Arbor, Edwards Brothers, Inc., 1957).
5. See Muzafer and Carolyn Sherif, *An Outline of Social Psychology* (New York, Harper & Brothers, 1956).
6. See Pierre Martineau, "The Personality of the Retail Store," HBR January–February 1958, p. 47.
7. Gunnar Myrdal, *An American Dilemma* (New York, Harper & Brothers, 1944), pp. 54–55.

8. Henry Allen Bullock, "Urbanism and Race Relations," in *The Urban South,* by Rupert B. Vance and Nicholas J. Demerath (Chapel Hill, The University of North Carolina Press, 1954), pp. 210–211.

9. See Kenneth and Mamie Clark, "Racial Identification and Preference in Negro Children," *Readings in Social Psychology,* edited by G. E. Swanson and Theodore Newcomb (New York, Henry Holt and Company, Inc., 1952), p. 551.

10. Eli S. Marks, "Skin Color Judgments in Negro College Students," *Readings in Social Psychology, op. cit.,* p. 116.

11. These figures have been aggregated from selected parts of U.S. Census, *Characteristics of the Population,* Volume II (Washington, D.C., Government Printing Office, 1952).

12. Allison Davis and Robert J. Havinghurst, "Social Class and Color Differences in Childrearing," *Readings in Social Psychology, op. cit.,* p. 543.

13. See Starke R. Hathaway and Paul E. Meehl, *An Atlas for the Clinical Use of the MMPI* (Minneapolis, University of Minnesota Press, 1951).

14. See Saul Rosenweig, Edith E. Fleming, and Helen Jane Clarke, "Revised Scoring Manual for the Rosenweig Picture-Frustration Study," *The Journal of Psychology,* October 1947, pp. 165–171; J. L. McCary, "Picture-Frustration Study Normative Data for Some Cultural and Racial Groups," *Journal of Clinical Psychology,* April 1956, pp. 194–195; and J. L. McCary and Jack Tracktir, "Relationship Between Intelligence and Frustration-Aggression Patterns as Shown by Two Racial Groups," *Journal of Clinical Psychology,* April 1957, pp. 202–204.

15

Henry Allen Bullock

Consumer Motivations in Black and White—Part 2

PART 1 of this article discusses in depth how the buying patterns of both Negroes and whites reflect each race's cultural system, and how advertisers have so far taken a distorted approach to the Negro as a consumer. To clarify this situation, the article analyzes both races' need to "belong"—Negroes wanting to be identified with the American society as a whole, whites desiring to remain generally acceptable but particularly exclusive. It then goes on to describe how the insecurities that both races feel influence their behavior in the market place, and to show how in each case the consumer trades money and credit for security.

In Part 2, businessmen are challenged to apply these new insights to create an "integrated" marketing program which is held to be the only effective, long-run method reaching the 17 million Negro consumers. These conclusions are based on an intensive analysis of the responses of over 1,600 Negroes and whites to various psychological tests and depth interviews, as reported in Part 1.

BUSINESS CHALLENGE

Social and behavioral scientists have given modern business many new leads as to methods of dealing with the problems of human relations in industry and commerce. But they are not businessmen, nor are they adver-

Reprinted by permission from *Harvard Business Review,* Vol. 39, No. 4, July–August 1961, pp. 110–124. Copyright © 1961 by the President and Fellows of Harvard College; all rights reserved.

tisers. None of their capital is directly risked in the use of their ideas; neither do their experiences qualify them for telling business executives or copy writers exactly what action to take in solving their respective problems. Theirs is to find truth and from it set limits within which executive action, if taken, has the highest probability of achieving some accepted end. It is within the framework of this limited role that we dare, in Part 2 of this report, to structure the implications of our research in the shadows of a new policy toward advertising.

As a result of our investigations reported in Part 1, we arrived at certain guidelines to administrative action in the field of selling, guidelines that will be especially helpful to those advertisers who wish to make the most of Negro and white markets under a common sales program. Specifically we will discuss:

- The motivations common to Negro and white consumers that can be used in appealing to both races.
- The media through which the two races can be most widely reached at the same time.
- The types of advertising patterns that are likely to have optimal effect on an optimum number of the two races.

These three guidelines are anchored to the point of view that a middle-ground advertising policy has greater promise of effectiveness than either the current practice of ignoring the Negro market or the current fad of creating a special advertising program to gain it.

JOINT APPEALS

As shown in Part 1, special appeals programs do not suit Negro aspirations, and racial differences in value systems are simply not sufficient to warrant their use. Just as Negroes reject radio stations beaming only to them, so do they reject advertising copy that has been given a black tone. Even where this policy is effective, the seller eventually gets in trouble. By drawing heavy Negro trade, he may get his product or store labeled as exclusively for Negroes and, in the end, alienate Negroes as well as whites. Since the catch-as-catch-can policy alienates Negroes equally as much, the middle-ground approach becomes an inevitable alternative for advertisers who seek to eat their cake and have it too.

DESIRE FOR DISTINCTION

The common motivations which advertisers can employ to influence Negro and white consumers alike are built around the desire for distinction.

This is a badge which the two races both wear. Negroes want to escape the group label and be counted as individuals; whites want to escape the pack and acquire something that represents them as being a little better off than the masses who dog their heels. Consumers of the two races concur in the view that such are the avenues to progress— to getting ahead. Therefore, the skillful marketer can give each camp the territory it desires without making either feel that it has lost what the other has gained. But to do this he must employ an approach which will make it possible for both groups to identify with the producer, brand, or seller.

There are only two warnings: (1) Negroes must not be included as a "type," and (2) white acceptance must not be strained beyond the limits of tolerance (which we shall define below). The marketer's strategy must also put to work those devices that make his product or service new and distinctive. The user should be made to feel that he is "getting there first" through this product. Such a theme, though very popular with whites, is not at all alien to Negro aspirations. In fact, it can be quite a clincher with the race. We were made quite aware of this when the proud Negro wearer of a pair of Stacy-Adams shoes told us: "The only ones who can afford them are rich white folks and well-off Negroes."

Another psychological characteristic that is common to consumers of both races is their low threshhold for stimuli of endorsement. Negroes are highly sensitive to what other Negroes buy, but are even more sensitive to the patterns of white consumers. They do not want to be Negro; but they do not want to be white either. They want to be *like* white people— to be able to live the way whites do, own the things whites have, enjoy the same privileges.

Whites are also sensitive to what other whites buy, provided the buyers are "name" people of the community. They want to be white, but they don't want to be like *most* white people. To utilize simultaneously these inclinations, a seller must stimulate the development of two paradoxical concepts about his product: exclusive acceptance and universal attainability. He should not worry about the stretch involved here. Everybody realizes that maid and mistress have been known to wear mink.

SEARCH FOR ADVENTURE

However, the task is bigger than that of providing escape from social typology or individual mediocrity. It requires provision for a chance to escape the boredom imposed by some modern shopping facilities. Nevertheless, here too is a common consumer quality which a seller can utilize to his advantage. If either Negro or white consumers are to be effectively influenced by a seller, the shopping experience offered must have a glow.

Supermarkets must be presented as institutions more often. They must be structured to accommodate greater freedom of customer-to-customer relations and greater opportunity for a buyer to express his or her personality. As consumers actually see food ads, these stores get the spotlight only indirectly and through the things they sell. Consequently, people acquire a "stomach image" of them. Finding this image unsatisfactory, the consumer is constantly in search of an image that better fills the bill. It may pay merchants to take advantage of this psychological readiness that Negro and white consumers share by tailoring their outlets more in line with consumer aspirations, or at least by making a shopping tour in their store a more exciting experience.

NEED FOR SAFETY

Like the motivation of belongingness, security needs also throw out guidelines and define certain areas of restriction for those interested in the simultaneous exploitation of Negro and white markets. Any seller who holds this interest must deal with a variable of fear whose continuum ranges from the simple feeling of personal inadequacy to a strong and complex anxiety about one's personal safety.

We have called attention to several kinds of situations in which consumers experience a feeling of personal inadequacy. It is important to note that all of the situations involve personal relations between an institution's personnel and its customers, suggesting those types of adjustments that appear to be essential for successful selling. For example:

Whether an individual buys through cash or credit does not appear to be an economic question entirely. It seems, in Negro and white cases alike, to depend on how safe the consumer feels in making the transaction. Negroes must believe themselves able to meet the notes. Whites must see themselves making a smart decision. Hence, sellers of big-money items must overcome consumer fears in order to lower consumer resistance.

Removing Negro fears in such instances seems merely to require that emphasis be placed on the company heart, showing that it has one and that it is a kind one. Emphasis for white consumers, conversely, should be placed on the economy of credit—capitalizing not only on the idea that people like to save money but also that they like to save face even more.

Both of these types of appeals can be made through the same advertising program, since they overlap the interests of the two races and, as will be shown later, the mind of those composing each will tend to interpret the situation in light of its own needs.

But, here again, the hand can be overplayed. People do not like to feel that others believe they *need* credit, nor do they like to feel that others expect them to pay cash in particular types of transactions. Their feeling of safety, therefore, must be supplied by the justifications which the salesman plants.

SALESMEN SERVICES

An implication that is even more specific pertains to the salesman himself. Simultaneous exploitation of both races naturally favors those salesmen who are highly adjustable in their personal make-up—those who sustain, as a result of their own aggressiveness, a constant flow of relationships between themselves and the customers whom they have served.

Consumer anxieties are naturally strongest in moments of crisis, and people are usually more inclined to seek relief from fear when the crest is highest. Both Negro and white consumers show a greater willingness to talk buying soon after the occurrence of some crisis which has probably exaggerated the need. Any consumer will admit that in moments like these the aggressive salesman who has maintained contact in the need area is the first person who comes to mind. Those sellers who have instituted the practice of sending periodic letters or cards as a means of perpetuating the friendly relations with old customers have probably experienced the profitable advantage of this policy. Such contacts not only place the salesman in the position of being able to exploit buyer readiness but also cast him in the more durable role of "rescuer."

What is more important, however, is the compulsion that the salesman's personality be balanced by courtesy and a flexibility that makes it possible for him to supply faith and confidence where racially different patterns of personal anxiety tend to lurk.

Thus, the salesman's relations with Negro consumers should be somewhat paternalistic but stripped of any sign of condescension. Although these consumers expect and indeed welcome counsel (especially about the use of the product and terms of payment), they are sensitive to any sign of discrimination, positive or negative.

The salesman's relations with white consumers should be more fraternalistic, revealing him to be a representative first of the consumer's interest and second of the company's interest. Even though the salesman must know his product well, it is of greater importance that he use the "soft sell." The last thing a white consumer wants to experience is a feeling that he has been a victim of high-pressure sales tactics.

HUMANE STORES

There is also the general problem of human relations within the walls of the retail enterprise. Here, the personality of the store is in focus even more sharply than that of the salesman. When he talks with you frankly, the average consumer in Southern cities readily admits that he is not completely at ease in large and overpowering shopping situations, especially in department stores.

Most of these consumers have not outgrown their rural back-grounds—their experiences in areas where shopping facilities are far more personal and considerably less complex. If we add to this cultural lag the Negro's intense race consciousness, we inevitably meet the pattern of customer insecurity as generated by the influences of traditional race rela-tions and by the technology of modern retailing.

There are two special ways of dealing with this problem which are to the satisfaction of Negroes:

(1) One method is to make the supervisor or floorwalker more conspicuously on duty. This makes the customer feel that he has some kind of protection from snobbery and discrimination. In telling us about large stores in which they feel insecure, many Negroes mention the supervisor. As one expressed it: "He'll come up and ask you if you need help when he sees you waiting too long." Another gained security in the feeling: "He keeps the clerks jumping."

(2) Another sales practice that apparently helps to relieve some of the in-store anxieties experienced by Negro customers grows out of the sustained personal touch. These customers admittedly like to be served by the same clerk each time they shop at a large store. Missing this, they like the next best thing—some sign that the clerk who does serve them is conscious of the fact that he is pinch-hitting. Calling them by name is very helpful, but this can be overdone. Salutations like "Honey," "Child," "Mary," or "Sam" have driven many potential Negro customers from fully stocked department store counters.

White customers are also sensitive to these store practices, but for different reasons. They are very quick to complain about some apparent neglect by a sales clerk, and they feel much more secure if one to whom they can complain is readily available. This is not because they fear discrimination but because they hate being underrated. Calling them by name is helpful, too. Although all shoppers are made to feel more wanted this way, whites especially get enough status to make them feel more secure.

FEARS AND PRODUCTS

Bigger and more dominating fears come into play when consumers turn their attention to special kinds of products. These fears are mainly about their physical welfare, though some need for ego defense is evident. The products are those like food, cigarettes, air conditioners, and auto-mobiles, but there are others calling for oral consumption like dentifrices and self-medicaments that may also be found to be areas of high sensitivity.

The seriousness of these anxieties makes it necessary for a seller to consider them in his sales campaign plans. At the same time, the degree of racial similarity involved in them makes it possible for this to be done under the cover of a common program.

Food   Since Negroes interpret eating more as a biological than a social activity, sellers would do well to emphasize the body-building power of a food product, especially as it relates to keeping the individual physically fit. This type of theme not only helps to relieve their fear of physical incapacitation but also, when mixed with the dollar-stretching power of a product, caters to the economic source of their anxiety.

The more indulgent attitude which whites have concerning food calls for a heavier emphasis on the pleasure principle. Closer identity between good food and good hosting should be established; advertisers will do well to realize that coffee and other such beverages are not the only food products that can be handled this way.

Nevertheless, one must not be led to believe that Negro and white consumers reach a complete parting of the ways at this point. Negroes gain a more social interest in food products as they climb the class ladder. A very effective common denominator, therefore, seems to be reached in the statement of a housewife of the Negro upper class who said: "She is a good hostess who serves nutritional foods." It is probably to a food seller's interest that his sales program be designed to encourage Negroes to conceive of food consumption more in the pleasure dimension of eating.

Smoking   The cigarette problem is much more serious, a fact which every account holder in the country knows by this time. According to the consumers we interviewed, to smoke or not to smoke is not the question. The problem area seems to rest mainly in the realm of consumption volume, for the pack-a-day habit elicits negative reactions from Negro and white consumers alike. Negroes tend to associate this habit with mental disturbances and physical incapacity; whites associate it with lung cancer and almost certain death.

Many of the product variation campaigns which cigarette makers are waging seem to be sharpening the consumer's point rather than blunting it. They are admitting that something is wrong and are projecting, according to consumer interpretations, a "trial-and-error scheme" in order to make corrections. At present, people as frightened as these are in a minority, but their ranks seem to be growing in direct ratio to the dissemination of health literature about smoking. Morally, both manufacturer and researcher are obligated to be right within reasonable limits. Marketwise, however, the seller must face the problem of bringing fear back into its proper proportions. To talk smoking moderation is to feed fear with fear. What people really want to hear is that the product has been modified according to the validated findings of medical research. "Then," as one frightened smoker explained it, "silence would not be giving consent."

Air Conditioning   Negroes and whites differ widely in their interpretation of air conditioning, but we do not know how much of this is due to a "fox and the grapes" attitude. Despite this limitation, there is probably some wisdom in slanting sales campaigns even more in the direction of the physiological values of air conditioning. Every manufacturer or seller of these appliances probably has bales of literature dealing with the impact of comfort on work efficiency and individual well-being, but little of this seems to have reached the consumer's mind.

In fact, most Negro consumers know nothing at all about it. Of our sample of more than 1,000 Negro households covered in Houston, 27% had window or central air conditioning, but only 3% of these owners knew anything whatever about comfort zones. It is possible that sales campaigns along this line would educate Negroes against some of their greatest fears and reinforce whites in the greatest attraction which air conditioning holds for them.

Health Products   On the other hand, the fears which consumers express concerning dentifrices and self-medicaments suggest that the health approach should be softened rather than hardened. If our survey information is correct, again all of these demonstrations about body cavities that need draining, membranes that need shrinking, and—according to one customer—"frowning faces that need smoothing" are frightening people out of their wits. Instead of relieving anxieties, these tricks of modern technology are building them. Demonstrations—chiefly those on television—are making hay fever and cold sufferers believe that they are more ill than they really are. So more of them are turning away from do-it-yourself medicine. (Despite some concern about fluorides, the Crest toothpaste campaign does not yet appear to be caught in the net of fear.) If self-medicaments are demonstrated, people want to see relief unadulterated by a prior state of agony. It is the agony that tends most to linger with them and to shape their image of the product.

Automobiles   Even automobile advertising has played on consumer fears. The excessive emphasis in past years on safety devices like seat belts, padded dashboards, and locking doors has pictured the automobile as a very dangerous thing. People are not always conscious of this fright, but their lack of awareness does not leave their consumer behavior untouched. In all their imagery about "good automobiles" the safety element is seldom if ever mentioned. Only when they talk about driving in traffic, crowded highways, and auto insurance does one get the feeling that they (especially whites) associate the automobile with certain death.

Ease and economy of operation are automobile selling features with both Negro and white consumers, but even here the *ease* is mainly in such matters as parking, changing gears, and steering. While manufacturers and advertisers of automobiles have some serious obligations to our much needed safety program, they still have the problem of feeding security rather than fear into the safety features of their product.

Until prices fall, our surveys indicate that the prestige image is virtually useless as an automobile sales pitch for the masses. If there is an exception, it is in the compact field. The compact owner says: "I have another one at home." The owner of the king-size compact (toward which some manufacturers seem to be moving) may turn out to say: "I didn't quite make it."

On the basis of all the statements whites and Negroes made about various products when questioned in our study, we are forced to conclude that consumers of both races are brothers in fear. And the seller who would exploit these markets simultaneously and without special programs for each must work within the limits of this fraternity.

INTEGRATED ADVERTISING

The idea that separate media are required to reach Negro and white consumers is more illusion than fact. There are certain strategic points at which the needs and the interests of these consumers converge in the stream of mass communication, hence suggesting specific channels through which they can be reached in common and effectively. (No *individual* medium is ruled out; rather each one simply is put to the test of how well it delivers an audience in competition with other available channels of communication, *regardless* of whether it is white or Negro.)

Media on which advertisers usually depend are also capable of covering large interracial audiences. As shown in Exhibit 3 [cf. Exhibits 1 and 2 in Part 1 of this article, pp. 180–181] these outlets present a gradient pattern according to their potential capability of reaching Negro and white minds. More specifically:

> Despite residential segregation, for example, the origin and destination of traffic behavior give racially common routes of traveling to and from work in Southern cities. In fact, there are certain streets over which more than 10,000 Negro- and white-operated vehicles with more than 25,000 people travel daily. It is possible for signs placed along these routes to be viewed over 500,000 times each month.

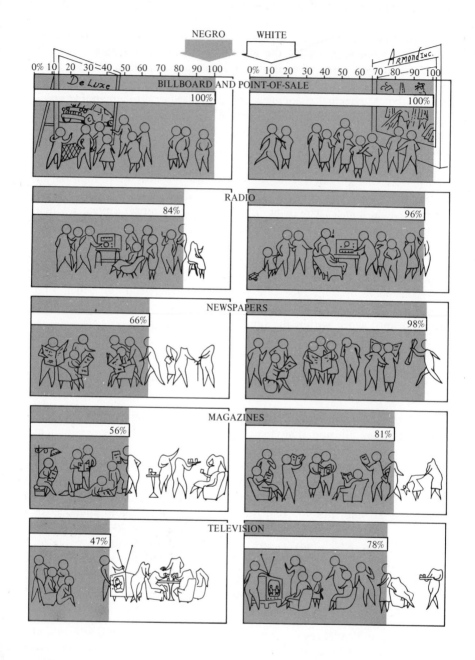

EXHIBIT 3 *Proportion of Negro and White Consumers Having Accessibility to Certain Mass Media*

- Again, every Negro or white buyer in these cities enters a supermarket at least twice per month (the tempo is usually higher than this).
- Finally, every major medium except television is available to more than half the Negroes and three fourths of the whites. And the rapid purchase of television sets among the former indicates that it, too, will join this family of common media that reach Negroes and whites alike.

Some difficulty does arise when we search for a common ground, however, because of the amount of claim various media make on the consumer's interest and time. We asked our subjects to name that particular medium with which they spend the greatest amount of time. The responses of those having equal access to all media are shown in Exhibit 4. Negroes seem to spend significantly more of their time with radio and magazines than do whites, while the latter apparently favor television and newspapers significantly more.

Yet, such differences need not be a stumbling block. The seller who uses radio and television together will gain the rather sustained attention of two thirds of the Negroes and of over half the whites. He will hardly be in any worse position if he combines radio and newspapers, since he will also be sending his message through channels that rate highest with more than one half the consumers of each group.

ATTENTION PATTERNS

This effectiveness can be made even stronger by those who turn creative and adjust their sales messages to the manner in which consumers

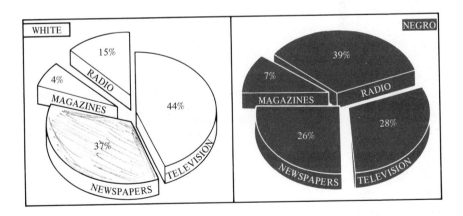

EXHIBIT 4 *Percent Distribution of Negro and White Consumers According to the Mass Medium with Which They Spend the Most Time*

of the two races synchronize the various media with the rhythm of their daily lives and the tonal qualities of their deepest aspirations.

Let us look at the timing element first, for nothing illustrates its power to guide advertisers to their target better than chronological accounts which subjects gave us concerning their habit patterns of media use. A far lesser proportion of Negroes have leisure time to be more responsive to eye-absorbing (as contrasted with ear-absorbing) channels of entertainment. There are many for whom radio is a constant companion—firmly married to their daily routine. This certainly showed up in the case of a Negro housewife, a part-time organist whose husband is a laborer. She gave us the following account of how radio fits into her daily living:

"I get up at 6:30 in the morning and fix breakfast for my husband. I go back to bed at 7:30 when he leaves for work. I get up again at 9:00, wash my breakfast dishes, and, if there are clothes to be washed, put them in the machine. The radio is going all the time. In fact, it moves with me from place to place."

Indicating this same pattern of companionship, another Negro woman, who is the wife of a taxi-driver, described her daily routine in these words:

"Radio wakes me up at 6:00 in the morning, and I keep it on while I am fixing breakfast and until 12:15. I don't listen steadily, but something often catches my attention. I fix lunch and look at the serials from 1:30 to 2:00. The children come in and take over the TV, so I get the rest of my work done by radio."

There are times when almost all of the mass media are neatly woven into a daily routine. This is illustrated very well by a housewife whose husband is a porter for a veterinary clinic:

"I am up at 6:00," she told our interviewer, "and I turn on the radio and listen to it until 11:00 A.M. Then I turn on TV, and it stays on all day— just going and nobody looking at it at times. After everybody is off to school and work, from about 8 to 10 I read the paper—radio going. I look at TV from 11 to 12, 12:30 to 1, and 3 to 4. I read magazines before I go to bed."

Negro housewives who are engaged in full-time employment normally follow a somewhat different media pattern. They use radio while working, the newspaper between work, and TV when at leisure. This account given by a Negro registered nurse whose husband is a public school teacher is fairly indicative of those who follow this pattern:

"I listen to the news on the radio while dressing. I continue to listen to the radio on my way to work. Before beginning to work I read the morning newspaper and I listen to the radio on my way home from work. Before doing my housework I may read a newspaper or magazine. When my housework is done, I look at TV before going to bed."

Whites also integrate the various media into the routine of daily living, but they do this in a different way, with different emphasis. They use the newspaper and television set as their daily companions. The paper is dominant with males, whereas TV leads with females. This account by a Jewish rabbi gives the newspaper center stage:

"After getting up, I read the newspaper—especially at breakfast. I read it during the evening when I am at home and during my reading hour. I guess I even try to read it when I am riding in the car."

Some whites, particularly women with leisure time, shut out newspapers and magazines and fill their lives with television. Such is the case of the wife of a mechanic who told us:

"I get up at 6:00; cook breakfast. My husband leaves. Then I have a time getting the kids off to school. This takes until 8:30. I have a cup of coffee and then start looking at TV. The little ones are home for lunch at 11:30. Then I eat my lunch. I may iron or sew but, I'm ashamed to say, it's mostly TV after that."

Even when time is at a premium, whites find a way to integrate the newspaper into their work and to build their leisure around television. A filling station operator indicated this tendency in his account:

"I open the station about 7:00. Around 8:00 things get slow and I can read the paper for a spell. I always keep it nearby. It kind of keeps me company when the boys are off. When I go home, I'm a bit tired. Spend most of the time looking at TV—the boxing, westerns, and features like that."

RECEPTIVITY PATTERNS

In some respects advertising is like bird shooting. The hunter must draw a bead on a moving target. Through narratives like these, therefore, consumers alert advertisers to the conditions according to which sellers must alter their sighting in order to make a direct hit. Respect for synchronism in the area of radio and television promises to prevent sellers from becoming absolute slaves to "prime time." It reminds them to define this kind of time as a function of media use as well as individual leisure. Thus:

> It has always seemed logical that one should encounter coffee ads near and around breakfast time. If such ads are sent out over the radio early in the morning, they tend to catch many Negroes at breakfast or, through automobile radios, on their way to work. That they are rendered more sensitive to the advertising message at this time is somewhat evidenced by the fact that four out of every five who reported having noticed coffee ads made contact with them through radio in the morning.
>
> A coincidence? Hardly. This frame of reference also makes the breakfast newspaper an excellent coffee communicator, especially for women who are avid ad-readers as well as coffee drinkers. Most of the white housewives who had noticed coffee ads got their message through the paper or television. Here, too, the morning hour was the time at which the hit was made.

Those who desire to exploit black and white markets through common sales programs can expect most of the racial difference in media appeal to melt away as television, especially where commercials are concerned, is made more suitable to the needs of consumers of both groups. In radio, the seller appears safe. In television, he appears in trouble. Negroes choose radio over television because of the greater opportunities for self-identification offered by the latter medium. Radio gives greater freedom to the imagination, freeing the Negro from the "left-out" feeling that a visual medium imposes. Whites also have their gripes with television commercials, feeling that they are "boring," "too interruptive," and "offer no lift."

That these attitudes are carried into the consumer's comparative evaluation of the advertisements he receives through these media is hinted at by data presented in EXHIBIT 5. In their judgments of ads encountered through various media, over half the consumers of each race were negative or indifferent, although mainly about TV commercials. On the other hand,

EXHIBIT 5 *How Negro and White Consumers Favor Ads Through Various Mass Media*

ATTITUDE	TELEVISION		MAGAZINES & NEWSPAPERS		RADIO	
	Negro	White	Negro	White	Negro	White
Entirely favorable	16%	5%	30%	35%	36%	32%
Favorable with reservations	32	30	32	20	34	25
Indifferent	20	5	25	19	15	10
Unfavorable with reservations	28	51	9	15	10	20
Entirely unfavorable	4	9	4	11	5	13

almost the same proportions held favorable attitudes toward commercials beamed by radio. Magazine and newspaper advertisements also elicited favorable feelings from both groups.

Nevertheless, television joins radio in being judged by both groups as an effective advertising medium. This is evidenced (in EXHIBIT 6) by the faith both Negroes and whites placed in the financial value of advertising through either medium.

To test this evaluation, we gave each interviewee a hypothetical budget to spend on an advertising campaign. That the average amount "spent" for the different media tended to favor television and radio confirms our position, although some of this hypothetical spending inevitably reflected a consciousness of the relative cost of the various media. A sound implication here, however, may be a black and white concurrence on the power of these media to sell and on the economy of creating a policy that renders the commercials beamed through them more acceptable to both races.

EFFECTIVE STRATEGY

In order to make the advertising message acceptable to Negro and white consumers at the same time, sellers must cater to the common motivations that influence their buying. To do this, they need not cling to a delicate thread, nor walk a crooked mile either. What they need to do is to consider which type of visual advertisements (the unstructured, the structured, or the cartoonized) is most likely to appeal simultaneously to both races.

UNSTRUCTURED ADS

Here, based on the principle of psychological selectivity, is an advertising policy which by favoring unstructured advertisements allows the consumer to project himself into the copy situation and to fit it to his own needs. He shapes his own thoughts; the seller merely manipulates them. This method is theoretically sound and empirically demonstrable.

As we have already shown, all of us have acquired a repertoire of motives embodying prejudices, aspirations, and anxieties. When we encounter a stimulus situation, this repertoire is called into play. It determines the particular element of the situation around which we anchor our attention, supplies the meaning we give it, and even guides the kind of response we make to its force. What is most important to the unstructured policy is the fact that the motive repertoire increases in effectiveness as the definiteness of the stimulus situation decreases. This means

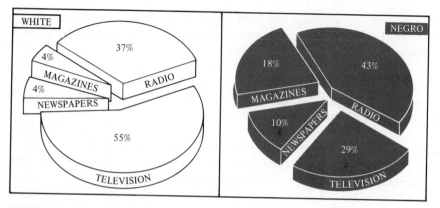

EXHIBIT 6 *The Proportion of the Advertising Budget Which Negro and White Consumers Would Spend with the Various Mass Media*

that people can be made to think of bread in all its softness without being bored by having to watch somebody squeeze a loaf. Indeed, they can identify with an ad without seeing "themselves" in it. To put it bluntly, we see what we want to see.

We observed this dimension of personality at work through a method patterned after the established Thematic Apperceptive Test, in which a subject is asked to look at sets of pictures and to compose a narrative concerning each. The narrative is organized around what he feels has happened, what is happening, and what will result. Pictures composing our test were taken from popular magazines in which they had appeared as advertisements or illustrations of feature stories. There was no textual material. In order to compare the self-projections made by Negroes and whites, each narrative was analyzed in terms of its theme and the kind of impact it made on the subject.

The narratives constantly reminded us that the interpretations people give to something they see depends on what they already have stored in their minds. Those elements of a picture that are singled out for emphasis and around which the entire pattern of response is organized show great correspondence with the individual's cultural background and motivations.

One illustration may be found in a set of responses which the subjects made to a picture of a doctor in conference with one patient while another is preparing to leave. The picture background is mildly structured for medicine and the character's costume emits a slight clinical tone. An unusual element prevails, however: the patients are white and the doctor is a Negro. Although there was some visual structuring, subjects of both races resorted to their respective cultural backgrounds as a means of resolving the mental conflict it fostered. Here is what happened:

White Responses given by the white subjects ranged from complete rejection of the doctor-patient fact to a guarded acceptance, toned by the implication that it did not happen in the South. One white female subject, after several futile attempts to compose a narrative, gave up in desperation by saying: "I can't make this out. Never saw anything like it. It's beyond me."

A variation from this perceptual block was shown by another white female who compromised with the picture's impact by restructuring the stimulus in accord with acceptable Southern traditions. The main portion of the narrative reads this way: "This is a poor area. The woman wants advice. The man is her husband. The Negro is a professional. It is a clinic? An apothecary? There's something odd in the picture."

However, most of the white subjects were more successful than this. They restructured the picture more decisively in favor of Southern interracial etiquette. The following statement made by a white male illustrates this tendency very well: "The two white people are apparently working people. Evidently this is a store the Negro man is running or owns. They're discussing something very serious, seem to be getting along together well. Looks like the Negro man said something that startled the white man. They will laugh it off, and the farm people will start back home before dark."

Only three of the whites who viewed the picture admitted the doctor-patient relationship. But here again the compromise mechanism was invoked. The doctor was not in the South; the setting was not his office. One female who employed these defensive tactics told her story this way: "Looks like a country doctor. The man is in a wheel chair. Must be up North as white people wouldn't go to a colored doctor down here. Looks more like a store than an office."

Black As for Negroes, they also restructured the situation in tune with Southern interracial etiquette. One of the new frontiers of advancement toward interracial harmony in the South is the growing tolerance of whites toward Negro salesmen. Several of the Negro subjects made the interracial elements of the picture more acceptable to their expectations by playing on this theme.

An example may be found in this narrative of a Negro female: "Is this a colored man talking to whites? Looks like some kind of business. I can't see very well. I'll say this is a colored salesman. . . . Seems as if he's gone to these people's homes. According to the clothes he has on, looks like he could be a doctor, but I'll say salesman anyway. He's trying to impress her that the bill of goods he's trying to sell is all he says it is, and she's almost ready to give in. Seems he's just about sold it. Being a salesman or a doctor, he's just about put over the point. She will believe what he's talking about whatever it is."

Approximately two thirds of the Negro subjects accepted the doctor-patient relationship but could see no specific good resulting from the incident. One woman representing this group said: "This is a colored doctor. Seems he is telling the white patient about her condition. The man is her husband listening to the doctor and he is surprised at what the doctor is telling her. I think what will happen is, *she will go to a white doctor.*"

These variations in perceptual responses are more than mere reflections of racial attitudes formed by diverse cultural backgrounds. They are also evidence of the individual's perceptual tendency to restructure the situations he encounters in the form and shape of his own needs and hopes. They tell us that an unstructured advertising policy is feasible and probably would be successful in a combined appeal to black and white markets.

Other forms of empirical evidence reinforce our faith in this policy. When Negro and white subjects were asked to select from a series of visual ad-patterns those that carried the greatest impact, the majority of both groups concurred in the selection of the hands. "An ad with mobility," exclaimed one white housewife. "Just enough to set you off," declared a white man who appeared charmed by its simplicity.

Negroes were equally moved. "It lets you think awhile," is the way a Negro minister judged it. "The hands talk to you," a Negro seamstress told the enumerator who placed the picture before her. Somehow, these responses seem to tell us over and over again that people see color only in faces; that the ad, after all, is a very private thing; that the company taking a chance on this one created an image of dignity for its product.

STRUCTURED ADS

Far less symbolic and much more conventional is the structured advertisement. Nevertheless, there are several ways in which it can be very effectively used in persuading both Negroes and whites to buy. Probably its greatest effect is in its power to lead members of each race to feel that they are included—that the advertising message is meant for them. One of these methods involves the skillful manipulation of foreground and background symbols. Here, also, psychological selectivity can be made more friend than foe. Where, against a special kind of foreground-background pattern, a variety of race symbols is employed to build an interesting composition, each race will take the initiative to put its familiar symbols in the foreground. In the end, everybody is satisfied.

Some of the most intriguing advertisements one can encounter, our Negro and white consumers told us, are those that inspire an exotic feeling. In trying to illustrate this point, they make their descriptions in the words and pictures of a tourist theme. These are often compositions in which tourists move against a relaxed background of native people, artifacts, foods, and ornamentations. Some advertisers use this horde theme much to the liking of both blacks and whites. In this instance, people of various races are presented in the aggregate and purely as individuals in pursuit of a product of apparent universal appeal.

From all the responses we have received, we are led to believe that both Negroes and whites would commonly be attracted by an ad, for example, that shows several automobiles of the same model operated with apparent ease by drivers of different racial groups in a crowded traffic situation. This technique of picturing a product in its natural use is not entirely new with advertisers, since many of them have used children of various races in playground settings. Three little girls, each of a different race, allowed consumers to identify with the child of their own race, while not rejecting the other children at the same time.

A second way by which an advertiser can put the structured policy to work in favor of his client's product is through the use of symbols which, though racial in nature, have prestige value for each group. As we have shown, Negroes hurriedly identify with those of their race who have achieved highly. They often go so far as to overestimate such achievements. Although whites do not identify with Negro "high achievers," they do join Negroes in overrating them.

This common ground, therefore, gives advertisers a chance to include both races in their ad situations. They can do this with a theme of dignity and without alienating either group. Of course, this has been undertaken many times. Gillette has done it well with baseball players—Elston Howard, for example, telling the audience how much he and his Yankee teammates like the product. Kent has presented Negro scientists who endorse that cigarette, and Revlon has been most aggressive of all. With Belafonte in main focus, Revlon allowed a network to telecast one of the most racially integrated programs in its history. While they give Negroes their greatest sense of identification with the sponsor's product, these highly structured advertisements do not seem to alienate whites. They sell because they make good sense. One of the most conservative white women in Houston said after viewing the Belafonte program: "A company would be silly not to exploit a popular talent like that." Probably this company's greatest protection against white alienation is not in the talent but in the psychological principle brought to light by Gerhart Saenger:

that readiness to accept Negroes in a given situation is a function of Negroes being there already. Prejudice seems to grow out of discrimination rather than discrimination out of prejudice.[1]

CARTOON ADS

The third type of advertising policy that seems to satisfy Negro and white motivations commonly is the cartoonized style which is gaining popularity so rapidly. Although the characters composing these types of situations are basically Caucasian, Negroes have been able to join whites in identifying with them mainly because of the cartoon's low capability of eliciting race consciousness. Also accompanying these cartoons is a comedy that carries a terrific force. It inspires laughter which, like music, is a universal language—capable of integrating all peoples. Consumers of both races consistently rate cartoon ads among the most pleasing which they encounter during a television program, in fact sometimes rating them over the main feature of the program.

Leading the parade of honor (around Houston) is Falstaff's Old Pro, who is now being challenged by the Jackson Brewing Comany's brew-buying Kangaroo. The only main feature that can outbill these characters, some consumers feel, is "The Flintstones."

We cannot overemphasize the weaknesses of beaming special advertising to Negroes and the strength of including them in the main stream. Using Negro models to push a product through Negro magazines and white models to push it through white magazines accumulates an undesirable attitude that grows in direct ratio to the Negro's integration aspirations. Showing that this attitude is already rising in ascendancy, one Negro consumer said the dual model policy looks like the seller is ashamed to be caught with Negroes. It is not necessary for advertisers to run this risk. They have not yet begun to approach the limits of tolerance drawn by the prevailing pattern of Southern interracial etiquette.

CONCLUSION

The report presented in these installments, though abbreviated by necessity, yields certain definite conclusions. Some can be derived directly from the facts that are involved, while others may be drawn indirectly from the normative dimensions of our society called into play by the implications of the study.

SELLING IMPLICATIONS

Advertisers have made two approaches to the Negro market: one, to give it special treatment; another, to give it no treatment at all. Neither of these extremes has been satisfactory. The former, inspired by the illusion that Negroes and whites are basically different, wins favor only with an economically unstable element of the Negro population while alienating the more economically stable group whose aspirations to be fully integrated into American life are blocked by this method. The latter approach, stimulated by an exaggerated fear of white reprisals, wins little or no favor with any element of the Negro population, since it gives these consumers a feeling of being left out.

Therefore, the main question has been: How can sellers win favor with Negroes without alienating whites? Although this has been a big question, we have found some workable answers. It is rather apparent that if sellers are to win one racial group without losing the other, their methods must become sufficiently inclusive to allow adequate identification on the part of those who compose the respective races. They must replace the "all" or "none" policies which they have followed in the past with one that desegregates the advertiser's source, message, and destination.

This new approach is made feasible by the operation of two factors:

1. The motivational forces guiding the behavior of black and white consumers, though different in detail, have common denominators which advertisers can manipulate in favor of the sale of a product or service. Both groups want to belong. Both have feelings of insecurity. When Negroes and whites buy goods and services, therefore, they are also buying belongingness and security.

2. The other factor that makes this new approach workable is its high degree of flexibility. The seller has a chance to make a choice as to how far he will venture to deviate from the norm of racial identification now defining current advertising practices. Barring the "all" or "none" methods, he can make use of unstructured schemes which, through the principle of psychological activity, allow individuals to decode the signal and restructure it in the image of their own aspirations. He may turn to cartoons which elicit very little race consciousness, or he may employ the use of black and white models on a prestige level which is acceptable to both races.

SOCIAL IMPLICATIONS

In addition to suggesting new points of departure in the field of selling, the implications of this report unavoidably throw our thoughts into the general realm of social norms. By showing advertisers what they *can* do to gain greater favor with black and white consumers, there is indirectly derived a value system concerning what they *should* do to keep this favor and to satisfy their own moral conscience.

There are two main advantages which sellers enjoy but which also challenge their moral strength as responsible citizens in a democracy:

- The freedom of mass communication which the sellers have inherited from our democratic tradition.
- The increased degree of skill in human persuasion which they have acquired through the development of their own insights and the aid of psychologists and social scientists.

These two advantages combine to impose on marketers the requirement that they be moral men as well as economic men. One of the great technological developments characterizing this twentieth century is our increased power of communicative efficiency—our power to spread ideas over a wider area and to a larger number of individuals. The radio, newspaper, and magazine are now pipelines that keep the family and all its members in constant touch with the pulse of our national life.

Therefore, communicators who use these media are invited into the privacy of American homes. Good taste requires that they be on their best behavior. Children, for example, do hear and learn the advertising message. They, too, are destinators. What kind of people they become is determined, at least in part, by the total quality of the advertisers' message. When sellers turn communicators, they inevitably become educators.

To the extent that advertisers gain control over the human mind, they also inherit some degree of responsibility for its content. Admittedly, there are Negroes who are greatly insecure about their health or color and who are sufficiently gullible to accept some of the absurd claims of sellers of "cure-alls" and "black-no-more's"—but this kind of mental outlook hardly justifies a reinforcement through repeated suggestions designed to exploit it economically. Admittedly, too, there are whites who would resent any presentation of the Negro image as a human being—but this is certainly not sufficient justification for repeated reinforcement of an attitude of racial intolerance.

Does not the seller have some responsibility in this, the most serious problem area involving our national unity?

[Notes]

1. Arnold M. Rose, *Race Prejudice and Discrimination* (Minneapolis, University of Minnesota Press, 1948), pp. 551–555.

16

Laurence P. Feldman
Alvin D. Star

Racial Factors in
Shopping Behavior

$\mathbf{A}$RE Negroes "different" in their marketing behavior? Or is Negro marketing behavior merely a manifestation of the low socio-economic status of the Negro and thus not really distinctive? These questions are increasingly raised as the relentless thrust of current events places the Negro squarely in the midst of contemporary marketing. The company president wants to know "What are we doing with the Negro market?" The marketing manager wonders if, in fact, there is a Negro market and, if so, how it is different from all other markets.

Two articles which have been written on this subject both stress the differences between white and Negro and, in effect, argue that a distinctive Negro market exists. Henry Allen Bullock has written that, in essence, the differences in white and black marketing behavior stem from differences in the way their respective needs for belongingness and security are manifested.[1] Raymond A. Bauer, Scott M. Cunningham, and Lawrence H. Wortzel have concluded somewhat similarly, that Negroes are different from whites because while the former have accepted white middle-class values they are at a disadvantage in attaining these values.[2]

Our purpose here is to test 1962 *Chicago Tribune* consumer shopping behavior data for real differences between whites and Negroes, and thus

Reprinted with permission of the American Marketing Association from *A New Measure of Responsibility for Marketing, Proceedings of the American Marketing Association National Conference,* a publication of the American Marketing Association, Keith Cox and Ben M. Enis, eds., June 1968, pp. 216–226. Appreciation is expressed to Mr. Don Klein and Mr. John Timberlake of *The Chicago Tribune* for making available the data on which this study is based.

205

verify the finding of the studies mentioned above with respect to shopping behavior. This paper is a report on preliminary findings using a simple cross-classification analysis, applying the Chi-square test of significance against a null hypothesis of "no difference." The research plan calls for subjecting this data to multi-variate analysis in the future.

THE DATA

The 1963 *Chicago Tribune* study, *Chicago Shops,*[3] was primarily concerned with obtaining information on shopping center trading areas and customer characteristics. The study was restricted to non-food shopping behavior. A random sample of telephone and non-telephone homes was employed with special attention given to obtaining a random sample of the non-telephone homes.[4] Of the total sample 1000 respondents resided within the City of Chicago and of those 760 were white and 240 were non-white. This subsample was chosen for our study because too few non-whites lived in the area outside the city. Use of the city subsample reduces the impact of suburban living, which may affect Negro and white shopping behavior differentially.

It should be noted that the *Tribune* study classified respondents as "white" and "non-white." However, in view of the fact that the non-white population of Chicago in 1962 was overwhelmingly Negro, little inaccuracy is introduced by using the terms Negro and non-white interchangeably in this paper.

Among the data collected from each respondent in the *Tribune* study were race, income, and eleven aspects of non-food shopping behavior. These last items can be classified into three groups each of which will be analyzed in turn:

1. Non-store shopping behavior
2. Store shopping behavior
3. The influence of price in shopping behavior

NON-STORE SHOPPING BEHAVIOR

Not all shopping behavior involves a visit to the store by the shopper. The question arises as to whether whites and non-whites differ significantly with respect to their non-store shopping behavior. We approached this problem by analyzing three sets of data: the availability of credit, the use of phone or mail-order in shopping, and the extent of purchasing from catalogs.

AVAILABILITY OF CREDIT

Although the availability of credit is not in itself a manifestation of shopping behavior, we feel that it is an important factor in determining the extent of this behavior in that it helps to make the process of ordering by phone or mail more convenient. Our data is limited to the extent that it includes only those respondents with credit at department stores (either at State Street or branch stores) and would therefore exclude those having credit with retailers selling exclusively from catalogs, for example, Aldens. However, this is a minor limitation because it is probable that respondents with department store credit would have no trouble opening accounts with catalog retailers should they desire to place an order.

Examining the data for the sample as a whole, we see in Table 1, that the proportion of whites having credit is 44%, while only 35% of non-whites have credit. The difference is statistically significant.

Classifying the respondents by income group, however, we find that there is no statistical difference between the proportion of whites and non-whites having credit in each income class. There is a generally similar and logical pattern for both racial groups, in that as income increases the proportion in each group increases. For each of the two highest income classes, the proportion of whites and non-whites having credit is virtually identical.

The lack of statistical significance in the differences between whites and non-whites in the two lower income classes show these differences to be more apparent than real. However, the direction of the differences may be explainable. In the lowest income bracket the proportion of whites having credit, while not high, at 23% is substantially higher than the proportion of non-whites, 10%. A possible reason for this difference is that a higher proportion of non-whites on this income level are on some form of public welfare, and are thus unable to secure department store credit.

In the $3,000–$4,999 bracket the situation is reversed, with the non-whites being the larger proportion with credit. This reversal may partly be a reflection of the differential attitude of whites and Negroes toward credit, as postulated by Bullock. He found that, in contrast to whites, Negroes had a more instrumental attitude towards credit believing that it should be used to buy goods which would otherwise be beyond their financial reach. On the other hand, whites appeared to justify their use of credit on less economic grounds.[5] It is possible that the differences between the two racial groups is more strongly manifested at this, than at any other income level.

USE OF PHONE OR MAIL ORDER

A direct manifestation of non-store shopping behavior is the extent to which the telephone or mail is used in the purchasing patterns. Specifi-

TABLE 1 *Credit at Major Department Store*

| | All Respondents* | | FAMILY INCOME | | | | | | | |
| | | | $0–2,999 | | $3,000–4,999 | | $5,000–6,999 | | $7,000–9,999 | |
	W	N	W	N	W	N	W	N	W	N
Have Credit (%)	43.7	35.1	22.9	10.0	36.3	47.2	37.0	37.2	51.6	52.6
Don't Have Credit (%)	56.3	64.9	77.1	90.0	63.7	52.8	63.0	62.8	48.4	47.4
Totals { Percent	100.0	100.0	100.0	100.0	100.0	100.0	100.0	100.0	100.0	100.0
Totals { Respondents	758[a]	228[a]	48	70	102	53	219	43	155	19

* Indicates statistically significant difference beyond p=.05.

[a] Totals include those with undisclosed incomes or incomes of $10,000 or more.

(Note: the above footnotes also apply to Tables 2–11)

TABLE 2 *Use of Phone or Mail Order*

| | All Respondents* | | FAMILY INCOME | | | | | | | |
| | | | $0–2,999* | | $3,000–4,999 | | $5,000–6,999 | | $7,000–9,999 | |
	W	N	W	N	W	N	W	N	W	N
Have Used (%)	29.6	12.9	18.4	6.4	19.6	9.6	20.8	16.3	34.8	15.8
Have Not Used (%)	70.4	87.1	81.6	93.6	80.4	90.9	79.2	83.7	65.2	84.2
Totals { Percent	100.0	100.0	100.0	100.0	100.0	100.0	100.0	100.0	100.0	100.0
Totals { Respondents	760	240	49	78	102	55	221	43	155	19

cally, our data was concerned with whether either of these means had been used by the respondent to make a purchase within the preceding twelve months.

From Table 2, we see that on an overall basis the proportion of whites shopping via phone or mail-order (30%), is more than twice that of the 13% proportion of non-whites. The difference is statistically significant.

The table also shows that when the data is classified by income there is, again, a general similarity in the pattern of phone or mail-order usage by both racial groups. As income increases the proportion of each racial group shopping via phone or mail order increases.

Although white phone or mail-order usage is consistently higher by income group, especially in the $7,000–$9,999 income bracket, there is no statistically significant difference between whites and non-whites except at the lowest income level. The difference at this level may be attributed to the point raised earlier relating to the smaller proportion of non-whites in this income class having credit.

CATALOG PURCHASERS

The final aspect of non-shopping behavior that was examined was whether a respondent had purchased through a catalog within the preceding twelve months. This class of purchase is a sub-class of mail or phone order purchasing, and one would expect to get results generally similar to those of the preceding discussion. That is, in fact, the case.

Here again, we see the statistically significant difference between whites and non-whites with respect to this measure when the entire sample is considered. In addition, as Table 3 illustrates, there is a similar pattern of increasing proportions of whites and non-whites at higher income levels up to $5,000–$6,999. Above this point the proportion of whites stabilizes at 48% while that for non-whites declines from 35% to 26%. This apparently large difference at the highest income level is not statistically significant.

The only statistically significant difference between the two racial groups is found at the lowest income level. Here, too, the explanation for this may be the lack of credit by non-whites at this income level in combination with a lower level of literacy. Both of these factors would tend to inhibit catalog purchases.

COMMENT ON NON-STORE SHOPPING BEHAVIOR

Several comments are in order with respect to the three preceding analyses of non-store shopping behavior. First, for the sample as a whole, there were statistically significant differences between whites and non-

TABLE 3 *Catalog Purchasers*

| | | | FAMILY INCOME | | | | | | | |
| | All Respondents* | | $0–2,999* | | $3,000–4,999 | | $5,000–6,999 | | $7,000–9,999 | |
	W	N	W	N	W	N	W	N	W	N
Have Purchased from Catalogue (%)	40.1	18.3	16.3	5.1	30.4	20.0	48.4	34.9	47.7	26.3
Have Not Purchased from Catalogue (%)	59.9	81.7	83.7	94.9	69.6	80.0	51.6	65.1	52.3	73.7
Totals ⎰ Percent	100.0	100.0	100.0	100.0	100.0	100.0	100.0	100.0	100.0	100.0
⎱ Respondents	760	240	49	78	102	55	221	43	155	19

TABLE 4 *Shopping Travel Time*

| | | | FAMILY INCOME | | | | | | | |
| | All Respondents* | | $0–2,999 | | $3,000–4,999 | | $5,000–6,999 | | $7,000–9,999 | |
	W	N	W	N	W	N	W	N	W	N
Travel Less Than Thirty Minutes (%)	18.9	22.4	30.4	31.9	29.7	18.9	15.1	16.3	15.1	10.5
Travel Thirty Minutes or More (%)	81.1	77.6	69.6	68.1	70.3	81.1	84.9	83.7	84.9	89.5
Totals ⎰ Percent	100.0	100.0	100.0	100.0	100.0	100.0	100.0	100.0	100.0	100.0
⎱ Respondents	746	228	46	69	101	53	219	43	152	19

whites for the three aspects of non-store shopping behavior which we have examined.

Second, we noted that, by income class, there were no significant differences between the two racial groups, except at the lowest income level in two instances.

Finally, the results obtained in the course of the analysis of this aspect of shopping behavior are generally consistent across all three sets of data, which gives us more support for our findings.

The preceding suggest that, with respect to non-store shopping behavior, the statistically significant differences between whites and non-whites which were observed for the total sample was the result of an income effect, rather than an ethnic effect.

STORE SHOPPING BEHAVIOR

When we turn to the actual physical aspects of store shopping there are two ways in which such behavior can be measured. One is to measure the number of different shopping areas or shopping centers visited in a given time period, and the other is to measure the number of such visits in a given time period. The data we are studying has both types of measurements, as well as information on other shopping habits which may be related to these measures.

For example, we would expect willingness to travel for long periods of time and whether an automobile is used for shopping purposes to be related to the number of shopping areas and centers visited per year for both whites and non-whites. Let us examine each of these factors and see if this is borne out by the data.

SHOPPING TRAVEL TIME

Table 4 shows the percentages of whites and non-whites who sometimes travel more than 30 minutes to shop for non-food items. For the entire sample the difference between whites (81%) and non-whites (78%) is small and not statistically significant. This difference is also small and not statistically significant for each of the income groups. (The same is true, even if the sample is broken down into groups that sometimes travel more than 60 minutes to shop which data is not presented here.)

However there is an association between travel time and income which shows up well in the table. Here it can be seen that for both whites and non-whites there is a strong relation between income and the percentage of respondents who sometimes travel more than 30 minutes to shop. For both races this percentage rises from about 70% for the lowest income groups to 85%–89% for the highest income group. This data then, like the recent Charles Goodman data for foods,[6] indicates that the lowest income shopper has a tendency to travel out of his neighborhood to shop, however higher income shoppers have an even greater tendency to do so.

AUTOMOBILE USE IN SHOPPING

Table 5 shows the percentages of whites and non-whites who drive their car when shopping. For the overall sample a significantly larger percentage of whites (67%) use their cars for non-food shopping than non-whites (57%). When the sample is broken down into income groups it is seen that lower income whites use their cars for shopping more than lower income non-whites. This difference is statistically significant for the $3,000–$4,999 income class but not the 0 to $2,999 income class. However, there is no significant difference in car usage for shopping between whites and non-whites with annual incomes of $5,000 or over. In fact there is an indication, though it is not statistically significant, that proportionately more higher income non-whites use their cars for shopping than whites, so that the overall difference in behavior stems from the lower income group influence.

SHOPPING AREAS OR CENTERS VISITED

Turning now to the Number of Shopping Areas or Centers Visited in the past twelve months (Table 6) we see that for the total sample there is a significant difference between the shopping "horizons" of whites and non-whites. A greater percentage of whites shop at many shopping centers and areas per year (7 or more) and a greater percentage of non-whites shop at few shopping centers and areas per year (1–3).

When the total sample is broken down by income groups the same general pattern is seen for each income group: whites have a broader shopping horizon and non-whites a more restricted shopping horizon, however the difference is not statistically significant for annual income groups of $5,000 or more. This is just the opposite of what is suggested by the travel time and car use data although few of the differences in all three tables are statistically significant. That is, the travel time and car use data would lead us to hypothesize that high income non-whites would have a shopping horizon as wide, or wider than high income whites. This hypothesis would follow from the indications that proportionately more high income non-whites use their cars for shopping than high income whites and that proportionately as many high income non-whites as whites sometimes travel more than 30 minutes to shop.

TABLE 5 *Car Owners Who Drive To Shop*

	FAMILY INCOME									
	All Respondents*		$0–2,999		$3,000–4,999		$5,000–6,999		$7,000–9,999	
	W	N	W	N	W	N	W	N	W	N
Do Drive (%)	67.2	57.1	72.7	50.0	63.3	37.1	58.6	63.3	68.3	84.6
Do Not Drive (%)	32.8	42.9	27.3	50.0	36.7	62.9	41.4	36.7	31.7	15.4
Totals { Percent	100.0	100.0	100.0	100.0	100.0	100.0	100.0	100.0	100.0	100.0
Totals { Respondents	564	105	22	8	60	35	157	30	139	13

TABLE 6 *Number of Shopping Centers and Areas Visited*

	FAMILY INCOME									
	All Respondents*		$0–2,999*		$3,000–4,999*		$5,000–6,999		$7,000–9,999	
	W	N	W	N	W	N	W	N	W	N
Three or Less (%)	22.6	44.2	34.7	47.4	25.5	52.7	22.2	39.5	15.0	36.8
Four to Six (%)	38.8	35.4	36.7	44.9	52.0	25.5	42.5	32.6	34.7	26.4
Seven or More (%)	38.6	20.4	28.6	7.7	22.5	21.8	35.3	27.9	50.3	36.8
Totals { Percent	100.0	100.0	100.0	100.0	100.0	100.0	100.0	100.0	100.0	100.0
Totals { Respondents	757	240	49	78	102	55	221	43	153	19

In view of the lack of statistical significance of these findings a definite statement cannot be made as to whether whites and non-whites really differ in shopping horizon, but there is a suggestion here that they do. Further study of this behavior is needed: application of multi-variate analysis to this data may shed additional light on these relationships.

Additionally we might note that the shopping horizon for both whites and non-whites expands with increasing annual income. This is, of course, what we would expect from the Travel Time and Car Usage data.

FREQUENCY OF SHOPPING TRIPS

The next area of shopping behavior examined is the frequency of shopping trips for whites and non-whites (Table 7). For the entire sample the data indicate that a significantly higher percentage of whites than non-whites are high frequency shoppers. Correspondingly a higher percentage of non-whites than whites are low frequency shoppers. In short it would appear from the overall data that whites shop more frequently than non-whites. However when the data is broken down by income groups the picture is not quite as clear.

For both high and low frequency shoppers there are some consistencies. In every income class, the percentage of white high frequency shoppers exceeds that of non-white high frequency shoppers. In addition, with the exception of one income class ($3,000–$4,999), the percentage of white low frequency shoppers is smaller than the percentage of non-white low frequency shoppers. For middle low and middle high frequency shoppers, however, the pattern is mixed. What can be observed is that in each income class, again except the $3,000–$4,999 income class, the frequency is lower for non-whites than for whites. Most of these differences are not statistically significant so that we cannot say that there is a real difference between white and non-white shopping behavior with regard to frequency of shopping trips, however, the data is suggestive that this is so. Again, further research is required before a definitive conclusion is drawn.

FREQUENCY OF DISCOUNT SHOPPING TRIPS

The frequency of shopping trips can be broken down in any number of ways. We will examine (1) the number of discount store shopping trips in the past twelve months and (2) the number of State Street department store shopping trips in the past twelve months.

The number of discount store shopping trips (see Table 8) for the total sample shows no significant difference between whites and non-whites with about 50% of both races making 1 to 9 discount store trips per year, about 30% making 10–29 such trips per year, and about 20% making 30 or more trips per year.

TABLE 7 *Frequency of Shopping Trips*

| | | FAMILY INCOME | | | | | | | | |
| | All Respondents* | | $0–2,999 | | $3,000–4,999 | | $5,000–6,999* | | $7,000–9,999 | |
	W	N	W	N	W	N	W	N	W	N
1–49/year (%)	17.4	28.4	19.6	32.8	21.8	20.7	14.1	39.5	16.4	31.6
50–99/year (%)	30.3	28.8	30.4	32.9	31.7	20.7	32.3	27.9	28.3	31.6
100–199/year (%)	34.0	30.6	23.9	25.7	29.7	49.1	40.0	20.9	36.9	21.0
200 or more (%)	18.3	12.2	26.1	8.6	16.8	9.5	13.6	11.7	18.4	15.8
Totals { Percent	100.0	100.0	100.0	100.0	100.0	100.0	100.0	100.0	100.0	100.0
Totals { Respondents	747	229	46	70	101	53	220	43	152	19

TABLE 8 *Frequency of Discount Shopping Trips*

| | | FAMILY INCOME | | | | | | | | |
| | All Respondents* | | $0–2,999 | | $3,000–4,999* | | $5,000–6,999 | | $7,000–9,999 | |
	W	N	W	N	W	N	W	N	W	N
1–9/year (%)	48.4	52.8	52.0	62.8	56.5	38.1	41.0	57.6	49.6	45.4
10–29/year (%)	31.0	29.4	24.0	18.6	21.7	49.9	37.0	18.3	31.4	36.4
30 or more (%)	20.6	17.8	24.0	18.6	21.7	11.8	22.0	24.2	19.0	18.2
Total { Percent	100.0	100.0	100.0	100.0	100.0	100.0	100.0	100.0	100.0	100.0
Total { Respondents	529	163	25	43	69	42	173	33	121	11

When the entire sample is broken down into income groups the difference between whites and non-whites is statistically significant only for the $3,000 to $4,999 income class, where there is a pronounced peak of non-white discount store shoppers in the middle frequency range. Interestingly, the $5,000 to $6,999 income group pattern while not significant statistically is almost the reverse of the $3,000–$4,999 income group pattern. This suggests that the discount store has its greatest appeal to whites in the $5,000–$6,999 income bracket and to non-whites in the $3,000–$4,999 income class.

FREQUENCY OF STATE STREET DEPARTMENT STORE VISITS

Table 9 shows that for respondents who have made 5 or more visits to State Street department stores in the past twelve months the difference between whites (87%) and non-whites (79%) is statistically significant. When the sample is broken down into income groups, however, only the difference in the $3,000–$4,999 income group remains significant. The difference for the $7,000–$9,999 income group is not testable because of low non-white frequencies.

The interpretation of this data is rather difficult because of the very small percentage of non-white State Street shoppers in the $7,000–$9,999 income group. When this group is disregarded the analysis is straightforward. Low income (0 to $2,999) shoppers of both groups frequently patronize State Street department stores to about the same extent (75% to 80% of each group). At the next income level, $3,000 to $4,999 per year, more whites (89%) but not Negroes (72%) become frequent State Street shoppers, and here the difference in patronage behavior is statistically significant. Finally, at the $5,000 to $6,999 income level we find that proportionately as many Negroes as whites are frequent State Street shoppers (both just under 90%). The data indicate that while a greater proportion of whites shop State Street department stores frequently when their income exceeds $3,000, an equivalent movement for Negroes does not occur until the $5,000 income per year "barrier" is passed. Bullock has noted that Negroes are more defensive about patronizing large department stores than whites.[7] Perhaps Negroes need the security of a larger income before they feel free to patronize downtown department stores as frquently as whites.

COMMENT ON STORE SHOPPING BEHAVIOR

The data presented here also do not yield any hard core evidence of white/non-white differences in store shopping behavior. Certainly the null hypothesis of no white/non-white differences generally holds for the data when income effects are eliminated. This conclusion is clearly valid for *Shopping Travel Time, Car Use, Frequency of Discount Store Shopping Trips,* and *Frequency of State Street Department Store Visits.*

When *Number of Shopping Centers and Areas Visited* and *Frequency of Shopping Trips* data are examined, however, we begin to see white/non-white differences in behavior which, while small and not necessarily statistically significant when income effects are considered, are consistent in pattern and suggestive of real differences in behavior. To generalize, the apparent difference is that whites shop in more places and more frequently than non-whites, and this is true even though for whites and non-whites shopping travel time and car use are about the same. These data then contain the suggestion of a real ethnic difference in shopping behavior. However, further research is required for validation of this quite tentative finding.

THE INFLUENCE OF PRICE

The shopper's attitude toward price is a major influence on shopping behavior. For shoppers for whom price looms large as an influence it is reasonable to expect a shopping preference pattern which differs from that of those for whom price is a less important influence. This section is concerned with the extent to which different attitudes toward price exist between whites and non-whites, and the degree to which this difference affects selection of the type of store in which to shop.

SHOPPING ATTITUDES

The data on shopping attitudes represent a three-way classification of responses to various questions relating to what the respondents looked for when they shopped. These classes described shoppers who were:[8]

Concerned with Price, Budgeting—These are the shoppers who feel that they ought to keep shopping until they have assured themselves that they are getting the best possible prices, and/or feel obliged to spend as little money as possible by stretching their budget. Their first concerns when making a purchase are: "Can I afford it?" and "Could I get it cheaper somewhere else?"

Concerned with Living Better—These women are mainly concerned that the purchases they do make will enrich their everyday lives, or will make their families' life more enjoyable. Their first concerns when considering a purchase are "Is this the item I want?" "Might not someone else have something I would more enjoy owning?"

TABLE 9 *Frequency of Visits to State Street Department Stores*

	FAMILY INCOME									
	All Respondents*		$0–2,999		$3,000–4,999*		$5,000–6,999		$7,000–9,999[a]	
	W	N	W	N	W	N	W	N	W	N
1–4/year (%)	13.4	20.6	20.6	25.0	10.4	27.8	12.5	10.5	10.0	31.3
5 or more/year (%)	86.6	79.4	79.4	75.0	89.6	72.2	87.5	89.5	90.0	68.7
Totals { Percent	100.0	100.0	100.0	100.0	100.0	100.0	100.0	100.0	100.0	100.0
Totals { Respondents	568	170	34	40	77	36	160	38	120	16

[a] Significance not testable, expected frequency<5.

TABLE 10 *Shopping Attitudes*

	FAMILY INCOME									
	All Respondents*		$0–2,999		$3,000–4,999		$5,000–6,999		$7,000–9,999*	
	W	N	W	N	W	N	W	N	W	N
Price (%)	33.0	55.1	54.8	60.9	41.2	64.1	35.6	50.0	32.7	57.2
To Live Better (%)	29.4	18.5	9.5	15.6	20.6	5.1	27.9	23.5	23.1	35.7
Get Money's Worth (%)	37.6	26.4	35.7	23.5	38.2	30.8	36.5	26.5	44.2	7.1
Totals { Percent	100.0	100.0	100.0	100.0	100.0	100.0	100.0	100.0	100.0	100.0
Totals { Respondents	707	178	42	64	97	39	208	34	147	14

Concerned with Being Sure, Satisfied with Purchases—These women are not as much concerned with price or product satisfactions as the first two groups. Rather they try to avoid making mistakes. They tend to depend upon store and brand reputation. They want to be sure that they've received their money's worth. When they shop, they start with two basic questions: "Can I trust the maker or seller?" "Is it a reasonable price for what I'm getting?"

White and non-white attitude toward price is brought out by the data in Table 10. Here, as in many of the other aspects of shopping behavior we have examined, we have a statistically significant difference between the total sample proportions of whites and non-whites.

The data by income class show that for whites "price" is unmistakably the most important of the three shopping attitudes for those with incomes less than $3,000. Above this level its importance declines until for incomes of $5,000 or more price becomes subordinate to "get money's worth" as an influence on shopping behavior.

On the other hand, for non-whites "price" is clearly the dominant attitude at every income level. However, the difference between the proportions of whites and non-whites is statistically significant only for the $3,000–$4,999 and $7,000–$9,999 income classes. In addition, for incomes of $3,000 and above, the desire "to live better" while subordinate to price, increases with income while "get money's worth" declines in importance. These findings tend to support Bullock's contention that Negroes are most interested in price when shopping, while whites place greater emphasis on value.[9]

DISCOUNT VERSUS DEPARTMENT STORE SHOPPING

Given the result of the preceding analysis, namely that for incomes over $3,000 non-whites place greater emphasis on price than do whites, one might expect that a manifestation of this attitude would be a differential patronage pattern. In particular it would be reasonable to hypothesize that non-whites, with their greater emphasis on price would make more frequent shopping visits to discount stores than to department stores.

Table 11 shows the proportion of respondents reporting more visits to discount stores than to department stores in the preceding twelve month period. For the total sample, the difference between whites and non-whites with respect to this aspect of shopping behavior is statistically significant. Furthermore, at all income levels a greater percentage of

TABLE 11 *Discount Versus Department Store Shopping*

	All Respondents*		$0–2,999*		$3,000–4,999		$5,000–6,999		$7,000–9,999[a]	
	W	N	W	N	W	N	W	N	W	N
More Visits to Discount than Department Stores (%)	8.2	16.9	9.3	24.1	11.4	16.3	10.7	18.4	5.3	6.7
More Visits to Department than Discount Stores (%)	91.8	83.1	90.7	75.9	88.6	83.7	89.3	81.6	94.7	93.3
Totals { Percent	100.0[a]	100.0	100.0	100.0	100.0	100.0	100.0	100.0	100.0	100.0
Totals { Respondents	686	189	43	54	88	43	196	38	150	15

FAMILY INCOME

(a) Significance not testable, expected frequency<5.

220

Negroes than whites report more visits to discount stores than to department stores. However, this difference is statistically significant only at the lowest income level. For higher incomes, the differences between the two racial groups are not significant and in fact become smaller. In the highest income class the proportion of each racial group visiting more discount stores is sharply lower and almost equal.

COMMENT ON THE INFLUENCE OF PRICE

Some might argue, citing Bullock's findings, that Negroes tend to avoid department store shopping, because they feel that their high visibility makes them conspicuous and engenders feelings of defensiveness.[10] This might be one reason why they favor discount stores with their more neutral atmosphere. However, support for the influence of price considerations in Negro patronage of discount stores is the Bauer, Cunningham and Wortzel statement that "... Negro women concentrate more on the economic transaction of exchanging dollars for goods."[11] On this basis, discount stores, with their emphasis on the "price" aspect of the transaction, are more likely to appeal to Negro than to white shoppers, and the data in this study tends to bear that out.

CONCLUSIONS AND IMPLICATIONS

Having concluded the discussion, what remains is to evaluate the influence of racial factors on shopping behavior. Much of what we have discovered in the course of this study is summarized in Table 12. Here we see that, for the sample as a whole, there are statistically significant differences between whites and Negroes on nine of the eleven dimensions of shopping behavior we have examined. One might conclude therefore, disregarding income, that whites and Negroes differed substantially in terms of their shopping behavior.

This substantial difference tends to disappear when income is considered, however. As can be seen from Table 12, whites do not appear to differ from non-whites in terms of non-store shopping behavior, except at the lowest income level.

For store shopping behavior, most of the comparisons by income class show no statistical significance between racial groups. In three of the aspects of store shopping behavior significant difference is found only in the $3,000–$4,999 income class. In only one instance, relating to the number of shopping centers visited, is a statistically significant difference observed in as many as two income classes both of which are below $5,000.

TABLE 12 *Pattern of Statistical Significance*

	All Respondents*	FAMILY INCOME			
		$0–2,999	$3,000–4,999	$5,000–6,999	$7,000–9,999
Credit at Major Department Store	S[a]	—	—	—	—
Use of Phone or Mail Order	S	S	—	—	—
Catalog Purchasers	S	S	—	—	—
Shopping Travel Time	—	—	—	—	—
Drive to Shop	S	—	S	—	—
Number of Shopping Centers	S	S	S	—	—
Frequency of Shopping Trips	S	—	—	—	—
Frequency of Discount Store Shopping Trips	—	—	S	S	—
Visits to State Street Department Stores	S	—	S	—	—
Shopping Attitudes	S	—	S	—	[b]
Discount vs. Department Stores	S	—	S	—	[b]

[a] "S" Indicates statistically significant difference beyond p = .05.
[b] Significance not testable, expected frequency < 5.

The one area in which a potential meaningful difference was discovered was in terms of attitude toward price as an influence on shopping behavior. Here, in two income classes including the highest, Negroes place a statistically significant greater emphasis on price than whites.

The reasons underlying the observed pattern of significant differences in shopping behavior may be inferred by drawing upon the work of Bauer, Cunningham and Wortzel. They have suggested that a "basic dilemma of Negroes is whether to strive against odds to attain middle class values (and the goods which come with them), or to give in and live without most of them."[12] We have seen that in only 2 of 11 aspects of shopping behavior was a statistically significant difference observed between whites and Negroes with incomes of $5,000 or more. It is reasonable to infer that Negroes with this level of income tend to resolve their dilemma in favor of middle class values because the level of their income is high enough to permit realistic aspirations for middle class status. Thus, they tend to be more similar to than different from whites in terms of the aspects of shopping behavior we have examined.

On the other hand, there do appear to be substantial differences between white and Negro shopping behavior for those with incomes less than $5,000, particularly with respect to store shopping behavior. For many Negroes at this level of income, aspiration to the middle class values of the dominant white culture is unrealistic and they have resolved the dilemma (if they have ever explicitly confronted it) by engaging in non-striving behavior. In addition, to the extent that Negroes at the lower levels of income are "first generation" urban immigrants with many of the consumption patterns of the southern rural culture of their origin, these differences in behavior would be exacerbated.

We would conclude that any broad generalizations relating to distinctive Negro shopping behavior is likely to be in error unless other factors are considered. A deficiency of our study has been that we have confined ourselves merely to the effect of income, and yet on this relatively crude basis the similarities between white and Negro residents of central cities for many aspects of shopping behavior tend to outweigh the differences.

The evidence does suggest tentatively that differences between the shopping behavior of the two groups tend to diminish with increasing income. The implication of this is that as Negroes better themselves economically, the differences in shopping behavior between the two groups which are now indistinct may well become negligible. To the extent that these differences are indicative of marketing behavior the "Negro market" may be a transient phenomenon in American life.

[Notes]

1. Henry Allen Bullock, "Consumer Motivations in Black and White–I," *Harvard Business Review* (May–June 1961), 89–104.
2. Raymond A. Bauer, Scott M. Cunningham, and Lawrence H. Wortzel, "The Marketing Dilemma of Negroes," *Journal of Marketing* (July 1965), 1–6.
3. *Chicago Shops* (Chicago: *The Chicago Tribune*, 1963). The data for the study was collected in 1962.
4. Same source as footnote 3, Col. I, 67–68.
5. Same source as footnote 1, 98–99.
6. Charles S. Goodman, "Do the Poor Pay More?," *Journal of Marketing* (January 1968), 18–24.
7. Same source as footnote 1, 99.
8. Same source as footnote 3, Vol. 1, 76.
9. Same source as footnote 1, 102.
10. Same source as footnote 1, 99.
11. Same source as footnote 2, 4.
12. Same source as footnote 2, 2.

17

Carl M. Larson

Racial Brand Usage and Media Exposure Differentials

$\mathbf{A}$N awareness of the Negro as a growing and vital force in the market place is developing. There are 23 million consumers with 30 million dollars to spend.[1] Unfortunately, there is little worthwhile information about the Negro market; therefore, stereotyped thinking provides most of the guidelines for selling action aimed at the Negro. Much of the good information is simply descriptive or demographic in nature. That is to say, data are available about such matters as the number of Negroes living in cities, the distribution of income to them, details on their family life, job opportunities, and their lack of educational opportunities.[2] However, market management cannot make meaningful decisions unless more is known about the products they prefer, and their brand preferences within the various product categories. This can be made available through proper market research which will separate the Negro market from the mass market. There is little question that Negroes are emerging as individuals who are proud of their race, and who wish to take their rightful place in the mainstream of American economic life.

IS THERE A NEGRO MARKET?

Apparently there is some disagreement as to whether there exists a Negro market. Mr. Leonard Evans, Editor and Publisher of Tuesday Publication, Inc. (and incidentally a Negro) thinks that Negroes can be

Reprinted by permission of the author and the American Marketing Association from *A New Measure of Responsibility for Marketing, Proceedings of the American Marketing Association National Conference,* a publication of the American Marketing Association, Keith Cox and Ben M. Enis, eds., June 1968, pp. 208–215.

separated out of the general market only because they are concentrated in the larger cities, and because of their lowly economic position. In other words, Mr. Evans believes that if the Negroes were dispersed throughout the nation on an equal basis, the Negro market would cease to exist.[3]

On the other hand, another Negro market practitioner, Mr. H. Naylor Fitzhugh, a vice president of Pepsi-Cola disagrees with Mr. Evans. He sees the Negro both as a consumer and a Negro, and he doesn't believe that the two roles can be separated.[4]

Other writers such as Lawrence E. Black and Raymond A. Bauer take the position that there is a Negro market and that it is a distinct and social reality.[5]

MEASURING THE NEGRO MARKETS

If there is a Negro market, it should be identifiable and measureable. This is the thought that Dr. John S. Wright and this writer had in mind when the Chicago Negro market was surveyed to determine Negro brand preference from a selected list of products. This report is concerned only with the results of this survey and a second survey of white Chicago households which was taken in order to make meaningful comparisons. The results speak only for Chicago and may not be representative of other markets.

RESEARCH TECHNIQUES

THE NEGRO SURVEY

From a list of census tracts of the city of Chicago, those with a concentration of twenty-five percent (or more) Negro households were identified. From this universe, twelve tracts were chosen through the use of a table of random numbers. Next from each tract, two blocks were chosen—again a table of random numbers was used. From the twenty-four blocks, chosen at random, a total of 210 households were selected and interviewed. For this survey reliability equals .95 with a standard error of proportion of 3.5 percent.

THE WHITE SURVEY

In order to make meaningful comparisons, two hundred white households were selected and interviewed. In this instance, only those tracts within the city of Chicago that were ninety-five percent white were selected as the universe. By using a table of random numbers, forty tracts were chosen. Next, using the random technique, five blocks were chosen from each tract. A single white household was selected to be interviewed from each of the two hundred blocks. The white survey also has a reliability of .95 with a standard error of proportion of 3.5 percent.

THE QUESTIONNAIRE

The questionnaire was divided into two parts. The first consisted of questions that related to the purchase of selected products in the thirty-day period preceding the interview. Demographic questions were also asked—Part II was a pantry inventory of products by brands that the households actually had in their possession at the time of the interview. No respondent had prior knowledge while answering the questions in Part I that their pantry would be inventoried before the interview was concluded. The same questionnaire was used for the Negro households and the white households.

INTERVIEWERS

In both surveys the interviewers were students of the University of Illinois at Chicago Circle. They were trained and supervised by this writer. Negro students were used to interview Negro households and white students were used in the white survey. Each interview took approximately one hour to complete.

REPRESENTATIVENESS

All good surveys should test the data they collect to check on its representativeness. The usual procedure is to take statistics that are gathered in the survey and compare them with known measurements (parameters) of the universe. If one is satisfied that there is no significant differences between the two sets of data, the assumption is that the sample is representative of the universe from which it has been taken. Tests using the chi-square analysis were made comparing educational levels attained as indicated by the sample data with known data regarding educational levels. A second test using income data was also made. Dr. Wright and myself were satisfied that the sample was indeed representative of the Negro population. Similar tests were made to determine the representativeness of the White Survey.

FINDINGS

All knowledgeable people recognize the fact that most Negro households receive less income than white households. Our surveys indicated this too. Table 1 records this data. Note that a typical white household has $3950 more income than a Negro household.

TABLE 1 *Family Income Before Taxes for Selected Chicago Households*

	HOUSEHOLDS	
Income Range	Percentage White	Percentage Negro
Under $ 3000	5	18
3000– 4999	6	25
5000– 7999	18	28
8000– 9999	22	15
10000–14999	32	11
15000–Over	16	3
Not determined	1	0
Total	100%	100%

Median annual income per family:
White=$9700
Negro= 5750

Source–Original Data, 1966, 1967.

HOME OWNERSHIP

Many differences that exist between the races are a function of their income rather than their race. An example could be home ownership. Table 2 shows this information.

TABLE 2 *Characteristics of Dwelling Places of Selected Chicago Households*

	PERCENTAGE OF HOUSEHOLDS	
	White	Negro
A. Own	59%	26%
Rent	41	74
Total	100%	100%
B. Single dwelling	49%	21%
Multiple unit dwelling	51	79
Total	100%	100%

Source–Original Data 1966, 1967.

Conclusions:

1. A significantly larger number of white householders (54%) own their dwelling places as compared to Negro householders (26%).
2. More white householders (49%) live in single dwelling units than do Negro householders (21%).
3. Future marketing research could be directed to testing the hypothesis that households of similar incomes have the same propensity to home ownership without regard to race. However, the fact that Negro households cannot move freely to all locations is a contributing factor to current dwelling patterns.

TABLE 3 *Automotive Ownership Patterns for Selected Chicago Households*

	PERCENTAGE OF HOUSEHOLDS	
	White	Negro
A. Own Automobile	83%	54%
Do Not Own Automobile	17	46
Total	100%	100%
B. Brands Owned:		
Chevrolet	25%	39%
Ford	19	22
Buick	11	6
Pontiac	10	5
Oldsmobile	7	5
Dodge	6	3
Rambler	5	1
Cadillac	4	4
Plymouth	3	—
Mercury	3	3
Volkswagen	2	—
Chrysler	1	4
Lincoln	—	5
Others	4	3
Total	100%	100%

NOTE: With a standard error of 3.5 percent, ownership patterns less than seven percent are not significant.

Source–Original Data 1966, 1967.

Conclusions:

1. Automobile ownership is higher among Chicago Negroes (1 out of 2) than some surveys find in other cities. For example in a study for station WLIB of the New York market by Pulse Inc., it was disclosed that one in three Negro families in New York owned automobiles in 1967.[6]
2. The Negro preference for automobile ownership is a function of income rather than race. Almost 61 percent of the Negro households owned either a Chevrolet or a Ford as contrasted to 44 percent for the white households.
3. The stereotyped idea that more Negroes own and drive Cadillacs and other luxury automobiles than their white counterparts was not borne out.

GASOLINE PREFERENCE

One of the checks that we employed to test the validity of the answers on automobile ownership was the following:

"Have you purchased gasoline in the past 30 days?" This was the answer.

	PERCENTAGE OF HOUSEHOLDS	
	White	Negro
Yes	88%	55%
No	12	45
Total	100%	100%

The purchase of gasoline follows closely the automobile ownership pattern, therefore the results seem to be valid. Table 4 indicates the brand preference for gasoline.

TABLE 4 *Gasoline Purchase Patterns for Selected Chicago Households*

	PERCENTAGE OF HOUSEHOLDS	
	White	Negro
A. Brand Name		
Standard	32%	52%
Shell	19	11
Sinclair	16	17
Clark	7	11
Martin	6	4
Texaco	6	1
Other	14	4
Total	100%	100%
	PERCENTAGE OF HOUSEHOLDS	
	White	Negro
B. Regular	50%	41%
Premium	50	59
Total	100%	100%

Source—Original Data 1966, 1967.

Conclusions:

1. Standard gasoline is the preferred brand for all Chicago households. However a significantly greater percentage of Negro households prefer Standard than white households.
2. Perhaps an anomaly of the lower income status of Negro families is the fact that they use more premium gasoline than do white drivers. It confirms an opinion that Negro families purchase better and more expensive brands.

FOOD STORE PREFERENCE

One of the most important hypotheses that were tested was the one which stated Negro households do more of their food shopping in "Mom and Pop" stores rather than in national chains. Table 5 discloses our results.

TABLE 5 *Food Store Preference Patterns for Selected Chicago Households*

	PERCENTAGE OF HOUSEHOLDS	
	White	Negro
Name of Store:		
Jewel Tea Co.	39%	13%
National Tea Co.	22	8
A & P Food Store	9	34
Certified	6	5
High-Low Foods Inc.	4	9
Kroger Co.	4	3
Dominick's	2	—
Hillman's Pure Food	2	5
Del Farm Food Co.	10	19
Total	100%	100%

Source–Original Data 1966, 1967.

TABLE 6 *Incidence of Product Usage in Chicago by White and Negro Households in Which Little Apparent Differences Exist*

	PERCENTAGE OF HOUSEHOLDS USING	
	White	Negro
Product:		
Milk	99%	97%
Bread	98	99
Toothpaste	96	92
Laundry Products	95	99
Potatoes (fresh)	93	95
Deodorant (women)	91	90
Spaghetti	80	80
Wieners	78	77
Deodorant (men)	74	69
Salad Dressing	84	83
Tea	68	62
Cologne & Perfumes	59	62
Barbeque Sauce	47	51
Cough Remedies	42	48
Cigarettes (men)	54	48
Canned soft drinks	38	44
Cigarettes (women)	40	43
Packaged boneless ham	35	34
Instant coffee	33	31
Bottled beer	27	24
Instant tea	20	17
Instant milk	12	13

Source–Original Data 1966, 1967.

Conclusions:

1. There was no evidence that Negro shoppers preferred "Mom and Pop" stores. Negroes shopped the national chains, although this preference for stores differed from white households, Jewel Tea Co. being preferred by white households and A & P being preferred by Negro households.
2. Since A & P has an image of low prices, it is not surprising that it is preferred by those who are the most disadvantaged in terms of income.

PRODUCT PREFERENCE

One of the major objectives of the Chicago surveys was to determine if there existed any significant difference in product usage by Negro and white households. Tables 6, 7, and 8 summarize the results.

Conclusions on Product Preferences.

1. There are significant differences in product preferences between white and Negro households at least as far as Chicago is concerned. Some of these differences may be accounted for by differences in income. One example that comes readily to mind is the automobile. Other differences may or may not be accounted for by economics.
2. The Chicago survey tends to agree with Charles E. Van Tassel that Negro households tend to purchase more cooked cereal, cornmeal, rice and flour than do their white counterparts.[7]

TABLE 7 *Incidence of Product Usage in Which Chicago Negro Households Exceed That of White Households*

| | PERCENTAGE OF HOUSEHOLDS USING | | |
	White	Negro	Difference
Product:			
1. Rice	83%	93%	10%
2. Plain flour	71	86	15
3. Cornmeal	14	81	67
4. Sliced luncheon meat	59	79	20
5. Cooked cereal	59	77	18
6. Pork sausage	48	57	9
7. Vitamins	32	41	9
8. Self-rising flour	16	34	18
9. Laxatives	22	32	10
10. Insecticides	23	30	7
11. Canned luncheon meat	9	20	11
12. Tonics	3	13	10

Source—Original Data 1966, 1967.

TABLE 8 *Incidence of Product Usage in Which Chicago White Households Exceed That of Negro Households*

	PERCENTAGE OF HOUSEHOLDS USING		
	White	Negro	Difference
Product:			
1. Soups (wet or dry)	97%	74%	23%
2. Detergent for dishes	96	76	20
3. Coffee (regular)	92	66	26
4. Cold cereal	92	84	8
5. Gasoline	88	55	33
6. Shampoo	90	45	45
7. Headache remedies	87	71	16
8. Passenger cars	84	54	30
9. Bottled soft drinks	81	70	11
10. Hair spray	76	21	55
11. Lipstick	66	50	16
12. Canned beer	56	43	13
13. Powder and rouge	50	40	10
14. Eye make-up	50	30	20
15. Whiskey (except scotch)	44	19	25
16. Dietary soft drinks	49	25	24
17. Wine	40	12	28
18. Tires (regular)	34	12	22
19. Hair coloring	32	11	21
20. Gin	21	9	12
21. Vodka	20	8	12
22. Brandy	14	6	8

TABLE 9 *Incidence of Product Usage of Specific Cosmetics by Selected Chicago Negro Households*

	PERCENTAGE OF FAMILIES USING	PREFERRED BRAND
Product:		
Hair straightener	21%	Ultra Sheen (20%)
Skin bleach	17	Artra (24%)

3. The Chicago survey also showed a preference by Negro households for packaged sliced luncheon meat, pork sausage, vitamins, laxatives, insecticides, and tonics.

4. The Chicago surveys indicate conclusively that white households purchase for home consumption a greater variety of liquors such as gin, whiskey, brandy, wine, etc. Approximately the same percentage of households purchase scotch whiskey, although scotch tends to be the leading liquor purchased by Negroes for home consumption.

   Raymond A. Bauer indicates that Negro consumption of scotch is three times as much as that consumed by white families.[8] This conclusion could be true since a Negro scotch drinker could consume a greater number of

TABLE 10 *Brand Preferences for Selected Products by Chicago Households As Disclosed in a Pantry Inventory*

Product:	PERCENTAGE OF HOUSEHOLDS White	Negro	Product:	PERCENTAGE OF HOUSEHOLDS White	Negro
1. Bread			11. Corn meal		
Wonder	17%	34%	Quaker	62	94
Silvercup	16	6	Aunt Jemima	23	3
Holsum	12	15	A & P	8	—
2. Packaged			12. Flour (plain)		
luncheon meats			Gold Medal	34	21
Oscar Mayer	88	69	Pillsbury	33	69
Swift	2	16	Ceresota	30	—
Super Right	2	8	13. Flour (self rising)		
3. Canned			Pillsbury	49	69
luncheon meats			Aunt Jemima	29	10
Armour Treet	38	17	Gold Medal	13	7
Hormel Spam	38	32	14. Soup (wet)		
Oscar Mayer	8	5	Campbell's	79	92
4. Boneless ham			Heinz	19	4
Swift	6	47	American Beauty	—	2
Agar	18	32	15. Soup (dry)		
Armour	24	—	Lipton	49	67
5. Bacon			Campbell's	21	—
Oscar Mayer	51	38	Mrs. Grass	21	—
Swift	11	18	Knorr	3	17
Cudahy	9	2	16. Macaroni		
6. Wieners			Creamette	26	16
Oscar Mayer	61	80	Red Cross	20	65
Ball Park	12	—	Fould's	18	7
Swift	3	10	17. Spaghetti		
7. Pork Sausage			Red Cross	31	84
Oscar Mayer	47	16	LaRosa	15	2
*Parker House	—	49	Fould's	14	7
Jones	19	—	18. Rice		
*Negro packing			Minute	39	2
house in Chicago			Riceland	35	77
8. Bar-be-que sauce			Uncle Ben	23	13
Open Pit	86	68	19. Coffee (regular)		
Kraft	10	12	Hills Bros.	42	43
Ann Page	1	4	Maxwell House	18	34
9. Cereal (hot)			Folger's	15	7
Quaker	75	91	20. Coffee (instant)		
Cream-of-wheat	14	2	Sanka	47	36
Farina	6	2	Maxwell House	28	36
10. Cereal (cold)			Hills Bros.	14	11
Kelloggs	60	69	21. Tea (regular)		
Post	20	15	Lipton	69	93
General Mills	12	9	Salada	12	—
			Jewel	8	2

TABLE 10—(Cont.)

22.	Tea (instant)			34.	Detergents (dishes)		
	Lipton	43	67		Joy	18	18
	Nestea	46	8		Ivory	17	16
	Tenderleaf	5	8		Trend	5	13
23.	Milk (fresh)			35.	Deodorant		
	Dean's	27	6		Right Guard	21	16
	Bowman	8	28		Ban	16	15
	Borden	13	18		Avon	1	11
	Joe Lewis	—	12	36.	Shampoo		
24.	Potatoes (fresh)	72	91		Prell	19	27
25.	Potatoes (instant)				Halo	7	17
	French's	33	17		Breck	17	—
	Borden	13	25		Alberto Culver	4	10
	Pillsbury	4	17		Fuller	—	10
26.	Salad dressing			37.	Toothpaste		
	Kraft	38	36		Colgate	27	53
	Wishbone	19	1		Crest	26	6
	Hellmann's	8	17		Gleem	14	18
27.	Beer				Macleans	12	2
	Budweiser	21	15	38.	Hairspray		
	Schlitz	21	26		VO-5	17	52
	Miller's	11	23		Aquanet	20	3
28.	Soft drinks				Just Wonderful	19	—
	Pepsi-cola	26	31	39.	Cold remedy		
	Coca-cola	20	20		Contac	37	19
	7-Up	14	5		Vicks	18	42
	Nehi	3	13		Dristan	10	7
29.	Hard liquor			40.	Cough remedy		
	Cutty Sark Scotch	7	31		Vicks	70	64
	Canadian Club	11	—		Pertussin	14	6
	Old Fitzgerald	2	13		666	—	8
	100 Pipers	1	13	41.	Headache remedy		
30.	Cigarettes (filter)				Bayer	28	31
	Winston	19	22		Anacin	20	30
	Viceroy	16	22		Excedrin	20	17
	Marlboro	16	4		Bufferin	16	12
34.	Cigarettes (non-filter)			42.	Laxatives		
	Pall Mall	33	70		Ex-Lax	35	46
	Camel	29	20		Phillips Milk of Magnesia	29	2
	Lucky Strike	20	10		Black Drought	—	15
32.	Cigarettes (menthol)			43.	Tonics		
	Kool	36	54		Geritol	79	41
	Salem	45	28		Father Johns	—	12
	Newport	13	4		Lydia Pinkham	7	12
33.	Detergents (laundry)			44.	Vitamins		
	Tide	30	34		One-a-day	37	46
	Cheer	12	17		Chocks	14	25
	Breeze	2	9		Poly-Vi-Sol	—	5

drinks away from home. Our survey, however, indicates that about the same number of households had scotch in their possession.

5. White households tend to consume much more of the following products than do Negro households: hair spray, shampoo, regular coffee, soups, cosmetics, and dietary soft drinks.

BRAND PREFERENCES

One of the important objectives of the Chicago study was to compare the brand preferences of specific products by white and Negro households to see if there were any important differences. It was also useful in corroborating the stated preferences for a specific brand and the actual brand on hand. Table 10 summarizes our findings. Only the top three or four preferences are used in this paper.

Conclusions about Brand Preferences.

1. There were several surprises. Negro smokers of menthol cigarettes preferred Kool by a wide margin over second choice Salem. (54% vs. 28%) The white smokers of menthol cigarettes chose the national leader Salem although Kool was a strong second.

2. Another surprise was toothpaste. Negro householders preferred Colgate over Crest by a 10 to 1 margin. White users of toothpaste divided almost equally between Colgate and Crest.

3. It was no surprise that Negro households are exceedingly brand loyal and give some of their favorites overwhelming support. Examples are as follows: Oscar Mayer in meat products, Quaker for hot cereals, Quaker for cornmeal, Kellogg's for cold cereal, Pillsbury for flour, Campbell's for soups, Red Cross macaroni and spaghetti, Riceland rice, Lipton tea, and Standard gasolines.

4. Again it was no surprise that products which depict an unfavorable Negro image such as Aunt Jemima and Uncle Ben are unpopular among Negro households. Perhaps these labels should be eliminated completely in all markets.

5. Companies which have made specific marketing appeals to the Negroes are successful in winning their support. Examples are Pepsi-cola, Coca-cola, Pillsbury and Continental Baking Company.

6. Negroes do display more loyalty to national products than private labels. An exception would be Parker House pork sausage. Parker House is a Negro-owned packing house which enjoys a fine reputation in Chicago among the Negroes.

RADIO LISTENING HABITS

An interesting objective of the Chicago surveys was to measure the radio listening habits of both Negro and white households. This was in response to the hypothesis that Negroes prefer Negro-oriented radio and white households prefer white-oriented radio. Table 11 gives the results.

TABLE 11 *Patterns of Radio Listenership by Selected Chicago Households*

	PERCENTAGE OF HOUSEHOLDS	
	White	Negro
A. Listeners to radio on day preceding interview.	72.90%	55.61%
Did not listen.	27.10	44.39
Total	100.00%	100.00%
B. Time of day preferred for radio listening.		
Morning	57.14%	43.75%
Afternoon	24.13	25.00
Night	18.73	31.25
C. Radio stations preferred.		
WVON (Negro oriented)	—	64.10%
WBEE	—	6.84
WCFL	11.73%	5.13
WIND	42.42	4.27
WGN	11.84	—
All Others	33.91	19.66

Source–Original Data 1966, 1967.

Conclusion:

1. A Negro oriented station such as WVON will attract most of the Negro listeners. This fact should be significant to advertisers who wish to reach the Negro market.
2. Stations such as WIND are not white oriented as such. They program for the mass market, hence they do have a number of Negro listeners, although their audience is primarily white.

CONCLUSION

There seems to be little question that American corporations are interested in improving their service to their Negro consumers. This can only come about when sufficient information is available. Once information is available, then it is the duty of the companies to evaluate this information from their own point of view. Some authors suggest that marketers should learn more about Negro attitudes, behavior and motivation. There is no disagreement with this suggestion, and perhaps a starting point can be surveys of the type that are presented in this article.

Information that discloses product and brand preferences will invariably lead to the "why" questions. That is to say—why do Negroes prefer brand "X" rather than brand "Y." In some cases companies might find that they have neglected this market and have made no special effort to improve their efforts to win the Negro households, other companies might find they use images which anger Negro consumers. In any case, Negroes are emerging as a proud people whose economic power is on the ascendancy. Negroes are like all consumers everywhere. They will purchase those products and brands which maximize their satisfaction—physical, sociological and psychological.

[Notes]

1. "Negro Consumers are Waiting," *Grocery Mfr.,* Volume 1, No. 11, November 1967, pp. 4–8 at p. 4.
2. Charles E. Van Tassel, "The Negro as a Consumer—What We Know and What We Need to Know," *Marketing for Tomorrow—Today, 1967 June Conference Proceedings,* Series No. 25, American Marketing Association, pp. 166–168 at p. 166.
3. "Is There Really a Negro Market?," Marketing Insights, Volume 2, No. 14, January 29, 1968, pp. 14–17 at p. 14.
4. *Ibid.* at p. 14.
5. Raymond A. Bauer, Scott M. Cunningham, and Lawrence H. Wortzel "The Marketing Dilemma of Negroes," *Journal of Marketing,* Vol. 29, No. 3, July 1965, pp. 1–6, and Lawrence E. Black, "The Negro Market Growing, Changing, Challenging," *Sales Management,* Vol. 91, No. 8, Oct. 4, 1963.
6. "Negro Earnings Rise, Survey Finds," *Marketing Insights,* Volume 2, No. 14, January 29, 1968 at p. 6.
7. Charles E. Van Tassel, *op. cit.* at p. 167.
8. Raymond A. Bauer, *op. cit.* pp. 1–6 at p. 2.

18

Raymond A. Bauer
Scott M. Cunningham
Lawrence H. Wortzel

The Marketing Dilemma
of Negroes

THE distinctive nature of the Negro revolution is that it is not a revolution to overthrow the established order so much as it is a revolution to achieve full membership in that order.

Because material goods have such an important symbolic role in American society, the acquisition of material goods should be symbolic to the Negro of his achievement of full status. This is not to say that all product categories have such a symbolic function for Negroes. In general, though, the symbolic status attributed to products by Negroes parallels that attributed to these products by whites.

Some exceptions, however, give the Negro market some distinctive characteristics. For example, it would appear that toilet soap, particularly as associated with deodorizing properties, has special importance for Negro women as compared with white women. Perhaps this is only a reflection of the middle-class dictum about cleanliness being next to godliness, perhaps also a reaction to the belief that Negroes smell different than whites.

The background of both the Negro revolution and the Negro's behavior in the marketplace is, of course, his relatively low socio-economic status. Despite an absolute income increase in Negro income since World War II, it is a moot point as to whether the Negro's relative position has

Reprinted by permission of the American Marketing Association from the *Journal of Marketing,* a publication of the American Marketing Association, Vol. 29, No. 3, July 1965, pp. 1–6.

improved. While two-thirds of Negroes reported a family income below $4,500 in the 1960 census, only one-third of the white families did so. Negro educational, occupation, and housing deprivations are also severe. These are some of the factors which account for the Negroes' increasing concentration in Northern urban "ghettos."

The socio-economic factors are so important that it may be asked whether there is a Negro market in any meaningful sense. Are there any special characteristics which distinguish the Negro from any other lower-income, lower-educated, and geographically concentrated group?

The answer is yes. And while income and education are the most important factors, they are not the only ones.

SOURCES OF DATA

The hypotheses developed here are derived from reanalyses of over a dozen surveys, both local and national, which have been studied during a period beginning in 1962.

To preserve continuity for the reader, the illustrative data will be drawn from only two studies: a survey of women's shopping habits in New York and Cleveland,[1] and a survey of male buyers of Scotch in Northern urban areas.[2] Many of the same patterns noted have been found in cross-sectional samples of the U.S. Negro and white population, as well as in some local surveys.

BASIC DILEMMA OF NEGROES

Negroes as a group have accepted the values of the majority white middle-class culture, but are at a disadvantage in acquiring the goods which represent some of these values.

In other words, *the basic dilemma of Negroes is whether to strive against odds to attain these middle-class values (and the goods which come with them), or to give in and live without most of them.*

It is easy to listen to the rising, increasingly militant, voices of American Negroes combined with the voices of African nationalism, and to conclude that the American Negro has not accepted white middle-class values, or that he may even be alienated from the white culture. However, even the publications of the Black Muslims reveal strong emphasis on the values of temperance and achievement, along with some racist content.

Certainly it is the consensus of both Negro and white students of the American Negro that Negroes have accepted white middle-class values.[3]

For convenience, we have been discussing Negroes and whites as though they were two distinct groups, each of which is in turn homogeneous. This is, of course, not so; but we are trying to emphasize some major trends and certainly various Negroes respond differently to the "basic dilemma" mentioned above.

DIFFERENCES IN CONSUMPTION PATTERNS

Any discussion of the Negro market needs to be based on general differences in Negro-white consumption patterns. A combination of societal restraints and cultural traditions leads Negroes to underspend, as compared with whites of equal income, in four major areas: housing, automobile transportation, food, and medical care (excluding certain categories of proprietary medicines). See Table 1.

TABLE 1 *Negro Versus White Spending Behavior: Controlled by Income*

	NEGRO SPENDING VERSUS WHITE SPENDING
Food	Less
Housing	Less
Clothing	More
Recreation and leisure	Mixed
Home furnishing	More
Medical	Less
Auto transportation	Less
Non-auto	More
Savings	More
Insurance	Less

Source—Marcus Alexis: "Some Negro-White Differences in Consumption," *American Journal of Economics and Sociology,* Vol. 21 (January, 1962), pp. 11–28.

This pattern of spending less on housing, automobile transportation, food, and medical care makes available to Negroes *proportionately* more money for the purchase of goods than is available to whites of comparable income. Thus, Negroes at a given level of income repeatedly have been found to spend more on clothing, furniture, and alcoholic beverages than do whites of the same income.

SYMBOLIC IMPORTANCE OF GOODS

The once prevalent stereotype that Negroes were uninterested in, or incompetent to judge, the quality of goods has long been displaced—with the contrary image now of Negroes being extremely interested in quality, and being even more concerned with the symbolic value of goods than are whites. Although this idea may sometimes be overdrawn, it seems

TABLE 2 *Proportion of Negro and White Women Showing "High-Fashion Interest"*[a]

FAMILY INCOME	NEGRO WOMEN		WHITE WOMEN	
	%	No.	%	No.
Under $3,000	34%	(113)	21%	(216)
$3,000– 4,999	38	(115)	36	(416)
$5,000– 7,500	56	(99)	47	(938)

[a] Of the Negro women who had $3,000 family income, 34% were "high fashion" in orientation.

close to the truth. Table 2 shows the proportion of white and Negro women in New York and Cleveland who scored high on a scale of fashion-consciousness.[4] Negro women were at least as fashion-conscious or more so than white women.

For another product category, liquor, a Negro family is likely to spend about 1.25 times as much money on alcoholic beverages as a white family with the same per capita income.[5] But the figures on buying Scotch are even more interesting.

Negroes drink at least 25% of the Scotch consumed in the United States, although they represent only 11% of the population. *Chicago Tribune* panel data (1961) indicate that 16.8% of Negro families report buying Scotch compared with 9.3% of white families. The distributors of White Horse have found that the average Negro Scotch drinker reports drinking almost twice as many drinks of Scotch per week as the average white Scotch drinker.

These data suggest that Negro *per capita* consumption of Scotch is *three times* as much as that consumed by whites. Other estimates have been of the same order.

Is Scotch related to status among Negroes? On a series of questions generally assumed to be related to the idea of Scotch as a high-status drink, Negroes indicate that drinking of Scotch is associated with high status. But perhaps a more crucial question is whether these attitudes vary according to whether a Negro sees himself moving upward or downward in society. We find that self-perceived mobility—that is, perceiving one's self as higher, the same, or lower in social class than one's father—is closely related to attitudes toward Scotch and toward reporting that one is a regular Scotch drinker.

Within the Negro group, such attitudes are much more highly correlated with self-perceived mobility than with present income. Those Negroes who see themselves as moving upward from their fathers' position in society are most likely to give answers which indicate they regard Scotch as a "status" drink, and are most likely to report being regular Scotch drinkers.

SEGMENTATION WITHIN THE NEGRO MARKET

To repeat what was stated above, the "basic dilemma" of the Negro is whether to strive against odds for middle-class values as reflected in material goods, or to give in and live more for the moment. It is the response of Negroes to this dilemma that creates two categories of persons whom we have labeled "strivers" and "nonstrivers." In turn, their responses to goods of high symbolic value, leads to an interesting segmentation of the Negro market.

Let us assume, therefore, that Negro women who are high on the scale of fashion-consciousness and Negro men who report they are regular Scotch drinkers are "strivers," and that the others are "nonstrivers," and then see where this leads us.

TABLE 3 *Social Activities Outside the Family*

	NEGROES				WHITES			
Income	High Fashion	No.	Low Fashion	No.	High Fashion	No.	Low Fashion	No.
Under $3,000	54%[a]	(38)	25%	(46)	30%	(45)	29%	(120)
$3,000–$5,000	46	(44)	21	(27)	44	(150)	38	(161)
$5,000–$7,000	53	(56)	28	(24)	54	(440)	48	(281)

[a] Of 38 high-fashion Negroes who had income under $3,000, 54% were involved in community activities.

Table 3 shows relationships between fashion interest and social activities outside the respondent's family. The pattern suggested by these data is: Among white women, social activities outside the family are almost entirely a function of family income, whereas for Negro women, once they have been identified by degree of interest in fashion, income no longer plays a role in the Negro group.

In every income category, those Negro women high on fashion-consciousness are twice as likely to take part in social activities outside the family as are low-fashion-conscious Negro women.

These data indicate that by comparing Negro women on the basis of interest in fashion, we have identified women with two basically different orientations toward the world outside the family. One group is actively engaged with the outside world; the other is more withdrawn from the world. This proposition would not be so interesting if it were not for the fact that this is *not* true for the white women in this sample.

The same sort of relationship holds for a whole series of questions on shopping habits: High-fashion-conscious Negro women are more than twice as likely as low-fashion-conscious Negro women to report that they

TABLE 4 *Combining Shopping with Other Activities: Controlled by Income*

Activity while shopping[a]	NEGROES		WHITES	
	Fashion-consciousness		Fashion-consciousness	
	High	Low	High	Low
Lunches	11%[b]	3%	7%	3%
Theatre	15	4	4	4
Seeing friends	7	—	6	3
Errands	3	5	2	3
Other	5	3	7	4
Don't combine shopping with other activities	60	84	73	83
Number =	(136)	(98)	(626)	(581)

[a] Multiple responses permitted.
[b] Of the 136 high-fashion-conscious Negro women, 11% reported eating lunch when they went shopping.

shop with others. Also, they are likely to combine shopping with social and recreational activities (see Table 4).

In short, the high-fashion-conscious Negro women (in the Rich-and-Portis shopping study) express their greater involvement with the world outside of the family in their shopping activities. Such differences among white women are in the same direction; but the differences, in general, are less than half the magnitude, either absolutely or relatively, as those among Negro women.

Thus, the Negro strivers are more actively engaged in the world about them than the nonstrivers; and shopping and attitudes toward symbolically important goods (interest in fashion) reflect this "striving" attitude.

ANXIETY ABOUT SHOPPING

Shopping can be an especially serious business for a social group that is moving up in society and very concerned with whether their funds are sufficient for buying the goods to which they aspire. We have found that Negro women are less likely to mention the secondary aspects of shopping—convenience, politeness of salesgirls, crowds, and so on—than white women. Rather, Negro women concentrate more on the economic transaction of exchanging dollars for goods. Compared with white women, what Negroes *like* best about shopping is getting new things and finding bargains; but they also are more likely to say that what they *dislike* about shopping is spending money!

Our discussion of shopping as an especially serious business for Negroes leads us to the expectation that there is a greater degree of anxiety among Negroes with respect to making shopping decisions generally. Table 5 shows that Negro women in general report greater difficulty

TABLE 5 *Proportion Having Difficulty Making Shopping Decisions: Controlled by Income*

	NEGROES FASHION-CONSCIOUSNESS		WHITES FASHION-CONSCIOUSNESS	
	High	Low	High	Low
	39%[a]	29%	25%	23%
N =	(158)	(110)	(1,472)	(979)

[a] Of the 158 high-fashion-conscious Negroes, 39% reported having difficulty making shopping decisions.

than white women, in making buying decisions. This becomes most acute among those Negroes who are "most involved" in the product category. The Negro women "strivers" are more committed to goods of high symbolic value (we identified them by their interest in fashion), more involved with the world outside the family, and show more concern over making shopping decisions.

A parallel may be found in the market for Scotch. Negroes are more likely than whites to report having an established brand preference, and at least as likely to specify a particular brand of Scotch when ordering a drink (see Table 6). Furthermore, the regular Scotch drinkers, both Negro

TABLE 6 *Brand Preference for Scotch: Controlled by Income*

	NEGRO DRINKERS		WHITE DRINKERS	
	Regular	Occasional	Regular	Occasional
Brand preferences "firmly established"	71%[a]	51%	67%	46%
(No.=)	(94)	(107)	(243)	(375)
Specify brand of Scotch when ordering in bars, clubs, restaurants	79%[b]	64%	77%	55%
(No.=)	(93)	(101)	(241)	(389)

[a] Of the 94 Negro regular Scotch drinkers, 71% claim that their brand preferences are firmly established.

[b] Of the 93 Negro regular Scotch drinkers, 79% claim to specify a particular brand of Scotch when ordering in bars.

and white, are more brand-conscious than occasional Scotch drinkers.

In response to the statement, "To obtain a good Scotch you have to order an old reliable brand," the regular drinkers among the whites are somewhat more likely to reject this statement.

This pattern conforms to a trend that has been discussed in marketing circles, namely, that persons more experienced with a product type probably will display their "expertise" by departing from accepted brands. But among Negroes, the reverse is true in the present instance. It is the regular drinkers, those most engaged in the product category, who report being reliant on the brand-name for assurance of getting a good Scotch (see Table 7).

TABLE 7 *Reliance on Brand Name: Controlled by Income*

	NEGRO DRINKERS		WHITE DRINKERS	
	Regular	Occasional	Regular	Occasional
State that to obtain a good Scotch you have to order an old reliable brand	61%[a]	53%	49%	60%
(No.=)	(98)	(114)	(247)	(416)

[a] Of the 98 Negro regular drinkers of Scotch, 61% agreed with the statement.

The inference we draw is that the regular Negro drinker of Scotch, in contrast with his white "opposite number," is more anxious about the possibility of making a mistake. His greater familiarity with the product (compared with the occasional drinker) does not decrease his reliance on brand names to avoid a mistake. This is analogous to the finding above, that fashion-conscious Negro women are more likely to report having difficulties in making buying decisions.

DISCUSSIONS

We have indicated that Negroes show a simultaneous high degree of involvement in material goods of high symbolic value, and a degree of anxiety associated with exchanging scarce resources for goods about which one does not want to make a mistake. Among Negroes, this leads to a good deal of talking about shopping. Negro women are more likely to say they find it useful to talk with someone when they have trouble making shopping decisions than are white women (52% v. 36%).

Furthermore, to the extent that they are involved with the world outside their family, they are more likely to turn to it for guidance. As can be seen from Table 8, high-fashion-conscious Negro women are much more likely to talk with and go shopping with friends than with husbands. This trend is not nearly so strong among the white group.

As to the market for Scotch, Negroes are more likely to report that they initiated and took part in discussions about brands of Scotch. Furthermore, regular drinkers (both Negro and white) are generally more likely to take part in such discussions than occasional drinkers.

Since regular Scotch drinkers have more friends who are also regular Scotch drinkers, they have more opportunities to talk about Scotch than do occasional Scotch drinkers (and in fact they do talk more). After per-

TABLE 8 *1. Proportion Finding It Helpful to Discuss Shopping with Various
Types of Persons*

	Negroes Fashion-Consciousness		Whites Fashion-Consciousness	
Person	High	Low	High	Low
Friend	55%[a]	32%	30%	20%
Husband	5	8	9	11
Other or no one	45	60	51	69
(No.=)	(158)	(110)	(1472)	(979)

[a] Of the 158 Negroes who were high-fashion-conscious, 55% found it helpful to discuss shopping with their friends.

2. Choice of Shopping Companions

	Negroes Fashion-Consciousness		Whites Fashion-Consciousness	
Companion	High	Low	High	Low
Friend	48%[a]	34%	37%	27%
Husband	9	32	23	24
Other or no one	43	34	40	49
(No.=)	(98)	(56)	(517)	(400)

[a] Of the 98 high-fashion Negroes who took someone with them when shopping, 48% selected a friend as a companion.

forming a statistical manipulation to equalize the number of regular Scotch drinkers each group has among its friends, we can look at their discussion habits as they would be if everyone had about the same opportunity to talk. This is the basis for the data presented in Table 9.

TABLE 9 *Word-of-Mouth Activity Relative to Scotch: Controlled by Friendship Patterns*

	Negro Drinkers		White Drinkers	
	Regular	Occasional	Regular	Occasional
Heard brand recommended	42%	39%	51%	39%
Heard brand criticized	25	6	21	11
(No.=)	(98)	(114)	(247)	(416)

The data in this table indicate that the regular Negro drinkers of Scotch are *not* appreciably more likely to report having heard of a brand recommended than the occasional drinkers of Scotch among the Negroes. However, they are at least four times as likely as occasional drinkers to report having heard a brand criticized.

This suggests that the regular Negro drinkers of Scotch are principally concerned with information that will help them to avoid mistakes. This fits with the picture sketched above of the regular Negro drinkers of Scotch being especially anxious about not making mistakes.

IMPLICATIONS

The data about drinking of Scotch fit the contemporary stereotype of high brand loyalty among Negroes. However, an all embracing notion of Negroes being brand loyal is, judging from our other studies, often too simple.

There are whole product categories, for example, facial tissues, which appear *not* to have high symbolic value with respect to middle-class cultural values (at least in the eyes of Negroes). In this product category none of the phenomena discussed with respect to Scotch and fashion have been found.

Furthermore, the Negro market is by no means homogeneous as to involvement with products of high symbolic importance. In fact, it is split between the strivers and nonstrivers.

Again, in some product categories, such as women's fashion, the same dynamics that might elsewhere lead the strivers among the Negroes to rely on brand names for reassurance drives them rather to other sources of information such as talking with friends.

Finally, in areas where brand names are important, Negroes tend to be brand-conscious, rather than brand-loyal. In the Scotch market we found evidence of Negroes being under cross-pressures—on the one hand, they had their own favorite brands; but on the other hand, they also reported being involved in many more discussions in which competing brands were recommended.

Compared with whites, Negroes show more concern, more anxiety, and more ambivalence over spending money for material goods. In this connection, it will be remembered that what the women liked most about shopping was getting things, and what they liked least was spending money.

While some Negroes will become increasingly secure in their status, it is probable that a growing proportion will become strivers as their expectations rise to the point where they work for a full place in American life. The proportion of nonstrivers will probably decrease as aspirations rise in general. But until Negroes' opportunities are brought in line with their aspirations, the basic dilemma we have discussed will remain.

[Notes]

1. Stuart U. Rich, with the assistance of Bernard Portis, Jr., *Shopping Behavior of Department Store Customers* (Boston: Division of Research, Harvard University Graduate School of Business Administration, 1963). The data presented are a result of reanalysis of the original data, and not to be found in Rich and Portis.
2. Made available through the cooperation of Browne-Vintners, Inc., distributors of White Horse Scotch.
3. For example, Thomas F. Pettigrew, *A Profile of the Negro American* (Princeton: D. Van Nostrand Company, Inc., 1964), Chapters 1 and 2.
4. Same reference as footnote 1.
5. George Fisk, *Leisure Spending Behavior* (Philadelphia: University of Pennsylvania Press, 1963), p. 145.

19

Broadus E. Sawyer

An Examination of Race As a Factor in Negro-White Consumption Patterns

THE PROBLEM

THE theory prevails in current consumer economics literature that at any given income level Negroes save more than Whites[1] and consequently spend less than Whites on consumption. Thus, by its continuous appearance in print, race becomes a factor in the determination of consumption patterns. Even though no study[2] sets forth the exact effect race has on consumption, the belief of a racial difference in consumption patterns remains unabashed.

This study holds that differences in consumption patterns both between and within ethnic groups do occur. Indeed, differences in the consumption patterns of the same individual vary with the fortuities of life. Differences in consumption patterns are caused by many factors, among which are one's station in life, his opinion of himself, availability of credit, income expectation, age, dependents, education, location, and financial reserves, to mention only a few. To date, no study has explained the effect of all these variables on consumption patterns. To attribute unexplained differences to race is not only misleading, but a disservice to the nation.

In addition, race is not a factor that may be isolated and its effect measured with ultimate precision. Indeed, there is much doubt of the validity of current race classification. M. F. Ashley Montague observes,

Reprinted with permission from *The Review of Economics and Statistics,* Vol. XLIV, No. 2, May 1962, pp. 217–220.

The idea of "race" represents one of the most dangerous myths of our time, and one of the most tragic. Myths are most effective and dangerous when they remain unrecognized for what they are.[3]

There is the much broader aspect to the problem and one that is not divorced completely from economic consideration. This aspect deals with the attempt by some persons to use any difference—real or apparent—between Negroes and Whites as a basis for declaring the former inferior to the latter. Such differences are seized upon in some sections of the country as justification for various discriminatory practices, which cause the United States irreparable harm in foreign eyes and are a contributory cause for the loss of numerous allies in times of international crises or at least loss of trade with otherwise friendly nations.

THE STUDY

If it is assumed that at any given income level Negroes spend less on consumption than do Whites at the same income level, it follows that observations on the regression line of consumption on measured income for Negroes will be continuously below that for Whites at the same measured income.[4] This proposition may be illustrated through the use of a diagram (Chart 1) where consumption expenditures are plotted along the Y axis and measured income is plotted along the X axis. If "a" equals the amount spent on consumption by Negroes with zero income, then the regression of consumption for Negroes may be represented by the line yy. The formula for the regression line may be set forth as

$$y = a + bx \qquad [1]$$

where "b" is equal to the amount of change in "y" for each unit of change in "x." The yy line represents the expected amount of consumption for Negroes at observed levels of income. The slope of line yy, "b," represents the marginal propensity to consume for Negroes.

If it is granted that at any given level of income Whites spend more on consumption than Negroes at that same level, then the intercept of the Y axis by the regression line of consumption for Whites would be some distance above "a"—which distance is designated as "r" (Chart 1). If it is further stipulated that "r" stands for race, then this value should be a constant at any observed income level.[5] If "r" is constant, then the $(y+r)(y+r)$ line, the regression of consumption of Whites will be parallel to the yy line, the regression of consumption line of Negroes. This function may then be represented by the equation

$$y + r = a + r + bx. \qquad [2]$$

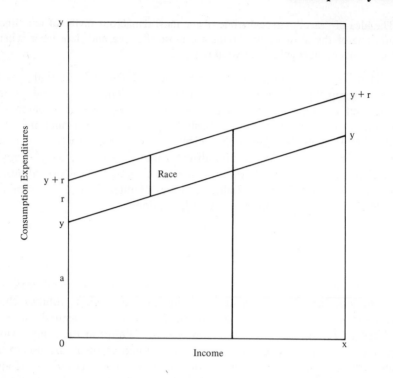

CHART 1 *Model Depicting Consumption Expenditures: Negroes and Whites
—Race a Factor*

The only difference between the amount of consumption for Whites and
Negroes at any given income level as represented by these two equations
is this constant *"r"* which by definition represents race. If *"r"* is added
to equation (1), it becomes

$$y + r = a + r + bx;\qquad\qquad\qquad [3]$$

but now equation (3) is identical to equation (2) and hence each term
contained therein must be equal. Then *"b"* in equation (2) equals *"b"* in
equation (3); but *"b"* is the marginal propensity to consume. It now
follows—if the hypothesis is valid—the marginal propensity to consume
of Whites is equal to the marginal propensity to consume for Negroes.

Table 1 shows calculated marginal propensities to consume for
Whites and Negroes from various sections of the country. Whereas it is
obvious that in no case are the marginal propensities to consume for the
two races the same, statistical tests reflect that the difference between the
two groups is no greater than the difference within each race. Since
the marginal propensities to consume for the two races are not the same,

TABLE 1 *Marginal Propensity to Consume*

	WHITES	NEGROES
Large Cities in the North	.49277	.76124
Suburbs in the North	.65657	.47206
Large Cities in the South	.54190	.84816
Suburbs in the South	.47237	.94520
Small Cities in the South	.68620	.82543
Large Cities in the West	.58133	.73529
Large Cities in the North—Individual Consumers	.58077	.90818
Large Cities in the South—Individual Consumers	.33019	.75459

Source: Computed from Table 15, Summary of Family Accounts, Bureau of Labor Statistics, *Study of Consumer Expenditures, Incomes, and Savings* (Tabulated by the Bureau of Labor Statistics for the Wharton School of Finance and Commerce, University of Pennsylvania, 1956), Volumes I and II, 137–148 each volume.

the regression lines will not be parallel. They will cross eventually and while they will not necessarily nullify the hypothesis that race is a factor in the determination of the consumption function, they may indicate strongly that factors other than race are at work.

Data from various sections of the country are analyzed for the purpose of ascertaining whether they support the proposition that the marginal propensity to consume of Negroes and Whites is the same.[6] Data for Large Cities in the North are used to illustrate the method followed in this study. Table 2 contains information relative to size of family, money income after taxes and consumption expenditures for Whites and Negroes. It is readily apparent that the size of families for the two races is not identical and adjustment therefore is required.[7] To put the information in comparable form, both money income after taxes (Col. 2) and consumption expenditures (Col. 3) are divided by size of family (Col. 1). Thus Cols. 4 and 5 are on a "unit of one" basis.

A trend line, by the least squares method is drawn for both the average expenditures on consumption for Whites and the average expenditures on consumption for Negroes (Chart 2). It may be noted that these two lines are not parallel as postulated in the linear hypothesis (Chart 1), but cross. Similar situations prevail for data taken from other sections of the country; in each case examined, the trend lines (as depicted in Chart 2) crossed.

One additional check was applied to the data. The calculated amount spent on consumption by Whites with $2,000 income was analyzed to determine if it differed significantly from the calculated amount spent on consumption by Negroes with $2,000 income. The answer was that the variance between the races did not differ significantly from the variance within the races. (See Table 2.)

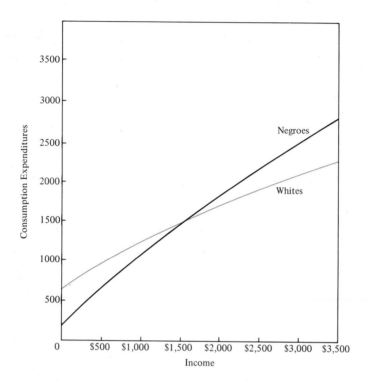

CHART 2 *Consumption Regression Lines for Negroes and Whites—Large Cities in the North*

THE FINDINGS

Since the regression lines for consumption of Whites and Negroes were not parallel in any situation examined, the hypothesis that race is a factor in the determination of consumption patterns is rejected. The calculated marginal propensities to consume vary greatly for both races in different sections of the country (Table 1) and this fact gives additional reason for rejecting the theory. The inference is clear that factors other than race are at work in the determination of consumption patterns. Although the data examined here do not rule race out as a factor in the determination of consumption patterns, they cast such serious reflections on the hypothesis as to make it, with all charity, useless. There are too many uncontrolled variables to warrant the conclusion that race alone is responsible for the difference in consumption patterns. It has become clear in this study that the concept of race as a factor in the statistical analyses of group

TABLE 2 *Schedule of Family Expenditures for Current Consumption Large Cities in the North*

Size of Family (1)	Money Income After Taxes (2)	Consumption Expenditures (3)	Unit of One	
			Money Income After Taxes (4) [(2) ÷ (1)]	Consumption Expenditures (5) [(3) ÷ (1)]
WHITE FAMILIES				
1.5	590	1,493	393	995
1.8	1,551	1,862	862	1,034
2.5	2,554	2,759	1,022	1,104
3.1	3,476	3,554	1,121	1,146
3.4	4,476	4,551	1,316	1,339
3.6	5,450	5,341	1,514	1,484
3.6	6,637	5,959	1,844	1,655
4.1	8,353	7,324	2,037	1,786
3.8	17,233	11,019	4,535	2,900
NEGRO FAMILIES				
1.3	682	739	525	568
2.1	1,493	1,608	711	766
2.9	2,542	2,667	877	920
3.3	3,464	3,353	1,049	1,016
4.1	4,373	4,406	1,067	1,075
3.5	5,401	5,914	1,543	1,690
3.6	6,447	5,631	1,791	1,564
7.0	8,221	7,775	1,174	1,110
5.7	11,959	9,682	2,098	1,699

Source: Bureau of Labor Statistics, *Study of Consumer Expenditures, Incomes, and Savings* (Tabulated by the Bureau of Labor Statistics for the Wharton School of Finance and Commerce, University of Pennsylvania, 1956), I, II, 138 in each.

economic behavior, such as in the assessment of so-called Negro-White savings and consumption patterns, has no more validity than left-handedness, eye pigmentation, or height.

Before any realistic comparison is made on the amount spent on consumption by Negroes and Whites, adjustments should be made for the difference in their income expectation, age, dependents, education, location, financial reserves, and similar factors. Once these adjustments are made, differences attributed to race may find their origin in other factors. For example,

(t)he tendency by Negroes to save more than whites at comparable income levels, which has been noted in previous studies, turns out to be completely attributable (except for incomes below $1,000) to the apparently much higher dissaving in cash and deposits by whites.

Professors and researchers have an obligation not only to find the truth but to make every effort to present their findings in such a way that they may not be distorted easily. The theory still prevails—even in academic circles—that at any given income level, Negroes spend less on consumption than Whites. The data examined here do not support that conclusion and there is an obligation upon the proponents of the theory to present data that support it.

[Notes]

1. The word "white," when it occurs as a noun, is capitalized as an aid to the reader.
2. See Milton Friedman, *A Theory of the Consumption Function* (Princeton, 1957); Horst Mendershausen, "Differences in Family Savings between Cities of Different Size and Location, Whites and Negroes," *The Review of Economics and Statistics,* XXII (August 1940); and James S. Duesenberry, *Income, Saving and the Theory of Consumer Behavior* (Cambridge, 1952).
3. M. F. Ashley Montague, *Man's Most Dangerous Myth: The Fallacy of Race* (New York, 1952), 1.
4. Cf. Friedman, 79–81.
5. Based upon the assumption that one has neither more nor less "race" as his income changes.
6. Data analyzed in this study are taken from Bureau of Labor Statistics, *Study of Consumer Expenditures, Incomes, and Savings* (Tabulated by the Bureau of Labor Statistics for the Wharton School of Finance and Commerce, University of Pennsylvania, 1956), Volumes I and II, Table 15, Summary of Family Accounts, 137–148 each volume.
7. There still remains within the data an unadjusted difference in the number of full-time wage earners between the two races in the various income classes.
8. Irving Friend and Stanley Schor, "Who Saves?" *The Review of Economics and Statistics,* XLI (May 1959), Part 2, 230.

20

Marcus Alexis

Some Negro-White Differences in Consumption

SINCE the end of World War II, there has been a growing interest in how Negro consumers spend their incomes. One of the reasons for this is the relative and absolute improvement in their economic position which has taken place since 1940.[1] American Negroes are now reported to command an annual spending power in excess of seventeen billion dollars.[2] Secondly, there is a marked migration of Negroes into urban centers in all sections of the country. Since Negroes for the most part reside in the heart of the larger cities and whites have been leaving for the suburbs in large numbers, there has been a large absolute and relative increase in the Negro population of most major cities.[3] The increase in relative market importance of Negroes in these areas has made it necessary to know more about their economic behavior. The belief of many sellers that Negroes spend their incomes differently from comparable income whites is a third reason for the interest.

The alleged difference in the spending behavior of Negroes and whites is attributed to the economic and social discrimination which has been part of the Negro's heritage. Not being able to live, relax or dine where they please, American Negroes are said to have developed consumption patterns different than those of their white counterparts.

In this article, budget data from several sources shall be analyzed to determine if there is any basis for the contention that Negro and white

Reprinted by permission from the *American Journal of Economics and Sociology*, Vol. 21, No. 1, January 1962, pp. 11–28. Some of the materials used here were developed for the author's Ph.D. dissertation at the University of Minnesota, "Racial Differences in Consumption and Automobile Ownership" (1959).

consumers with comparable means allocate their income differently to the following budget items: savings, food, housing, clothing, recreation and leisure, house furnishings and equipment and transportation (non-automobile and automobile).

1. SAVING BEHAVIOR

Major contributions to the literature of Negro and white saving behavior have been made by Mendershausen, Brady and Friedman, Tobin, Klein and Mooney and the Bureau of Labor Statistics.[4] With the exception of Klein and Mooney, whose data are from the Federal Reserve Board's Surveys of Consumer Finances, and the Bureau of Labor Statistics which collected its own data in a series of postwar surveys, the source of the data used is the *Consumer Purchases Study* of 1935–36.

In 1940, Mendershausen found differences in the savings of Negro and white families which were significant at the one per cent confidence level. He found that Negroes had smaller deficits or larger surpluses than comparable income whites and that the break-even income for Negroes was fifty per cent of what it was for whites.[5]

Brady and Friedman and Duesenberry also found that at comparable incomes Negroes save more than whites. They explain this by observing that it is the relative income position rather than the dollar income which determines savings. That is, savings are related to one's decile or per-centile rank in the income distribution. The higher the relative income position, the greater the savings. If separate income distributions are computed for Negro and white families, it will be found that a given income occupies a higher relative position in the Negro distribution than it does in the white. Consequently, one should expect Negroes to save more than whites. The same phenomenon exists in the savings of urban and rural families with equal incomes.

Brady and Friedman do not consider the relative income hypothesis to be capable of explaining all differences in savings between Negro and white families. They hold that the absolute differences in incomes of Negro and white families in the same relative income position are too large to be overcome by the relative income position.

Duesenberry, on the other hand, is satisfied with the results obtained when an adjustment has been made for the decile positions of the two groups.[6]

Professor Tobin's study supports the higher Negro savings findings of Mendershausen, Brady and Friedman and Duesenberry. He offers a competing hypothesis to explain observed differences. In this hypothesis assets play an important role.

The saving behavior of families below their break-even point will depend on the financial resources at their command. If they have no asset holdings or credit, their savings will be zero or positive to the amount of their contractual saving. But if they have asset holdings or credit, they will dissave or at least save less than their contractual saving. Availability of credit is to a large extent dependent on asset holdings and families are, if only because of the cost of borrowing more willing to draw out their own savings than go into debt. Therefore, the asset holdings of the families below their break-even point will determine the amount of their dissaving.[7]

The work of Klein and Mooney is the most exhaustive treatment of Negro and white saving behavior included in this paper. Their definition of saving is essentially a measure of change in net worth. This definition excludes changes in cash on hand from saving. This is an important fact because they find that upper-income Negroes save less than southern whites or northern Negroes with the same incomes. Because prosperous southern Negroes are sometimes reluctant to reveal how well off they are, they may choose not to use such conventional means of saving as saving accounts, ownership of marketable securities or life insurance, but may choose to hold cash instead.[8] Another possible explanation is that upper-income Negroes in the south have much greater social responsibilities which compel them to have higher consumption standards than comparable income whites, but not as high as white community leaders with much higher incomes.

In his study of the urban Negro consumer, Edwards reached the same conclusion as Klein and Mooney regarding the social responsibilities of upper income Negroes. He reported that these individuals often do not have the income of the leaders of the white society, and as a result cannot maintain the same standards of consumption. He also noted that leaders of the Negro community spend beyond their means when compared with whites having the same incomes. However, since their economic foundation cannot support truly high consumption patterns, their consumption falls far short of the standards they emulate.[10]

Other important findings are: northern Negroes save more than comparable income northern whites; at the lower ranges of disposable income, southern Negroes save more than southern whites, northern whites or northern Negroes.[11]

Klein and Mooney find assets to be important in all income groups except upper-income southern Negroes. They also support Tobin's assertion that at lower income levels the higher saving of Negroes is attributable primarily to smaller average decreases in their liquid asset holdings and not to miscellaneous saving.[12]

It is interesting to note that the higher savings of Negroes at comparable income levels persist when purchases of consumer durables are included in the definition of saving.

Several explanatory variables are found to be statistically significant either by themselves or in combination with other variables at the one per cent confidence interval. These variables are: liquid assets (at the beginning of the year); disposable income X liquid assets; race X disposable income X liquid assets. A group of variables related to job security are also found to be significant at the one per cent confidence interval. They are: disposable income and job security; disposable income, job security and liquid assets; race, liquid assets and job security.

The significant interactions found between job security and other variables are largely the result of the saving behavior of one group—the self-employed but not working. This group is responsible in large measure for the relatively great dissavings shown by whites at the lower income levels.

The significant interaction between race, liquid assets and job security fits into the scheme of Negro job security and asset holdings described by the AFL-CIO Economic Policy Committee.

> Since most of them were employed in lower paying jobs before they were laid off, they have slimmer resources to fall back on when unemployment strikes.[13]

Negroes have poorer job security; when they are employed, their jobs are generally those yielding lower incomes. Consequently, their assets are not great. Their incomes are not high enough for them to accumulate much savings. Thus the market for Negro labor affects all the variables found to be significant: income, assets, and job security.

Klein and Mooney also sought institutional explanations for their findings. They observed that at the lower income levels, non-farm, non-business Negroes were more often than comparable whites employed in occupations in which they received non-money income. The inclusion of the dollar value of this income would move the savings ratios of low income Negroes closer to those of comparable whites.

Two hypotheses, that Negroes have greater difficulty obtaining credit, and that Negroes have less income mobility, are not confirmed by Klein and Mooney. The credit hypothesis is rejected on the basis of the higher proportion of credit sales to Negroes than to whites. It is realized that this test is by no means conclusive, but in the absence of other empirical information to the contrary, they accept it. An alternative measure of the credit availability of Negroes would be the acceptance rate of Negro applicants and the acceptance rate of comparable white applicants. Credit may be more rationed to Negroes because of their lower income levels, but if comparable whites are rejected at the same rate, this cannot be said to be attributable to race.

No evidence was found to substantiate the belief that a greater proportion of whites have incomes which are down temporarily than do Negroes. This does not constitute a complete rejection of the hypothesis that Negroes have less income mobility than whites. It would still remain to be shown that the income horizon of Negroes is no lower than it is for comparable whites. If people could predict their future incomes with a reasonably high degree of accuracy, say within twenty per cent of the actual income achieved in ten or twenty years, the potential income could possibly influence current purchases.

Perhaps one of the more significant contributions of Klein and Mooney is their observation that economic variables alone do not reveal the factors making for the differences in the consumption of Negroes and comparable whites.

> Negroes can work only in certain occupations; they have less job security than whites; they are not freely permitted to buy certain types of goods and services; they have a different family structure; they have a peculiar population distribution. Surely these factors cannot be altogether neglected while one looks only at income and wealth variables for the study of savings behavior. It is to be emphasized that income and wealth variables are not reliable indicators of the noneconomic variables needed. They are only partially correlated with some of these additional variables.[14]

Usable information from the Bureau of Labor Statistics study of family income and expenditures in 1947 is broken down by race for Washington, D.C. As in previous studies, total consumption expenditures of Negroes are shown to be less than they are for the comparable income whites.[15]

In 1948, the Bureau of Labor Statistics conducted a series of budget studies in the cities of Denver, Colorado; Detroit, Michigan; and Houston, Texas. Data for Detroit and Houston are available by race. In both cities, the savings of Negro families were greater than they were for comparable income white families.[16] The 1949 Memphis study produced similar results.[17]

In both the 1947 and the 1948 studies, not only were aggregate savings more for Negro families, but a breakdown of the average surpluses and deficits of families reporting one or the other revealed that the average surpluses were higher, and average deficits were lower for Negro than they were for white families.

The studies of Mendershausen, Brady and Friedman, Duesenberry, Tobin, and Klein and Mooney and the Bureau of Labor Statistics consistently reveal a higher propensity to save for Negroes than for whites at comparable income levels. It follows that if Negroes save more than whites at each income level, Negroes and whites must differ in the way they allocate their incomes to various classes of consumer goods. More specifically, there must be at least one class of consumer goods for which Negroes and whites in the same income class spend different amounts. If this were not true, it would be impossible for Negroes and whites to have different amounts of saving (or dissaving) at the same income levels.

In the presentation below, attention will be focused on investigations which shed light on the differential expenditure patterns of Negro and white consumers for food, housing, clothing, house furnishings, recreation, medical care, transportation (non-automobile and automobile). Several studies shall be analyzed in order to arrive at general conclusions regarding racial patterns of consumption of these goods.

2. EXPENDITURES FOR FOOD

The most comprehensive studies of urban Negro consumption available are those of Paul K. Edwards.[18] He presents an integrated economic and sociological approach to the subject.

In comparing the food expenditures of Nashville Negroes with Bureau of Labor Statistics estimates for white labor families, Edwards found:

> For practically every income class of white labor families in the several southern cities included in the Bureau's analysis, the adjusted food expenditure percentages are considerably higher than those for Nashville Negro labor families. This would tend to indicate that the southern urban Negro labor family spends a smaller proportion of its income for food than do white families of like occupation and income. This finding is not surprising in view of the fact that large numbers of Negroes are employed in domestic service and in restaurants and hotels, where the food they consume on the job does not enter in home food costs. For instance, 44 percent of the women gainfully employed in the sample of Negro labor families studied in Nashville with incomes ranging from $1200 to $1500 per annum were in domestic service.[19]

Using data taken from the Consumer Purchases Study for the monumental study by Myrdal of the Negro's status in American life, *An American Dilemma*, Richard Sterner calculates that Negro families in southern villages spend 43 per cent of their income and Negro families in Atlanta and New York spend 34 per cent of their incomes for food. White families in the southern villages, and in Atlanta, spend on the average between 28 and 32 per cent of their incomes for food. These estimates are based on the average income of Negro and white families respectively.[20]

These percentages must be viewed cautiously. A greater relative expenditure for food by Negro families might be due to the operation of Engel's law. Low income families will certainly spend a greater proportion of their incomes on necessities than families with higher incomes. Since Negroes usually have lower incomes than whites in the same communities, this is very likely an income effect. There is evidence, moreover, that after data have been adjusted for differences in incomes, Negro units spend a smaller proportion of their incomes for food than whites.

Sterner, himself, supplies the evidence to support the belief that the relatively greater food expenditures for Negro families do not hold up when an income adjustment is made. He indicates that Negro families devote a smaller proportion of their incomes to food than do comparable income whites. With increases in incomes, however, Negro families increase their consumption of protein foods more rapidly than do white families. This is very likely traceable to another finding of Sterner, namely, that Negro families tend to spend less for milk, cream, cheese, vegetables, and fruits than white families in the same income class. With a rise in their incomes, these Negro families increase their consumption of foods which are not adequately represented in their diets at the lower income levels.[21] A related phenomenon is reported by Humes. She found that though Negroes spent less per person for food than whites at given income levels, this difference was due to the types of food purchased, not the quantity.[22] This observation helps to explain how Negro families manage to spend less for food.

In 1947 the Bureau of Labor Statistics found that Washington, D.C., Negroes spent slightly more for food than comparable income Washington, D.C., white families at the $1,000–$2,000 and at the $3,000–$4,000 income levels.[23]

A breakdown of consumption expenditures made in the 1948 Bureau of Labor Statistics study revealed that Detroit Negro families spent less for food than comparable income white families at every income level, except the $2,000–$3,000. This is in spite of the fact that the average size of Negro families was at least equal to the average size of white families at all income levels. Houston Negroes spent fewer dollars for food at every income level than did whites.[24]

The Bureau of Labor Statistics survey of consumer spending in Memphis exhibits the same food expenditure pattern found in Detroit, Houston, and Washington. At all income levels, except the $4,000–$5,000 level, Negroes spent less for food than did comparable income whites, in spite of the fact that Negro families were larger than comparable income white families. At the $4,000–$5,000 level, the larger average family size of Negro consumers was enough to compensate for the smaller expenditure per person, but at this level also, the expenditure per person for Negro families was less than it was for white families.[25]

A Washington, D.C., Afro-American study offers additional evidence. The section of the study dealing with food consumption by the 525 Negro and 525 white families sampled showed the same behavior already noted in previous studies. Negro families spent less for food than white families with whom they were compared. This is so despite the fact that the average size of Negro families was 4.3 persons, and that of white families was 3.4 persons.[26]

Using data collected by the Bureau of Labor Statistics in 1950 and 1951 and tabulated at the Wharton School of Finance and Commerce, Friend and Kravis calculated food expenditures for selected groups of Negroes and whites. They report their findings in terms of the relative per cent of Negro and white expenditures. Negroes were found to universally spend less for food than comparable income whites except for small cities in the south at the $2,000–$3,000 income level. Here, Negroes spent a mere .9 percent more than comparable income white families.[27]

These studies indicate an overwhelming tendency for Negro families to spend less for food than comparable income white families. One commodity group for which Negroes and whites spend differently has been found. The extent to which this is true for others is explored below.

3. EXPENDITURES FOR HOUSING

Sterner's research on housing indicated that Negro and white families spent the same proportion of their incomes for housing in the southern villages. In a metropolitan area such as New York City, however, the proportion spent on housing by Negro families was slightly higher than it was for white families.[28] Here again, we find evidence which is probably an income effect. Negroes probably spend a greater proportion of their incomes for necessities than do whites because they have lower incomes.

It is interesting to note that in Sterner's study, the proportion of income spent for housing by Negro and white families in southern villages was the same. Friend and Kravis found that for Negro and white families with the same incomes in the south in general, and this included some small southern cities, Negro families spent a smaller proportion of their incomes for housing than did whites.[29] This evidence adds weight to the belief that Sterner's observation is an income effect.

The 1947 Bureau of Labor Statistics budget studies analyzed by Humes revealed that Washington, D.C., Negroes spent more for housing than did comparable income whites at all income levels except $2,000–$3,000. The 1948 and 1949 studies yield results which are the direct opposite of the 1947 study. At every income level in these cities (Detroit, Houston, and Memphis), Negro families spent a smaller proportion of their incomes for housing than similarly situated whites.[30]

The 1948 and 1949 Bureau of Labor Statistics and Friend and Kravis' data are more current, more detailed, and more inclusive than Sterner's. Since these data are classified by income class, the observations are not due to the greater frequency of low income families among the Negroes than among the whites. Sterner's data suffer from a lack of income comparisons of this type. Hence more confidence should be placed in the Bureau of Labor Statistics and Friend and Kravis' observations.

A general conclusion which may be drawn on the basis of the evidence presented is that Negroes spend less for housing than do comparable income whites.

4. EXPENDITURES FOR CLOTHING

Expenditures for clothing are important budget items. Furthermore, there are characteristics of the demand for clothing that suggest that this commodity serves as more than a protective covering for the body. For example: it is commonly argued that Negroes spend more for clothing than do whites. It is further argued that Negroes are not as price conscious as white buyers. The greater emphasis of Negroes on clothing is attributed to the inability of Negroes to purchase some forms of recreation and shelter. Clothing becomes a substitute for these inaccessible alternatives. Such price behavior is difficult to understand when one considers the typically lower incomes in the Negro population.

Extensive investigation carried out by Edwards in Nashville, Birmingham, and Richmond, Virginia, supported the general notion that Negroes were paying at least as much for clothing as white individuals with equal income. Specifically, it was found that Negro common laborers were paying as much for their clothing as were white semi-skilled workers. Negro professionals were paying as much, and in some cases more for their clothing, than white teachers, nurses, clergymen, and merchants. The interesting fact here is that the Negro professional group sampled consisted largely of teachers. The income of these Negroes could not be considered as high, especially when contrasted with the white merchants who constituted a large proportion of the white professional class.[31]

Edwards' observations refer to total expenditures for clothing, not to the prices paid for specific articles. In Edwards' work, there is ample evidence that the assumed lack of concern about prices attributed to Negroes is an accurate representation of their actual behavior.

In view of the relatively low earnings of the great majority of Negro families on the one hand and of their keen desire for wearing apparel on the other the Negro is a persistent shopper or bargain hunter, particularly in the purchase of small articles of clothing and also shoes.[32]

It is not surprising . . . 55.4 percent of the housewives and the family heads interviewed in Birmingham, 72 percent of those interviewed in Atlanta, and 75 percent in Richmond have mentioned price as the most important determinant of the direction of their trade.[33]

In a study of Negro newspapers, Consuello Young found Negro readers to be unhappy about the absence of price-line advertising in the Negro press. Furthermore, she pointed out that Negro readers consulted their local newspapers for this information. This indicates that Negro shoppers are indeed concerned about price.[34]

Some observers seem to be confused by the difference between buyers interested in quality or prestige merchandise and those who do not relate price to quality. Negro buyers certainly do not fall into the latter category. There are some very good nonprice reasons why Negro consumers should be particular about the merchandise they purchase. Several investigators have certified that in community there is a strong desire to wear fashionable clothes, drive expensive automobiles, and generally engage in conspicuous consumption because this is the means by which one gains status.[35] There are also alternative explanations of any observed tendencies on the part of Negroes to shop at the better stores.

The purchases of clothing in the better stores by Negroes may be explained on the basis of the protection such stores offer and for which Negro consumers are willing to pay. A history of having shoddy merchandise passed off on them has made Negroes skeptical of unbranded merchandise.[36] Credit availability is also important. Negroes have been able to afford some higher priced garments because they have not had to purchase as many units as comparable income whites. This is a by-product of the relatively large Negro employment in domestic services. The receipt of second-hand clothing by domestics releases some income to pay higher prices for the units purchased.

Several interesting observations regarding the importance of clothing to Negro and white families are found in *The Negro's Share.* Urban Negroes are found to spend a slightly greater proportion of a given income for clothing than comparable income city whites. As incomes rise, both races increase their consumption of clothing at a faster rate than they increase total consumption. It is also found that wives, without regard to race, increase their expenditures for clothing more rapidly than their husbands when incomes rise.[37]

According to the Bureau of Labor Statistics, Detroit Negroes spent more for clothing at all income levels than did whites. In Memphis and Washington, D.C., Negroes spent more for clothing than did whites at all but one income level (the Memphis and Washington, D.C., income levels referred to were not the same). In Houston whites spent more at all income levels than did Negroes except one. Friend and Kravis also report that Negroes consistently spend more for clothing than whites.[38]

5. EXPENDITURES FOR RECREATION AND LEISURE

It is reasonable to expect that the restrictions on leisure and recreation will produce racial expenditure patterns for them which differ in kind and possibly in magnitude also. Edwards found that Negroes in his sample allocated a larger share of their budgets to social requirements than did whites with comparable incomes.

> Social requirements . . . seem to make relatively larger financial demands upon each of the several occupational classes of the Negro community than upon the corresponding class of the white community. This is particularly true of the business and professional groups whose social and civic responsibilities fall early because of leadership responsibilities and small numbers.[39]

This view is not supported by Sterner, who observed:

> Negroes spend less than whites for recreation both in general and at corresponding income levels.[40]

He also observed that with increases in income the amount spent on recreation and the varieties of recreation increased pronouncedly.

In the Bureau of Labor Statistics studies, Detroit Negroes spent more for recreation at all income levels than did comparable white families. In Houston, Negro families spent more for recreation than did comparable white families at all but one income level. Memphis Negroes, on the other hand, spent less on recreation at all but two income levels than did comparable whites, and Washington, D.C., Negroes spent less than did their white counterparts at all income levels.[41]

Friend and Kravis found expenditures for recreation by Negro consumers to be less than the recreation expenditures of comparable income white consumers. In the large cities of the north, expenditures of Negroes more closely approximated the level of whites. Even here, however, Negro consumers spent at least 12.7 percent less than did their white counterparts.[42]

The apparent inconsistency between the findings of Friend and Kravis, and Edwards and the Bureau of Labor Statistics data for Detroit and Houston may be nothing more than a matter of definition of terms.

Friend and Kravis use a catch-all term, "recreation etc." as their measure of social expenditures. The Bureau of Labor Statistics, however, separates recreation from reading and education. Negro families usually spend less for reading and education than comparable income white families. Thus if the "recreation etc." measure is employed, it could very easily result in a smaller expenditure for "social responsibilities" for Negro families than it does for comparable income whites. While this may serve to explain differences in the data of Friend and Kravis and the Bureau of Labor Statistics data for Detroit and Houston, it does not reconcile differences within the Bureau of Labor Statistics data which are not due to differences in definition. It is possible that the differences observed within the Bureau of Labor Statistics' data are due to basic differences in the social structure of the cities of Detroit and Houston on the one hand and Memphis and Washington, D.C., on the other.

Frazier has observed that the consumption standards of upper-class Negroes are set by the wealthiest members of the class, and that as Negroes become integrated into the life of the community, the clerical worker or professional man or woman escapes from the social obligations of his (her) upper-class role in the Negro community.[43]

The average length of time upper-class Negroes have been in desegregated communities and the degree of desegregation might serve as good indicators of their assimilation of white consumption patterns. Other factors to consider are the percentage of Negro professionals in the total population and the recreational outlets available to Negroes.

6. EXPENDITURES FOR HOUSE FURNISHINGS AND EQUIPMENT

Edwards' data on expenditures for house furnishings and equipment by Negro and white low income urban families reveal that Negro families have smaller average expenditures.

> On the average, the Negro common and semi-skilled labor family probably does not spend more than one or two percent of annual income for house furnishings and equipment, whereas the low income urban white family budget will usually yield in the vicinity of 4% for this purpose.[44]

Sterner's findings corroborate Edwards'. He finds that Negro families spend less than their white counterparts for house furnishings and equipment.

> Even when Negro families had the same incomes as white families they spent less on the average for furnishings and equipment. Among both groups average expenditures for such goods increased with income, but in neither group was the proportion of the total budget allotted to this category clearly related to income.[45]

Friend and Kravis report that average expenditures for furniture and equipment of Negro families at the $2,000–$3,000 income level in large cities in the North and in the South at the $4,000–$5,000 income level, are larger than for white families with equal incomes.[46]

The Bureau of Labor Statistics data are not entirely consistent with those of Sterner and Edwards or Friend and Kravis. Negro families in Washington, D.C., spent less for furniture and equipment than did comparable whites at all income levels. Detroit Negro families spent more for furniture and equipment than did comparable white families at all income levels. Houston Negro families, for whom less information is available, spent less than did white families at the $1,000–$2,000 income level, but spent more at the $2,000–$3,000 income level, and as much at the $3,000–$4,000 income level. Memphis Negroes spent more at two income levels and less at three.[47]

Time seems to be an important factor in determining the relative levels of furniture and equipment expenditures for Negro and white families. The Sterner and Edwards studies are older than the Bureau of Labor Statistics and Wharton School data used by Friend and Kravis. This, though, does not explain all observed differences, especially in later data.

As in the case of recreation Detroit Negroes spent more than comparable income whites and Washington, D.C., Negroes spent less. Much of the net emigration out of southern rural communities is accounted for by the movement of Negroes.[48] Negro families are more apt to be in the process of making the transition from rural to urban life. Consequently, they are most likely to need household equipment and furniture. It would be valuable to have a measure of the relative number of Negroes in Washington, D.C., Detroit, and Houston who are newcomers to urban living. Estimates of the absolute and relative growth of the Negro urban populations are available, but they do not reveal the migrants' point of origin.

Another possible determinant of expenditures for household equipment and furniture could be the average annual income of the respondents over a period of say, five or ten years prior to the survey. A plausible hypothesis is that families which had low average annual incomes prior to the reference period and whose incomes have increased by more than the cost of living will probably be the families making the largest outlays for furniture and equipment within the various income groups. Relatively more Negroes have been making the transition from low income rural employment to higher income unskilled urban employment since 1940. Thus, one would expect outlays for furniture and equipment by Negro families in the post-1940 studies to be higher in general—and this is the case. Needless to say, this discussion is all conjecture. Before any more valid statements can be made, research on the kinds of data suggested would have to be made.

7. EXPENDITURES FOR MEDICAL CARE

Sterner found that Negroes devoted a smaller share of their budget to medical care than did white consumers.[49]

Since his data are not classified by income classes, it is quite possible that Edwards' comparisons are of the type suggested earlier, namely, lower relative shares of the budget of low income Negroes being devoted to non-necessities than is true for higher income whites. However, in each of the Bureau of Labor Statistics surveys, Negroes are also found to spend less for medical care at all income levels than their white counterparts;[50] and Friend and Kravis also found Negro consumers spend less for medical care at all income levels.[51] The record is quite clear. Negroes spend less at every income level for medical care than comparable income whites.

A possible explanation for the low medical care expenditures consistently reported for Negroes is that Negro families having become urbanized more recently are not as well habituated to seeking professional counsel for some of their ailments. They make greater use of home remedies and patent medicine.[52]

8. EXPENDITURES FOR NON-AUTOMOBILE TRANSPORTATION

The discussion of the expenditures of low income Negroes and whites to be found in "Distinctive Characteristics of Urban Negro Consumption" is an excellent example of the effect of social conditions of market behavior.

> . . . Negroes in domestic service commonly receive carfare to and from work in addition to wages. This reduces personal transportation costs to a point considerably below the level of expenditures for this item by white laborers. Studies of the Bureau of Labor Statistics indicate an average expenditure of about 9 percent for transportation by low income white families; only 2 percent by low income Negro families.[53]

Since the completion of Edwards' study, Negro employment in the service industries has experienced a secular decline. Consequently, carfare as a part of total compensation has declined in importance. At the same time, there is evidence that the frequency of automobile ownership among Negro families is lower than among comparable income white families.[54] Thus one would expect that non-automobile transportation expenditures would be higher for Negro than white families in the same income grouping. An investigation of the Bureau of Labor Statistics studies of 1947 and 1948, and of the data interpreted by Friend and Kravis indicates that this is true for the cities of Washington, D.C. (except at the $1,000–$2,000 income level), Detroit, Houston and Memphis (at all income levels), and is generally the case in the Friend and Kravis data also for comparable income groups. Thus, one can state that in general Negroes spend more for non-automobile transportation than comparable income whites.[55]

9. AUTOMOBILE TRANSPORTATION

The only data available on outlays for automobile transportation are to be found in the Bureau of Labor Statistics studies and in the work of Friend and Kravis.

The Bureau of Labor Statistics and Friend and Kravis indicate an overwhelming tendency for white consumers to spend more for automobile expenses at comparable income levels than Negro consumers. Whites at all income levels in Washington, D.C., and Houston spent more for automobile services than did Negroes with equal incomes. Detroit whites spent more than Negroes at all income levels except the $4,000–$5,000. In Memphis, whites spent more for automobile services than did their Negro counterparts at all income levels below $5,000. The data for incomes above $5,000 are not truly comparable. But Memphis Negroes in the $5,000–$7,000 income bracket spent more for the services of their automobiles than did whites in either the $5,000–$6,000 or the $6,000–$7,000 income brackets. Friend and Kravis also report that Negroes spend less for automotive services than do whites at comparable income levels. There is no question that these data consistently point to lower automobile expenditures for Negroes than comparable whites.[56]

10. CONCLUSION

Table 1 summarizes the findings presented in the data introduced in the hope of shedding some light on potential differences which might exist in the consumption propensities of Negroes and whites. When all the data have been digested, the following major findings emerge:

1. Total consumption expenditures of Negroes are less than for comparable income whites, or, Negroes save more out of a given income than do whites with the same incomes.
2. Negro consumers spend more for clothing and non-automobile transportation and less for food, housing, medical care and automobile transportation than do comparable income whites.
3. There is no consistent racial difference in expenditures for either recreation and leisure or home furnishing and equipment at comparable income levels.

Because of the increased importance of Negro consumers in urban markets, it is prudent to state that race as a consumption variable warrants more attention from economists and marketers than it has received thus far.

It is impossible to predict with any accuracy when Negroes shall be accorded all the rights and privileges which whites take for granted. It is very likely, however, that observed differences in consumer behavior will continue to be influenced by differences in the socio-economic environment.

TABLE 1 Summary Statement of Findings for Studies Covered by Whether Negroes Spent More or Less Than Comparable Whites

Study	Food	Housing	Clothing	Recreation and Leisure	Home Furnishings and Equipment	Medical Care	Auto Transportation	Non-auto Transportation
Edwards	less	less	more	more	less	—	—	—
Sterner	less	more[a]	more	less	less	less	—	—
B. L. S. Detroit	less	less	more	more	more	less	less	more
B. L. S. Houston	less	less	less	more	less	less	less	more
B. L. S. Washington	more	more	more	less	less	less	less	more
B. L. S. Memphis	less	less	more	less	mixed	less	less	more
Friend and Kravis	less	less	more	less	more	less	less	more
Fact Finders	less	—	—	—	—	—	—	—

[a] In the southern villages there was no difference.
Edwards and Sterner discuss transportation, but do not make a breakdown by auto and non-auto.

272

[Notes]

1. *Negroes in the United States: Their Employment and Economic Status,* United States Department of Labor, Bulletin No. 1119, Washington, U. S. Government Printing Office, 1952, p. 24.
2. Arch Parsons, Jr., "Mitchell Cites Progress by Negroes in 15 Years," *New York Herald Tribune,* Nov. 25, 1957.
3. "The Vast Buying Power of Negro America for Your Products," Chicago, *Ebony Magazine,* 1958, p. 4. Jay M. Gould, "What Population Boom Means to You," *Marketing in Transition,* ed. Alfred L. Seelye, New York, Harper, 1958, p. 3.
4. Horst Mendershausen, "Differences in Family Savings Between Cities of Different Size and Location, Whites and Negroes," *Review of Economic Statistics,* 22 (August, 1940), pp. 122–37. Dorothy S. Brady and Rose D. Friedman, "Savings and the Income Distribution," *Studies in Income and Wealth,* New York, National Bureau of Economic Research, 1947, pp. 247–65. James S. Duesenberry, *Income, Saving and the Theory of Consumer Behavior,* Cambridge, Harvard University Press, 1949. James Tobin, "Relative Income, Absolute Income and Saving," *Money, Trade and Economic Growth,* New York, Macmillan, 1951, pp. 135–56. Lawrence R. Klein and H. W. Mooney, "Negro-White Savings Differentials and the Consumption Function Problem," *Econometrics,* 21 (July, 1953), pp. 425–46. Helen H. Humes, "Family Income and Expenditures in 1947," *Monthly Labor Review,* 68 (April, 1949), pp. 389–97. This article is reprinted as Bureau of Labor Statistics Serial No. R. 1956. All references are to Serial No. R. 1956. "Consumer Spending: Denver, Detroit and Houston, 1948," U. S. Bureau of Labor Statistics, Serial No. R. 1948. Mary C. Ruark and George H. Mulcahy, "Family Spending in Memphis, 1949," *Monthly Labor Review,* 72 (June, 1951), pp. 655–61.
5. Mendershausen, *loc. cit.,* p. 131.
6. Duesenberry, *op. cit.,* p. 50.
7. Tobin, *loc. cit.,* p. 144.
8. Allison Davis, Burleigh B. Gardner and Mary R. Gardner, *Deep South,* Chicago, University of Chicago Press, 1941, pp. 454, 466, 474, 481, 482.
9. Klein and Mooney, *loc. cit.,* p. 455.
10. *Cf.* Paul K. Edwards, "Distinctive Characteristics of Urban Negro Consumption" (Unpublished D. C. S. dissertation, Harvard University, 1936), pp. 137–8; E. Franklin Frazier, *Black Bourgeoisie,* Glencoe, Illinois, Free Press, 1957, pp. 195–212.
11. Klein and Mooney, *loc. cit.,* pp. 428–9.
12. *Ibid.,* p. 450.
13. "Still the First to Be Fired: Negro Unemployment," *Economic Trends and Outlook* (May–June, 1958), p. 3.
14. Klein and Mooney, *loc. cit.,* p. 430.
15. Humes, *loc. cit.,* p. 5.
16. "Consumer Spending: Denver, Detroit, and Houston, 1948," *loc. cit.,* pp. 5, 13.
17. Ruark and Mulcahy, *loc. cit.*
18. *Cf.* Paul K. Edwards, "The Negro Commodity Market," *Harvard Business School Bulletin,* 8 (May, 1932), pp. 242–44. Paul K. Edwards, "Distinctive Characteristics of Urban Negro Consumption," *loc. cit.* Paul K. Edwards, *The Southern Urban Negro as a Consumer,* New York, Prentice-Hall, 1932.
19. Paul K. Edwards, *The Southern Urban Negro as a Consumer,* pp. 42–3, n. 14.
20. Richard Sterner, *et al., The Negro's Share,* New York, Harper, 1943, p. 95.
21. Sterner, *op. cit.,* p. 95.

22. Helen H. Humes, "Family Food Expenditures, 1947 and 1948," *Monthly Labor Review* (June, 1949), p. 628.
23. Humes, "Family Income and Expenditures in 1947," *loc. cit.*, p. 5.
24. "Consumer Spending: Denver, Detroit and Houston, 1948," *loc. cit.*, pp. 5, 13.
25. Ruark and Mulcahy, *loc. cit.*
26. Fact Finders Incorporated, *Analysis of 525 Washington, D.C., Negro Families Who Read the Afro-American Compared With 525 White Families Living in Homes of Similar Rent or Value,* Washington, D.C., Afro-American Newspapers, 1953, p. 7.
27. Irwin Friend and Irving B. Kravis, "New Light on the Consumer Market," *Harvard Business Review,* 35 (January–February, 1957), p. 113.
28. Sterner, *op. cit.,* p. 99.
29. Friend and Kravis, *loc. cit.*
30. Humes, "Family Income and Expenditures in 1947," *loc. cit.* "Consumer Spending: Denver, Detroit and Houston, 1948," *loc. cit.* Ruark and Mulcahy, *loc. cit.*
31. Edwards, "The Negro Commodity Market," *op. cit.,* p. 244.
32. Edwards, *The Southern Urban Negro as a Consumer,* p. 96.
33. *Ibid.,* pp. 96–7.
34. Consuello Young, "Reader Attitudes Towards the Negro Press," *Journalism Quarterly,* 21 (June, 1944), p. 149.
35. David, Gardner and Gardner, *op. cit.,* pp. 243–4. Frazier, *op. cit.,* pp. 200–03.
36. "The Forgotten 15,000,000. . . . Three Years Later," *Sponsor,* 3 (October 24, 1949), p. 76.
37. Sterner, *op. cit.,* pp. 137–9.
38. Humes, "Family Incomes and Expenditures in 1947," *loc. cit.,* p. 5. "Consumer Spending: Denver, Detroit and Houston, 1948," *loc. cit.,* pp. 7, 11. Ruark and Mulcahy, *loc. cit.* Friend and Kravis, *loc. cit.*
39. Edwards, "Distinctive Characteristics of Urban Negro Consumption," *loc. cit.,* pp. 137–8.
40. Sterner, *op. cit.,* p. 156.
41. Humes, "Family Income and Expenditures in 1947," *loc. cit.* "Consumer Spending: Denver, Detroit and Houston, 1948," *loc. cit.* Ruark and Mulcahy, *loc. cit.*
42. Friend and Kravis, *loc. cit.*
43. E. Franklin Frazier, *The Negro in America,* pp. 294–5, 300.
44. Edwards, "Distinctive Characteristics of Urban Negro Consumption," p. 155.
45. Sterner, *op. cit.,* p. 133.
46. Friend and Kravis, *loc. cit.*
47. Humes, "Family Income and Expenditures in 1947," *loc. cit.* "Consumer Spending: Denver, Detroit and Houston, 1948," *loc. cit.* Ruark and Mulcahy, *loc. cit.*
48. Gould, *loc. cit.*
49. Sterner, *loc. cit.,* p. 99.
50. Humes, "Family Income and Expenditures in 1947," *loc. cit.* "Consumer Spending: Denver, Detroit and Houston, 1948," *loc. cit.* Ruark and Mulcahy, *loc. cit.*
51. Friend and Kravis, *loc. cit.*
52. H. A. Haring, "Selling to Harlem," *Advertising and Selling,* 11 (October 31, 1928), pp. 18, 50.
53. Edwards, "Distinctive Characteristics of Urban Negro Consumption," p. 156.
54. Marcus Alexis, "Racial Differences in Consumption and Automobile Ownership," (Unpublished Ph.D. dissertation, University of Minnesota, 1959), chapter 5.
55. Humes, "Family Income and Expenditures in 1947," *loc. cit.* "Consumer Spending: Denver, Detroit and Houston, 1948," *loc. cit.* Ruark and Mulcahy, *loc. cit.*
56. *Ibid.*

21

James E. Stafford
Keith K. Cox
James B. Higginbotham

Some Consumption Pattern Differences Between Urban Whites and Negroes

DURING the past 20 years, the "Negro market" has been virtually ignored in the United States, except by a few farsighted companies. Most mass-market–oriented firms assumed that the advertising message, as well as the product itself, reached the Negro, even though both were directed almost exclusively at the white audience. As a result, few companies have realized their potential with Negro consumers, and many opportunities have been overlooked. In recent years, however, increased political, social, and economic pressure has forced more companies either to consider for the first time, or to re-evaluate, the nature of the Negro market.

A very basic question being asked is, "Does a Negro market really exist?" The answer appears, on the surface, to be a simple and straight-forward "yes." If the problem is carefully delineated, however, it is found that there are several sides to the question, and they must be uncovered, evaluated, and integrated before a definitive answer can be stated. Several studies, for example, have noted that the Negro market is a distinct geographic, social, and psychological reality based not only on certain physical characteristics, but also on common experiences of exclusion and depriva-tion.[1] Similarly, from an economics standpoint, there is little doubt that

Reprinted by permission from the *Social Science Quarterly*, Vol. 49, No. 3, December 1968, pp. 619–630.

Negroes constitute a segment of the population separate from the majority of whites. The Negro's relatively low economic status is clearly demonstrated by the fact that 35 percent of Negro families had incomes below $3,000 in 1965, compared with only 14 percent of white families. At the other end of the spectrum, 42 percent of the white families had family incomes greater than $8,000, while only 16 percent of the Negroes had comparable family incomes.[2] When these facts, plus other enlightening economic comparisons, are coupled with the severe educational and housing deprivations suffered by Negroes, it should be no great revelation to learn that, on an aggregate basis, Negroes have distinct consumption patterns, relative to whites.[3] Some of these same economists, however, have argued that even when income discrepancies are controlled statistically, comparable Negroes and whites still allocate their incomes differently. The alleged difference in spending behavior of Negroes and whites is attributed to the economic and social discrimination which has been part of the Negro heritage. Not being able to live, relax, or dine where they please, American Negroes are said to have developed aggregate consumption patterns different from those of their white counterparts.[4]

It is apparent from the foregoing discussion that Negroes, as a group of individuals having certain characteristics and behavior patterns in common with—yet distant from—whites, could be viewed as a "market." To marketers, however, such a segment exists only to the extent that Negroes *behave differently* from whites *as consumers*. A group of individuals with certain characteristics in common does not, in itself, constitute a realistic market segment. Only when people have common characteristics as consumers may they be thought of as a market segment.

Marketers, therefore, are basically concerned with determining if consumption-pattern differences exist between Negroes and whites and, if they do, whether they are attributable to income differentials, racial differences, or other factors often overlooked.[5] It may be that race, for example, is secondary to income as an influence on purchase behavior; in fact, it is conceivable that 100 percent of the consumption-pattern differences between Negroes and whites could be accounted for by income and other sociodemographic differentials. Klein and Mooney reach somewhat the same conclusion when they state that "this explanation of racial differentials is not solely adequate" to explain consumption differences. They go on to say that the "effects of [socio]demographic variables have been found to be statistically significant. . . . but not clear in direction."[6]

In the study reported here, the authors hoped to shed light on the problem of Negro-white consumption-pattern differences over and above that shed by earlier studies. These studies approached the comparisons on a macro-economic level, that is, their basic concern was to make aggregate comparisons of how Negroes and whites allocated their incomes. More specifically, the purposes of the present study were (1) to determine if there existed between Negroes and whites consumption-pattern differences which were not accounted for by income differentials, and (2) to specify, where possible, the nature or possible origin(s) of those differences.

METHODOLOGY

SAMPLE

The consumption-pattern data for both Negro and white housewives was taken from a large-scale commercial survey conducted in the Houston Standard Metropolitan Statistical area in 1967. A probability sample of 1,546 housewives was obtained through personal interviews in the respondents' homes. This sample survey was cited by Advertising Research Foundation as conforming to the standards set forth in ARF's *Criteria for Marketing and Advertising Research*. With no substitutes allowed in the sample survey, a completion rate of 80 percent was achieved by the researchers, who made up to eight call-backs to housewives who were not at home. The accuracy of the field interviewing was verified by ARF, which conducted a 100 percent verification of the field interviewing, using FACT (Field Audit and Completion Test).[7] Because of the procedures used in this survey, the usual problems of sampling errors (and non-sampling errors due to interviewing) were considered to be minimal.

LIMITATIONS

Due to the nature of the original proprietary survey, several limitations were imposed on this study. First, since the search objectives of the company conducting the project were much broader in scope than a simple study of Negro-white consumption patterns, they made no attempt to be all-inclusive in the product categories chosen. As a result, the present study was restricted to a survey of only a small list of household product purchases. Second, even though the Negro sample selected was unusually large (see Table 1), it was still not large enough to permit a completely

TABLE 1 *Sample Breakdown by Income Classifications*

Income	WHITES		NEGROES	
	N	Percent	N	Percent
Under $3,000	151	11.3	86	40.8
$3,000–5,999	236	17.7	77	36.5
$6,000–7,999	298	22.3	26	12.3
$8,000 and Over	650	48.7	22	10.4
	1,335[a]	100.0	211[a]	100.0

[a] These are the base numbers used hereafter in each of the tables except where stated differently.

TABLE 2 Total Sample Breakdown by Income and by Various Sociodemographic Characteristics (in percent)

Sociodemographic Characteristics	ANNUAL FAMILY INCOME							
	Less than $3,000		$3,000–5,999		$6,000–7,999		$8,000 or more	
	Whites	Negroes	Whites	Negroes	Whites	Negroes	Whites	Negroes
Occupation								
Prof/semi-prof/tech	—	—	4	4	8	8	19	9
Prof/mgr/official	—	—	6	1	9	11	22	14
Clerical/sales/kindred	3	5	16	6	15	11	16	18
Craftsmen/foremen/kindred	6	3	24	25	34	8	26	23
Operatives/service	10	48	24	49	26	31	12	14
Farm/laborers	3	14	8	8	2	19	1	9
Retired	77	30	18	6	5	8	3	9
Others/not reported	1	—	—	1	1	4	1	4
Total	100	100	100	100	100	100	100	100
Education								
Less than high school	48	53	28	26	15	19	7	9
Some high school	22	23	26	30	23	23	15	9
High school grad.	18	17	26	31	34	31	27	14
Some college	9	3	15	9	18	8	25	32
College graduate	2	1	2	—	7	8	17	23
Graduate or prof. training	1	—	1	—	3	8	9	9
Not reported	—	3	2	4	—	3	—	4
Total	100	100	100	100	100	100	100	100
Sex—head of household								
Male	40	48	77	83	94	88	96	91
Female	60	52	23	17	6	12	4	9
Total	100	100	100	100	100	100	100	100
Age of household head								
Less than 24 years	3	9	14	6	9	4	2	9
25–34 years	1	10	16	27	31	31	21	32

35–44 years	7	26	16	32	27	31	33	27
45–54 years	10	19	19	22	18	22	26	23
55–64 years	18	20	18	13	11	8	15	9
65 years or older	60	14	16	—	4	—	3	—
Not reported	1	2	1	—	—	4	—	—
Total	100	100	100	100	100	100	100	100
Total living in household								
1	44	17	11	4	2	—	1	—
2	43	32	33	20	21	15	22	14
3	7	13	25	22	23	20	21	36
4	3	13	11	18	26	23	27	14
5–7	3	19	18	23	26	38	27	32
8 or more	—	6	2	13	2	4	2	4
Total	100	100	100	100	100	100	100	100
Total no. employed in household								
None	75	17	14	3	4	4	2	5
1	21	50	64	47	70	46	58	18
2	4	29	19	44	24	50	33	68
3	—	2	2	5	2	—	6	9
4 or more	—	—	1	1	—	—	1	—
Not reported	—	2	—	—	—	—	—	—
Total	100	100	100	100	100	100	100	100
Stage in life cycle								
Younger children only	3	12	18	14	25	11	12	23
Younger and older children	1	16	15	26	21	27	17	27
Older children only	9	23	16	35	29	35	36	18
None—head less than 45	3	15	10	10	7	8	7	9
None—head over 45	31	14	27	9	16	19	24	18
None—single head over 45	52	19	14	4	2	—	3	5
Not reported	1	1	—	2	—	—	1	—
Total	100	100	100	100	100	100	100	100

satisfactory breakdown of income classes, particularly at the middle
($3,000–$6,000) and upper ($8,000 plus) levels. Similarly, multiple
cross-classifications by income and other sociodemographic characteristics
were impossible, due to inadequate cell sizes. Isolation of the impact of
these other sociodemographic characteristics on consumption patterns was
limited to inferences drawn from Table 2. Great care, however, was taken
by the authors not to become over-enchanted with implying cause and
effect relationships relative to these characteristics. Finally, any generalizations from this study must be tempered with the realization that the data
were collected from one large urban metropolitan area located in a
Southern state.

RESULTS

While of general interest to marketers, aggregate income-allocation differences do not provide any information about actual product- or brand-
choice comparisons, which are so vital to marketing strategy decisions. It
may be, for example, that even though Negroes spend more money on
food, their product and brand choices are very similar to those of whites
in comparable circumstances. In this study (see Table 3), specific usage
comparisons were made between Negroes and whites for ownership of a
selected number of household products (by holding income constant). An
evaluation of brand preferences will be left to a future study.

CONSUMPTION DIFFERENCES

1. Food Products   Table 3 clearly demonstrates that, at every income level,
Negroes consumed more butter than did whites. In fact, Negroes at
the lowest income level (under $3,000) spent more on butter than did
whites at the highest level of income ($8,000 and over). Obviously, factors
other than income must account for these variations, but none of the
sociodemographic characteristics shown in Table 2 seem to provide any
substantial clues.[8]

Nondietary soft drink consumption varied drastically across income
classes between the two groups. Negro usage was double that of whites
at the lowest income level, but then tended to decline with increasing
wealth. Among whites, consumption followed somewhat a reverse trend,
with usage rising as income increased. Consumption differences at the
low-income level can be attributed primarily to dissimilarities in occupations between the groups. The data in Table 2 indicate that the 77 percent
of the low-income whites were retired, as compared to only 30 percent of

TABLE 3 *Percentage of Negroes and Whites Who Had Recently Purchased or Who Owned Various Items Shown Premium*

Products	Annual Family Income							
	Less than $3,000		$3,000–5,999		$6,000–7,999		$8,000 or more	
	Whites	*Negroes*	*Whites*	*Negroes*	*Whites*	*Negroes*	*Whites*	*Negroes*
Food Products[a]								
Butter	6.6	23.3	8.0	31.2	7.7	26.9	14.1	45.4
Margarine	58.3	61.6	63.6	72.7	69.8	57.7	69.5	81.8
Frozen vegetables[b]	30.5	31.4	28.0	50.6	39.6	34.6	47.1	54.6
Canned vegetables[c]	20.5	35.6	35.6	44.5	37.9	40.4	40.6	43.2
Dietary soft drinks	7.3	17.4	11.9	23.4	20.8	23.1	25.5	13.6
Nondietary soft drinks	26.5	60.5	55.5	71.4	62.4	23.1	67.1	45.4
Liquor								
All respondents[d]	15.2	26.7	29.7	39.0	39.3	46.2	56.5	54.6
Scotch[e]	3.3	9.3	4.2	22.1	7.7	34.6	19.7	27.3
Bourbon[e]	7.3	15.1	20.3	23.4	29.2	7.7	40.9	40.9
Personal Hygiene Products[f]								
Shampoo	42.4	41.9	59.3	52.0	74.5	65.4	72.6	50.0
Deodorant	39.7	65.1	56.8	79.2	74.5	92.3	76.6	81.8
Toothpaste	48.3	76.7	75.0	89.6	86.9	88.5	89.1	86.4
Mouthwash	43.7	61.6	58.5	75.3	56.7	88.5	63.5	86.4
Disinfectants	52.3	69.8	56.4	80.5	70.1	61.5	68.6	86.4
Home Appliances[g]								
Auto. washing machine	47.4	19.8	57.6	29.9	78.6	50.0	85.5	72.7
Auto. clothes dryer	12.6	5.8	16.5	7.8	34.2	15.4	54.9	27.3
Auto. dishwasher	2.0	—	5.5	—	14.1	3.8	33.8	—
B&W television	87.4	91.8	89.5	98.7	83.7[h]	97.9[h]	—	—
Color television	3.3	0.6	5.7	1.9	24.3[h]	6.2[h]	—	—
Home Ownership								
Own home	68.3	39.5	49.4	57.1	70.8	73.0	81.5	77.3

[a] Purchased within the past seven days.
[b] Includes all types of frozen vegetables.
[c] Includes canned corn, peas, green beans, and tomatoes.
[d] Percentage to total respondents purchasing some alcoholic beverages within past 12 months.
[e] Percentage of Scotch and Bourbon purchases among total respondents.
[f] Purchased within past 30 days.
[g] Percentage "having" in the home.
[h] Last two income classes were combined because of small number of respondents.

the Negroes. As a result, the low-income Negro families were considerably larger and had more children than the average low-income white families. Why Negro consumption of nondietary soft drinks was so erratic in the high-income brackets is difficult to answer.

Dietary soft drinks were more popular with Negroes until the highest-income bracket was reached. At this point, usage among whites was almost double that among Negroes. Again, the larger size of Negro families probably is sufficient to explain larger consumption patterns in the low-income groups. At the highest income level, it may be that Negroes are less diet-conscious than are whites and, as a result, have turned their attentions to other "drinks."

2. Liquor Negroes, in every income bracket but the highest, purchased more liquor than did whites. For both groups, however, liquor consumption rose steadily with increases in income. Scotch whiskey was preferred to a substantial degree by Negroes in almost every income group, when compared with whites. This observation supports the findings of several other studies, which indicate that Negroes drink at least 25 percent of the Scotch consumed in the United States, although they represent only 12 percent of the population.[9] Scotch, among all consumers, has always been thought of as a "quality," high-class product. Therefore, it appears likely that, among Negroes, drinking Scotch has become associated with high status. Bauer also found that "those Negroes who see themselves as moving upward self-perceived mobility from their fathers' position in society are most likely to ... regard Scotch as a 'status' drink, and are most likely to report being regular Scotch drinkers."[10]

3. Personal Hygiene Products In 11 of 12 possible income groupings, Negroes purchased more deodorant, toothpaste, and mouthwash than comparable groups of whites. Negroes, on the other hand, did not purchase as much shampoo, although the differences were slight in most cases. More household disinfectants were used by Negroes, except in one income group.

The bulk of the differences, particularly at the lower income levels, can be attributed to larger Negro families with more children. Higher rates for usage of household disinfectants by Negroes probably result from the difficulty of keeping their average substandard housing facilities clean.

4. Major Home Appliances and Home Ownership A very striking point was that, except for the lowest income bracket, almost as many Negroes owned their own home as did whites. The difference at the lowest income level can be explained by the occupational discrepancies mentioned earlier.

Substantial differences in ownership of various major appliances were noted between the two groups at all income levels. Ownership differences for washing machines, clothes dryers, and dishwashers were particularly apparent. Part of the reason for these differences is income; for example, ownership of washing machines among Negroes increased across each income level until it was fairly close to the white ownership level. Another reason which helps explain the differentials is that many of the dwellings occupied by Negroes, regardless of income, are not equipped with the plumbing and electrical connections necessary for installation of those appliances. The additional installation cost makes it impractical or impossible to purchase washers and dryers. A further comment on automatic dishwashers is in order, since ownership variances are so prominent, even at the highest income level. The reason for these variances is that the majority of dishwasher sales are made to home builders who install them in new homes. Since even higher-income Negroes have had limited opportunity to purchase new homes, it should not be surprising that dishwasher ownership is so low.

Color television ownership was much higher among whites at every income level, although the reverse was true for black-and-white television. No simple explanation is available for this phenomenon, unless Negroes: (1) do not care much about color TV, or (2) cannot afford or are not willing to replace a working black-and-white TV for a new color set.

CONSUMPTION SIMILARITIES

A major finding of this study was that, for many household products, consumption-pattern differences were small both in number and magnitude. In fact, many similarities existed. For example, purchases of margarine, frozen and canned vegetables, and bourbon were nearly identical for both groups. Even among those products for which group differences existed, there were similarities in overall consumption patterns (for example, high total usage of personal hygiene products in both groups) as well as expanding usage as income rose.

DISCUSSION

Most of the earlier economic studies were concerned with comparing and analyzing aggregate consumption-pattern differences between Negroes and whites. They concluded that, essentially, the consumption differences were a reflection of the greater need of Negroes to save, rather than a result of cultural differences. This type of aggregate analysis, however, tends to conceal any internal variations in consumption which might exist within each group.

Although extensive consumption-pattern differences were found for a variety of household products, most of the discrepancies could be explained by income and/other sociodemographic differentials between the two groups. Consider, for example, major home appliances, for which ownership appears to be primarily a function of income and a lack of proper utility connections. Even though a large portion of the consumption differences could be attributed to economic and sociodemographic considerations, usage patterns for several products—particularly Scotch, butter, soft drinks, and frozen foods—could not be so explained.

One reason behind the varying consumption patterns in the Negro market versus the white market is the Negro's narrower spectrum of choice:

> The Negro has less selectivity in the purchase of a home, of a vacation, of travel, dining, entertainment, etc. This results in a greater expenditure per unit in the things that are available to him. Whites have more places to put their discretionary income while Negroes, even in the same income level as whites, use their dollars differently because of their narrower selectivity.[11]

Another reason for consumption differences is that minority groups today are apt to engage in compensatory consumption. Most Negro families have little opportunity to base their self-respect on occupational, educational, or other accomplishments. This poverty of opportunity tends to reinforce for these families the significance of consumption as at least one sphere in which they can make progress toward the American dream of success. Appliances, automobiles, and a home of their own can become compensations for blocked social mobility.[12] Bullock agrees and notes that "the main criterion for determining social class in many urban Negro communities of the South is overt consumption rather than wealth, family background, or church affiliation."[13] Similarly, Negroes who are insecure in their status or who believe their status is not widely accepted may participate in conspicuous consumption. "For instance," according to Broom and Glenn, "those who have recently improved their economic standing may buy conspicuously expensive items to communicate the fact that they have 'arrived.' "[14]

Because material goods have such an important symbolic role in American society, their acquisition symbolizes to the Negro his achievement of full status. Yet, this often creates a dilemma for the Negro consumer: whether to strive against odds for middle-class values, as reflected in material goods, or to give in and live for the moment.[15]

SUMMARY AND IMPLICATIONS

A probability sample of 1,335 whites and 211 Negroes was interviewed in Houston, Texas, to determine if, and to what extent, consumption patterns varied for a selected list of household products. The results for both groups were broken down and analyzed across four income categories. Sample variations for other sociodemographic characteristics were noted and utilized in explaining the resulting product-usage differences.

For the five product categories evaluated—food, soft drinks, liquor, personal hygiene products, and major home appliances—variations in consumption were found between Negroes and whites. A substantial portion of these differences, however, were explainable more in terms of income or sociodemographic variations than by purely "racial" influences. The evidence, in fact, disclosed as many similarities as differences in consumption patterns. There were, however, certain products for which unexplained differences in consumption patterns still existed between Negroes and whites even after an attempt was made to separate out the influence of income and other sociodemographic factors. Two such examples were butter and Scotch. No economically "rational" explanation exists why Negroes at every income level consume more of these products than do whites. The two most likely reasons put forth by this and other studies are compensatory consumption and status or conspicuous consumption. Unfortunately, too few products were studied to ascertain accurately which types of people or products would most likely be subject to these influences.

In conclusion, it can be said from a businessman's point of view that a Negro market does exist, not so much identifiable by color as by patterns of consumption. Marketers who assume that product buying in Negro households is roughly a match for that in white families of similar economic circumstances are far from correct. A combination of societal constraints; cultural traditions; and differences in values, preferences, and psychological needs have led Negroes not only to spend a larger proportion of their incomes on food, drink, clothing, and home entertainment than do whites, but also to vary their expenditures across different products and, probably, brands compared with whites.[16] However, as the Negro continues to climb the economic and social ladder, some of these patterns of consumption will undoubtedly change, as the more prosperous persons raise their sights from compensatory spending to financing nice homes, education, medical care, and travel. In other words, it is likely that a smaller percentage of the Negro's income will be channeled into traditionally popular product categories—food, clothing, liquor, and entertainment—while there will be an increase in forms of consumption which heretofore have been either unattainable or unwanted. This means that opportunities will continue to expand very rapidly for companies willing to cultivate the Negro as a market. If this is to be, then marketing must keep up with the changes occurring inside and outside this market.

[Notes]

1. See T. F. Pettigrew, *A Profile of the American Negro* (Princeton, N.J.: D. Van Nostrand Company, 1964); Talcott Parsons and K. B. Clark, eds., *The American Negro* (Boston, Mass.: Houghton-Mifflin Company, 1966); Henry Bullock, "Consumer Motivations in Black and White," *Harvard Business Review* (May–June, July–Aug., 1961), pp. 89–104, 110–124; L. E. Black, "The Negro Market," *Sales Management,* 91 (Oct. 4, 1963), pp. 42–47; Raymond Bauer *et al.,* "The Marketing Dilemma of Negroes," *Journal of Marketing,* 29 (July, 1965), pp. 1–6; and Leonard Broom and Norval D. Glenn, *Transformation of the Negro American* (New York: Harper & Row, 1965).

2. U.S., Bureau of the Census, *Current Population Reports,* Series P-60, No. 53, "Income in 1966 of Families and Persons in the U.S.," (Washington, D.C.: U.S. Government Printing Office, 1967), p. 19.

3. Horst Mendershausen, "Differences in Family Savings between Cities of Different Size and Location, Whites and Negroes," *Review of Economic Statistics,* 22 (Aug., 1940), pp. 122–137; Dorothy Brady and Rose Friedman, "Savings and Income Distribution," *Studies in Income and Wealth,* 10 (New York: National Bureau of Economic Research, 1947), pp. 247–265; J. Duesenberry, *Income, Saving and the Theory of Consumer Behavior* (Cambridge, Mass.: Harvard University Press, 1949); Marcus Alexis, "Some Negro-White Differences in Consumption," *American Journal of Economics and Sociology* (Jan., 1962), pp. 11–28.

4. Alexis, *ibid.,* p. 11.

5. At least one writer argues very strongly that most studies to date have deemphasized the consideration that many factors other than race influence the determination of consumption patterns. In fact, he concludes that because of the number of uncontrolled variables, "the concept of race as a factor in the statistical analyses of group economic behavior . . . has no more validity than lefthandedness, eye pigmentation, or height." B. E. Sawyer, "An Examination of Race as a Factor in Negro-White Consumption Patterns," *The Review of Economics and Statistics,* 44 (May, 1962), p. 220.

6. L. R. Klein and H. W. Mooney, "Negro-White Savings Differentials and the Consumption Function Problem," *Econometrics* (July, 1953), p. 455.

7. Pilot Study of FACT, Arrowhead Study No. 4 (New York: Advertising Research Foundation, Inc., 1968).

8. Among other possible explanations, two stand out as likely sources of influence. The first is "status." Bauer, in a recent study, stated that Negroes are extremely interested in quality and are "even more concerned with the symbolic value of goods than are whites." (Bauer, "Marketing Dilemma," p. 2.) The possibility exists, therefore, that a certain amount of status usually is associated with highly conspicuous goods—clothing and automobiles. A more likely explanation is that Negroes are compensating for their narrower spectrum of choice relative to potential uses of their income. In other words, since the Negro has less selectivity in the purchase of a home, of a vacation, etc., he spends more per item on the things that are available to him.

9. "The Negro Market, Accent on Quality," *Media-scope* (April, 1964), p. 77.

10. Bauer, "Marketing Dilemma," p. 3.

11. "Is There Really a Negro Market?," *Marketing Insights,* Jan. 29, 1968, p. 14.

12. David Caplovitz, *The Poor Pay More* (New York: The Free Press, 1963), pp. 12–13, 181.

13. H. A. Bullock, *Pathways to the Houston Negro Market* (Ann Arbor, Mich.: Edwards Brothers Publishing Co., 1957), p. 190.

14. Broom and Glenn, *Transformation,* pp. 28–29.

15. Bauer, "Marketing Dilemma," p. 3.

16. Marketers should keep in mind, however, that the indications in this study are that the Negro market is not completely homogeneous. Even as Negroes at the top income levels find the lines separating them from the rest of America becoming less of a barrier, those at the bottom income level still find themselves essentially isolated from their total environment. As a result, there has been increasing economic and cultural stratification within the Negro community which, among other things, has led to internal consumption-pattern variations.

22

Bernard Portis

Negroes and Fashion Interest

IN the 1950s and 1960s businessmen have come to recognize that the American Negroes' collective purchasing power has grown considerably and that the Negro market represents an important economic opportunity for the entrepreneur. In addition, they have become more aware of the Negroes' increasing effective demand for expensive and fashionable goods, and they are currently paying more attention to the Negro consumer of such goods. But contradictory clichés often make it difficult for businessmen to decide whether Negroes really represent a desirable market for prestige products. For example, Negroes are said to be too poor to buy the more expensive goods, and yet they are reportedly seeking prestige or status by means of such purchases. Little factual information exists about Negro purchasing behavior which would enable businessmen to choose among such beliefs. In this paper I attempt to distinguish between fiction and fact about the Negro fashion market: first, by citing current popular beliefs about Negro purchasers of fashion goods; and then by comparing these beliefs with data derived from a recent survey on the characteristics of the Negro fashion market.

"Fashion" is a difficult term to define. Oscar Wilde's remark, "Fashion is a form of ugliness so intolerable that we have to alter it every six months," is witty but not very helpful. Fashion can be defined very narrowly, in terms of the "haute couture" practiced by a privileged few, or more broadly, as a set of ideas which influence great numbers of people. In this paper I adopt the broader definition, that is, "Fashion is a concep-

Reprinted by permission of The University of Chicago Press from the *Journal of Business,* Vol. 39, April 1966, pp. 314–323.

tion of what is currently appropriate."[1] This conception or attitude is expected to affect a variety of activities by many people. "Fashion influences human activities and shapes the forms of our possessions. It affects the things we do, the things we say, the things we wear, and the things we use."[2]

The evidence presented here is necessarily limited to clothing fashions. This evidence shows that Negroes, though an important market for fashionable clothing, may not constitute a *special* market. Indeed, there is some danger in treating Negroes as a special market, particularly if this results in a failure to recognize separate and important segments within the Negro market. Although there has been some recent recognition of Negroes as a segmented rather than a homogeneous market, this segmentation or stratification has been visualized mostly in terms of city-by-city differences.[3] Segmentation within the Negro market also can proceed from more subjective considerations.[4] In particular, this paper shows that disparities among Negroes in fashion interest leads to differences among them in their methods of following fashions and shopping for clothing.

BELIEFS ABOUT THE NEGRO MARKET

In the past, most statements about the Negro market have referred to characteristics common to all Negro consumers rather than to a segmented Negro market. For example, prior to World War II, businessmen generally believed: (1) Negroes lacked the purchasing power to buy expensive merchandise, and (2) they were not interested in fashions.[5] During that same period, national advertisers seldom made special appeals to Negro consumers through Negro media. The advertisers assumed that Negroes, as a result of their experiences in domestic service occupations, as well as their exposure to general communications media, imitated white spending patterns to the best of their ability.

Since World War II, Negro media and advertising trade magazines have worked hard to combat such skepticism about the Negro market. As early as 1947, *Tide* magazine pointed out that population shifts from the rural South to urban areas of the South and North were helping to make Negroes a more promising market.[6] Negroes were obtaining better jobs in the urban areas and therefore had more money to spend.

The trade journals and Negro media have claimed that some firms were especially successful in selling to Negroes. Articles appeared entitled, "Why a Handful of Advertisers Dominate Negro Markets," and "Case Studies: How Several Firms Have Succeeded in Selling the Negro Market."[7] Some of these articles tended to assume that special advertising or promotional campaigns undertaken by firms were the reason for these firms' success in the Negro market. Other articles claimed that success came only to those advertisers who took into consideration special characteristics of Negroes. For example, a poll of Negro radio stations yielded the following recommendations on the special practices needed in advertising to Negro consumers:

1. Negroes, despite lower than white income levels, prefer the best of brand-name merchandise and respond well to air advertising for such products.
2. Negroes are proud and sensitive Americans and can spot a chauvinistic advertising approach every time.
3. Negroes have some specialized quirks concerning radio commercials and radio offers.
   a. Negroes do not go for sight-unseen premiums of jewelry, and other "gimmick" inducements to product buying often used as part of radio campaigns.
   b. Negroes in general do not like to send in cash in advance for mail-order items, nor do they usually like to write in for sample or trial offers.
   c. Negroes often respond more readily, on the other hand, to merchandising gimmicks.
   d. Negroes resent any kind of advertising stunt that makes a differentiation between white and colored listeners, either directly or by implication.
   e. Negroes are very cautious about "bargains."
4. Negroes make a startling amount of luxury purchases, with relation to median income, but it is best to aim air advertising at their basic needs.[8]

A survey of Negro magazines or newspapers would probably bring similar recommendations, except that these media would also suggest using Negro models in picture ads in order to increase reader interest.

The Negro radio stations portray Negroes as much more desirable customers than businessmen have believed. Rather than presenting Negroes as too poor to purchase expensive merchandise, these radio stations maintain that Negroes want prestige goods by stating that Negroes "prefer the best of brand merchandise," "are very cautious about bargains," and "make a startling amount of luxury purchases." They also indicate that Negroes, far from being unresponsive to advertisements, are actually "proud and sensitive Americans" with "some specialized quirks concerning radio commercials and radio offers." If such claims are correct, it would then follow that the Negro media, which presumably know Negroes best and are most trusted by them, should be used in advertising to this sensitive audience.

There is reason for skepticism about the claims and recommendations of the marketing magazines and the Negro media. They have provided little evidence that supposedly successful advertising campaigns actually increased any firm's share of the Negro market or its profits. The recommended use of Negro media for advertising does not necessarily follow from their description of Negro consumer characteristics. On the basis of his motivational research of Negro consumers, Bullock has argued for using general media and integrated advertisements rather than specialized advertising.[9]

The problem is not that trade journals and Negro media have made poor recommendations but that they have presented inadequate evidence in support of their recommendations. New evidence is presented here about Negroes' fashion interest—in particular, about the ways in which Negro women follow fashions and make their purchases of new clothes. Fashions are of particular interest because clothing is one of the principal means open to Negroes for achieving prestige or status. The Johnson Publishing Company, publisher of *Ebony* and other Negro magazines, has stated that Negroes are especially likely to seek prestige or status in their purchases of clothing and home furnishings because they are generally prevented from achieving status in other purchases, such as housing. Cited as supporting evidence are statistics gathered by the Bureau of Labor Statistics, which show that Negroes spend a smaller proportion of their income on housing and more on home furnishings and clothing than do whites with comparable incomes. It should be noted that these statistics are aggregate statistics and do not explain individual motives or purchasing behavior.

MEASURING FASHION INTEREST

This new information about Negroes' interest in clothing fashions comes from a 1962 survey of women shoppers in New York and Cleveland.[10] Since keeping up with fashions was expected to be an important shopper interest or motive, women were questioned both directly and indirectly about their interest in fashion. The following question from the survey directly asked women to summarize their over-all interest in fashion.

Question 25
Which one of the statements listed on the card best describes your reaction to changing fashions?
1. I read the fashion news regularly and try to keep my wardrobe up to date with fashion trends.
2. I keep up to date on all the fashion changes although I don't always attempt to dress according to these changes.
3. I check to see what is currently fashionable only when I need to buy some new clothes.
4. I don't pay much attention to fashion trends unless a major change takes place.
5. I am not at all interested in fashion trends.

This question is "doubled barreled," in a sense, because it refers both to a general attitude about fashion as well as to purchasing behavior. (Other survey questions, to be considered later, more clearly separate interest in fashions from actual purchasing behavior.) The above question provides a convenient summary of respondents' over-all concern with fashion and is therefore a useful question to examine initially.

In Table 1, the fashion interests of white and Negro women are com-

TABLE 1 *Fashion Interest and Race*

EXTENT OF FASHION INTEREST	RACE OF RESPONDENT* (PERCENT)	
	White	Negro
1. I read the fashion news regularly and try to keep my wardrobe up to date with the fashion trends	13	15
2. I keep up to date on all the fashion changes although I don't always attempt to dress according to these changes	35	27
3. I check to see what is currently fashionable only when I need to buy some new clothes	18	25
4. I don't pay much attention to fashion trends unless a major change takes place	19	18
5. I am not at all interested in fashion trends	13	11
6. Don't know	2	4
Total	100	100
Number	3,074	375

* Puerto Ricans and other women in New York and Cleveland not classified as white or Negro are excluded from this and succeeding tables. Most respondents were interviewed by women of their own race, as interviewers lived in or near the neighborhood in which they did their interviewing. No record of interviewer's race was kept.

pared, as measured by the above question. On the whole, Negro and white women are quite similar in their responses to this question. For example, the differences in the more extreme statements, 1 and 5, are very small (15 versus 13 percent and 11 versus 13 percent), and all are well within the range of sampling error. In the remainder of this paper, categories 1 and 2 are combined to allow simple presentation of data, and this gives whites a higher percentage (48 versus 42 percent).

This evidence, showing white and Negro women to be similar in fashion interest, tends to contradict the two poles of thought about racial differences in purchasing expensive or prestige merchandise. Negro women are neither a poor market for style merchandise, as many national advertisers believed at one time, nor an exceptionally good market, as put forth by the Negro media. Of course, this lack of evidence of racial differences in fashion consciousness need not be true for all prestige merchandise.

Before entirely dismissing Negroes as a special market for clothing fashions, we need to consider other characteristics of Negro fashion interest as well as some significant social factors in this regard. One important social factor is family income. Since Negro women generally have lower family incomes than do whites, they would be expected to have less opportunity to keep their wardrobes up to date. Low income and difficulty in making frequent clothing purchases could even depress a woman's interest in fashion. Katz and Lazarsfeld found fashion interest to be lowest among those with least income or of lowest social status.[11]

TABLE 2 *Extent of Fashion Consciousness* at Various Income Levels*

	RACE OF RESPONDENT (PERCENT AND NUMBER)	
LEVEL OF FAMILY INCOME	White	Negro
Under $3,000	21 (216)	34 (113)
$3,000–5,000	36 (416)	38 (115)
$5,000–7,500	46 (938)	57 (99)
$7,500 and over	58 (1,377)	48 (27)
All respondents	48 (3,074)	42 (375)

* Fashion-conscious women are those who picked either statements 1 or 2 in question 25, concerning fashion interest.

In Table 2, family income is held constant in reporting Negro and white women's interest in fashion. For all levels of family income, except the highest of $7,500 and over, Negro women more frequently expressed higher interest in fashions than did white women. The opposite tendency among Negro women in the high-income category is probably not too reliable because there were comparatively few Negroes in the sample with incomes of $7,500 and over. Thus the data in Table 2 can be interpreted to give some support to the claims that Negroes are an especially good market for prestige merchandise.

FOLLOWING CLOTHING FASHIONS

For businessmen, the most immediately practical or useful data about interest in fashions involve the ways women follow clothing fashions and make their purchases. There are such data in the shopper survey reported here.

A note of caution: The reader should recognize that this information refers to behavior as reported by respondents and not to behavior actually observed by researchers.

The interviewees were questioned about how they followed fashion news, and their answers are of interest to advertisers who promote fashion goods. The replies of Negro women especially supply information about the extent to which they use the general media in following clothing fashions. Unfortunately, media specially prepared for Negro consumption were not noted by the interviewers. On the basis of this survey's data, we cannot settle the controversy about the relative value of using general media, as opposed to specialized media, in advertising to the Negro market.

In Table 3, women are compared according to both race and fashion

TABLE 3 *Fashion Interest* and Methods Used to Follow Fashions*

METHOD USED TO FOLLOW FASHIONS	NEGRO SHOPPERS BY FASHION INTEREST		WHITE SHOPPERS BY FASHION INTEREST	
	High Fashion Interest	Low Fashion Interest	High Fashion Interest	Low Fashion Interest
Going shopping in stores themselves	59%	41%	67%	61%
Looking at newspaper ads	51	58	73	63
Reading the fashion magazines, such as *Vogue* and *Harper's Bazaar*	50	15	34	13
Reading articles about fashion in newspapers	45	27	56	30
Discussing fashions with other women	43	22	36	23
Watching television	41	33	30	27
Observing what other women wear	40	30	50	46
Reading magazines other than the fashion magazines	25	18	37	19
Going to fashion shows	17	9	11	4
Listening to the radio	11	4	6	3
No answer	0	8	0	2
Average number of reasons by those giving reasons†	3.8	2.8	4.0	2.9
(Number of cases)	(158)	(158)	(1,473)	(1,189)

* Women of high fashion interest are those picking statements 1 or 2 in question 25 stated in the text. Women picking statements 3 or 4 are those of low fashion interest. Women who expressed no fashion interest, and chose statement 5, were not even asked how they followed fashions.

†Multiple reasons and, therefore, total exceeds 100 percent.

interest in the ways they follow fashion news. Fashion interest makes more of a difference in the way women follow fashion news than does race, as measured by the questions from Tables 1 and 2. For example, if quantity of methods used is noted, the more fashion-conscious women in both groups use more methods (whites, 4.0, and Negroes, 3.8) than do the less fashion-conscious women (whites, 2.9, and Negroes, 2.8). In a more qualitative vein, fashion-conscious women surpass the less fashion conscious in the following three categories: reading the fashion magazines (for example, whites, 34 versus 13 percent; and Negroes, 50 versus 15 percent), reading articles about fashion in newspapers, and discussing fashions with other women. These three methods are especially likely to provide detailed information about current fashions and may even require more interest and effort on the part of the women than the other methods of following fashions.

The fashion-conscious white and Negro women do not differ markedly in the ways they follow fashion. There is no clear qualitative or quantitative difference in methods chosen to follow fashion. The only noteworthy and, indeed, surprising difference between fashion-conscious Negro and white women is that the fashion-conscious Negro women rely more on fashion magazines, such as *Vogue* and *Harper's Bazaar* (50 versus 34 percent). These particular fashion magazines make less direct appeal to Negroes in their articles and ads than do any of the general media. This is an illustration of how an absence of special appeals to Negro readership has not alienated or reduced its following among fashion-minded Negroes.

Fashion consciousness in clothing is related not only to methods by which women follow news about clothing fashions but also to their choice of stores for clothing purchases. As can be seen in Table 4, the fashion-conscious and less fashion-conscious women differ to a moderate extent with respect to the stores shopped most for clothing. Among Negro women, the fashion conscious are more likely to shop at department stores for their better dresses and for children's clothing. The fashion conscious among white women differ from their less fashion-conscious sisters in doing more shopping at high-priced specialty stores, such as Bonwit Teller or Saks Fifth Avenue. Thus, while fashion consciousness may affect both Negroes' and whites' store preferences, the effect is somewhat different. If the sample of Negroes were larger, it would be interesting to pursue further the reasons why fashion consciousness is related to greater preference for department stores among Negro shoppers. The relation of fashion consciousness to preference of department stores is rather complicated because department stores differ considerably in their fashion appeal or image.[12] A more refined analysis is necessary in order to determine which department stores attract the more fashion-conscious Negroes and for what reasons.

One thing that all the shoppers have in common, regardless of race or fashion consciousness, is that they do more shopping for better dresses at department stores and high-priced specialty stores than they do for children's clothing and undergarments in these same stores. Discount stores, in

TABLE 4 *Fashion Interest* and Stores Shopped Most Regularly for Clothing (Percent)*

	GOOD DRESSES		HOUSEDRESSES AND UNDERGARMENTS		CHILDREN'S CLOTHING	
	High Interest	Low Interest or None	High Interest	Low Interest or None	High Interest	Low Interest or None
Stores shopped most by Negro women:						
High-priced specialty	1	3	0	1	1	1
Department	50	38	37	36	31	21
Discount	16	15	28	19	31	36
Local	21	28	24	27	31	26
Other	11	3	2	2	5	16
None	1	13	9	15	1	0
Total	100	100	100	100	100	100
(Number)†	(141)	(195)	(155)	(197)	(118)	(145)
Stores shopped most by white women:						
High-priced specialty	14	8	6	3	7	4
Department	42	46	43	40	32	31
Discount	10	9	14	16	20	22
Local	25	26	25	26	24	23
Other	4	4	2	2	16	19
None	5	7	10	13	1	1
Total	100	100	100	100	100	100
(Number)†	(1,421)	(1,492)	(1,442)	(1,513)	(1,127)	(1,030)

* Fashion interest is measured by question 25 as in preceding tables. Statements 1 and 2 indicate high fashion interest, and statements 3, 4, and 5 indicate low or no fashion interest.
† Numbers vary from question to question because not all women shop for all types of clothing.

particular, seem to be gaining over department stores in sales of undergarments and children's clothing. It is noteworthy that the fashion conscious as well as the less fashion conscious apparently try to save money in purchases of utility clothing.

The fashion conscious of both groups are active shoppers, as indicated by the variety of ways they follow fashion news and the variety of stores they use. These fashion-conscious shoppers in both groups also appear to be "trading up," which has resulted in increased shopping at department stores by the Negro women and more shopping at high-priced specialty stores among the whites. The fashion-conscious shoppers are therefore likely to be good customers.

The picture of the fashion-conscious Negro shopper, as presented by the Negro media, does not entirely fit the evidence from this survey about the ways Negro women actually follow fashions. The Negro media seem to be on safest grounds in describing fashion-conscious Negroes as good customers. The implication that Negroes are not interested in bargains does run somewhat contrary to the tendency of fashion-conscious women to do much of certain types of shopping at discount stores. Most upsetting of all to the image of the Negro consumer presented by Negro media is the reliance the fashion-conscious Negroes place on the general media, especially *Harper's Bazaar* and *Vogue,* as a source of fashion news. Once again, it must be noted that the survey did not obtain use of special media, such as the Negro newspapers or magazines.

PROFILE OF NEGRO FASHION SHOPPERS

Thus far, more information has been provided about the Negro shoppers' methods of following fashion trends than about the personal characteristics of the fashion-conscious and less fashion-conscious Negro shoppers. A profile of the fashion-conscious Negro shopper should aid those businessmen, especially department store executives, who wish to promote or sell goods to this important segment of Negro shoppers. Information as to how the fashion-conscious and less fashion-conscious Negro shoppers differ in personal characteristics can suggest explanations for segmentation within the Negro market.

Some social factors associated with fashion interest and fashion leadership have been identified in previous research by Katz and Lazarsfeld. In brief, these authors found the following characteristics among all the more fashion-conscious women represented in their study: They had high socioeconomic status, they were gregarious in their social contacts, and they generally tended to be young and unmarried.[13] As their research was done on a cross-sectional sample in Decatur, Illinois, it is interesting to see how well their findings also apply to the women within the major metropolitan areas of New York and Cleveland who were surveyed in the Stuart Rich study.

Besides the differences of locale in these two studies, there are differences in defining fashion interest, socioeconomic status, life cycle, and gregariousness. The differences in defining these latter social factors are rather minor, but the definition of fashion differs in a significant way. Katz and Lazarsfeld broadly defined fashion interest so as to include keeping up with makeup and grooming trends as well as following clothes styles.

Despite the difference in definitions and samples, the findings between these two studies are very similar. As shown in Table 5, the fashion-conscious women, regardless of race, are more affluent, young, and gregarious (active in organizations) than are the less fashion-conscious women. Indeed, the only difference in the metropolitan sample of women shoppers and the cross-sectional sample of Decatur is that the more fashion-conscious women in Cleveland and New York are mostly found among the young married women while the fashion-conscious women in Decatur were most likely to be young unmarried women. The most likely source of this discrepancy comes from the difference in defining fashion interest. The broader definition in the Decatur study, which includes personal care, could well give special prominence to the young unmarried women.

The factors of family income, life cycle, and social participation (shown in Table 5) account for only part of Negro fashion interest. It is

TABLE 5 *Social Characteristics and Their Fashion Interest**

	NEGRO SHOPPERS BY FASHION INTEREST		WHITE SHOPPERS BY FASHION INTEREST	
	High	Low	High	Low
Level of family income:				
Under $3,000	25%	37%	3%	10%
$3,000–5,000	29	35	10	17
$5,000–7,500	37	21	32	35
$7,500–10,000	6	4	23	19
Over $10,000	3	3	32	19
Total	100%	100%	100%	100%
(Number†)	(152)	(201)	(1,402)	(1,451)
Life cycle:				
Under 40—no child	9%	10%	9%	4%
Under 40—child	62	55	47	36
Over 40—no child	14	15	16	29
Over 40—child	15	20	28	31
Total	100%	100%	100%	100%
(Number) †	(158)	(201)	(1,469)	(1,544)
Social activities:				
Participate in community, social, or sports activities	53%	29%	55%	42%
Do not participate in such activities	47	71	45	58
Total	100%	100%	100%	100%
(Number) †	(158)	(208)	(1,463)	(1,535)

* Fashion interest is defined as in preceding table.
† Number varies slightly from question to question due to non-response about social characteristics.

likely that many Negroes are interested in fashion because of personal needs rather than as a reflection of low circumstances. The sources of Negroes' fashion interest and expenditures for fashion need to be explored in further research.

SUMMARY

Although knowledge about Negroes' fashion interest is still incomplete, evidence presented here allows some preliminary conclusions.

Special appeal to the fashion-conscious Negro woman may not be required. There is little indication in the data presented that Negro women follow clothing fashions in ways which are much different from white women. Fashion-conscious Negro women are likely to read fashion magazines, such as *Vogue* and *Harper's Bazaar,* even though these magazines make no direct appeal to Negroes. The over-all frequency of fashion-conscious shoppers among white and Negro women is quite similar, except that Negroes at the lower- and middle-income levels are somewhat more interested in fashion than their white counterparts. All the reasons for Negroes' interest in clothing fashions are not yet known, and presumably there could be special circumstances affecting this interest. On the basis of data presented here, differences between white and Negro women in following fashions appear to be more a matter of degree than of substance.

There does appear to be segmentation of Negro women shoppers according to interest in clothing fashions. Almost by definition, the more fashion-conscious Negro women are those who read more news about fashion changes and keep their wardrobes up to date. There is some indication that Negro fashion shoppers trade up by buying at department stores. These fashion-conscious Negro women can provide an important demand for stylish clothing, a factor which clothing marketers might take into account in trying to reach this segment of the Negro market.

In conclusion, the marketer should recognize that he may be trying to reach some fashion-conscious women who happen to be Negro rather than Negro women who happen to be fashion-conscious. Fashion interest is at least as important a factor as race in describing the methods women use to follow fashions and to purchase clothes. This is probably not too surprising to the sophisticated marketing analyst who tries to understand consumers rather than to label them. Fashion consciousness is an attitude or need which women possess as individuals and can only be understood on an individual basis. Race is a label applied to groups, and, although it provides some indication as to a particular group's social situation, it bears no necessary relation to the shopping habits or needs of individuals.

[Notes]

1. Alfred H. Daniels, "Fashion Merchandizing," Malcolm P. McNair and Harry L. Hansen (eds.), *Readings in Marketing* (New York: McGraw-Hill Book Co., 1956), p. 114.
2. *Ibid.*
3. "The Negro Market: Accent on Quality," *Media Scope* (April, 1964), pp. 77–78.
4. Raymond Bauer *et al.,* "The Marketing Dilemma of Negroes," *Journal of Marketing,* July, 1965, pp. 1–6.
5. "The Negro Market: An Appraisal," *Tide,* XXI (March 7, 1947), 15.
6. *Ibid.*
7. David J. Sullivan, "Why a Handful of Advertisers Dominate Negro Markets," *Sales Management,* LXV (September 15, 1950), 65; "Case Studies: How Several Firms Have Succeeded in Selling the Negro Market," *Tide* (July 20, 1951), pp. 25–47.
8. "Selling to Negroes: Don't Talk Down," *Sponsor* (July 28, 1952), p. 36.
9. Henry Allen Bullock, "Consumer Motivations in Black and White," *Harvard Business Review,* May–June, 1961 and July–August, 1961.
10. For a full report of this research, see Stuart U. Rich, *Shopping Behavior of Department Store Customers* (Division of Research, Harvard Business School [Cambridge, Mass.: Harvard University Press, 1963]). A point peculiar to this article is that respondents, for the most part, were approached by an interviewer of their own race.
11. Elihu Katz and Paul F. Lazarsfeld, *Personal Influence* (Glencoe, Ill.: Free Press, 1955). The authors indicate their study was based on a cross-sectional sample of women in Decatur, Illinois, but did not state racial composition of the sample.
12. Stuart U. Rich and Bernard Portis, "The Imageries of Department Stores," *Journal of Marketing,* XXVIII (April, 1964), 10–15.
13. Katz and Lazarsfeld, *op. cit.*

Selected References

Akers, Fred C. "Negro and White Automobile Buying Behavior," *Journal of Marketing Research,* 5 (August 1968), 283–290.

"Arithmetics of Negro Spending Review," *Advertising Age,* 35, November 30, 1964, 27.

"Birmingham's Race Conflict Has Small Effect on Sales," *Advertising Age,* 34, November 11, 1963, 1ff.

Brimmer, Dr. Andrew F. "Economic Trends in the Negro Market," *Marketing Information Guide,* Vol. 11, No. 5 (May 1964).

Consumer Dynamics in the Super Market. New York, N.Y.: Progressive Grocer, 1965.

"Consumer Expenditures and Income, with Emphasis on Low-Income Families" (BLS Report 238-6). Washington, D.C.: U. S. Department of Labor, Bureau of Labor Statistics (July 1964).

"Getting a Ghetto Back in Shape," *Business Week,* March 23, 1968, 103–106.

Gibson, D. Parke. "Guess Who Is Coming to Market," *Sales Management,* 100, May 1, 1968, 44–46.

Gibson, D. Parke. "Negro Consumer," *Aerosol Age,* 12 (March 1967), 34–35.

Goodman, Charles S. "Do the Poor Pay More?," *Journal of Marketing,* 32 (January 1968), 18–24.

Grayson, W. P. "Economic Pressure of Negro Consumer Expanding," *Advertising Age,* 32, August 28, 1961, 32.

Groom, Phyllis. "Prices in Poor Neighborhoods," *Monthly Labor Review,* 89 (October 1966), 1085–1090. Washington, D.C.: U. S. Department of Labor, Bureau of Labor Statistics.

Holloway, Robert J., Richard N. Cardozo, *et al. The Low Income Consumer: An Exploratory Study.* Minneapolis, Minn.: School of Business Administration, University of Minnesota, February 1969.

"Inside Negro Buying Habits," *Grocery Manufacturer* (November 1967), pp. 9–11.

Johnson, J. H. "Negro Market Will Be Controlling Factor in Profit Margins of Big U. S. Companies in 15 Years," *Advertising Age,* 35, September 21, 1964, 119–120.

Krugman, Herbert E. "White and Negro Responses to Package Designs," *Journal of Marketing Research,* 3 (May 1966), 199–200.

"Negro Business Pressure Grows," *Business Week,* 1599, April 23, 1966, 31ff.

"Negro Buying Power," *Negro Historical Bulletin,* 25 (March 1962), 126.

"The Negro as a Consumer," *The New York Herald Tribune Inc.,* Business and Financial Section, No. 5, September 2, 1962.

"The Negro Consumer," *Electrical Merchandising Week,* Vol. 96, No. 17, April 27, 1964.

"Negro Consumers Are Waiting," *Grocery Manufacturer* (November 1967), pp. 4–8.

"Negro Consumer: What Broadcasters Have Learned About Him," *Sponsor,* 18, September 14, 1964, 36–40.

"The Negro's Force in the Market Place," *Business Week,* 1708, May 26, 1962, 76ff.

"Negro Groups Put Economic Pressure On," *Business Week,* 1591, February 27, 1960, 26–28.

"Negro Market: Buying Power Changes Market Place," *Printers' Ink,* 284, August 30, 1963, 9ff.

"The Negro Marketing Power," *Dun's Review and Modern Industry,* 82, November 1963, 61.

"New Facts Require New Look at Market," *The Gibson Report* (November 1967).

"New Marketing Profile of U. S. Negro Emerges," *Sponsor,* 19, July 26, 1965, 38–43.

"Probing the Negro Market: The Brand Loyalty Barrier," *Sales Management,* 102, March 1, 1969, 44.

"Retailing: Black Christmas," *Newsweek,* 72, December 9, 1968, 79–81.

"Selling to the Negro," *Newsweek,* 60, November 5, 1962, 92.

Wright, John S., and Carl M. Larson. *A Survey of Brand Preferences Among Chicago Negro and White Families.* Chicago: College of Business Administration, University of Illinois, 1967.

Strategic Implications for Market Interaction

The preceding parts of this book establish a frame of reference, state of the market, and current consumption patterns of black consumers. The articles in Part 4 discuss the implementation of pertinent marketing strategies designed to achieve the potential represented by the black-consumer market and indicate the need to recognize, identify, and develop methods for the effective distribution of goods and services to the black consumer.

D. Parke Gibson, in "Setting of Realistic Marketing Goals," emphasizes the necessity of clearly defining and planning the procedure required for successful development of the black-consumer market in a comprehensive sense. Consumer satisfaction and favorable sales result with the understanding only of attitudes toward a product or service and the development of marketing programs with these consumer attitudes in mind. Bowling businesses located in predominately black areas or adjacent to them exemplify this approach.

In "Customer Strategy for Negro Retailers," John V. Petrof describes the locational aspect of the black consumer as a significant advantage possessed by black retailers for serving black consumers—an appropriate marketing strategic condition. By capitalizing on their inherent opportunity to cater to the black patron, they can achieve a position of differential advantage in the American business community.

Determining and implementing the most desirable strategies for reaching the black consumer require constant effort, particularly in the magazine and newspaper media. "The Negro and American Advertising, 1946–1965," by Harold H. Kassarjian, analyzes magazine advertisements in which blacks have appeared. Findings indicate that over a twenty-year period, although there was an increase in the social role of the black and the appearance of integrated advertising, advertisements that treated the black as an equal were conspicuously few.

In "Reaching the Negro Market: A Segregated Versus a General Newspaper," John V. Petrof suggests that sellers of general-use products and services can communicate more effectively and economically with the black consumer through general newspapers rather than through segregated newspapers. However, the black newspaper is the more effective medium for communicating messages about products and services used exclusively by blacks.

Recent research indicates various socioeconomic characteristics of the black, which provide a consumer structure for strategy decisions. W. Leonard Evans, Jr., in "Ghetto Marketing: What Now?," examines the social stratification of this market segment and the implications for marketing and advertising for communication purposes. The inability of the ghetto consumer to participate in the high standard of living enjoyed by others seems to indicate the necessity for different marketing strategies. As a result of this inability to participate in American affluence, the ghetto market segment represents an important marketing opportunity.

Market information about this ethnic group is unquestionably of high priority to businessmen. Charles E. Van Tassel's excellent article, "The Negro as a Consumer—What We Know and What We Need to Know," indicates that a lack of general knowledge about the black consumer hampers the development of realistic marketing programs. For example, information about black purchasing patterns, black attitudes, and black motivations would be basic to the decision-making process when strategy considerations are analyzed. There is a critical need for reliable attitudinal and motivational information that companies can use to reach black consumers, while recognizing that this segment of the market is in a perpetual state of change.

23

D. Parke Gibson

Setting of
Realistic Marketing Goals

MANY of the companies desiring to increase their sales in the Negro market often do not take into consideration the essentials needed for successful market development. They do not plan for sales, nor do they work the plan.

Instead of applying crude guesses, blind hunches, and unintentionally stereotyped thinking to sales efforts in the market, companies should apply a clearly defined procedure by which sales development can be planned and measured for possible future sales growth.

Company thinking on sales forecasting and quota setting in the Negro market ranges from application of white-oriented, across-the-board thinking to asking a newly employed Negro salesman what he thinks should be the sales quota in the territory assigned.

With some marketing and sales executives the Negro market is often considered a "necessary evil," but no real thinking is given to its development. It is relatively easy, for example, to take a single market factor, apply it against the market, and then write the market off as unimportant.

The application of a single market factor can conceivably be one of the most expensive write-offs a company could experience. Serious consideration given to the use of several market factors, on the other hand, may prove to be an effective guide for setting attainable marketing goals.

Once a company discovers the market factors that could be favorable to increased distribution and sales, it should not be inclined to optimism

Reprinted by permission of The Macmillan Company, Collier-Macmillan Ltd., London, from D. Parke Gibson, *The $30 Billion Negro.* © 1969.

solely for this reason. There is the danger that an estimate based on optimism alone would not be logical in performance.

One of the most effective ways of planning for increased sales is to do as some companies are beginning to do: send sales people into the field to get an accurate picture of how sales are currently being developed among Negroes. A first-hand view enables a salesman or marketing executive to understand the demands of the market, general conditions in the marketplace, new products being introduced, and Negro-oriented advertising and promotional programs currently in use.

One consultant on the Negro market has suggested that if a company's sales force in major markets just once a year spent a day "as a Negro," sales could be increased by over 18 percent in some product classifications. The sales executives and salesmen would have to read at least two Negro-oriented magazines and newspapers, listen to Negro-oriented radio stations, make purchases in retail outlets that have predominantly Negro traffic, and talk with some consumers.

Too often, cold statistics never reflect marketing conditions in the Negro market and the sales results that are obtainable. While companies often know their products and services thoroughly, sales executives often fail to use tested methods to learn about Negro consumers, to learn to "speak their language," or even to consider how sales can be increased.

The "token gesture" is a poor method of quota setting or planning for increased sales.

Many times sales quotas are based on previous years' sales; and, while they might be considered a good sales volume, the actual potential may be considerably greater. Often companies are unwilling to make their campaigns in the market more flexible, but continue year after year to plod a time-worn track. While sales may remain level or show a slight increase from doing the same thing continually, the sales potential might be in actuality appreciably larger through application of new techniques and thinking.

In some product categories, companies that once held the sales lead among Negroes are being forced by market conditions, competitive programming, changes in the thinking of the consumer, or for other reasons either to refocus their efforts or to accept less than their sales potential and share of market.

Any company that plans for sales in the Negro market—by doing realistic forecasting and quota setting and by transmitting this information effectively—and works this plan, instead of haphazardly setting sales quotas, can expect favorable sales results.

In marketing to Negroes, attitudes and approaches become very important considerations. We have helped a number of clients crystallize their attitudes and approaches. We ourselves have learned considerably more about the Negro as a consumer through these experiences, for example, our experience with the bowling business.

Our firm was retained by American Bowling Enterprises, Inc., a Rochester, New York-based company that owned eight bowling centers in the Southeastern United States. Each of the centers was a new, modern, fully equipped bowling center with American Machine & Foundry (AMF Pinspotter) equipment, and each was built at the cost of a million dollars. All were located in predominantly Negro areas or adjacent to them and easily accessible in Atlanta, Birmingham, Charlotte, Chattanooga, Memphis, Nashville, Richmond, and Savannah.

In each community the bowling lanes were a brand-new experience, and they quickly became social gathering spots. At the time white lanes were still closed to or unused by Negroes. Entire families turned out as soon as the lanes were opened, and individuals of all ages were throwing bowling balls, pushing them, or correctly bowling through experiences remembered from service life or learned in other cities.

The lanes had each been built in quick succession. As soon as one was going full steam, another was built in one of the cities on the schedule until the eight were completed. And then it happened. Business dropped off for no apparent reason. Yet there was an explainable reason.

The client told us that no market research had been done either by themselves or by the American Machine & Foundry Bowling Group. They had either gone ahead after an initial experience or used experiences gained in other cities. As I then told the client, it was hard for me to believe that over eight million dollars in property, equipment, and salaries could be extended by themselves and AMF Pinspotters without even knowing the market.

As we do with almost all of our clients, we made an evaluation of the company's relations with the market by talking with management at the home office and in the field. Three centers were visited initially.

We learned that each center had a Negro manager who had been trained by the company itself and was qualified. Community organizations were using the well-appointed meeting rooms at the centers. We also learned that an AMF competitor was in the marketplace and in some cities had lanes competitive to those of our client.

The Bowling Division of Brunswick Corporation, the major competitor for equipment to AMF, had done an exhaustive market study, which gave us an indication of what we had already come to believe—education in the sport of bowling was essential in the Negro community.

Most American Bowling Enterprise magazines, while having beautiful bowling lanes, the latest equipment, and trained help, had a market of considerable size and potential that had not been conditioned to the sport of bowling.

AMF Pinspotters' national advertising and promotional campaigns were primarily white oriented and had little effect in the Negro community. Press relations and community relations were practically nonexistent in this community. The bowling centers were in the same position, with the exception of releasing bowling scores to Negro-oriented newspapers and radio stations in the cities where they were operating.

The problem that we faced was the fact that the attitudes of the community needed to be favorably developed toward the sport of bowling. The community had bowled initially with enthusiasm, but then the activity seemed to have receded in much the same manner. A change was necessary.

As part of the campaign to reshape opinions and to rekindle the enthusiasm, we recommended the creation of a booklet that would serve as an introduction to the sport of bowling. Since there were no nationally known Negro stars in bowling (as there were to be later), like the Negro athletes in other sports, whom we could identify with the sport of bowling, we recommended use of the three Negro members of the AMF Staff of Champions.

While the trio was known in bowling circles, we had the immediate task of getting them known in the communities in which our client operated. Several occasions, such as an opening, had brought them into some of the cities and had provided instruction on a limited basis.

The booklet *How-to-Bowl* was developed by AMF Pinspotters for us, and it was sponsored by the Coca-Cola Company. It featured the AMF Staff of Champions' trio, Eric deFreitas, Rosemary Morrow, and Don Scott, and outlined the basic rules for learning the game of bowling.

Thousands of copies of the booklet were distributed, not only in our client's bowling centers, but in lanes across the United States. In addition, it received wide coverage on the sports pages of the Negro-oriented press. Importantly, the booklets were distributed in quantity to all of the predominantly Negro schools in the cities where our client operated, to teachers and instructors in athletics. These included junior high schools, high schools, and colleges in the eight cities.

We had assisted in marshaling forces for the client in a number of directions and advised on specific activity in each market, which developed into a cohesive plan of action, particularly in the educational phase.

There had previously existed a communications problem among the managers of the client's lanes, and while there were occasional meetings, one manager was successfully running a program of which another manager in the same company was unaware.

We helped the client develop a plan to which the managers contributed and which became the guideline for more effective development of the Negro market. Here are some of the recommendations that appeared as guidelines:

1. Marquee Advertising   As part of the effort to achieve universality of approach, suggestions were made for the effective use of marquee advertising, such as "free instruction," and these were put into practice.

2. "Operation Kids"   Each manager was provided a manual describing a very effective school program in operation at one of the bowling centers. It was a step-by-step review of the operation that later became standard practice at other lanes, as it involved predominantly Negro schools.

3. Publicity Manual   Each manager was provided a public-relations and publicity manual that served as a guideline in each community. It contributed significantly to improved press relations and publicity for the sport of bowling in the communities.

4. Manager Publicity   We took advantage of the opportunity to publicize the fact that the eight managers, all of whom were Negro, had the responsibility for administering property and equipment valued at more than eight million dollars. This publicity was well received.

5. AMF Fashion Line   With the cooperation of the AMF Fashion Line, the organization within AMF responsible for the promotion of fashions and bowling accessories, publicity pictures were taken with an attractive Negro model for the first time and released to the Negro press nationally, with specific handling in our client's markets. This proved extremely popular with women. (Although we no longer counsel in the sport of bowling in the Negro market, we are proud that annually the AMF Fashion Line now continues to service Negro-oriented media with such pictures.) In addition, AMF provided bowling bags, shoes, and other accessories that were used as prizes in bowling centers to attract more women to the sport, and these products were used in fashion shows as well.

What we helped the client to do was to refocus the attitude of the market and the approaches to the Negro market by the client. We in turn helped the client to understand the market and how the service it provided could fit into their lives. We then sought to develop a plan by which this could be accomplished most effectively.

The attitudes that exist toward a product or service in the Negro market should be clearly understood, if at all possible, especially before a new service or a new product is introduced. If could be particularly dangerous to assume that the Negro consumer has the same attitude as the white consumer toward a product or service and then proceed strictly along those lines. There often needs to be some preconditioning of the

Negro market, and if consumer education can be employed, it could prove to be an excellent means of promoting sales in itself.

Once the attitudes of the market toward a product or service are determined, the correct approaches to it become much clearer. Then, too, the setting of marketing goals can be much more realistic.

24

John V. Petrof

Consumer Strategy for Negro Retailers

A growing body of evidence seems to indicate that the Negro consumer possesses some distinctive characteristics. The pattern of the Negro's behavior as a consumer, of course, is influenced by his relatively low socioeconomic status. The importance of differences in socioeconomic factors have led some people to question the existence of a separate Negro market in any meaningful sense. According to this viewpoint, there are no special characteristics that differentiate the Negro from any other lower income, lower educated group of people; however, time and again studies have indicated that income and education are not the only factors that determine the behavior of Negroes in the market place.[1]

BACKGROUND

With few exceptions, the great bulk of Negro business consists of small concerns in retail trade and services, employing from two to ten people.[2] Harding B. Young and James Hund in their study of Negro entrepreneurship in the South estimate that approximately 94 percent of total Negro businesses fall in this category.[3]

Historically, Negro retailers of all sizes have maintained their existence by taking advantage of opportunities created by segregated society.

Reprinted by permission from the *Journal of Retailing*, Vol. 43, No. 3, Fall 1967, pp. 30–38.

These avenues of opportunity were open because comparable white institutions generally refused to recognize and cater to the needs of an important market segment of the American society. By adapting their behavior to the problems and opportunities created by their environment many Negroes have served their communities and at the same time amassed personal wealth.

Political, social, religious, and economic forces have been advancing racial integration at different speeds in the various walks of American society. As this country moves ahead in solving its "dilemma," both white and Negro businessmen are being forced to reevaluate their age-old policies and assumptions concerning the Negro consumer.

The incomes of Negro consumers in recent decades have been rising, and their patronage has been increasingly solicited by firms outside of the Negro business community. The relative improvement of the Negroes' socioeconomic status in our society and recent discussions on the theory of market segmentation have caused many executives to focus more direct attention on the Negro market. Awareness of a separate Negro market which is segmented on psychological as well as other significant grounds has led many business firms to use Negro communications media more extensively in order to communicate more effectively with the Negro consumer.[4] In order to counteract any gains made by white businesses in the hitherto isolated Negro market, the Negro businessman has been advised by many Negro leaders to broaden his market coverage by going after the general domestic market.[5] Such people contend that attempts on the part of Negro entrepreneurs to capitalize on ostracism based on race represent a short-sighted market strategy.[6]

Of course, the criticism that the Negro businessman is preoccupied with the Negro consumer to the exclusion of other consumers is not new. Many social scientists have criticized the Negro businessman for having a racial rather than an economic orientation;[7] however, an examination of such statements reveals that they represent nothing more than emotional and subjective generalizations derived from idealistic and heroic assumptions.

Although never stated explicitly by its advocates, the recommendation that Negro business firms expand their market coverage is based on three assumptions: (1) that race is not a factor in a Negro consumer's decision to patronize a given business establishment, (2) that Negro businesses have no difficulty in locating near white consumers when convenience and service factors make physical proximity to markets a necessity, and (3) that Negro businesses which by definition have limited resources can compete in the general market against stronger and more experienced white business with equal success. The following paragraphs will examine the validity of the above assumptions.

DO NEGROES PREFER TO SHOP AT
NEGRO-OPERATED STORES?

In a free enterprise system business exists to satisfy consumer wants and preferences. Consumer wants cannot be determined on an *a priori* basis; they must be verified empirically. If Negro consumers show a patronage preference toward Negro-owned or identified business firms, this may provide such firms with a differential advantage. Since a sound business strategy should always lead from strength, it would be unwise indeed for Negro firms not to capitalize on a customer preference which gives them a differential advantage *vis-à-vis* other firms in their locality.

Research conducted in the past has indicated that Negroes tend to reduce their purchases from white retailers during periods of racial strife.[8] In order to determine the attitudes that Negroes have toward Negro and white establishments it was necessary to conduct a survey in a tension free period. To reduce the possibility of including white respondents in the sample, only areas consisting of census tracts with 90 percent and above nonwhite population falling within the geographical limits of Metropolitan Atlanta were included in the survey. Twenty-six census tracts comprised the universe. These census tracts had a total population of 142,118 and represented 41,010 housing units. The survey sample consisted of housing units selected from the twenty-six census tracts on a random basis. In selecting respondents a systematic multistage sampling design was used. Respondent rejections amounted to less than 4 percent. The existence of a few rejections might have biased the results on the affirmative side, but the quality and magnitude of the sample offset this bias to a large extent.

The data collected in this survey reflect opinions and statements of the sampled 315 Negro household heads. Insofar as statements might differ from facts, the results might not conform to reality. Some respondents might not have been completely truthful in answering certain questions. An interview is useful in determining attitudes but not actions. Accepting the sociological proposition that an individual's statement of events is made from a perspective that is a function of his position in a group, one can interpret statements in this case to be an individual's perspective on the point involved, that is, the attitude of the Negro consumer toward patronizing Negro and white business establishments.

During the survey interviewers attempted to find out if, other things being equal, Negroes show a preference toward patronizing Negro-operated establishments. In addition to asking direct questions on the subject, interviewee attitudes on the matter of store preference were also checked through an indirect approach. For example, respondents were asked such questions as whether they would prefer being waited on by a Negro or a white salesclerk in a department store. An overwhelming majority, 92 percent of the respondents, indicated that other things being equal they prefer patronizing Negro-operated establishments. The standard error of this percentage is:

$$\text{Standard Error} = \sqrt{\frac{.92 \times .08}{315}} = \pm .015$$

or, in percentage form 1.5 percent. To put it more simply, 95 times out of 100 any other sample drawn randomly from the Negro population of Metropolitan Atlanta would indicate that 92 ± 3 percent, or between 89 and 95 percent, of Negroes prefer to deal with a Negro-operated business firm.

No significant relationship was found between the geographical origin of the respondents and race as a factor in determining their store preference. However, the coefficient of correlation between years spent in formal education and race as a factor influencing store preference was +.754. Although statistical association is by no means an indicator of a cause and effect relationship, one may assume that prolonged education makes Negroes more race conscious in their patronage of stores.

CAN NEGRO-OPERATED FIRMS SERVE WHITE CONSUMERS EFFECTIVELY?

TABLE 1 *Reasons Interviewed Negroes Patronize Stores**

REASON	FREQUENCY OF PREFERENCE
Service	107
Price	90
Locality	80
Assortments	68
Personality of Store Personnel	63
Credit	44
Other	6
Total	458

* Total frequencies exceed the number of interviewees because some respondents indicated more than one reason for patronizing a given store.

As can be seen from Table 1, Negro shoppers place more emphasis on convenience and other nonpecuniary factors in selecting a given store. A study by G. P. Stone indicates that most urban shoppers patronize stores for noneconomic reasons.[9] Based on the data in Table 1 one may easily conclude that in this respect Negroes are no different from most consumers in American society.

TABLE 2 *Types of Goods Bought by Interviewed Negroes from White and Negro Businesses*

	PERCENT OF TOTAL BOUGHT FROM WHITE BUSINESS	PERCENT OF TOTAL BOUGHT FROM NEGRO BUSINESS	TOTAL
Shopping	48	52	100
Convenience	29	71	100
Specialty	69	31	100

Table 2 indicates respondent purchases of goods and services from white- and Negro-owned establishments by type of goods. The category "shopping goods" covers commodities which the consumer usually wishes to purchase only after comparing quality, style, and price in a number of stores. Furniture, clothing and shoes, rugs, millinery items, jewelry, and piece goods are prominent in this category. "Convenience goods" are commodities that the consumer usually desires to purchase with a minimum of effort from the most conveniently located store. Groceries, meats, drug items, tobacco, small hardware items, and gasoline are important examples. "Specialty goods" are those which have a particular attraction for the consumer so that he or she will go out of his way to purchase them. Examples are men's high-grade clothing and shoes, fancy groceries, expensive perfumes, and fine watches.

As can be seen in Table 2, Negroes satisfy a larger proportion of their demand for shopping and convenience goods among Negro- rather than white-owned establishments. One may make an *a priori* assumption that in addition to race, store location and other convenience factors are important in determining store preference in the purchasing of such items by Negroes.

In the category of specialty goods Negroes buy twice as much from white firms as they do from Negro-owned establishments. The reason for this shopping pattern is rather obvious. Many items in this category, such as brand-name appliances, cars, and other exclusively distributed products in many communities can be obtained only from businesses operated by white people. Empirical evidence, although isolated, indicates that when given a choice Negroes prefer to purchase such items from Negro-operated establishments.[10]

Since location is important in selling convenience and shopping goods, it is not likely, as long as segregated neighborhood patterns exist, that Negro businessmen will be allowed to operate establishments in areas where they can cater efficiently to the demands of the white market. Even if one assumes that white Americans are indifferent or even have a strong preference toward patronizing a Negro-operated store, it is highly unlikely that they would be willing to travel across town to purchase their convenience and shopping goods. All consumers expect to obtain such goods with a minimum expenditure of effort. Social pressures and customs deny Negro entrepreneurs the location they need in order to serve the white market properly.

The only area where Negro-operated establishments can compete effectively for the dollar of the white customer in spite of their locational disadvantage is in the distribution of specialty goods; however, with few exceptions, such as night clubs and other forms of entertainment, this area shows a rather limited growth potential. Most white consumers have limited use for many products and services designed especially for Negroes. Beauty salons, hair preparations, and certain food products are examples of goods and services which have little or no appeal for white consumers when manufactured or offered as services by Negroes.

DO NEGRO-OPERATED FIRMS HAVE THE RESOURCES TO COMPETE?

In addition to the aforementioned locational disadvantage, Negro retailers face a financial disadvantage vis-à-vis most of their competitors. It is a well-known fact that most Negro businesses are small. Even the larger ones are of a lilliputian nature when compared to similar enterprises in American society.

In a free enterprise system there is a direct relationship between the size of a firm's financial resources and its ability to compete. Most Negro firms could improve the return on their limited promotional funds by aiming them toward a concentrated Negro market rather than spreading their promotional efforts over a large market area, since a given amount of advertising can create a larger degree of firm awareness and preference when aimed toward a smaller market than it can if it is dissipated over a larger market.

CONCLUSIONS

The findings of this survey indicate that an overwhelming majority of Negroes prefer to patronize Negro-operated establishments. In addition, due to segregated housing patterns Negro businesses have a locational advantage in serving Negro customers and a locational disadvantage in catering to the demands of a white clientele.

According to economic theory the holder of a comparative advantage should capitalize on it.[11] In other words, in trade relationships a nation, a firm, or an individual should lead from strength. If the employment of Negroes in diplomatic service is considered a plus factor in furthering the interests of the United States among African nations,[12] it is rather contradictory to assume that race is of no significance in dealing with domestic Negroes.

This article has indicated through deductive reasoning as well as empirically that Negro retailers do possess a comparative advantage in serving the Negro market. Failure to capitalize on this advantage would be very foolish indeed.

The recommendations of Fitzhugh, Young and Hund that attacking the white market is the best defense for Negro businesses is a short-sighted policy. Such conclusions are derived from idealistic rather than realistic hypothesis and if adopted may lead Negro businesses to disaster.

The Negro politician was able to secure for himself a place under the sun as a result of Negro bloc voting. Bloc purchasing can accomplish the same objective for Negro businessmen.

This article does not advocate the practice of racism. It simply substitutes reality for wishful thinking. If some of the current environmental limitations prohibiting Negro businessmen from competing for the dollars of white consumers are removed, then Negro businesses should by all means take advantage of such changes. However, in pursuing the white market Negro retailers should never neglect the Negro customer. By capitalizing on the advantage they have in serving the Negro patron, Negro firms can provide themselves with a differential advantage in the American business community. In the foreseeable future the white market can be of only marginal importance for the great majority of Negro establishments.

[Notes]

1. Raymond A. Bauer, Scott M. Cunningham, and Lawrence H. Wortzel, "The Marketing Dilemma of Negroes," *Journal of Marketing* (July 1965), pp. 1–6.
2. H. Naylor Fitzhugh, ed., *Problems and Opportunities Confronting Negroes in the Field of Business* (Washington, D.C.: United States Department of Commerce, 1962), p. 23.
3. Harding B. Young and James N. Hund, "Negro Entrepreneurship in Southern Economic Development," from Melvin L. Greenhut and W. Tate Whitman, *Essays in Southern Economic Development* (Chapel Hill, N.C.: University of North Carolina Press, 1964), p. 138.
4. "Colored Car Buyers," *The Wall Street Journal,* December 2, 1966, p. 1.
5. Fitzhugh, *op. cit.,* p. 7.
6. *Ibid.*

7. Charles S. Johnson, *The Negro in American Civilization* (New York: Henry Holt and Company, 1930), p. 101.

8. John V. Petrof, "The Effect of Student Boycotts Upon the Purchasing Habits of Negro Families in Atlanta, Georgia," *Phylon* (Fall 1963), pp. 266–70.

9. Gregory P. Stone, "City Shoppers and Urban Identification: Observations on the Social Psychology of City Life," *The American Journal of Sociology* (July 1954), pp. 36–45.

10. *The Wall Street Journal, op. cit.,* p. 1.

11. Paul A. Samuelson, *Economics,* 3d ed. (New York: McGraw-Hill Book Company, Inc., 1955), p. 643.

12. Fitzhugh, *op. cit.,* p. 89.

25

Harold H. Kassarjian

The Negro and American Advertising, 1946-1965

IT has become almost axiomatic to claim that mass media of communication, and advertising as a subset, reflect the culture and society in which they exist. For example, since mid 1963 civil rights organizations and specifically the Congress of Racial Equality and the National Association for the Advancement of Colored People "have brought direct pressure upon advertisers to include Negroes in advertising layouts, to use more Negro actors in television programming, and to hire more Negroes into the advertising industry"[1]. The *New York Times* described these Negro moves for integration as follows: "The wider representation of Negroes in conventional middle-class settings will, Negro groups believe, do much to erase the undesirable stereotypes of the Negro that exist in the white community" [3, p. 229].

Few recent studies have been found that indicate how the Negro has been portrayed in the mass media or, more specifically, in advertising. *Advertising Age* reproduced seven ads from print media to illustrate how black models were being used. Interestingly, there were two airlines, two utilities, two department stores, and one insurance company, undoubtedly representing an extremely small portion of the kind of products on which the Negro spends his estimated 25 to 30 billion consumer dollars [3, p. 229].

Reprinted by permission of the American Marketing Association from the *Journal of Marketing Research,* a publication of the American Marketing Association, Vol. VI, No. 1, February 1969, pp. 29–39. Numbers in brackets refer to sources listed in the reference notes, which are on page 341.

Boyenton [3] in 1964 informally sampled issues of four metropolitan newspapers and their Sunday supplements and found, among 7,400 pages of print, 12 ads that could be said to contain Negro models, some with exotic African backgrounds. A sampling of 1964 issues of some 2,500 pages of *Life, Good Housekeeping,* and *Atlantic Monthly* yielded four ads with Negroes. In an unpublished study [4] conducted for the American Civil Liberties Union (ACLU) a television content analysis indicated that Negroes are given .65 percent of the speaking roles in commercials and 1.39 percent of the nonspeaking roles.[1]

The difficulties with both the ACLU study and the Boyenton study have been their limited time span and the informal or unsystematic content analysis either because of financial or time demands. Hence it became the purpose of my study to:

1. determine the frequency in which Negroes appeared in mass circulation magazine advertising
2. determine depiction of the Negro's role in print advertising
3. examine changes, either in frequency or role, that occurred over the 20-year period since the end of World War II.

HYPOTHESES

Three years—1946, 1956, and 1965—were chosen for the study. In 1946 consumer advertising had again begun to appear, and civil rights pressures tended to be minimal. The armed forces were not yet integrated, and the Negro had not achieved his rightful citizenship. By the early 1950's "civil rights" pressures increased with such threats as economic boycotts; public transportation had achieved some semblance of desegregation, and the 1954 U. S. Supreme Court decision on school desegregation and other demands of the middle class Negro began to show some effect on the white society.[2] Hence 1956 was chosen as the second year of study. By this time some changes in the portrayed role of the Negro could be expected. By the mid 1960's the term, "white backlash," appeared, and the summer of 1965 produced the Watts riots affecting all of America. To avoid contamination by the supposed appearance of black-white societal polarization and library accessibility of print media, the third year chosen for the study was 1965.

It was hypothesized that in 1946 the Negro was portrayed as a servant, laborer, and background slave, e.g., the Uncle Tom and Aunt Jemima. By 1965, the Negro's occupational role as depicted in advertising would tend to be the stereotyped servant-laborer-slave, but rather tend to be more middle or lower middle class.

Although the change in role was hypothesized to be linear, the frequency of the Negro's appearance in advertising layout was hypothesized to be U-shaped or curvilinear. The logic of this expectation is based on the reasoning that in 1946 the Negro in his servant-laborer role posed little threat to middle class white society or to the general advertiser concerned about the need-value systems of his public. By 1956 the pressures of the civil rights movement and society's changing attitudes prevented extensive use of the stereotype of Uncle Tom. Hence, it was assumed that advertisers reacted by not using Negroes as much. Finally by 1965 the advertiser, unable to hide from his social responsibility, again began to employ Negro actors, models, and celebrities for his advertising layout; now, however, not in the slave role but in a more realistic occupation. Nevertheless, it was expected that fewer Negroes would appear in 1965 than in 1946 since the advertiser might still fear consumer reprisal.

However, it must be emphasized here, that this study is a systematic content analysis—an objective, quantitative analysis of the role portrayed by the Negro model in magazine advertising and a measure of his appearance frequency. There is no attempt to measure interpretations placed on the ad by the consumer or magazine reader. The author was not interested in how the ad was perceived by the audience, and in fact experimental measures were taken to reduce perceptual or selective differences among interpreters. Moreover, no evidence is collected about the communicator's intent, whether it be the magazine editor or advertiser. This study is not concerned with why a Negro model was or was not used, or even whether the communicator expected a particular actor to be recognized as a Negro by the audience. The research concerns neither the effects of the communication on any particular group or audience nor the intent of any particular communicator; it is rather, according to Berelson [2], an "objective, systematic, and quantitative description of the manifest content of the communication." Nevertheless inferences about the communicator and the audience can be made.

SELECTION OF MEDIA

Magazines were selected as the media for study rather than television, radio, or newspapers because of the availability and permanence of any particular ad over a 20-year period. Yellowing newspapers or microfilm were obviously inadequate and the unavailability of TV or radio commercials evident. Using the December 27, 1965, issue of the Standard Rate and Data Service publication on consumer magazines, all magazines in excess of 250,000 paid circulation were stratified by magazine type and circulation. A random sample was chosen. Unfortunately many magazines within the sample, mainly those with a lower middle class or lower class appeal—categories such as romance, babies, motion pictures and television—were unavailable over the 20-year period studied, either from libraries or used-magazine dealers.

Hence, the media used, rather than being representative of mass circulation magazines, was selected as follows. All magazines published between 1946 and 1965 available at the University of California, Los Angeles Library, the Los Angeles Public Library and the Santa Monica Public Library with circulations over 250,000 as of December, 1965, were listed alphabetically. From this list Negro publications such as *Ebony* were eliminated. The remaining were randomly numbered and 11 selected for the study. Another magazine, *Sports Illustrated,* was added even though it was first published in 1954 because of the many Negroes that appear in its editorial content. This author was curious if more Negroes would appear in the advertising of this particular publication. The final selection of magazines in the sample is shown in Table 1.

METHODOLOGY

AD SELECTION

A research assistant, carefully trained to be sensitive to Negro and other minority and ethnic group differences, studied each magazine systematically and methodically looking for ads with any non-Caucasian. If any possibility existed that any given actor, model, character, photograph, or cartoon might represent a Negro or other non-Caucasian, it was to be recorded with the total number of pages in each issue. At first other data such as total number of all ads, ad size, product advertised, and color in ad were also recorded, but the size of the task in relationship to available funds led to the elimination of this phase.

A second research assistant spot-checked many issues independently, recording similar data. Comparing the two records led to the conclusion that there was little disagreement in the selection of ads that purportedly contained a Negro. That is, extremely high reliability existed between the two research assistants although a few ads with other races were overlooked by one of the assistants.

Next the two sets of recorded data were given to a third research assistant who again went through the entire sample of magazines, this time not independently, but with the two sets of records in front of him, checking for overlooked pictures of Negroes and eliminating Orientals and other ethnic groups.[3] After completion of this stage, the magazines were taken to a professional photographer, and 35 mm. slides were prepared of all ads that might contain a Negro. The final determination on a Negro characteristic was to be made later by judges.

A fourth assistant independently rechecked the number of pages in each issue of the magazine sample. Some disagreements resulted mainly from the practice of some magazines of putting regional edition advertising on unnumbered pages. The page counts presented in Table 1 are those of

TABLE 1 *Magazines Studied*

MAGAZINE	CIRCULATION[a]	PAGES PUBLISHED[b]
Esquire	923,997	7,018
Fortune	431,006	9,305
Good Housekeeping	5,435,775	9,362
Harper's Bazaar	430,266	8,248
Life	7,327,185	20,817
Mademoiselle	642,963	8,213
New Yorker	466,847	20,480
Newsweek	1,825,994	15,767
Popular Mechanics	1,375,176	9,706
Sports Illustrated[c]	1,134,993	9,024
Time	3,138,585	17,480
Vogue	440,130	12,290
Total	23,572,917	147,710

[a] Standard Rate and Data Service as of December 27, 1965.
[b] These page counts are approximate—see text.
[c] *Sports Illustrated* was not published in 1946.

the research assistant rated to be most careful in his page counts; however, they still may contain errors.[4]

The slides were checked against the original ads for accuracy, then numbered and placed, using a table of random numbers, in slide projector trays in preparation for judging. Then lists were prepared of all ads with multiple insertions. Generally, if the exactly identical ad was run in different issues of the same magazine or in different magazines, a single photograph was taken.

CATEGORIES FOR ANALYSIS

In the procedure for content analysis judges were expected to categorize the sign-symbol material of the content using explicitly formulated rules. That is, the judges in the study's major phase were given a series of operational definitions or explicitly formulated rules and asked to categorize the content (here, the ad) only according to the rules.

The rules, themselves, were operationally structured such that several judges working independently would give identical results. This procedure

was followed to prevent casual categorizations of the content and minimize the effects of selective perception. In a series of several pilot studies,
judges were independently asked to categorize the ads according to the
explicit definitions given to them. Where disagreements among the judges
existed, category definitions and operational rules were enforced, and in
some cases entire categories were eliminated if instructions could not be
rewritten to ensure lack of confusion or disagreement. For example, one
of the categories to be judged was whether the Negro appearing in the
ad was American or non-American. Definitions of "American" and "non-
American" were presented to the judge with sample ads to differentiate
the two categories. The judge was to use the cues available to him in
the ad to make the decision, including dress, exotic background, scene
location, props in the photograph, etc. He was not to make any assumptions not explicitly in the rules. For example, he was not to make any
assumptions about the actual birth place of the model used in the ad
(who may have been American). Instead, by using cues in the picture
or cartoon he was to categorize the nationality of the Negro character in
the ad.

The study's final categories follow:

1. Is there a Negro in this ad?
   a. American Negro
   b. Non-American Negro
   c. No Negro
   d. Don't know
2. How sure are you that the characters are Negro?
   a. Recognize the person (e.g., Eartha Kitt, Pearl Bailey)
   b. Very sure a Negro but do not recognize the models
   c. Possibly a Negro
   d. Very sure not Negro
   e. No Negroes, recognize every character
3. Type of figure (picture)
   a. Photograph of actual scene
   b. Photograph of a photograph (photo of book jacket or record album
      cover)
   c. Drawing
   d. Cartoon
4. Importance of the Negro in the ad
   a. Small (hard to find, not important to the message)
   b. Average
   c. Very important (Negro is predominant figure)
5. Racial makeup
   a. All characters Negro
   b. Separate pictures (panel ad, record albums with white and Negro per-
      formers placed next to each other, no Negroes and whites presented
      in the same scene)

    c. Mixed Negro-white, but in a nonpeer relationship (waiter with white patron)

    d. Mixed Negro-white, a peer relationship between Negro and white (Negro and white children playing together)

6. Kind of interaction
   a. Ad contains one individual only
   b. Social interaction—characters are interacting with each other at a party, while relaxing at a social gathering
   c. Work interaction—characters are interacting but in a work environment; waiter taking an order, two or more men digging a ditch
   d. Noninteraction—characters are in the same scene but not in contact with each other, not looking at, talking to or touching each other; conceivably not even aware of each other's existence

7. Sex of each Negro
8. Age of each Negro
   a. Child (under 14 years old)
   b. Young adult (13 to 30 years old)
   c. Adult (31 to 60 years old)
   d. Older (over 60)
9. Occupation of each Negro (to be written in).[5]

The product advertised and the size and color of ad were also recorded.

JUDGES

Under ideal conditions several judges would have been trained in the categorization or judging procedure, and all judges would have been given the same stimuli. This would produce a reliability measure based on the number of times the judges disagreed with each other and hence a measure of the results' stability. Unfortunately this was impossible here since the judges could process and categorize about 30 ads per hour. Besides the extensive training involved, more than 600 slides were to be judged. Hence 23 graduate students were asked to volunteer for the study and were trained in the categories used in the analysis.

Each judge processed 40 slides. At least 20 of these ads were processed by one or two other judges to get a measure of reliability. Both in the training procedure and in the actual sample of ads to be judged, several control slides with no Negroes were inserted to prevent a set within the viewer that all ads necessarily contained a Negro.

Table 2 shows the results of the judging procedure. In all, 664 ads were judged by the 23 judges, of which 546 were the study's actual stimuli. An additional 96 slides were duplicates of other slides. In all, 225 of the ads were processed by more than one judge. For each slide, between 1 and 42 judgments or categorizations were made. The agreement

TABLE 2 *Composition of Slides Shown to Judges*

ITEM	NUMBER	PERCENTAGE
Number of dissimilar ads judged	546	
Number of duplicated ads judged	96	
Control ads (no Negroes)	10	
Number of slides which were not ads	7	
Number of ads with Oriental or non-Negro native	5	
Total slides judged	664	
Slides processed by three judges	160	24.1%
" " by two judges	65	9.8
" " by single judge	439	66.1
Total	664	100.0%
Number of multiple judged ads	225	
" " judgments made	4,782	
" " disagreements among judges	392	
Total errors in judgment		8.2%
Reliability of judgments		91.8%

among judges, or the reliability of the content analysis, is 91.8 percent. That is, in 92 percent of the multiple judgments made, the judges agreed on the categorizations.

For content analysis research this is indeed respectable, and in fact the true reliability is somewhat higher. Most errors in agreement occurred in judging ages of characters in the ad, whether the character was a recognized person such as a baseball star, and whether the ad was a cartoon or a drawing. Since these categories are unimportant for the study, the true reliability of the remaining categories is considerably higher. Amazingly little disagreement occurred in the central categories, such as existence of Negroes, kind of interaction, racial composition and characters' occupation.

RESULTS

In total, 546 separate different ads containing a Negro were found in the nearly 150,000 magazine pages studied. Estimating the number of ads among these pages, the number of Negro ads comprise less than one-third of one percent of the total. This is considerably less than the one percent found in the ACLU study on television advertising and not dissimilar to the results Boyenton obtained in his more casual analysis of magazines.

The first problem in processing the data, however, was whether one should consider each as a unique entity to be counted just once, or whether, in the case of multiple insertions of any given ad, each insertion rather than each dissimilar ad should be processed. Processing only the dissimilar ads might bias the results in that maybe an ad for Kodak showing a Negro and white child playing with each other would be counted as occurring only once when, in fact, the identical ad may have run a dozen times in half a dozen magazines. However, counting this specific ad a dozen times might give the misleading impression that print media are saturated with Negro and white children playing together. To reduce this kind of possible ambiguity, the data were processed using both categories, dissimilar ads and total ads. Table 3 contains some classificatory

TABLE 3 *Classification Data*

CHARACTERISTIC	DISSIMILAR ADS	TOTAL ADS
Number of ads	546	808
Size of ad		
2 pages	14.9%	12.6%
1.0–1.9 page	61.6	58.5
0.5–0.9 page	9.9	9.3
0.25–0.49 page	7.4	8.2
Less than .25 page	6.2	11.4
	100.0%	100.0%
Color of ad		
Black and white	56.7%	58.8%
Color	43.3	41.2
	100.0%	100.0%
Kind of figure		
Photograph	52.3%	49.8%
Photograph of photograph	14.2	11.6
Drawing/cartoon	33.3	38.5
Don't know	0.2	0.1
	100.0%	100.0%

information, indicating fairly clearly that the two schema of data processing will tend to produce minimal differences, although it appears that the multiply inserted ads tend to be smaller, black and white, and drawings or cartoons.

Table 4 contains demographic data on sex and age of the Negroes appearing in the dissimilar set and total set of ads. Of the 546 dissimilar ads and 808 total ads that the researcher and his assistants presumed to contain Negroes, the judges found only 503 and 751 ads, respectively, that contained a Negro according to the rules of categorization. Examination of the deviant cases indicated that if a Negro did exist, he played a small or insignificant role or lacked sufficient Negro characteristics to be so classified.

On the reasoning that Negro females and children would be less threatening than Negro males or adults, it was hypothesized that more Negro females than males would appear in the ads and that more children would appear than adults. The results in Table 4 clearly reject this

TABLE 4 *Demographic Data*

CHARACTERISTIC	DISSIMILAR ADS	TOTAL ADS
Number of ads	503[a]	751[a]
Number of Negroes	821	1,187
Mean Negroes per ad	1.63	1.58
Sex		
Male	80.5%	79.5%
Female	19.5	20.5
	100.0%	100.0%
Age		
Child (0–14 years)	5.6%	5.3%
Young adult (15–30)	47.6	48.1
Adult (31–59)	44.7	45.2
Older (60 and over)	2.1	1.4
	100.0%	100.0%

[a] Of the 546 dissimilar ads, 503 were judged to have a Negro. Similarly, of the 808 total ads, 751 were judged to have a Negro.

hypothesis. Among the 821 Negroes that appear in the set of 503 different ads, 80 percent are male and 92 percent are adult. Very similar results are obtained in the analysis using the total set of ads. One possible explanation for these results may be that, as shown later, Negroes are often depicted in the service, laborer, and entertainer occupations, roles which tend to be dominated by male adults.

Table 5 presents the results of judging on the category related to the Negroes' nationality within both the total and the dissimilar set of ads. Results for the dissimilar set indicate that 68.2 percent of the ads contained American Negroes, and 23.9 percent contained Negroes of other nationalities, mainly African or Caribbean countries. An additional 7.9 percent of the ads were judged with "no Negro" or "don't know" responses. As mentioned, these eight percent are generally ads in which the Negro is sufficiently insignificant not to be noticed or lacks sufficient Negro characteristics to be classified as Negro.

THE HYPOTHESIS OF CURVILINEARITY

The first of the study's major hypotheses was that the frequency in which Negroes have appeared in mass circulation magazine advertising would tend to be a curvilinear relationship from the years 1946 to 1965

(Table 5). Of the 372 dissimilar ads in this study with American Negro models or characters, 35 percent appeared in 1946, 25 percent in 1956 and 40 percent in 1965. An overall chi-square statistic indicates that these percentages are significantly different from each other ($x^2 = 12.49$, df $= 2$, p .01). Moreover, the number of ads appearing in 1956 is significantly smaller than in either 1946 ($x^2 = 5.50$, df $= 1$, p .02) or 1965 ($x^2 = 12.44$, df $= 1$, p .001). However 1946 is not significantly different from 1965. Therefore, the hypothesis that the frequency with which Negroes appear in magazine advertising would be a U-shaped relationship is supported for the dissimilar ads containing American Negroes. It was further expected that the 1946 ads would contain more Negroes than those in 1965. This expectation was not confirmed; in fact, considering only raw numbers, the results indicate the opposite. For the total set of ads, the statistical results and conclusions are identical.[6]

TABLE 5 *Nationality of Negro Models by Year*

Year	American	Non-American	"No Negro" (don't know)	Total
		Total ads		
1946	36.3%	25.9%	36.8%	33.8%
1956	27.4	31.5	28.1	28.5
1965	36.3	42.6	35.1	37.7
	100.0%	100.0%	100.0%	100.0%
Sample size	554	197	57	808
		Dissimilar ads		
1946	34.7%	25.2%	34.9%	32.4%
1956	25.3	35.1	34.9	28.4
1965	40.0	39.7	30.2	39.2
	100.0%	100.0%	100.0%	100.0%
Sample size	372	131	43	546

For the non-American Negro in Table 5, the results are obviously not similar. Among the 131 dissimilar non-American ads, 25 percent appeared in 1946, 35 percent in 1956, and 40 percent in 1965. Although an overall chi-square statistic indicates that these percentages are not significantly different from one another, there appears to be a trend of greater use of the non-American Negro role in magazine advertising over the 20-year period rather than the U-shaped relationship that appeared with the American Negro. Using the total set of ads in Table 5 does not refute this interpretation.[7]

If one may be allowed interpretations beyond the available data here, these results lend some credence to the reasoning given earlier that the 1946 Negro posed little threat to middle-class white America; hence

American Negroes could comfortably be used in their servant-laborer role with little repercussion from the Negro market. By 1956 changing pressures from within the society may have led to a lesser use of American Negroes, but not a lesser use of him in the foreign Negro role. By 1965 the use of the non-American Negro role continued to increase, significantly surpassing the 1946 level. The American Negro, although in 1965 depicted more often than in 1956 ads, merely reached the 1946 level of use. Perhaps the non-American Negro was not perceived to be quite as threatening in 1956. Moreover, by 1965 the continued increase of non-American Negroes reflects pressures to increase Negro representation and is a less controversial solution.

One possible difficulty in testing the hypothesis that the frequency of using Negro characters varies over the 20-year period is related to the number of pages which varies in the sample magazines. Obviously if ten times as many pages were published in 1965 as in 1956, one should expect there to be fewer Negroes appearing in 1956. To account for this variance, an index number was computed to control the number of pages.

The results are presented in the next to the last row of Table 6. In 1946 there were 5.83 ads using Negro models per thousand pages of magazines published. By 1956 the index had dropped to 4.60 and by 1965 had risen to 6.00. The trend is again in a predicted U-shaped curvilinear direction with fewer Negroes appearing in 1956 than in either 1946 or 1965. Note that these index numbers are based on the total sample of Negro ads, including both American and non-American groups, and hence tend to be quite conservative. The curvilinear hypothesis did not apply to the non-American Negro sample; in fact, this group tended to show a linear increase over the 20 years. If this group were eliminated from the index and only the American Negro considered, the drop in use of Negroes in 1956 relative to the other two years would be considerably greater.[8]

Also, Table 6 points out the differences from magazine to magazine. Whether one considers the actual number of ads or the index number (ads per thousand pages) and therefore controlling differences in number of pages published, the results are quite similar. Most magazines show the expected U-shaped frequency of published ads with Negro characters. *New Yorker* and *Vogue* do not indicate a decline in 1956 but show a healthy increase in the number of Negro ads published in 1965. *Fortune* shows a continuing and dramatic decrease over the 20-year period in use of Negroes. (One can only hope this does not reflect the attitudes of its obviously business-oriented readers.) Finally *Esquire* produces data opposite to most of the sample publications. Relatively few ads with Negroes were published in 1946. By 1956 when use of Negroes in other publications tended to drop, *Esquire* showed more than a five-fold increase, and

TABLE 6 *Negro Ads Appearing in Selected Magazines*

MAGAZINE	1946		1956		1965		TOTAL	
	Percentage of Total	Ads 1000p	Percentage of Total	Ads 1000p	Percentage of Total	Ads 1000p	Percentage of Total	Ads 1000p
New Yorker	18.7%	10.72	35.2%	10.96	39.7%	14.52	31.3%	12.35
Life	21.2	8.73	16.6	4.76	14.8	7.26	17.5	6.77
Time	17.9	8.59	11.7	5.00	11.5	5.48	13.7	6.35
Newsweek	17.6	8.90	8.7	3.71	8.5	5.20	11.6	5.96
Fortune	9.9	8.73	5.2	3.94	1.6	1.58	5.5	4.73
Esquire	3.3	3.17	15.7	17.60	6.2	8.90	7.9	9.12
Sports Illustrated[b]	—	—	4.8	2.66	6.2	3.89	3.7	—[b]
Popular Mechanics	2.2	1.77	—	—	0.3	0.36	0.9	0.72
Good Housekeeping	2.6	2.13	0.4	0.32	3.0	3.07	2.1	1.82
Mademoiselle	3.3	2.67	—	—	3.9	5.05	2.6	2.56
Vogue	1.5	0.79	1.3	0.89	2.3	1.81	1.7	1.14
Harper's Bazaar	1.8	1.50	0.4	0.43	2.0	2.29	1.5	1.45
Total	100.0%	5.83	100.0%	4.60	100.0%	6.00	100.0%	5.47
Base	273		230		305		808	

[a] Total ads.
[b] *Sports Illustrated* was not published in 1946.

by 1965 tended to decrease the publication of ads containing Negroes. Undoubtedly the results from *Fortune* and *Esquire* compared with the rest of the media must be accounted for by some logical set of factors such as changes in readership, management or magazine appeal or format.

An early expectation in designing this study was that magazines with lower class and lower middle class appeal would show Negroes less often than upper middle class magazines. Unfortunately, as mentioned, magazines appealing to the lower strata of society were unavailable for this study. However, note that the *New Yorker,* with its appeal to the higher strata, consistently accounted for a large proportion of Negro ads in the study. Yet, *Popular Mechanics* and *Good Housekeeping,* which presumably appeal to a lower strata, publish relatively few ads with Negro models. It is also interesting that the three fashion magazines, *Mademoiselle, Vogue,* and *Harper's Bazaar,* show relatively few Negroes, although by 1965 all three show an increase in their use of the Negro. The data relating to *Sports Illustrated* was rather surprising. In the editorial pages one encounters more Negroes than in any other magazines in the sample; the magazine presumably has a larger Negro readership, yet one finds few Negroes in the advertising pages.

Since Table 6, in presenting the number of Negro ads in the various magazines, combines American Negroes and non-American Negroes, Table 7 presents the number of ads that depict only American Negroes per

TABLE 7 *Index Number of American Negro Ads Appearing in Magazine Sample*[a]

Magazine	Ads / 1000p
New Yorker	6.35
Life	6.10
Time	4.75
Newsweek	4.38
Fortune	3.22
Esquire	6.13
Sports Illustrated[b]	2.55
Popular Mechanics	0.31
Good Housekeeping	1.82
Mademoiselle	1.58
Vogue	0.49
Harper's Bazaar	1.21
Total	3.75
Base	554

[a] Total ads.

[b] *Sports Illustrated* did not publish in 1946. Data are based only on 1956 and 1965.

thousand pages of publication. A comparison of Table 7 with Table 6 produces few startling results. The ranking of magazines according to the ads-per-thousand-pages index number is almost identical. *Popular Mechanics* still has the fewest number of ads and *New Yorker* the greatest number. Note, however, that the margin of the *New Yorker* over the other magazines virtually disappears, and of the remaining ads, a great many are for night clubs and restaurants featuring Negro entertainers such as Pearl Bailey and Harry Belafonte. These results even further dilute the consistently high index of published Negro ads in the *New Yorker*.

In any case, the outstanding finding shown in Tables 6 and 7 is the small number of ads that exist among the some 150,000 magazine pages studied for the 20-year period with a combined, but not necessarily mutually exclusive, circulation of 24 million copies per year. The readership of these magazines may well be one-half the population of the United States. Including all Negroes considerably fewer than six ads containing a Negro per-thousand-published pages exist. And if one considers only American Negroes the ratio drops to less than four ads per thousand pages.

Before the discussion of another main part of this article, two other minor hypotheses should be examined. Based on the same reasoning that led to the curvilinear hypotheses in the frequency of appearance of Negroes, it was expected that the 1946 Negro would be included in ads for "atmosphere" and would not be very important to the ad but that he would be obviously a Negro. By 1956, the hypotheses would state that the new, improved version of the Negro, if he appeared at all, would be buried in the advertising, show minimal Negro characteristics and, in fact, be difficult to recognize as a Negro. By 1965, it was expected that he would be a dominant part of the ad.

Unfortunately these hypotheses were most difficult to test reliably. In the final categorizations, two questions were asked the judges: How sure are you that there is a Negro in the ad? How important is the Negro to the ad's layout and theme? The results are shown in Table 8.

These data must be interpreted cautiously. The majority of disagreements among judges were, at this point, seriously questioning the reliability or stability of the results. In any case, the hypotheses must be rejected. Negroes tended to be more easily recognized as Negroes in the 1956 ads than in either the 1946 or 1965 versions, and the relative importance of the Negro to the entire ad was greater in 1956 than in either 1946 or 1965. The results, if valid, are in the exact opposite direction from those expected. Again to generalize beyond the data, one wonders if the Negro were being less anxiously characterized in 1946 and 1965 than he was in 1956. The author intends to replicate this study with 1969 ads to see what effects serious Negro unrest may have had.

TABLE 8 *Characteristics of Negro by Year*[a]

CHARACTERISTIC	1946	1956	1965	TOTAL
How sure person is Negro?				
Recognize person (known Negro)	7.5%	23.5%	21.0%	17.3%
Very sure	64.4	55.7	53.3	57.6
Possibly	24.1	16.8	21.9	21.2
Don't know	4.0	4.0	3.8	3.9
	100.0%	100.0%	100.0%	100.0%
Importance of Negro in ad				
Small	43.1%	39.9%	38.4%	40.4%
Average	39.1	28.4	34.6	34.3
Very important	16.1	30.4	26.1	24.0
Don't know	1.7	1.3	0.9	1.3
	100.0%	100.0%	100.0%	100.0%
Sample size[b]	174	149	211	534

[a] Dissimilar ads.

[b] For 12 ads that were judged to contain no Negro, data were not recorded.

THE ROLE OF THE NEGRO

If one were to judge role and occupational relationships between white and black in American society and had available only magazine advertising on which to base his conclusions, what would his analysis of the Negro's role indicate? Table 9 shows the judged occupations of American Negroes that appeared in the ads present in the sample of periodicals.

In 1946, 78 percent of American Negro actors or models were depicted in the ads as having laborer or service jobs: maid, waiter, slave, field hand, personal servant, the Aunt Jemima, or the Uncle Tom. The higher status occupations (including police and firemen) shown in the ads constituted three percent of the American Negroes; an additional 15 percent were entertainers or sports participants.

By 1956 the number of American Negroes depicted as sports heroes or entertainers increased to 36 percent, and the number of occupations in the service and laborer categories dropped to 52 percent. The number of Negroes shown as members of white-collar or professional occupations remained constant at one ad per year. The data suggests that by 1965 Negro incomes must have increased many fold if the occupations depicted in magazine advertising are to be a valid indicator of the Negro's role in society. Professional, managerial, and clerical occupations rose from less than one percent to nine percent in 1965. By this time, entertainment and sports constituted the greater majority of Negro occupations depicted in the ads—nearly 60 percent. However, few Negroes were found in menial tasks, the percentage dropping from 78 percent in 1946 to 13 percent in

TABLE 9 *Negro Occupations by Year*[a]

OCCUPATION	1946	1956	1965	TOTAL
	American			
Professional	0.5%	—	5.2%	2.4%
Managers, clerical, sales	—	0.9%	3.5	1.6
Craftsman	1.5	1.7	1.8	1.7
Operative	1.5	6.0	1.8	2.6
Service	52.3	35.0	9.6	30.5
Laborers	25.7	17.1	3.9	14.6
Entertainer, model, sports	14.9	35.9	59.4	38.2
No occupation	3.6	3.4	14.8	8.4
	100.0%	100.0%	100.0%	100.0%
Sample size	195	117	229	541
	Non-American			
Professional	—	5.0%	5.3%	3.7%
Managers, clerical, sales	3.6%	1.0	0.9	1.4
Craftsman	3.6	4.0	2.6	3.3
Operative	5.4	5.0	0.9	3.3
Service	21.4	24.0	23.5	23.3
Laborers	26.8	14.0	20.0	19.2
Entertainer, model, sports	8.9	20.0	30.4	22.2
No occupation	30.3	27.0	17.4	23.6
	100.0%	100.0%	100.0%	100.0%
Sample size	56	100	115	271

[a] Dissimilar ads.

1965. How well advertising reflects the occupational status of the Negro can be found by comparing the data in Table 9 with the non-white occupations in the United States from the 1950 to 1960 *U. S. Census of Population*. Fairly consistently, 50 percent of the Negro jobs have been in the service and laborer categories, compared with 13 percent found in 1965 advertising. Note also that a little less than 20 percent of the non-white occupations in the nation are in the professional, clerical, and white-collar categories. These categories within the sample of ads consisted of 0.5 percent in 1946, 0.9 percent in 1956 and 8.7 percent in 1965. The poorest inroads made by the Negro, however, as might be expected, were in the craftsman and operative categories. Although the occupations of skilled and semiskilled labor represent one-quarter of the jobs held by Negroes, ads showing Negroes in these occupations accounted for 3.0 percent of the total ads for 1946 and 3.6 percent for 1965.

The study's hypothesis stated that changes would occur over the 20-year period. To test statistically this relationship, American Negro occupations in Table 9 were collapsed into four categories (white collar/

professional, skilled/semiskilled labor, unskilled labor, entertainment), forming a 3 x 4 chi square. The chi-square statistic was 179.51, with six degrees of freedom, significant well beyond the .001 level. Obviously it is the unskilled labor and entertainment categories that account for these results.

Another interesting set of conclusions can be generated by comparing the American Negro occupations with the non-American Negro occupations, Table 9. The use of non-American Negro entertainers also tended to increase but not at the rate of the American Negro. Interestingly the category of service and laborer occupations showed no significant changes, remaining just under half of all occupations depicted over the 20-year period. Note also that more white-collar and professional occupations are found among 1946 and 1956 non-American Negroes than among American Negroes. This relationship is also true for the occupational categories of skilled and semiskilled labor. By 1965, however, few differences existed between the American and non-American Negro's appearance in the higher status occupations. Perhaps in earlier years, it was safer to depict a non-American Negro in a higher status job, and by 1965 only the non-American Negro could comfortably be a maid, stable boy, or porter. The American Negro of 1965 apparently showed primary competence as a high fashion model, football player, or TV, night club, or recording star.

A chi-square analysis performed on the non-American Negro data in Table 9 produced a statistic of 11.72 with six degrees of freedom (not significant). The hypothesis of an occupational role change is confirmed only for the American and not for the non-American Negro. However, even with the non-American Negro the advertiser still lacked the courage to show the Negro in higher occupations. In raw numbers, one ad portrayed the American Negro in a professional, semiprofessional, or technical occupation in 1946. In 1956 no ads appeared, but in 1965 12 ads were among the more than 500 separate ads with American Negroes in the three years studied.

A second measure of the changing role of the Negro is shown in Table 10. The data represent racial composition within the ads and the kind of interaction among the characters in the ad. For example, the segregated kind of ad in which all characters are American Negro remained an approximately constant 15 percent throughout the three sample years. However the panel ad in which both white and black appear together, but in which white and black are in separate photographs or drawings, increased significantly over the 20-year period. This kind of ad has either entirely different scenes or perhaps has numerous record album jackets in the layout. It is interesting that by 1965 the greatest number of ads presenting an American Negro were of this kind. Two other outstanding findings are evident. Again with the American Negro the

TABLE 10 *Interaction Role by Year*[a]

	AMERICAN			NON-AMERICAN		
CATEGORY	1946	1956	1965	1946	1956	1965
Group composition						
Panel ad/separate						
pictures	15.5%	29.8%	38.9%	12.1%	8.9%	15.4%
All Negro	14.7	18.1	16.1	36.4	33.3	26.9
Mixed nonpeer	62.8	36.2	12.8	51.5	44.5	46.1
Mixed peer	6.2	15.9	32.2	—	13.3	9.6
Don't know	0.8	—	—	—	—	2.0
	100.0%	100.0%	100.0%	100.0%	100.0%	100.0%
Interaction						
Single individual	10.9%	26.6%	28.2%	27.3%	20.0%	19.2%
Noninteraction	30.2	30.9	41.6	30.3	17.8	23.1
Work interaction	56.6	40.4	15.4	39.4	46.6	42.3
Social interaction	2.3	2.1	14.1	3.0	15.6	15.4
Don't know	—	—	0.7	—	—	—
	100.0%	100.0%	100.0%	100.0%	100.0%	100.0%
Sample size	129	94	149	33	45	52

[a] Dissimilar ads.

number of ads in which white and black are peers and appear in the same scene increased over the time span measured, but the whites and blacks appearing in a nonpeer relationship decreased quite dramatically. A non-peer relationship almost always presented the Negro in a service or inferior role, such as a waiter taking an order from white patrons. In the entire sample, only two ads existed in which a mixed race, non-peer relationship was found, where the Negro might be considered to have a superior role. Both appeared in 1965, one showing a Negro nurse pushing a white patient in a wheel chair, and the other showed a non-American Negro nurse tending a white child.

Interestingly among non-American Negroes the relationships are somewhat different. Considerably more segregated or all-Negro ads were found, and at least in the later years there were more integrated ads showing Negroes in inferior nonpeer roles. Again it seems that in the later years the American Negro is handled far more delicately than the non-American Negro.

Regarding the kind of interaction among characters in the ad, it is apparent from Table 10 that use of a single American Negro with no other characters increased over time as did use of American Negroes with other characters in the scene, but in which there was no interaction. However, interaction scenes that involved work or employment situations decreased. This latter category includes ads such as a Negro shoeshine boy accepting a tip. Quite apparently with a shift in the occupation of the Negro from the service-laborer class, he began appearing either singly in the ad or in a situation requiring no interaction. However, for the non-American Negro many of the trends take the opposite direction.

As another step in the data analysis, a cross-break was prepared (Table 11) comparing the kind of interaction among characters indicated by the ad's racial composition. For example, in the mixed non-peer racial composition, most ads in 1946 and 1956 involved a work interaction showing the Negro in an inferior role. By 1965 a substantial proportion moved away from interaction in an inferior role to a noninteraction kind of layout. By 1965 most segregated, all-Negro ads tended to consist of a single individual, typically a singer, actor or other type of entertainer, or a sports hero. Unfortunately the number of ads that include racially mixed groups on a peer level are too few to be meaningful. However, the number of ads depicting a socially interacting mixed peer group has increased from two in 1946 to fourteen in 1965. Sixteen ads in all, from a total of 546 ads that include Negroes and perhaps 100,000 to 200,000 ads altogether that appeared in the sampled magazines during the three years studied—an overwhelming one-hundredth of one percent!

TABLE 11   *Group Composition by Kind of Interaction*[a]

CATEGORY	PANEL AD/ SEPARATE PICTURES	ALL NEGRO	MIXED NON-PEER	MIXED PEER
1946				
Single individual	25.0%	47.4%	—	—
Noninteraction	75.0	15.8	22.2%	37.5%
Work interaction	—	31.6	77.8	37.5
Social interaction	—	5.2	—	25.0
	100.0%	100.0%	100.0%	100.0%
Sample size	20	19	81	8
1956				
Single individual	42.9%	76.5%	—	—
Noninteraction	57.1	23.5	17.2%	28.6%
Work interaction	—	—	77.1	71.4
Social interaction	—	—	5.7	—
	100.0%	100.0%	100.0%	100.0%
Sample size	28	17	35	14
1965				
Single individual	42.4%	73.9%	—	—
Noninteraction	57.6	8.7	42.1%	43.5%
Work interaction	—	8.7	52.6	26.1
Social interaction	—	8.7	5.3	30.4
	100.0%	100.0%	100.0%	100.0%
Sample size	59	23	19	46

[a] American Negroes only; dissimilar ads.

This kind of ad typically advertised a hard liquor, showing Negro and white drinking together, small children playing with each other or rather exotic high fashion ads with models in bizarre positions. Two of the 16 ads showed Sammy Davis, Jr., one sitting on the floor with a high fashion model and the other advertising a record album, *Golden Boy,* with a pen drawing of a Negro obviously kissing a white girl.

TABLE 12 *Products Using Negroes in Advertising*[a]

PRODUCT	1946	1956	1965	TOTAL
Travel/tourism	5.1%	14.3%	10.8%	10.0%
Hotels/resorts/night clubs	1.7	9.1	8.5	6.5
Railroads	25.1	6.5	0.5	10.1
Airlines	2.3	3.3	6.6	4.2
Car rental/tires/parts	4.6	1.9	1.9	2.7
Clothing/fabrics	6.3	5.2	16.0	10.0
Liquor/beer/wine	10.3	9.1	5.6	8.1
Foods/cereal/wax/soap	10.9	3.3	3.7	5.9
Perfume/jewelry/stationery	4.0	2.6	1.4	2.6
Records	4.0	16.2	15.5	12.0
Newspapers/books/TV-radio/ movies	4.6	4.5	5.6	5.0
Cameras/film	—	0.7	4.7	2.0
Industrial supplies/equipment	10.3	10.4	3.7	7.7
Banks/insurance/investments	1.7	5.2	8.5	5.3
Institutional ads	3.4	3.9	2.8	3.3
Ideological crusades	2.3	1.9	1.9	2.0
Miscellaneous others	3.4	1.9	2.3	2.6
	100.0%	100.0%	100.0%	100.0%
Sample size	175	154	213	542

[a] Dissimilar ads.

Finally Table 12 presents a summary classification of the product categories advertised in this study's sample of ads. As evident, certain product categories decreased their advertising using Negroes and others increased the number of ads with Negroes. The most significant decrease is found among railroads. Twenty-five percent of the ads appearing in 1946 were those of railroad companies portraying Negro porters, shoe-shine boys and luggage handlers. By 1965 only one railroad ad with a Negro appeared. Obviously railroad advertising, itself, has diminished considerably, and these results may affect some of the conclusions previously stated. Other important decreases in the frequency of using Negroes appear for industrial equipment and supplies, which tended to use Negro laborers, and foods and cereals.

Major increases in the use of Negroes can be found in travel, tourism, and airline ads which tend generally to portray exotic non-American

Negroes in varied settings. The increase of using Negroes in ads for hotels, night clubs, and resorts is primarily portrayals of Negro entertainers. Two other product categories—clothing and fabrics, banks and insurance companies—show significant increases in the use of Negroes. For fabrics and clothing, the Negro is typically a high fashion model in mixed peer groups, and for financial institutions one finds portrayals of children playing together or white-collar employees, white and black, interacting in peer roles.

Conspicuous by their failure to use Negroes in ads are advertisers with large advertising budgets, such as manufacturers of patent medicines, automobiles, and personal hygiene products, such as toothpastes and deodorants. Missing also are producers of ready-to-eat cereals, detergents, and soap products.

SUMMARY

In summary the hypothesis that the frequency of Negroes appearing in magazine advertising would be U-shaped over the years 1946, 1956, and 1965 was confirmed both for the total set of ads studied and for those depicting only the American Negro. The frequency of appearance of ads with a non-American Negro tended to show a continuing increase. The portrayed occupational role of the American Negro has changed considerably over the 20-year period with considerably more Negroes portrayed in the higher status occupations in recent years. The occupational role of the non-American Negro has shown no significant change since 1946. The social role of the Negro and the appearance of integrated advertising in which black and white are shown as peers has also tended to increase recently. However, the ads that treat the Negro as an equal are so few that neither can the civil rights groups be acclaimed successful nor can the advertising industry take particular pride in their supposedly newly found social responsibility.

[Notes]

1. Some results of the study are also reported in [1].
2. See, for example, Simon [5].
3. A phase of the study on other non-Caucasian races and ethnic groups was eliminated at this stage because of costs.
4. Page counts were not checked against publisher's records or secondary sources such as *Advertising Age* to keep the study as independent as possible of the

communicator's claims and because of some concern that use of regional editions available at libraries may lead to errors.

5. Occupations were later coded according to the U. S. Census occupational categories, except that a separate category of "entertainer, model, sports" was created. The occupations of policeman and fireman (in two or three ads) were not classified under *service* (with porters, maids, and janitors) but under *craftsmen*. It would be misleading to put Negro policemen and custodians in the same occupational category.

6. Table 5—American Negro statistical significant test (total ads):
   Overall chi square=8.67, df=2, $p<.02$
   1946–1956; $\chi^2=6.80$, df=1, $p<.01$
   1956–1965; $\chi^2=6.80$, df=1, $p<.01$
   1946–1965; not significant.

7. Table 5—Non-American Negro statistical test (total ads):
   Overall chi square=8.60, df=2, $p<.05$
   1946–1965; $\chi^2=8.06$, df=1, $p<.01$
   1956–1965; not significant $(p=.10)$
   1946–1956; not significant.

8. As shown later, changes in the kind of product advertised over the 20-year period may counterindicate the curvilinear hypothesis. Railroad ads that tend to picture Negro porters decreased significantly in incidence during the 20-year period, but travel and tourism ads that tend to picture non-American Negroes increased.

[References]

1. Arnold M. Barban, "Negro and White Reactions to 'Integrated' Advertising: Some Preliminary Findings," Unpublished paper, Department of Advertising, University of Illinois, August 1967.

2. Bernard Berelson, *Content Analysis in Communication Research,* Glencoe, Ill.: The Free Press, 1952, 18.

3. William H. Boyenton, "The Negro Turns to Advertising," *Journalism Quarterly,* 42 (Spring 1965), 227–35.

4. Fred H. Schmidt, "A Guest in the Home: A Survey of Television and the American Negro," Unpublished paper, Institute of Industrial Relations, University of California, Los Angeles, January 1966.

5. Rita J. Simon, "An Appraisal of Changes in the White Attitudes Toward Negroes and Civil Rights Over Three Decades," Unpublished paper, School of Communications, University of Illinois and forthcoming in *Public Opinion Quarterly.*

26

John V. Petrof

Reaching the Negro Market: A Segregated Versus a General Newspaper

THE objective of this paper is to furnish the businessman with some information concerning the value of using a segregated vs. a general medium in trying to communicate with the Negro customer. In addressing a seminar of the Southern California Council of the American Association of Advertising Agencies, Mr. Arthur A. Porter (1966), senior vice-president of Campbell-Ewald Company, said that special markets, such as ethnic groups, can be reached more productively through publications designed for them. Such statements seem to be logical conclusions from the theory of market segmentation. However, in dealing with consumers, regardless of their race or creed, it is extremely risky to base decisions on ivory-tower inductive reasoning. Even if they subscribe to ethnic publications, members of minority groups may not be influenced by the commercial messages presented in such media. Advertisements in media cutting across ethnic lines may reach the so-called special markets more efficiently.

In advertising, as in all forms of business endeavor, it is impossible to measure efficiency unless results can be compared with some predetermined goals. This study attempts to determine the difference in awareness created among Negro consumers when two advertisements, one by an institution patronized primarily by Negroes and the other by a firm catering to both races, are presented through a Negro and a general readership newspaper. This information is of great importance to many advertisers, since the fact that most of them buy space in general readership

Reprinted by permission from the *Journal of Advertising Research*, Vol. 8, No. 2, June 1968, pp. 40–43. Copyright © Advertising Research Foundation, 1968.

and minority publications simultaneously can be taken as *prima facie* evidence that they suspect or believe that each type may have a different impact on a Negro prospect.

COMMUNITY BACKGROUND

Atlanta, known also as the Gateway to the South, is the largest metropolis in that region. As of April, 1965, the nonwhite population of metropolitan Atlanta amounted to 253,773, which was 22.2 percent of the total. As in most metropolitan centers, a large proportion (41 percent) of the nonwhite population lives in the central city. The area also ranks tenth in median Negro family income, about $4,900 a year (Petrof, 1963).

In Atlanta the general press is represented by the *Atlanta Constitution* and the *Atlanta Journal,* both publications of Atlanta Newspapers, Inc. The *Atlanta Constitution* was selected for this study since it is most comparable to the only daily Negro newspaper in Atlanta. The *Constitution* is a morning daily with a circulation of 200,165. The Negro press is represented by the *Atlanta Daily World* which is also a morning paper with a circulation of 30,000. The price of space in the general newspaper is approximately three times as expensive as comparable space in the Negro newspaper; however, when one compares the two media on the basis of audience exposure rather than absolute cost of space, the general newspaper gains a seven to one edge over the Negro newspaper because of its larger circulation. Exposure figures by themselves give no indication of the ability of a given advertisement to create product or firm awareness in a prospect. If a publication with a smaller circulation is capable of creating greater awareness among a large percentage of its audience than the larger, one may say that advertising in the small publication is more effective—assuming that greater awareness leads to more sales.

METHODOLOGY

With the cooperation of two local retailers, one patronized primarily by Negroes and the other by both races, two advertisements featuring a sale at both stores appeared in both the above-mentioned local newspapers on a Thursday morning. The size, appearance and wording of each store advertisement were identical in both papers; however, it was not possible to secure the same location in both newspapers, mainly because the general publication on that date was seven times the size of the Negro newspaper. This tends to put the advertisement in the general paper at a disadvantage, since it has to compete against a larger number of messages to attract a reader's attention. But since the larger newspaper's circulation was also seven times that of the Negro publication one may assume that a sizeable circulation will to a large extent offset this disadvantage.

By securing the cooperation of the circulation managers and delivery men of both publications, it was possible to develop an address list of Negroes who regularly purchase both papers in the various neighborhoods of the community. Based on the author's knowledge and opinions of knowledgeable people in the area, such neighborhoods were classified into three socioeconomic groups consisting of the upper, middle and lower classes of the Atlanta Negro community. Most people familiar with the locality and the dwelling patterns of its minority groups can perform this classification without much difficulty. Also, in order to check and evaluate the validity of respondent classification, interviewers were supplied with questionnaires containing questions that further verified the accuracy of the classifications.

The size of the total Negro population in each socioeconomic group was determined by fitting population figures provided in census tracts into the geographical dimensions of the three socioeconomic classes as defined for the purposes of this study. In a community with segregated housing this can easily be accomplished, since a great majority of census tracts consist of 100 per cent nonwhite population. After determining the size of its population, a random sample was selected for each social class from the list of Negroes who purchase both papers. The number of people interviewed in each group was in the same proportion as the population in each class had to the total Negro population in the area. A total of 612 adult Negroes subscribing to both papers were interviewed on the evening that the advertisements appeared. To help the respondents identify the medium in which the advertisements appeared, interviewers used aided recall. After attempting to identify the first advertisement with its source, respondents were asked to repeat the same procedure for the other advertisement.

FINDINGS

Negro readers, like their white counterparts, are interested mainly in local news (Bureau of Advertising, 1951). In all three socioeconomic classes an overwhelming majority of the Negroes who purchase the Negro newspaper do so because it gives better coverage of local Negro news. Negroes from all social classes believe that the general newspaper provides superior and more effective news coverage. However, since the general newspaper does not include detailed news concerning the local Negro community, as far as Negroes are concerned it fails to fulfill its most important community function. A great majority of Negroes who purchase the race oriented publication because it gives better coverage of their community still think that information concerning political news, local store advertising, job vacancies, etc., can be obtained more effectively through the general newspaper. Lack of Negro news coverage by the general media is obviously the main justification for the existence of the minority newspaper in most American communities.

The advertisement of the firm catering primarily to Negroes was noticed in the Negro newspaper by 46 percent of the sample (see Table 1). However, only 82 percent of those who claimed to have seen

TABLE 1 *Awareness and Identification of Advertisement with Its Source*

| | NEGRO NEWSPAPER | | GENERAL NEWSPAPER | |
	I	II	III	IV
	Interviewees who claimed to have seen the ad.	Interviewees in Col. I who correctly identified the ad.	Interviewees who claimed to have seen the ad.	Interviewees in Col. III who correctly identified the ad.
Ad. of Retailer Catering to Negroes	46%	82%	29%	40%
Ad. of Retailer Catering to Both Races	31%	39%	64%	90%

the advertisement were able to identify it correctly. The same advertisement drew claims of having been noticed in the general newspaper by 29 percent of the sample, and the percentage of those who correctly identified it was 40 percent.

The advertisement of the retailer catering to both races was noticed by 64 percent of the interviewed Negroes in the general newspaper; 90 percent of those were able to identify the advertisement with its correct source. The same advertisement appearing in the Negro newspaper was noticed by 31 percent of the respondents; only 39 percent of this group could identify the advertisement with its proper source.

These figures lead one to believe that only products and firms catering primarily to Negro customers can make a more effective impact on their prospective clients by using a segregated publication in their newspaper advertising. It is obvious that the majority of Negroes notice advertisements in Negro newspapers only when such messages concern products or firms exclusively used by Negroes, e.g., hair products and special foods. The advertiser who markets products and services of general use can increase the mileage he gets from his advertising expenditures by using general newspapers in his attempt to communicate with his prospective Negro customers. For example, a local car dealer who desires to convey a message to a Negro prospect improves his chances of accomplishing this objective by better than 100 percent when he does so through a general instead of a Negro newspaper. However, this situation practically reverses itself when the advertising of products and services with an exclusive Negro use is involved. In such cases Negroes notice advertisements better in minority oriented news media.

Although this general relationship of advertisement impact by medium holds true for all classes, the effectiveness of the Negro newspaper reaches its height among the middle and lower classes. Upper class Negroes noticed the Negro retailers advertisement better in the general newspaper. Although this difference is not significant one may speculate that from an advertiser's viewpoint newspapers lose their communicative effectiveness as Negroes reach the upper classes. It is also possible that upper class Negroes are less race conscious (see Table 2).

TABLE 2 *Impact of Newspaper Advertisements on Negroes by Social Class and Medium of Presentation*

	FIRMS PATRONIZED PREDOMINANTLY BY NEGROES			FIRMS PATRONIZED BY BOTH RACES		
	Upper Class	Middle Class	Lower Class	Upper Class	Middle Class	Lower Class
Percent of total interviewees who correctly identified the ad in the Negro newspaper	18%	55%	68%	5%	43%	47%
Percent of total interviewees who correctly identified the ad in the general newspaper	21	38	6	41	56	52

IMPLICATIONS

This study brings out some interesting implications about the future of Negro newspapers. Practically all the interviewed individuals admitted that in their opinion the general newspaper is superior to the Negro newspaper in performing what they believed to be the functions of a newspaper. They purchased the Negro publication because the general paper does not provide enough news of their community. The fact that they keep subscribing to the general publication is *prima facie* evidence that this deficiency is more than offset by the more efficient way the general newspaper handles its other functions. One may hazard a guess that if the general readership newspapers in many American communities with large concentrations of Negroes would give more coverage to news concerning the Negro community, many of the so-called Negro newspapers would have difficulty in justifying their existence.

Since the impact of Negro newspapers is highest among the lower classes and tends to go down as the Negro moves upward along the socio-economic spectrum, it is possible that the current efforts of government authorities and private sources to assist the American Negro in improving himself both culturally and financially may prove disastrous for many Negro newspapers. As Negroes become full-fledged citizens they tend to act like the average American and not as Negroes. Without stereotyped Negroes the current Negro newspaper will find itself without a market unless, of course, it can adapt itself to changes in the social structure.

CONCLUSIONS

Many firms selling products and services of a general use purchase space in minority publications on the assumption that their advertisements will have a better impact on the members of the minority group. This study questions the validity of this hypothesis. Atlanta Negroes notice only advertisements featuring exclusively Negro products and services better in the segregated medium. Even then this relationship tends to disappear when they move upward along the social scale. Advertisers selling products and services of general use can communicate with the Negro consumer better and at a considerably lower cost if they beam their messages through general newspapers.

For products and services used exclusively by Negroes the Negro newspaper proves to be a more efficient medium in conveying the business-man's message. It appears that age old customs of the American society have shaped the cognitive structure of the average Negro consumer in such a way that he refuses to perceive certain advertising messages until they are channeled to him in a culturally acceptable manner. This social conditioning of the Negro consumer may be objectionable from a philosophical viewpoint; however, for the businessman who markets products of general use and whose main concern is to improve service to his customers through better communications, the Negro newspaper does not seem to provide the proper means.

To be sure, the findings of this study are of a local nature and may not be applicable to the entire national market. However, to the best of the author's knowledge this is the only study of this subject conducted by a sponsor with no vested interest in the results. Its national implications should be obvious to all persons familiar with this "American dilemma."

[References]

1. Bureau of Advertising. *What Happens When Newspapers Don't Hit Town.* New York: Bureau of Advertising, 1951, pp. 4–5.
2. Petrof, John V. The Effect of Student Boycotts Upon the Purchasing Habits of Negro Families in Atlanta, Georgia. *Phylon,* Fall, 1963, p. 267.
3. Porter, Arthur H. Battle Line Shaping for Markets of Mind. *Marketing Insights,* October 10, 1966, p. 4.

27

W. Leonard Evans, Jr.

Ghetto Marketing: What Now?

THE subject of "Ghetto Marketing: What Now?" suggests a discussion of the prognosis without an understanding and interpretation of the symptoms, an evaluation of the diagnosis and the ingredients of remedy. Once we have completed these basic phases, we can discuss the prognosis. Therefore, I will begin with a brief summary of the cause and the symptoms so that we may have a starting point. We may arrive at different diagnoses, but I think we can all agree that the patient is ill.

GHETTO MARKETING

First, what is ghetto marketing? It is simply marketing in any geographical area in any city in the United States where black people live and buy. It is an area usually designated as being occupied by low-income groups. It is in reality occupied by groups with the same basic segmentation that we find in any broad market spectrum.

For example, in the ghetto 3% of the people are in the upper-upper status group, 12% are in the upper status group and 45% are in the middle status group. This group represents a new middle-income group with upward mobility.

Reprinted by permission of the American Marketing Association from *Marketing and the New Science of Planning, Proceedings of the American Marketing Association National Conference,* a publication of the American Marketing Association, Robert L. King, ed., Fall 1968, pp. 528–531.

349

We find 40% in the lower status group which is broken down like other markets: The poor, but proud, representing 10% of the 40% that will not accept welfare of any kind; the poor, but decent, status group which represents 15% of the 40% and accepts welfare, but lacks high morals and traditions; the poor, but defeated, group which represents 10%, most of which are on welfare, but have no hope for a better life; the poor and defiant, representing 5%. The defiant ones in the Negro community may be slightly different because they throw things and for some reason these things burn.

EDUCATION AND THE ILLNESS

Many competent observers are quick to designate education as the primary cause of the illness. Education is very definitely a contributing factor, but one needs to probe beneath the surface to determine whether education in its present form meets the needs and desires of the black economic community.

Negroes in the United States have become specialists in humanities—some have been educated to be teachers, lawyers, even government clerks. But the black people in this country have neither been encouraged nor guided into such fields as architecture, engineering, banking, etc. Commerce and industry are subjects in education that have somehow eluded the black curriculum. There has been an improper diagnosis of the causes of the illness, in my opinion, which results in a lack of understanding of the proper treatment necessary for a cure. The illness of the resident of the ghetto is simply that he buys everything, but neither produces nor sells anything.

All of this has resulted in the ghetto's suffering from what economists call a deficit balance of payments. Ghetto residents are perhaps the only group in the world that can be classified as total consumers, because Negro communities as a whole have not been trained to be productive in our society; they only consume what America produces from the outside. This creates a deficit balance of payments of the worst kind. Collectively, in the United States the Negro community represents an annual income of approximately $32-billion. This means that the black ghettos in this country, if they were evaluated as a nation, would rank tenth in annual income among the nations of the world. We can conclude that the Negro in the United States is not poor individually, but richer collectively than most nations.

For example, in 1863 at the time of the Emancipation Proclamation, there were 2-million blacks in the United States with an estimated $30-million in assets. Today, blacks have grown to 25-million and have an estimated $200-billion in assets and an annual income that is expected to grow to $50-billion by 1975.

RELATIONSHIP TO MARKETING

My studies of the market problems in the major metropolitan ghetto areas of the United States over a period of some thirty years have made this basic logic incontrovertibly clear: All social and political ills have economic roots. It is impossible to make meaningful progress in one area unless one makes corresponding progress in all of the others. To put the matter more forcibly, we are observing in our cities today grave symptoms of economic death that are being delayed by an infusion of inadequate economic treatments, transfusions and injections of social welfare dollars and other ineffectual remedies. The patient needs surgery, not aspirin. The ghetto, in its present form, is an economic ghost town, thrashing in a death agony; yet paradoxically, it holds the greatest concentration of consumer purchasing power per square mile in the United States, and possibly the world. The symptoms, in my opinion, are very clear. The patient is dying of economic malnutrition—over-consumption and under-production.

DIAGNOSIS

The diagnosis, like the present prognosis, is relatively simple. The essential truth is that the cause of economic malnutrition in the black communities stems from the fact that black money was never segregated in this country—although everything else was. Capitalism, money, investment—call it what you will—have never been visible nor functional in the ghetto because there was no practical method by which to accumulate capital. The Negro earns money working for a white employer. He spends his money with the white businessman, and if there was anything left over, he put his money in a white bank. If he had an opportunity to develop a business for himself, the white banker always had any number of reasons why he could not make the loan.

We are discussing "Ghetto Marketing" because we have faith that the patient will survive. He represents one of the great consumers of the world. He is geographically located in major metropolitan areas; he is easily identified; and in spite of his economic dilemma, he purchases national brands in goods and services. It is a wealthy market collectively. The question that concerns us is whether his healthy attributes will be destroyed by the social cancer that threatens to disrupt our marketing economy. What can we, as marketing men, do?

It is again paradoxical that the patient will live and live healthily with three acute symptoms—integration, separatism and co-existence. There is no reason why integration, separatism and co-existence cannot be utilized to develop a healthy economy, as they guarantee a freedom of choice to the individuals. There are a number of blacks being irreversibly integrated every day which simply means that they are being absorbed into the white business world, never to return as a producer in the black community. They should have this right. Then there are those blacks who seek to find their success in the black community and make its basic economy work for material acquisition by means of a basic concept of separatism. There are those blacks who represent the great majority of the black community who practice and believe in the principal of co-existence, which simply means living in both the white and black worlds and making the most of the opportunities that are available. The principal of co-existence is making a start, and tremendous progress is being made in many cities.

THE REMEDY

The acute economic malnutrition being suffered by the ghetto is best remedied by a balanced diet of integration, separatism and co-existence. This is paradoxical, but true. This treatment requires surgery, not just a few pills. As the patient becomes economically viable, there will be certain positive readjustments to be made in ghetto marketing. Post-operative care must be intensive, and treatment is to be based upon an historic concept in seeking to restore economic health: One must not only be able to buy, but one must be able to produce and sell that which is produced. To produce, one must first have capital to invest. When the black man is able to do these things—buy, produce and sell—he will then attain equality among his fellow men and live to experience the true meaning of economic health and freedom.

The recuperative forces of the remedy reduce the high fever of the ghetto by retarding the outflow of capital and profits. A basic readjustment in the balance of payments will correspondingly reduce the pain. This can be done by a proper utilization of the top skills and talents within the black communities, not by a continued export of these skills and talents to the outside white economic areas. No economy rebuilds its strength with its least efficient laborers and its non-productive elements.

Marketing strategies must be adjusted accordingly. More consideration must be given to the fact that ghetto purchases have tremendous weight outside the ghetto, not just inside. In fact, there is a tremendous mobility outside of the ghetto by the black consumer.

ECONOMIC PROGNOSIS

The Negro shopper is structured by basic status groups which are as follows:[1] 15%, upper group; 45%, middle group and 40%, lower group. This status grouping reveals the Negro life style as well as where Negroes shop. We find that 80% of the Negro consumers shop outside of their immediate neighborhoods. The remaining 20% which are in the lower group actually confine their purchases to their own neighborhoods because of their lack of money and mobility. The 80% of the market buy not only in the central business district, but in the outlying areas. We have included, for your study, some comments—and possibly advertising and marketing implications—which were the basis of the study by Social Research, Inc. of Chicago (see Appendix).

When economic vitality is pumped into the ghetto community by self-determination, by new investment, and by new, sophisticated economic and financial creativity, e.g., in the number of supermarkets per square mile, per thousand consumer, etc., there will be shifts and changes in management and ownership of wholesale distributing facilities. There will be greater participation of black people in controlling the economics of their community.

At the present time, the Negro income of $32-billion is actually controlled by white sources. The Negro controls less than 2%. Any adjustment in the economics of the ghetto has to affect marketing strategy. For example, computerized marketing will have a dramatic effect on the future of the ghetto advertiser. In the past, these areas have been considered too poor to buy national brands. Many advertisers, to their surprise, are going to find a very high percentage of sales to the various segments within the Negro community.[2] We already know from a computer marketing analysis of product usage among heavy users of toilet soap, that black consumers represent more than 48% of the total users who consume eight bars or more per month in the city of Chicago. The Negro represents only 27% of the city's population.

CURRENT RESEARCH

Another vital development will create some changes in strategy in ghetto marketing. During the remaining years of this century, the ghetto community will become involved in the purchase of capital shares of major industrial and consumer good companies. This equity will begin to create a flow of dividends into the black communities which, along with the gradual restriction of the outflow of profits and capital, will develop a better balance of payments. A new era of economic vitality will develop from this base of capital accumulation and economic power.

We students of ghetto marketing remain puzzled today regarding the possible implications and effects on the marketing of national brands that may result from the civil rights revolution of the '60's. For example, we do not know whether the new consumers—the young consumers—who have lived through the civil rights revolution will maintain the brand loyalty and brand preference of their parents and grandparents. We do know, however, that there are symptoms of erosion of the national brand among high-income groups in such cities as Detroit, Chicago and Washington. There is a shifting to buy, not by brand, but by price—an unusual trend in ghetto marketing.

On the other hand, there has been in the past four years strong evidence of a market revolution in the form of brand disloyalty. For example, where alcoholic beverage brand A and brand B collectively enjoyed 94% of the market in the past, today the market is split between A, B, C, D and E, all representing the same price level, making the disloyalty horizontal rather than vertical in price character. These trends may be temporary, but for the future, the impact on marketing strategy can be serious.

In my opinion, this is part of the assertiveness of ghetto residents. It is a part of their new feeling of pride and ability to make a choice with selectivity. The effective invitation to purchase will be significant in the future sales cycle.

The crisis in our ghetto is, in part, the pent-up demand for new goods and services beyond comprehension. American marketing has created the desire for a higher standard of living, making the inability of the ghetto consumer to participate in this affluence a major cause of the urban crisis.

Marketing to the ghetto resident has a dynamic potential—an unprecedented demand for goods and services. Marketing men can fulfill this demand by recognizing and accepting the challenge. The ghetto market challenge is not a barrier to profitability, but an unusual opportunity to develop a viable black economic community and eliminate basic causes of urban crisis. Everyone can win in this crisis by accomplishing these goals with profitable results to all.

APPENDIX:
SOCIAL RESEARCH, INCORPORATED, 1968

Negroes As Shoppers

- Shoppers first, Negroes second
- What the Negro shopper wants
- Where Negroes shop
- Possible implications for marketing and advertising

Shoppers First—Negroes Second
  The "right" way is to seek economic self-interest in a free and open market.
Shop wherever the "best buy" can be found.
Desire to want advertised items—same brands, same labels as they imagine the *best* white Americans have.
Practical Shopper, first and foremost—way to express and realize values and aspirations as *Negro Human Beings.*
What the Negro Shopper Wants
  Quality and Price
  Credit and Exchange
  Guidance and Confirmation
  Protocol and Propriety—and Promise
Where Negroes shop
  Needs and selections and rejections influenced by social class levels and corresponding variations in residential and life-style patterns.

IMPLICATIONS FOR MARKETING AND ADVERTISING

(1) Negroes want belief that purchases reflect quality, value and good taste. Ads and labels—

SYMBOLIC * PICTORIAL * REASONS WHY

with background information, origin—how and why it is to be used. To be welcomed as: "Educational," Acculturative—guiding and helping the customer into understanding and doing the "right" thing.

(2) Edibles and other items directly consumed. Fresh and imperishable—same high quality as when packaged by reputable brand name processor. Feature: stoutly sealed and durable cans and boxes—ensuring freshness and purity. Reputation of processor *compensates for deficiencies of the retailer.*

(3) Wearing apparel
  Quality of manufacturer has been maintained—unsoiled. "Fresh" new styles and rot-resistant fabrics—safeguards to buy with confidence.

(4) Newly arrived middle-class . . . (and aspirants)
  Good casual clothes—a promising market. Life today—relaxed, informed for easy-going outlook—transmit a confidence to compensate for uncertainties about propriety.

(5) Negro shoppers value . . . guaranteed product replacement opportunities. Reassure the policies and commitments—cheerfully overcome possibility that customer believes he may: Wait, cringe, and plead for replacement of a defective item.

(6) Promote Personnel . . . considerate, helpful, knowledgeable, and expert (not friendly). Need for sharing knowledge for those who seek it.

(7) Capitalize on Negro Quest for Individuality—Distinctive Identity
  Subtly reinforce products and product messages—much is being done successfully with efforts directed to white audiences.

NEGRO STATUS GROUPS

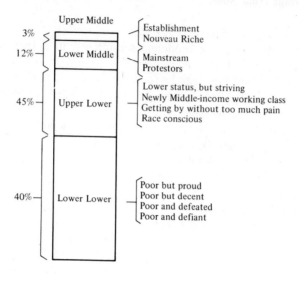

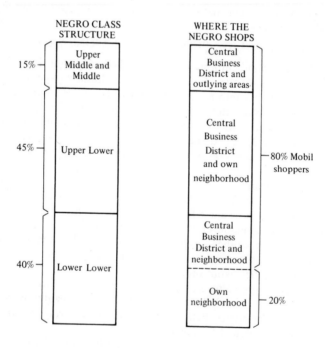

FIGURE 1 *Negro Status Groups*

[Notes]

1. Social Research, Inc., *Negroes as Shoppers,* Part I, Chicago, Illinois, 1968.
2. Brand Rating Corporation. *The Brand Rating Index,* Part I, New York, New York.

28

Charles E. Van Tassel

The Negro As a Consumer— What We Know and What We Need to Know

$\mathbf{D}$URING the past few years, there has been a substantial increase in interest and in research effort on the part of marketing management regarding the Negro as a consumer. More and more companies are paying more and more attention to the Negro as they search for market expansion opportunities, and their action is prompted primarily by four factors.

First of all, there has been an increased economic awareness of the Negro in recent years. The sheer size of the Negro population and the magnitude of its purchasing power have certainly heightened the business-man's interest in what is commonly referred to as "the Negro market". Second, there is an ever-increasing social awareness of the Negro. Organized efforts ranging from local neighborhood demonstrations against various forms of discrimination to relatively large and powerful national groups such as the NAACP and CORE have been quite effective in increasing the awareness of the Negro by American industry. A third factor pertains to increased political involvement. The most obvious example of this, and one which has profound implications for the business community is the passage of the Civil Rights Bill. Government action, then, has been in part responsible for business being more attentive to the Negro. The fourth factor which has been instrumental in spurring business interest in the Negro relates to the increased availability of market information about Negroes.

Reprinted by permission of the American Marketing Association from *Marketing for Tomorrow—Today, Proceedings of the American Marketing Association National Conference,* a publication of the American Marketing Association, M. S. Moyer and R. E. Vosburgh, eds., June 1967, pp. 166–168.

358

While the economic, social, and political dimensions are certainly of profound importance, it is the fourth element, the nature and extent of market information currently available about Negroes, which is of prime importance to the marketer.

NEGRO MARKET DEMOGRAPHIC INFORMATION

Most of the data available now on the Negro market are of a demographic or descriptive nature. For example, it is known that:

a. The Negro population rose from 13 million in 1940 to approximately 21 million today—an increase of over 60 percent. By comparison the white population increased in size by about 45 percent during the same period.
b. Negro median family income is approximately one-half that of white median family income.
c. Negroes have an aggregate annual purchasing power of between $25 billion and $30 billion—about 7 percent of the U.S. total.
d. Negro consumers represent a rather compact sales target. While about one-seventh of the white population lives in the 25 largest cities in the U.S., one-third of all Negroes are concentrated in these 25 cities.
e. The Negro market is relatively young. Median age for whites is about 30. Median age for Negroes is around 23.

Additionally, there is a wide range of data available concerning such areas as geographic location, population mobility, job status and employment stability, educational levels, and family life, including such details as divorce, death, and illegitimacy rates.

This sort of factual knowledge is, of course, fundamental to an understanding of the basic dimensions of any market. It is not enough, however, to serve the purposes of management in setting policy relative to the Negro market.

NEGRO MARKET PURCHASING PATTERNS

While most of the information about the Negro market is of a demographic nature, some data are being developed about Negro purchasing patterns.

In terms of relative purchase quantities, it is known, for example, that:

a. Negro families tend to buy substantially more cooked cereals, corn meal, household insecticides, cream, rice, spaghetti, frozen vegetables, syrup, and vinegar, among others, than do their white counterparts.
b. The average Negro male supposedly buys 77 percent more pairs of shoes during his lifetime than the average white male and pays more for them.

c. Reportedly, Negroes purchase as much as one-half of all Scotch whiskey consumed in the U.S.
d. Negroes also apparently consume somewhat more flour, waxes, toilet and laundry soap, shortenings, salt, peanut butter, fruit juices, and canned chili than whites.

While Negro purchase habit information is not as readily available as descriptive market data on Negroes, a fund of knowledge is being developed in this area which should serve marketers well in the future. But the combination of information in these two areas is still not sufficient upon which to base a rational approach toward this market.

NEGRO MARKET ATTITUDES AND MOTIVATIONS

One area remains to be explored: attitudinal and motivational dimensions of Negro consumer behavior. And it is here that the greatest void of knowledge exists.

Of course, some reliable information, some hypotheses, and some plausible suggested explanations are available regarding why Negroes act and react as they do in the market place. For example, many marketers have suggested that Negroes frequently attempt to emulate white society through purchases of products with high quality images. If this is true, it would at least partly explain the Negro's relatively higher expenditures on well known brands of Scotch, expensive clothing, quality furniture, appliances, and the like.

Another thesis is that Negroes as a group have accepted the values of white middle-class society, but, at the same time, experience difficulties in purchasing products which represent some of these values. A basic dilemma arises where the Negro must choose whether to strive, frequently in the face of formidable odds, to attain white middle-class values, and the products which are associated with these values, or simply give up and live without most of them.[1]

There are a variety of other explanations regarding why Negroes behave as they do in their roles as consumers. There is one major area, however, where relatively few explanations are available. This is also the area which probably provides the single greatest opportunity to influence the purchase behavior of Negroes—communications.

COMMUNICATIONS RESEARCH

Probably the most frequently raised and most perplexing issue relates to the advisability of adopting an "integrated" approach toward advertising. Some questions frequently asked by companies regarding how to communicate most effectively with Negroes are:

a. Should our advertisements be integrated or segregated; that is, should we use all white, all Negro, or white and Negro models?

b. Should we attempt to reach the Negro consumer by placing our traditionally "white" advertisements in Negro media, or should we have specially designed advertisements for Negro media?

c. If we produce integrated advertisements, should these advertisements be restricted to Negro media, or should they be exposed through general media?

d. If Negro media are used, which media in particular are best?

e. Does the Negro feel complimented or honored when he sees an advertisement specially designed to attract his attention and interest, or does he view this sort of thing as just one more reminder that he is different?

f. How would our white customers react to integrated advertisements in general media?

A certain amount of research has, of course, been completed in this general area. Something is known, for example, about viewing, reading, and listening habits. It has been established that radio is the major medium for Negroes, followed by television, newspapers, and magazines. And this pattern is known to be different than that for whites. Studies have shown that radio stations employing rather tasteless music and advertising programming appeal to the Negro working class and frequently offend and alienate middle and upper class Negroes. Evidence is available to show that advertisements which are apparently designed to appeal to Negro buyers, but which show Negroes in a situation which the Negro viewer recognizes as unrealistic can do more harm than good.

Some work has also been done on Negro reactions to various advertising stimuli. It was found in one fairly recent study that when people were presented with a series of general concepts, such as integrated advertisements, segregated advertisements, and various media alternatives, there was a great similarity in responses by Negroes and whites. Whereas advertising strategies of many large companies would lead one to expect sizeable differences in reactions of Negroes and whites to these alternatives, they were surprisingly alike.[2]

Other research studies indicate that the use of Negro models can be quite favorable, as long as the advertisements are presented in a dignified meaningful, and realistic way. And, importantly, it has been determined that Negroes frequently view companies which run integrated advertising campaigns as more progressive, more friendly, more desirous of the Negro's business, a fairer employer, and more anxious to work out today's social problems than companies which do not participate in integrated advertising.

Reactions of white respondents are also frequently more favorable than might be expected. They often view integrated advertisements which are tastefully presented as pleasant, appealing, meaningful and dignified. In addition, they too view a company which runs integrated advertising as generally more friendly, more progressive, and a fairer employer.

Research efforts of these types, however, are infrequent. Too little effort has been extended to date, in terms of uncovering Negro attitudes and motivations in the market place. The widely varying approaches taken by so many companies in an attempt to communicate with the Negro consumer strongly suggest that the answers to fundamental marketing questions simply are not available. It has been stated that, "Insufficient knowledge of the Negro consumer's motivations has led to sharp controversy over the direction advertisers should take to reach this market."[3]

While opportunities for the future lie partly in continuing to develop descriptive data and actual purchase behavior information on Negroes, significant gains will be primarily dependent upon ability of marketers to develop and properly interpret attitudinal data such that a sound basis can be established for understanding and communicating with the Negro as a consumer.

A LOOK AT THE FUTURE

In addition to reviewing past and present strengths and weaknesses regarding marketing to the Negro, it is useful to consider some expected future developments which will likely affect the approach taken by marketers in reacting to the ever-changing composition and requirements of the Negro market.

First, it is reasonable to expect a continued growth in the size and importance of the Negro market. It is expected that by 1970 Negroes will number somewhere around 25 million, and personal income should rise to about $45 billion. The influence of Negroes as consumers will be increasingly felt.

Second, geographic shifts will continue as the Negro becomes increasingly more urban. During the 1970's there will likely be a trend away from the central city to the suburbs as social barriers fall and as income and educational levels rise for the Negro. These developments will certainly affect consumption patterns.

Third, there will be increased pressure applied by special interest groups and by the government for a speeding up of the aggregation of Negroes into the mainstream of American life, which will, in turn, influence purchase behavior.

Fourth, basic social and economic forces will serve to radically change Negro expenditure patterns. For as incomes increase, and as intellectual and social horizons are broadened for Negroes and whites alike, expenditures of Negroes will shift in favor of goods and services which will upgrade their levels of living. Many products which have long received a disproportionately large share of the Negro's income, such as food, clothing, liquor, and entertainment will probably realize much slower growth in the future. A higher percentage of the Negro's income will be channeled toward such items as education, housing, medical care, automobiles, furniture and appliances, travel, insurance, and banking and credit facilities—that is, forms of consumption which have heretofore been unattainable.

Finally, substantial changes will be required in corporate policies directed toward the Negro in the future. Companies which have avoided meeting this problem and this challenge will be forced to become actively involved. This, in turn, will place added emphasis upon the need for collecting and properly interpreting data on the Negro as a consumer. Companies which have been actively involved in recruiting Negroes as customers will find a need to change their strategies and upgrade their abilities. For whereas the Negro may react favorably to an integrated advertisement now, no matter how ill conceived and how poorly presented, simply because it does finally represent a step forward, he will become more discriminating in his tastes over time and less tolerant of marketing programs borne out of inadequate knowledge on the part of management.

CONCLUSION

If one general observation can be made from this brief analysis, it is that the Negro market is in a perpetual state of change, and that the change is of a more revolutionary than evolutionary nature.

The challenge of keeping pace with this change is based upon the recognition of two prerequisites which must be accepted in order to establish effective marketing policies directed toward the Negro. First, a complete understanding of the Negro as a part of American life is required. One must be aware of the deep-rooted social and economic forces which are changing the Negro's role in society. For these forces will, in turn, shape the Negro's role as a consumer. Second, marketers must develop more and better information regarding the true attitudes, experiences, and motivations which influence the Negro's behavior in the marketplace.

Until these two things are accomplished, companies will be placing themselves in the dangerous position of taking action based upon hunch and intuition. For only when a true understanding of the Negro is reached regarding his emerging role as a member of society, as well as the forces which specifically influence his purchase activities, will it be possible to develop intelligent programs designed to optimize the opportunities presented by this important segment of the ethnic market.

[Notes]

1. Raymond A. Bauer, Scott M. Cunningham, and Lawrence H. Wortzel, "The Marketing Dilemma of Negroes," *Journal of Marketing*, Vol. 29, July, 1965, pp. 1–6 at p. 2.
2. Arnold Barban and Edward Cundiff, "Negro and White Responses to Advertising Stimuli," *Journal of Marketing Research*, November, 1964, pp. 53–56.
3. "Ad Men Straddle the Color Line," *News Front*, Vol. 10, No. 1, February, 1966, pp. 10–15 at p. 10.

Selected References

"Ads in Negro Market Media Do Double Duty with Negro Buyers: Interview with G. Zimmer, R. Bechtos," *Advertising Age,* 35, January 13, 1964, 72.

"Advertising: Reaching Vast Negro Market," *New York Times,* Business and Financial Section, September 12, 1965.

"Air Media and the U. S. Negro Market 1964," *Sponsor,* 18, August 17, 1964, 31–54.

Alexis, Marcus. "Pathways to the Negro Market," *Journal of Negro Education,* 28 (Spring 1959), 114–128.

Bauer, R. A. "Negroes More Brand Conscious than Whites," *Advertising Age,* 35, March 23, 1964, 73.

Black, L. E. "Negro Market: Growing, Changing, Challenging," *Sales Management,* 91, October 4, 1963, 42–47.

"Boycott by Negroes (Demand That Ads Show Negroes as well as Whites)," *Printers' Ink,* 284, August 23, 1963, 5–6.

"Breakthrough in TV Alerts Advertisers (to Negro Market)," *Sponsor,* 16, October 22, 1962, 10–12.

Danzig, Fred. "Negro Marketer Gets Bigger Role as Awareness of Specialized Field Grows," *Advertising Age,* 33, September 10, 1962, 96ff.

Fitzhugh, Naylor H. *The New Mood of the Negro: Some Implications for Market Developers.* Washington, D.C.: Howard University, 1963.

Gibson, D. P. "How to Plan a Negro Market Campaign," *Sales Management,* 102, April 15, 1969, 55–56.

Gibson, D. P. "Marketing to Negro Is Not Segregation in Reverse," *Advertising Age,* 36, September 27, 1965, 27.

"Heavy Buying by Negro Households Is Shown by WWRL," *Advertising Age,* 34, August 26, 1963, 242ff.

"How Do You Sell to Urban Negro Consumers?," Chicago: Johnson Publishing Company, Sales Promotion Department.

"How to Sell Today's Negro Women," *Sponsor,* 20, July 25, 1966, 49.

"Integration in Ads: The Next Step?," *Printers' Ink,* 283, May 31, 1963, 31.

Jeffries, L .W. "Treat Negro Equally to Get His Business," *Advertising Age,* 34, October 7, 1963, 62.

Johnson, John H. "Does Your Sales Force Know How to Sell the Negro Trade?," *Management Review,* 41 (July 1952), 449–450.

"Know-How Is Key to Selling Negro Today," *Sponsor,* 15, Part II, October 9, 1961, 9–10.

"Major Breakthrough in Integrated Ads New York Committee Says," *Advertising Age,* 35, February 17, 1964, 58.

"Making It in a Ghetto Super," *Chain Store Age* (September 1967), p. 84.

"Marketing to the Negro Consumer: Special Report," *Sales Management,* 84, March 4, 1960, 36–44.

"Negro Boycott Could Have Serious Lasting Effect on Sales, Study Shows," *Advertising Age,* 34, September 30, 1963, 3ff.

"Negro Brand Preferences: They Are Different," *Sponsor,* 21 (July 1967), 38–41.

"Negro Radio's Clients," *Sponsor,* 15, October 9, 1961, 31–32.

"New Tactic Is Pinpointed on Special Needs," *Sponsor,* 16, October 22, 1962, 13.

Rosenthal, Richard. "After the Riots—A Position Paper for Retailing," *Stores* (December 1967), pp. 11–20.

Russel, H. C. "Ads Alone Won't Win Negro Market," *Advertising Age,* 34, October 21, 1963, 3ff.

"Same Ad Intelligently Done Can Sell to both Whites and Negroes," *Advertising Age,* 32, June 12, 1961, 23.

"Should Products Be Created for the Negro Market," *The Gibson Report* (March 1968).

"30 Billion Negroes Tell How Best to Sell Negro Market," *Advertising Age,* 40, April 14, 1969, 61.

"Welcoming Service Offers New Approach to Negro Market," *Advertising Age,* 36, March 1, 1965, 38.

"Will an Ethnic Pitch Sell the Black Market?," Business Week, April 12, 1960, 88.

EPILOGUE

The Future
of the Black-
Consumer
Market

During the past few years, there has been a significant increase of
interest in the black as a consumer. Business concerns now realize the
importance of this ethnic market and are developing strategies
to meet the challenge.

Various factors account for the economic potential of the
black-consumer market. The magnitude of the black population,
approximately 11 percent of the present total population, or 22 million
people, presents a tremendous marketing opportunity. A desirable
characteristic of a population segment is that it be accessible.
Geographically and locationally, blacks are a rather collective group,
which expedites the communication and distribution functions
related to the provision of demanded goods and services. One-third
of all blacks live in the twenty-five largest cities, and 55 percent
live in central cities.

According to population projections, by 1975 blacks will increase to
over 12 percent of the total population. In 1990 nonwhites will
comprise approximately 14 percent of the total United States
population. The nonwhite population estimate is approximately 28
million in 1975 and, in 1980, 32.5 million. The black population should
account for one-fourth of the net increase in the total population
for the period 1968–1980.

The labor force participation rate for the next decade for nonwhites
is predicted to remain stable, approximately 60 percent. By 1980,
an estimated 12 million nonwhites will be in the labor force. Additional
changes will be reflected in the number of nonwhites under the age

367

of twenty-five who will be in the labor force (60 percent of the nonwhite population will be under twenty-five in 1990) and, therefore, the young black family structure will be an important marketing consideration. The employment picture for nonwhite teen-agers is expected to improve, although they will have to make a concentrated effort to increase their technical competence and to acquire marketable skills. Further trends toward a larger number of adult women in the labor force will augment the employment outlook.

If nonwhite jobs continue to gain in the 1970s at the same rate as in the preceding decade, in 1980 the occupational distribution between whites and nonwhites will be significantly different.

Projections of the labor force show nonwhites constituting 12 percent in 1980. A distribution of this labor-force composition suggests that nonwhites may hold 10 percent of the professional and technical jobs and 4 percent of the managerial, official, and proprietary occupations. Significant gains are expected to occur in the clerical, sales, and craftsmen occupations. A decline is expected in service-type employment when measured relatively.

A major determinant of this expected improvement in the occupational structure is the substantial progress anticipated in the educational achievement of the nonwhite citizen, which is certain to be followed by associated income increments.

The Bureau of Census figures show that in 1967 aggregate income was $487 billion, with the nonwhite population receiving $35.7 billion of this amount. Estimates for 1980 based on current trends show that aggregate money income may reach $843 billion, with a $74 billion portion accruing to nonwhites. The magnitude of these gains for both the white and nonwhite populations will have a tremendous impact on consumption patterns and on all demand for goods and services. The increase in per capita income for nonwhites might be as high as 50 percent. The relative improvement for nonwhites when expressed in aggregate money income and in per capita terms will be substantially greater than that of whites.

The social, political, cultural, psychological, and economic changes expected as a result of the foregoing predictions will be reflected in the black-consumer market. The changing role of the black in society will unquestionably shape the role of the black as a consumer. It is paramount to understand the attitudes, experiences, and motivations that influence marketplace behavior. Businessmen will have to make adjustments to secure and thereby benefit from this important market segment.

The periodical references and comparisons of whites and nonwhites show that data concerning the nonwhite market are available to businessmen. With the rapid changes that are developing, however, there should be a constant updating of such facts as the continued geographic shifts by the black. As social barriers are overcome, the move from the periphery of the central city to the urban environment will be common and the blacks' expenditure and subsequent consumption patterns will radically change with the pressures of social and economic forces. It is logical to assume that there will be a shift in his financial allocations.

As previously stated, attitudinal and motivational factors of the black consumer must not be overlooked. Blacks are developing a strong sense of ethnic pride, and they want to reflect this pride while attaining a higher standard of living. More research in this relatively unexplored field is necessary to establish effective communication with this growing market.

Some of the growth of the black-consumer market will come through the development of black-owned-and-operated business firms. History teaches that ethnic groups in the United States who have successfully broken out of the ghetto did so through the entrepreneurial route. A strong and prosperous middle class is essential to achieve economic, social, and cultural progress.

Although there is no way to identify the nonwhite's share of the gross national product, it is expected that the per capita measurement of GNP will be $5,650 in 1980, about a one-third increase since 1968. The 1980 United States economy is expected to operate at almost a trillion dollars, assuming a reasonable growth rate. With the economy growing at such a rapid pace, change is bound to occur.

A survey of the past few years emphasizes the magnitude of change in the black-consumer market, and it is desirable to view the future prospects from a marketing perspective. To a rather significant degree, the marketplace itself will influence the black and his style of life, his motivations, his attitudes, and his demands. Intelligent programs must be designed and developed if the promise of the black-consumer market is to attain its potential.